TWO YEARS IN REVOLUTIONARY CHINA 1925-1927

By
Vera Vladimirovna
Vishnyakova-Akimova

Translated by
Steven I. Levine

蘇俄顧問遊記

Harvard East Asian Monographs

HARVARD EAST ASIAN MONOGRAPHS

40

TWO YEARS IN REVOLUTIONARY CHINA, 1925-1927

TWO YEARS IN REVOLUTIONARY CHINA
1925 — 1927
(Dva goda v vosstavshem Kitae, 1925-1927
Moscow, Izdatelstvo "Nauka," 1965

by
Vera Vladimirovna Vishnyakova-Akimova
Translated by
Steven I. Levine

Published by
East Asian Research Center
Harvard University

Distributed by
Harvard University Press
Cambridge, Mass.
1971

The East Asian Research Center at Harvard University administers research projects designed to further scholarly understanding of China, Japan, Korea, Vietnam, and adjacent areas. These studies have been assisted by grants from the Ford Foundation.

Library of Congress No. 78-148942
SBN 674-91601-8

CONTENTS

INTRODUCTION

On June 25, 1925, in the company of two fellow-students, Vera Vladimirovna Vishnyakova, a twenty-year-old student from the Eastern Department of Far Eastern State University in Vladivostok, boarded a nondescript Chinese freighter bound for Chefoo. Like so many young students from the West who journeyed to China she was propelled there by the twin motives of service and adventure, and in the course of the next two years she had ample opportunity to satisfy both impulses. As a translator-interpreter and secretary she served in almost all the areas where Soviet military and political missions were active—in northwest China (with Feng Yü-hsiang's Kuominchün), in Canton with Borodin and Blyukher, and finally in Wuhan during the climax of the revolutionary events of the mid-twenties. With her husband, V.M. Akimov, a Soviet military adviser whom she had married while in China, she left Wuhan in June 1927 on Borodin's advice and returned home while the last act in the uneasy collaboration between the Russians and the Chinese revolutionaries was being played out.

Some forty years after her sojourn in China, in the year before her death in 1966, Mme. Vishnyakova-Akimova's historical recollections were published in Moscow.[1] This interesting volume is one of a growing number of memoirs by the Soviet Union's old China hands which have been published in the USSR over the past several years. These include works by the military advisers A.I. Cherepanov, N.I. Konchits, and V.M. Primakov as well as a volume by M.I. Kazanin, a Chinese specialist on Blyukher's staff.[2] Taken as a whole these memoirs, remarkably

1. Mme. Vishnyakova-Akimova continued to work in the China field after her return to the USSR. She published articles in the Soviet periodical press and worked for the General Staff. For a listing of her articles and translations see the first and second editions of P.E. Skachkov, *Bibliografia Kitaya* (Bibliography of China; Moscow, 1930, 1958).

2. A.I. Cherepanov, *Zapiski voennogo sovetnika v Kitae* (Notes of a military adviser in China; Moscow, 1964); A.I. Cherepanov, *Severnyi pokhod natsionalno-revoliutsionnoy armii Kitaya* (The Northern Expedition of the National Revolutionary Army of China; Moscow, 1968); V.M. Primakov, *Zapiski volontera: grazhdanskaya voina v Kitae* (Notes of a volunteer: the Civil War in China; Moscow, 1967). This book was originally published in 1930 under the name of Henry Allen, an Anglicized form of Primakov's Chinese pseudonym Heng-li Lin, and purported to be the reminiscences of an English volunteer instructor in Feng Yü-hsiang's army. N.I. Konchits, *Kitayskie dnevniki 1925-1926* (Chinese diaries 1925-1926; Moscow, 1969); M.I. Kazanin, *V shtabe Blyukhera: vospominania o Kitayskoy revoliutsi* (In Blyukher's headquarters: Reminiscences of the Chinese revolution; Moscow, 1966). This memoir material would have been considerably enriched had either Borodin or Blyukher set down their recollections as was their intention. But both Blyukher, shot in 1938 at the height of his career, and Borodin, who survived in obscurity till 1949 when he too was arrested and died, went to their graves without adding to the literature on China.

rich in historical detail, unquestionably represent an important new source for the history of the Soviet involvement in China during the 1920s.[3] It is in the hope of making available to a wider audience at least one of these memoirs that the present translation of Mme. Vishnyakova-Akimova's book is being published.

What accounts for the recent flowering of Soviet works on the Chinese Revolution of the mid-twenties? In the Soviet Union to an even greater extent than in most countries political considerations are of paramount importance in determining what is written and published. Mme. Vishnyakova-Akimova herself makes it clear that during the long, terror-ridden night of Stalin's rule the well-rooted tradition of Russian sinological studies was virtually destroyed through the purges of the thirties and forties. The pages in which she reminisces about advisers and China specialists read like a roll call of the dead. Only through an act of imagination can we who know the numbing effect of McCarthyism in America on China studies even begin to grasp the consequences of Stalinism for Soviet China studies.

In the past decade, however, Soviet scholarship on modern and contemporary China has once again begun to produce a growing number of serious monographs on various aspects of Chinese history. If Soviet historiography still lacks the excitement generated by impassioned disputes between scholars of different generations, outlooks, and experience, this may in part be due to the continuing necessity for a united front of serious scholars against the political hacks qua historians who dominated the preceding decades. In this context the publication of the works under discussion is a hopeful sign. In each case they have been ably edited by senior Soviet specialists on China. We can only welcome the unique contribution which Soviet historians, with access to important archival materials, are in a position to make to our general understanding of China.[4]

Without in any way negating the importance of the above-mentioned works from a scholarly standpoint, it may be suggested at the same time that their

3.   In addition to the works dealing with the 1920s, in the last year the Russians have published a large volume of memoirs by General Kalyagin who was one of the Russian advisers to Chiang Kai-shek during the anti-Japanese War. A. Ya. Kalyagin, *Po nyeznakomym dorogam* (Along unknown roads; Moscow, 1969). Is it too much to hope that those of us dealing with problems in post-war China will before long receive the benefit of memoir and other primary materials from the Soviet advisers and specialists who served in China during 1945-1960?

4.   Dan Jacobs notes in his review of the Soviet literature on China, "Recent Russian Material on Soviet Advisers in China: 1923-1927," *China Quarterly*, No. 41 (January-March 1970), p.112, that Soviet scholars and memoirists have been given access both to the Ministry of Defense Archives and the Central Party Archives of the Institute of Marxism-Leninism.

publication along with that of recent academic works on the same subject [5] also serves a contemporary political purpose. In the words of a recent writer:

> An objective analysis of the history of the Chinese Revolution, especially the role of the Comintern and its contribution to the working out of the theoretical and practical problems of the Chinese Revolution has today the utmost significance because the history of the Chinese Revolution and of the CCP over the course of many years has been the object of crude and ever deepening falsification not only on the part of bourgeois historiography but also on the part of Mao Tse-tung and his group. The goal of this falsification in the first place is to put the history of the CCP and the Chinese Revolution in the service of Mao Tse-tung's cult of personality and, secondly, to present individual aspects of the CCP's experience, and most of all the ideas of Mao Tse-tung as universal truth, as a necessary recipe for the revolutionary movements of all countries and all peoples.[6]

Recent Soviet works on China in the 1920s, then, share the desire to restore the Soviet contribution to China's revolutionary development to a place of honor, and to undercut the historical claims of the present Chinese leadership. The memoirs of Soviet advisers are a perfect vehicle for achieving this end. Memory itself is a way of putting a lien on the past, a form of historical possessiveness. But the memoirist does not merely repossess the past by reliving it in his pages. He is as well a prestidigitator with time. Through his art he makes the past seem present, dim figures from history emerge to take on the immediacy of contemporary personalities. When the memoirs are written after a gap of forty years between the event and the telling thereof this effect is even more enhanced.

The appearance of these memoirs comes at a peculiar juncture in time. The old China hands from the Soviet Union's revolutionary past are in the twilight of their lives. (As noted above, Mme. Vishnyakova-Akimova died the year after her book was published.) Those who survived the purges, heavy with years and with honors, possess an authority which no mere historian can hope to match. The political situation, moreover, is most favorable for the appearance of these works.

5.   For example, M.F. Iurev, *Revoliutsia 1925-1927 gg v Kitae* (The Revolution of 1925-1927 in China; Moscow, 1968). This is a full-scale academic treatment of the subject. R.A. Ulyanovsky et al., eds., *Komintern i Vostok* (The Comintern and the East; Moscow, 1969).

6.   V.I. Glunin, "Komintern i stanovlenie kommunisticheskogo dvizhenia v Kitae (1920-1927)" (The Comintern and the formation of the Communist movement in China, 1920-1927) in *Komintern i Vostok, pp. 242-243.*

The Soviets are long past the point in their relations with China when they must beware of offending the historical sensibilities of the Chinese leadership. Quite the contrary; these historical works serve to reenforce a popular theme in recent Soviet discussions of China—that of Chinese ingratitude. The personal testimony of Cherepanov, Konchits, Kazanin, Primakov, and Vishnyakova-Akimova all point to the magnitude and significance of the Soviet Union's contributions to the Chinese Revolution. (This too is the burden of recent Soviet works on the succeeding decades of Chinese history.) From this perspective it is not difficult to conclude that Peking's present posture is not only politically indefensible but morally reprehensible as well. Paradoxically one of the effects of these memoirists who, in the course of their common struggle, came to feel genuine affection for the Chinese as a people may be to reenforce the unfortunate tradition of Russian Sinophobia.

Having said all this it must be stated that what Mme. Vishnyakova-Akimova has written is only in part a political book, although it is much more than a personal memoir. As she states in her preface, "I have endeavored to write this book so that from its pages other voices which are now stilled forever would resound—the voices of my comrades in labor including my husband." In this she succeeds. But though she deals with the broad range of political events in China in the mid-twenties she adds very little if anything to the familiar Soviet interpretation of that decade. On all the questions which have intrigued Western historians—Soviet policy itself, the inner workings of the CCP-KMT alliance, the strategy of the Comintern, the role of Stalin and other leading figures—she is virtually silent. One must look elsewhere for a discussion of these problems. But time and again she illuminates the larger political questions by a revealing anecdote or comment: the tremendous frustration experienced by the Soviet advisers in their attempts to modernize and politicize Feng Yü-hsiang's army ("Just what are we? Some kind of medieval mercenaries?" one of them raged); the backwardness of northwest Chinese villages where the peasants thought the Russian advisers were missionaries, and knew nothing about Sun Yat-sen, the Kuomintang, or the National Revolution; the shocked indignation of the Russians at Canton on learning of Chiang Kai-shek's coup of March 20. In all of these pages her personal knowledge is richly amplified by extracts from the meticulous notes and diaries of military advisers such as the chief of staff of the Kalgan mission, Ivan Korneev (Anders). Madame Vishnyakova-Akimova is fully aware of the complexity of social and political change in China and of the great diversity of the country itself. This is evident in her pages on Kuo Sung-ling's revolt and the intricacies of warlord politics and in her evocation of the climate and customs of Kalgan, Canton, and the villages of North and South China.

Yet the special attraction and virtue of this book lies in the strength of Madame Vishnyakova-Akimova's powers of observation and her literary facility for being simultaneously the young student and the knowledgeable China expert. Through its pages breathes the enthusiasm of her former self, the young girl who traveled to China so many years ago. "I was probably more cheerful and carefree than befitted a girl of my age," she says in mild self-reproof. One takes exception to this remark when it is recalled that she was all of twenty at the time, yet it reminds us that by and large the Soviet community of advisers and supporting personnel was a youthful group. G.N. Voytinsky, the Comintern representative, was twenty-seven at the time of his first meeting with Sun Yat-sen. Borodin was virtually a patriarchal figure at the age of forty!

One of the striking themes of this book is the confrontation between Mme. Vishnyakova-Akimova's youthful, revolutionary idealism and touching naivete on the one hand and the realities of China on the other. Imagine her shock, for example, when she discovered on her first morning in Peking that Soviet diplomatic personnel rode around in rickshaws just like the wicked imperialists. This concession to prevailing custom was dictated by the rickshaw pullers themselves whose livelihood was imperiled by the idealism which rejected such exploitation of human labor. Possessing the liberated spirit of Soviet post-revolutionary women, Mme. Vishnyakova-Akimova, in her student clothes, mannish bob and worker's cap nearly induced an apoplectic fit in the Soviet Consul in Chefoo. Later in Kalgan she had to be transferred from her duties as an interpreter because the officers of the Kuominchün were affronted by the presence of female interpreters. (Yet in Canton the formidable Mira Sakhnovskaya worked as the chief of staff in the Russian military mission, and gave lectures at the Whampoa Academy while visibly pregnant!)

There is much in Madame Vishnyakova-Akimova's account of a timeless quality revealing the foreigner's reactions to China—the thrill which she felt as a student of Chinese on first hearing the living language, the discovery of the richness and profusion of Chinese marketplaces. It is an unadventurous soul indeed who cannot identify first with her hesitation and then her delight in downing a bowl of her favorite *ju ssu mien* at a tiny village restaurant of dubious cleanliness, or share her sense of mystery at witnessing the lighting of the "miniature rattlesnakes," the snake-green coils of mosquito incense. From a different perspective one is reminded of the more than physical distance which separates most Russians from China when Mme. Vishnyakova-Akimova, in recounting her first Chinese banquet, feels it incumbent to tell her readers that bread is not served with Chinese meals, and that Chinese cuisine is served sliced in little pieces. This is a far cry from the American world of canned or frozen "Chinese" dinners.

In Mme. Vishnyakova-Akimova one recognizes a fellow-lover of things Chinese, a woman who is at once naive and a cognoscente at the same time. That oldest form of Western accounts of China—the traveler's tale of the exotic East—is an integral part of this book. Her enthusiasm and affection lend an immediacy and vividness to her descriptions of the cities where she resided and the places through which she journeyed which is sometimes lacking in the writings of more professional travelers. (Compare, for example, her description of Canton's "narrow streets" with that of Harry Franck in *Roving Through Southern China,* Chapter IX.) Tourism rather than Marxism-Leninism seems, at times, to be her natural ideology though she is nothing if not a sincere Soviet patriot. Her social consciousness prevents her from ever romanticizing poverty or human degradation. In drawing a contrast between the pomp of a rich man's funeral and a poor man's she hauntingly evokes in a few quick sentences the pathos of poverty in China. As the citizen of a still revolutionary society the young Miss Vishnyakova empathized with the emerging labor and peasant movements. She fully realized the revolutionary significance of the fact that, as Malraux expresses it in *The Conquerors,* "Today coolies are beginning to discover that they exist, simply that they exist." Yet she does not belong to the "downtrodden masses" school of literature.

From the historian's point of view Mme. Vishnyakova-Akimova's most noteworthy contribution lies in her description of the community of Soviet advisers and supporting personnel in China during the 1920s. Her first service lies in identifying a considerable number of the advisers by their proper and assumed names. (In the Russian revolutionary tradition and in order to conceal their background and qualifications almost all of the Russian advisers utilized noms de guerre.) More than this, however, through a series of rapid portraits she breathes life into men whom we know only as gray-masked engineers of revolution, dour-faced, no-nonsense manipulators of Chinese men and social movements. We see here, rather, gay, light-hearted young people, dedicated to their work but capable also even of frivolity. We learn that A. Ya. Kantorovich, the legal counselor of the Soviet Embassy, was a Dickens enthusiast who quoted whole pages by heart; A.A. Argentov (Marino), a military adviser, knew no Chinese but refused the services of an interpreter and managed with the aid of a notebook full of Chinese military terms. (Incidentally, if possible, one should supplement these portraits of the Soviet advisers with the fascinating photos of many of them in Cherepanov's memoirs.) Her portraits of Borodin and Blyukher are sympathetic and respectful yet Borodin especially remains a somewhat shadowy figure from her account.

The sketches of leading Chinese figures are less successful. Partly this lack derives from her subordinate position from which she saw but did not know these Chinese. Her portrait of Chiang Kai-shek as a stoop-shouldered, blustering, irresolute man given to fits of hysterics is little more than a caricature. Of Mao Tse-tung whom she saw while serving as an interpreter for M.O. Razumov, Soviet adviser to the Kuomintang Agrarian Commission in April 1927 she says nothing at all.

What kind of men were the Russian advisers in China? Their youthfulness has already been referred to. All of them had shown their mettle in the Russian civil war. Many were graduates of courses on Asia in the Frunze Military Academy. One is constantly impressed by their training and experience. China undoubtedly provided an outlet for a number of Russian officers whose experience and talents were going begging after the end of the civil war. We are given no inkling that they seriously questioned the nature of the mission they were trying to accomplish though some of their gripes are recorded. Their dedication to their task, of course, gave them no immunity from error. A report by the acting chief of the Canton mission, V.A. Stepanov, in March 1926 noted the following mistakes:

> 1) Too rapid centralization of military power . . . 2) Excessive supervision of the generals and the various organs . . . 3) Inappropriate radical propaganda in the Army on the problems of imperialism, the peasantry and communism . . . We normally pay no attention to Chinese habits, customs and etiquette.[7]

7. C. Martin Wilbur, ed., *Documents on Communism, Nationalism and Soviet Advisers in China, 1918-1927* (New York, 1956), pp. 250-251.

The insularity, cohesiveness, and self-containment of the Soviet community in China is a particularly striking feature. Apart from their obligatory professional contacts with the Chinese, most of the Russians apparently kept to themselves. Their social lives revolved around the mission clubs. (A recent newspaper report from Cairo notes that the numerous Russian community of advisers in that city lives in a special section called Zamalek or Russian Island with its own club, schools, hospital and recreational grounds.)[8] Mme. Vishnyakova-Akimova does not mention having had any Chinese friends. In fact Chinese appear in the work only as political actors, service personnel, and people on the street. It should be added at once, however, that this did not reflect either condescension or a chosen attitude of aloofness on the part of Miss Vishnyakova and the others. They were under strict orders to avoid social contacts with the Chinese. With evident disappointment she notes:

> It is true that much of Peking of that day remained unknown to us. We dreamed of spending some time in at least one of the famous Peking universities so as to discuss things with our fellow-students, to meet Chinese workers, to mix in the ranks of the demonstrators and listen to what they were speaking about, to drop in on a peasant *fangtz* and much more. Alas, it was impossible. Our sincere desire to become acquainted with the Chinese people undoubtedly would have been regarded by the Chinese authorities and imperialist agents in Peking as "subversive activity" which might have led to undesirable political consequences. To this day I cannot recall without bitterness these vexatious limitations which deprived me of many interesting meetings.[9]

Even in revolutionary Canton the same restrictions were in effect, "in order to avoid any kind of idle talk and accusations to the effect that we were spreading Red propaganda."[10] In consequence, the Russians, especially the military advisers, conspicuously remained foreigners in China. Moreover, they lived under a double isolation—rejected by and in turn rejecting the enclavism of the Western treaty port concessions, and cut off from the surrounding Chinese community as well. They were in China but not of it. This was inherent in their official status. Against the background of Sino-American relations, for example, it is important to note that there were no Russians in China in other than official capacities (except for the generally despised White emigrés). As a result one does not meet in the history

8. *New York Times* (Jan. 18, 1970).
9. See below, p. 79.
10. See below, p. 231.

of modern Sino-Russian relations the profusion of individual and private institutional bonds and relationships which form so important an element in the contact between the United States and China. The enormous intellectual influence of Marxism-Leninism and the Russian Revolution was transmitted by and mediated through only a relative handful of foreigners. Perhaps ultimately this expedited the process of Chinese adaption of the revolutionary theory and practice.

What may be said in conclusion about the political meaning of the Soviet involvement in China in the 1920s as exemplified by the role of the advisers? This is not the place for an extended essay on the question but a few comments may be in order. In the first place, as Harold Isaacs noted many years ago, "The history of this period . . . can be made intelligible only in terms of the interaction of the Chinese and Russian revolutions."[11] It is misleading to view the Soviet involvement as simply a cynical attempt to exploit and subvert a foreign revolutionary movement (the Kuomintang) through its own instrument (the CCP) for purely realpolitik reasons. In an age when great powers including the Soviet Union and more particularly the United States manipulate client states with practiced finesse it is easy to view Russia's relationship to the Canton revolutionary regime in like terms. But the relationship between the USSR and the Kuomintang government until the break was more of a symbiotic one of mutual advantage to both sides. Each side tried to use the other to its best advantage, to be sure. Despite the influence and prestige of men like Blyukher and Borodin, and the virtual domination for a time of Soviet "advisers" in the command structure of the National-Revolutionary Army, the USSR lacked the mechanisms to control Chinese revolutionary developments. The CCP of that era was far from being a Bolshevized Communist party properly obedient to Moscow's will. Within the KMT-SU-CCP triangle the process of bargaining was always a possibility. (For example, the modus vivendi worked out between Chiang and Borodin after the former's coup of March 20, 1926.) Finally it must be remembered that both the Kuomintang and the CCP in the 1920s were revolutionary parties struggling for power amid a welter of competing political forces many of which had ties to the imperialist powers. To describe the Soviet support of the revolutionary forces in terms of infiltration, penetration, and subversion is to view events through a conservative prism. Still it must be acknowledged that insofar as the Soviets departed from the

11.   Harold Isaacs, *The Tragedy of the Chinese Revolution* (Stanford, 1961), 2nd rev. ed., p. 37.

role of revolutionary model and adviser to assume an active, guiding role in China they failed, perhaps inevitably.

The historical recollections of Mme. Vishnyakova-Akimova raise by implication but do not answer or deal in depth with the abiding questions of the Chinese revolutionary experience of the mid-twenties. Mme. Vishnyakova-Akimova, for all her keenness of observation, is never introspective. She does not (at least in this memoir) ponder the meaning in intercultural terms of her presence in China, or examine the role she is playing. Perhaps such consciousness of self is rare among foreign personnel in regard to their activity unless external events compel the growth of such awareness. Yet her memoirs with their many comments on the men and events of a turbulent period of Chinese history retain their fascination as a human and historical document.

August 1970

Steven I. Levine

PREFACE

The history of the Chinese revolution of 1924-1927 until now has been insufficiently represented in our literature. Even less has been written in our country about how scores of Soviet volunteers worked hand in hand with Chinese revolutionaries on Chinese soil. Moreover, the penpushers of the "free world" have spread the most absurd slanders about this fraternal collaboration which has presented so many remarkable examples of friendship between the two nations.

My husband, Major-General Vladimir Mikhaylovich Akimov, who served as one of the advisers to the Chinese revolutionary forces in the years 1925-1927, wanted to make his contribution to the illumination of these problems. Retiring in 1956, he intended, in collaboration with me, to write his reminiscences of the revolutionary events in China of which we were eyewitnesses.

Alas, it turned out that I had to work alone, without the help and guidance of the person who should have been the chief author of the book. Since it was no longer possible to adhere entirely to the original intention it became necessary to change the plan of the book. Now it is only the reminiscences of a China hand who during 1925-1927 worked on the staff of military advisers and in the office of the chief political adviser to the Central Executive Committee of the Kuomintang, Mikhail Markovich Borodin. But these are not simply my reminiscences. I have endeavored to write this book so that from its pages other voices which are now stilled forever would resound—the voices of my comrades in labor including my husband who wholeheartedly loved the Chinese people and labored tirelessly in the field of practical implementation of Sino-Soviet friendship until the Great Patriotic War. To their bright memory I dedicate this book.

My heartfelt thanks to all those comrades who participated in the discussion of my book which was organized by the Chinese Division of the Institute of the Peoples of Asia of the USSR Academy of Sciences, in particular T.N. Akatova, N.P. Vinogradov, R.V. Vyatkin, R.A. Mirovitsky, V.N. Nikiforov, and S.L. Tikhvinsky. I am much obliged to the surviving eyewitnesses of the revolution of 1924-1927 in China: Z.S. Dubasova, Ts. A. Kalinovskaya; and to the participants in it: A.A. Argentov, A. Ya. Klimov, N.I. Konchits, A.M. Kravtsov,

M.F. Kumanin; and to the Moscow sinologists V.I. Antonov, V. Ya. Sidikhmenov, and T. Ya. Tsvetkova for much valuable advice and clarification.

V. Vishnyakova-Akimova

Chapter I

TO CHINA FOR FIELD WORK

Day of Departure

In summer Vladivostok is quite a southern city. There is no cause for surprise; it is situated further south than Sevastopol which it elusively resembles. Not without reason does one hear in the geographical terms for Vladivostok and its environs—Black Creek, Golden Horn Bay, Admiral's Pier and others— echoes as it were of its older brother, the renowned city on the shore of the Black Sea. Despite the severe climate, there is much sunshine in Vladivostok, the colors are vivid as in the south, the sea is likewise beautiful.

On June 25, 1925, the sun shone everywhere when the last group of student field workers from the Eastern Department of the Far Eastern State University in Vladivostok, to be more precise V. Novoselov, A. Shirshov and the author of these lines, who had successfully advanced to the third course, departed for China. The glass gaily glittered in the windows of the blindingly white little houses which swept down toward the bay from the hilly shore. The sea barely lapped at the salt-corroded moorings. Chinese sampans with enormous stern oars skillfully handled by sun-blackened, white-toothed Chinese skidded up and down the surface of the bay which sparkled in the sun. Their passengers were young students celebrating the end of their studies.

At the pier lay a rather unprepossessing freighter of medium tonnage with three large characters painted on the side. This was the Chinese commercial vessel *Hsinp'inghai* which had been chartered by the Soviet Commercial Fleet. Loading of cargo had already been completed; indeed there was little to load. The entire hold for this voyage had been set aside for Chinese coolies—seasonal workers who, as always, were returning to their native land in summer and autumn. Boarding had already begun. Chinese hurriedly ran up the narrow gangplank supporting heavy parcels of their belongings on their heads with both hands. Their faces glistened from sweat.

An incredible din and noise arose. Separate sharp cries could be heard, a clamorous wrangling in Shantung dialect.[1] The ship's hold gradually filled

---

1. The Chinese seasonal workers who traveled to and fro from Vladivostok by sea were natives of Shantung as a rule.

with this animated, agitated mass of human bodies. Only aft could one see the dark, silent shapes of three Chinese coffins made of heavy wood. From time to time a light sea breeze wafted the heavy, stifling odor of decay onto the wharf where we stood surrounded by our comrades who had come to see us off. The dead were also returning to their motherland so that in accordance with the tenets of the Confucian faith they might find peace in the ancestral burial-ground of their forebears. Papers with addresses were pasted to the lids. The departed ones would be unloaded at one of the ports of Shantung—Chefoo (Yent'ai) or Tsingtao and they would begin their journey on their own. The pious countrymen would take pains to ensure that their kinsman would be buried on native soil. Hundreds of persons would voluntarily carry the heavy coffin until after a long journey, perhaps even of several years' duration, the dead man would reach his home.

This day was a great holiday for us. Our long-cherished dream had come true. The sinologists in the Eastern Department of Far Eastern State University were generally considered to be men possessed. We were all in love with China, with her rich yet laconic language, the difficult but descriptive characters, her ancient, distinctive culture and her history. But most important, before us was the bold people's liberation struggle which was unfolding then on Chinese soil. The revolution had already entered its second year, but in 1925 it reached an unprecedented tempo. The treacherous shooting down of unarmed demonstrators by the imperialists on Nanking Street in Shanghai on May 30, 1925, was, to some degree, for China what the ninth of January was for us. Instantly all of China exploded with anger and indignation. An anti-British boycott began and took an especially sharp form in the south where the famous Hong Kong-Canton strike flared up.

In the beginning of June the Executive Committee of the Comintern published an appeal which called upon the proletariat of the whole world to support the Chinese workers. A very tense situation had developed in Peking where we were headed. The Legation Quarter was on a war footing. The frightened imperialists, fearing the vengeance of the masses, had reinforced the guards at the gates of the Quarter and scarcely appeared beyond its limits. The Chinese boycotted them. Rickshaw pullers fastened placards on their vehicles with the message "No English or Japanese."

Even the Japanophile government of President Tuan Ch'i-jui was forced to make concessions to the intensity of the revolutionary mood. The papers carried notices saying that by decision of the government several palaces in the Forbidden City—the former imperial residence—had been converted into museums and were open to visitors in order to collect funds for Shanghai's striking workers.

On June 10, 1925, an unprecedented demonstration took place in Peking. For the first time tens of thousands of workers and peasants appeared on the streets of the capital and for the first time they were singing the "Marseillaise." Traffic was halted. Passions were inflamed to the limit. One of the demonstrators, a member of the Society for Pedagogical Reforms, yielding in a frenzy to the feudal habits of old China, cut off a finger and with his blood wrote on a wall the slogan "Down with imperialism" after which he fell into a dead faint.

On the day of our departure a new imperialist crime in China became known—the shooting of demonstrators on the twenty-third of June in Canton on the Shakee Embankment. This heralded a new outburst of the anti-imperialist struggle. It is easy to understand our mood as we left for China.

Let me say a few words about the conditions under which the administration of Far Eastern University sent us on foreign assignment. At that time our higher educational institutions could not boast a sufficiency of funds. Now it is even difficult to imagine how it was, but we received nothing at all apart from our passports and credentials which indicated the purpose of our journey and requested all Soviet establishments in China to extend all possible aid to us. The fortunate graduates who had completed all three years of the Eastern Department were given a small sum which was supposed to suffice for their travel expenses and two weeks of modest existence. We who, only yesterday, were in the second year had to be content with our own small savings. However, the miraculous paper saying "all possible aid" worked like a charm. Till this day I cannot forget how graciously we were received and with what touching attention the Soviet workers in China treated us.

The exchange of Soviet for Chinese currency was exceedingly simple at that time. You made a declaration in the bank about how many Chinese *tayen* you needed, and at the appointed hour a Chinese appeared before the teller's window where you exchanged the currency in the presence of a Soviet bank employee.[2] So that for the first few days we were provided for, but then we had to secure work—no easy task inasmuch as the staffs of Soviet overseas bureaus were recruited within the Soviet Union.

On the pier, my landlady, Aunt Dusha, dissolved in tears, thrust at me a small purse with sweet rusks . . .

Because of monetary considerations we decided to go by ship rather than rail. The Soviet Commercial Fleet agreed to land us in any Chinese port on their itinerary free of charge on the single condition that we travel without any conveniences, in the hold filled with Chinese seasonal workers. This did not disturb us and we ordered tickets to Chefoo from where we would have to make our own way to Peking. Fortune smiled upon us at the very beginning of our trip. As soon as the bustle of loading was finished, a jolly, fat supercargo approached us, and having asked who we were, joyfully offered us two empty cabins for ship's officers on the upper deck.

Animatedly my comrades began to drag our typically student belongings— bedding tied together with straps, baskets of books, skinny, tattered suitcases— to the place made available to us. They gallantly freed me from these worries. I stood at the railing looking at the remarkable city which was spread out like an amphitheatre along the shore of the bay. Preparing to cast off, the *Hsin- p'inghai* got up its steam with difficulty. The anchor chain clanked, the ship's ladder was taken up, bells rang, a whistle sounded, sailors ran by me, and one could hear the captain uttering oaths on the bridge. Soon our ship would sound its horn, move away from the pier, and after several minutes Vladivostok would be hidden behind high banks. Now is the time to say a few words about it in farewell.

Perhaps some of my readers will not quite understand this picture of Chinese seasonal laborers who were storming onto a Soviet ship with a non-Russian name, or the Chinese coffins on deck, or some Chinese changing money in a Soviet bank. How did all of this come about in a Russian, in a Soviet city? Truly it takes a real effort to recapture some of this; after all it was so long ago. For the present I want only to say that it was precisely the opportunity to learn through direct contact the Chinese language and the national life of the Chinese without leaving the boundaries of the Soviet Union which, during the

---

2. *Tayen*, yuan, Mexican dollar are various names for the Chinese monetary unit of that time which was equal to 80 Soviet kopecks.

summer of 1924, moved me to transfer from the second year of the Moscow Institute of Sinology to a parallel course in the Eastern Department of the Far Eastern State University. Somehow my friends procured a free rail pass for me.

I remember the crowded platforms of Yaroslavl Station, the long lines of coaches so crowded with persons carrying parcels and tea kettles that people had to be turned away. The Vladivostok-Moscow train went once a week and was always jammed. A gay crowd of students seeing me off surrounded me. Yet my relatives were crying and still trying to dissuade me from undertaking this dangerous trip. I was nineteen years old and leaving home for the first time. I didn't know a soul in Vladivostok. What a distance, what an anxious time! Where could I get money for the return trip if something should happen?

This was the longest trip by rail which I ever had occasion to make. Our train traveled for sixteen days. And the further east one went the more one encountered traces of the civil war and the intervention, the more strongly one could sense the bitter aftertaste of the recent tragic events.

Beyond the Urals, on both sides of the railroad embankment lay derailed, blown-up trains, witnesses to and participants in the great battles which re-sounded in the spaces of Siberia. There was so much terrible pathos, so much material for the human imagination in the heaps of piled up rusty metal! Many bridges lay in ruins, and temporary, wooden ones had been constructed by their sides. The train barely crept across them and the passengers listened to the creaking of the cross-beams with bated breath. At Khabarovsk, the train crossed the Amur on a ferry—enormous barges with rails laid on the deck. The locomotive remained on the shore and on the opposite shore another one was already waiting with its steam up. The enormously long bridge had not yet been restored. The barges loaded with railroad cars passed by gigantic girders with their ends lying out of the water.

Beyond Khabarovsk the trains proceeded under escort. Cheerful Red Army soldiers in Budyony jackets filled the platforms of the cars, hung onto the steps, and stood near the machine guns on the engine and tender. White bands which had just been driven away frequently raided our Far Eastern borders, even attacking trains.[3] We very quickly departed from the schedule and no one could say for certain when we would arrive at a particular place.

---

3. The members of one such band were brought to court in Vladivostok in a show-trial toward the end of 1924. The court chamber was located across from the university and we attended the trial almost every day.

At all the stations there was a terrible crush and cursing at the boiled water spigots. And no wonder. The train sometimes stopped for an hour or longer, or again the wheels would make a slow revolution and once more begin to move, and the ill-fated passengers, without having succeeded in getting boiled water, would dash off at full speed, and help each other jump onto the moving train. Often the train stopped not at the station but somewhere in the taiga. A gay crowd of youths swarmed out, lit bonfires, and sang Siberian songs. The old folks spoke of old times and about Vladivostok. The city stood before us clothed in a mist of poetic legends and marvelous stories about the heroism of the Russian people in the Far East.

We got to Vladivostok late in the evening. There was no point even in thinking about looking for a room or a student dormitory. The luxurious portal of the Versailles Hotel on Lenin Street—the main street of the city— caused me to panic. There was nothing to be done; I had to take a room. Before going to sleep I set off with my traveling companions to look over the town. We even rode on a sampan. The silent Chinese boatman imperturbably swayed on the stern, rowing with a huge oar, and we could not look enough at the field of lights or their reflection in the dark water of the bay.

At dawn beneath the window people began to bustle about, the animated voices of the Chinese began to jabber, just like birds who awake at the sun's first rays. A chorus of clear voices, interrupting each other, rang out fresh and buoyant in the morning air, just like a choir although it seemed there were but three persons talking. I caught the words "scow," "fish," and "bazaar." At times the voices rose to such a pitch that it seemed that people were quarreling and would come to blows at any moment. The lively, temperamental speech of the Chinese often produces precisely this impression on an inexperienced person. I heard this for the first time not in the speech of Liang K'un, a teacher at the Moscow Institute who spoke simply so that he would be better understood, but in the real, people's speech such as it actually was.

I ran downstairs and went out into the street. A new day had come with all its cares; people hurried about on their errands. And I followed after them, turning off into an alley. Among the still small number of passers-by my eyes sought . . . and found!

Coming towards me along the road to the port were Chinese porters with their yokes for transporting weights on the back. Further on some Chinese carried large, four-sided American kerosene cans on flat yokes, some filled with water, some with slops. In Vladivostok at that time only Lenin Street had sewers. A Chinese peddler stopped me and offered some trifle for sale. I still did not understand Shantung dialect—in the institute we were taught the official Peking dialect—therefore I stopped and stared fixedly at the peddler's mouth, thereby causing his utter bewilderment. All the Chinese were dressed in jackets and trousers in the national style, and if you stood close enough to them you could catch a whiff of the distinctive *cheremsha* which the Chinese are so fond of and which is rich in vitamins. (It is a wild garlic.)

Somewhat later a handsome Chinese youth in a cap and field-shirt walked quickly and assuredly by in a group of Russian fellows. At the end of the street a Chinese of dignified mien appeared dressed in a long gown and black satin skull-cap. He was perhaps the owner of one of the private shops which existed at that time in Vladivostok.

As I quickly discovered, the Chinese students, especially the Komsomol members, and many Chinese workers who had permanently settled in Vladivostok and had Russian wives, dressed in European style and lived in a new way, but the majority of Chinese observed their national customs, ate and dressed in their own ways, sang their typical songs, and observed their own lovely holidays. Those were something to hear and to see.

Old China could not feed its working population. No other country in the world has produced so many emigrants. Distance has not served as an obstacle. In San Francisco and other port cities of the USA, despite the harsh immigration laws against "colored" in the past, one encounters Chinatowns. There are many Chinese immigrants in Malaya, Singapore, the Philippines, the Hawaiian Islands, etc. According to statistical data, during those years there were half a million Chinese emigrating yearly from South China alone.

In our Far Eastern territories Chinese immigration began in the second half of the last century. Every year at the end of the agricultural season, thousands of unemployed from Manchuria and Shantung crossed the border. In spring and summer, the flow reversed itself. Only the men took up the seasonal work; they left their families at home. Living in Vladivostok for a year, I saw not a single Chinese woman.

The seasonal laborers did not intend to settle permanently. They considered death on foreign soil far from their native burial-ground as the most terrible unhappiness. Some of them got bogged down, but still they did not lose hope of returning home. I met decrepit old men with pigtails. Having left China during the Manchu dynasty, they still hoped to return home and feared that the absence of pigtails would prevent their doing so.[4] The Manchus cut off heads for such freethinking.

Rich Chinese too lived in Vladivostok, and I don't even want to tell just how they had come by their riches. You cannot begin to count how many of their fellow countrymen became the victims of their insatiable greed. Often these were the big shots of the underground, criminal world—usury, the keeping of opium dens, contraband, espionage—they were not fastidious about anything.

Insofar as the Chinese were the most unfortunate people in the city with few among them having skills the Chinese problem was especially complex during the first days of Soviet power in Vladivostok. It was a difficult time— unemployment, economic dislocation, an insufficiency of all things. And still it was necessary to arrange things somehow for the Chinese, to guarantee work and decent housing for them, to teach them (almost all were illiterates), to give them medical care and to organize them. The Russians and the very small number of Chinese Communists of that time were kept busy with these tasks. When I arrived, various courses for Chinese were already in existence, and many Chinese were studying in Soviet party schools. A Chinese paper, the *Kung jen chih lu* (Worker's path) was being published in the simplest conversational language which in itself was an unheard of innovation. Over the entrance to a fine private residence near the Semyonov Bazaar hung a sign in Russian and Chinese saying "The May First Chinese Club."

When a vessel of some colonial power came to port an incident foreign to the spirit of the Soviet city might occur. It happened that once a foreign officer tried to insult and even to strike a Chinese. Such incidents were settled on the spot. On the eve of our departure for China the mate of an English vessel was fined 400 roubles[4] by decision of a city show trial because, having suspected a Chinese porter of theft, he manacled him to the side of the vessel and kept him there for an hour until our police intervened.[5]

---

4. The Hsinhai Revolution of 1911 overturned the Manchu dynasty.
5. This was a big sum at that time. The real value of the rouble equalled its present value.

The Eastern Department of FESU where I went to study was the pride and joy of Vladivostok, or such was the firm conviction of all its students. It was the direct descendant of the Eastern Institute which had been founded in 1899 and had been located in the same building. This was a four-story white house on a small alley off the main street of the city. Two symbolic Chinese lions made of white stone goodnaturedly bared their teeth at the entrance.

The very location of the Eastern Institute, far away from the academic center of Russian sinology in Petersburg, indicated that its goals were in no way academic in nature. In fact, according to the plan of the tsarist government, the Eastern Institute was supposed to prepare not scientific workers but, first and foremost, cadres for the propagation of tsarist imperialist policies in the Far East. Officials of the Ministry of Foreign Affairs, officers of the General Staff, future military translators, and missionaries all studied there. The languages and countries of the Far East were studied in their contemporary aspect. Along with Chinese and Japanese, Korean, Manchurian, and Mongolian were taught. Judging by the composition of its students, the institute became relatively democratic on the eve of the First World War and especially in the following years.

The Eastern Institute had a reputation as one of the internationally known centers of sinology. This undoubtedly bespoke the influence of the great Russian scholars who guided its scientific activity. The talented sinologist Apollinaire Vasilevich Rudakov, the author of many works on the language, history, and geography of China, held the post of director of the institute for longer than anyone else. Regularly, until 1919, *Vostochnogo Instituta Izvestiia* (News of of the Eastern Institute) was published (sixty volumes appeared). At its press the institute published its own works in seven oriental languages and scholars in Europe, Asia, and America subscribed. In 1920, in conjunction with the creation of the Far Eastern State University, the institute became the university's Eastern Department with two divisions—Chinese and Japanese.

On the faculty I still found many old professors of the Eastern Institute— the Japanese specialist Ye. G. Spalvin who was, incidentally, married to a Japanese who also taught that language; the Manchurian specialist A. V. Grebenshchikov, and N. V. Kyuner who taught the cultural history of the peoples of the Far East. P. P. Shmidt, whose textbook *Opyt mandarinskoi grammatiki* (A sketch for a Mandarin grammar) we used in the first year, had already returned to his native land, to Riga, but A. V. Rudakov continued to work despite his advanced years and serious illness. Almost every day he took a cab to school, his legs already stood him in poor stead. Later on, students went to his apartment in Pigeon Ravine to study with him. A corpulent, good-hearted man, he loved to tell stories and he told them superbly.

Konstantin Andreevich Kharnsky, a man of great erudition and a great eccentric, taught the administrative structure of China. He despised restrictions and routine, he dreamed of reorganizing the instructional system in higher educational institutions and he usually improvised his lectures on the theme of the latest events in China. It was a real punishment to take one of his exams. He never asked about what appeared in the syllabus but concerned himself with the "general development" of the material in question, asking the most unexpected questions such as, what is the distance to the nearest star, where are sardines found, what is Batavia, is it only a city on Java, etc. He passed no one on the first round and it was obligatory to be shamed and told to come around once more. No matter how he tortured us we still loved him sincerely, so interesting a man was he. In 1929 his book *Kitai s drevneishikh vremen* (China from antiquity) appeared. Towards the end of the 1930s Kharnsky died tragically, becoming one of the victims of the cult of personality.

Boris Klimentevich Pashkov taught us newspaper Chinese. Ch'i Shih-hsi taught practical conversational Chinese; the elderly Manchurian Te Hsing-ko taught Manchurian and calligraphy. Ch'i Shih-hsi was young and sociable; he wore a simple gray gown. But Te Hsing-ko evidently remembered the privileged condition of his kinsmen in old China—he was stand-offish and flaunted a luxurious *kurma*[6] of tight, shiny satin. At the end of the 1930s, Te Hsing-ko, by then an instructor at the Moscow Institute of Sinology, was arrested and perished.

On October 21, 1924, the Eastern Department as the successor to the Eastern Institute celebrated its twenty-fifth anniversary. Students took a most active part in the event. High up near the ceiling of the assembly hall we tossed the heroes of the day—the professors and representatives of the administration, elderly persons, were evidently frightened by such honors. Below the dependable, young hands of their pupils carefully received them. Higher than everyone else flew the withered little figure of the university doorkeeper, Ivan Matveevich, who had served in the Eastern Institute from the day of its founding,

---

6. *Kurma* is a kind of jacket with wide sleeves, a high collar and a clasp on the right side or the center. Instead of buttons and buttonholes there is a special kind of lacing.

and was known as a severe and good "father" to all the student confraternity. In the period of the occupation he saved more than one student from the Japanese secret service.

The department conducted extensive social services among the Chinese. Students taught them Russian, led political circles, and spoke at meetings. Not counting the May First Club which our department looked after, and where in consequence many of our fellows spent their days and nights, there was not a single Chinese corner which we did not penetrate.

At that time, in Vladivostok as everywhere in the country, however, it was not easy to live a student's life. Not everyone received a stipend and some even had to pay for tuition. For those who had not yet mastered a specialty it was difficult to get a job. The period of restoration had not yet been ended so there was still unemployment. I remember how we all envied a certain girl, a student of the Eastern Department who, on the recommendation of the local party committee of the university, became a messenger for the office of the People's Commissariat of Foreign Affairs in Vladivostok. The position of messenger in such a place seemed like the first step on the ladder of success in the diplomatic field.

The hoarse, drawn-out horn of the *Hsinp'inghai* sounded sadly. The ship said farewell to the city. We were sailing. Farewell, Vladivistok, we will not soon see you again . . .

The *Hsinp'inghai* slowly leaves the bay, passing by Russian Island. In tsarist times troops were stationed there guarding the entrance to the harbor. During the intervention the Japanese were quartered there, but now it is unpopulated. From the high upper deck one can clearly see the abandoned barracks from which even the galvanized iron roofing was carried away by the interventionists. Many anonymous graves are there. Russian Island was the site for executions during the occupation.

Not long before our departure we spent a whole day on the island, access to which was given without any special formalities. We visited these graves, stood over them, and then plunged into the green thickets which were suffused with the sharp, fresh smell of lillies of the valley. They flowered underfoot, untouched, snow-white, lush and unusually large. Distracted by them, one of us clods lost the cover from a large, pretty well dented enameled teapot which had been taken, alas, from the kitchen without the permission of our landlady,

Aunt Dusha. Imagine our horror—women treasured their dishes at that time, and it was nowhere to be found. Fortunately, thrifty Aunt Dusha had another cover.

Russian Island was slowly left astern. It seemed that in the water at the edge of the shore lay large, round, remarkably blue pebbles. These were jellyfish which the ebb-tide left at the shore. The *Hsinp'inghai* left whole masses of them, blue and red, astern as it went out into the open sea. Delightful in color and shape, they swayed gracefully in the water, but to the swimmer who encountered them they promised little joy. The sting of a red jellyfish causes a high temperature for several days.

There were several passengers besides us on the upper deck of the *Hsinp'inghai*. One of them caught our attention. He was thin with very sharp non-Russian features, as it seemed to us, and he wore an excellent foreign suit. In his mouth gold teeth glittered in a complete horseshoe shape. He kept apart from the others, rarely left his cabin and spoke to no one. At once we decided that we had encountered an "international imperialist shark" as some of our most fiery orators frequently expressed themselves at the time. Just think, gold teeth like a millionaire's! Of course, he was not going to China with good intentions. We all conceived a hatred of the stranger, and from a distance we cast him the fiercest glances (though filled with curiosity), to which, however, he paid no heed. What was there to do? We had somehow to coexist with him. The presence of the "shark" really spoiled our mood in the first days of our voyage.

In the Port of Moji

The *Hsinp'inghai* steamed slowly southward. It became hotter and hotter. An almost dead calm prevailed. By day we were surrounded by the blue radiance of the sky and the sea; by night we were enchanted by the endless column of moonlight which lay to portside. After three days we reached the Japanese port of Moji.

We were struck by Japan's rather toylike beauty—her bright green islands were so pretty, so were her twisted, dwarf pines, fragile little houses, her diminutive boats. We were charmed by this scene but subsequent events soon shocked us out of this romantic mood. The *Hsinp'inghai* stopped at Moji for coal, and while she was unloading it we thought of getting off to have a look at Japan with which we had but recently concluded the Peking Convention. The Soviet Union had made serious concessions for the sake of stabilizing the situation in the Far East. We thought that after this relations should have improved and we would be treated well.

We had just succeeded in buying a large quantity of ripe bananas and pungent, tender, pink persimmons from the countless boats which surrounded the ship and we were delighting in their cheapness when we saw a Customs launch heading towards us. We had studied international law and we knew that the deck of a ship, even when in a foreign port, is the territory of the country whose flag she flies. Therefore, none of us thought to get excited merely because Japanese Customs wanted to make our acquaintance. On the contrary, we looked with curiosity at the little launch which was quickly approaching our ship amidst the Japanese boats which yielded the way to it, and at the strange gold-braided coats. Only later did it become evident that Japanese intelligence officers in the guise of Customs men were favoring us with their presence.

Two brothers, one ten years old and the other sixteen, were traveling together with us on the upper deck. I don't remember whom they were going to see; their tickets were to Shanghai. At the time I am speaking of, the younger one was peeling a banana which had just been purchased and threw the skin overboard. By accident it fell right on the face of a "Customs officer." A furious roar resounded. The little boy paled and hid himself instantly.

The Japanese officer with features distorted bounded up the lowered ladder. He was on deck in an instant. Small, puny, with protruding upper teeth, and wearing horn-rimmed glasses, dressed in a stiff parade tunic, he looked just as if he had come off a poster depicting a Japanese imperialist. He looked us over with his dull eyes, searching for his "foe." We all looked at him silently, dumbfounded.

The samurai code of honor transformed Japanese officers into maniacs capable of losing their human aspect over the most insignificant cause. They considered themselves the divine descendants of the goddess Amaterasu, representatives of a race of rulers predestined to hold sway over the earth.[7]

---

7. According to Japanese religious beliefs, Amaterasu is the goddess of the sun, the progenetrix of the ruling Japanese dynasty and the whole Japanese people. Right up until 1945 when, after the wartime defeat, the emperor was forced to renounce publicly pretensions to divine descent, this myth was an officially recognized dogma in Japan.

And suddenly there was a banana skin from the deck of a Soviet ship, a greeting, so to speak, from that country where not long before the unsuccessful pretenders to world power and foreign property had been thrown out shamefully.

We were summoned to the lounge. A "verification of documents" ensued. Only afterwards did the captain explain to us that Japanese Customs had no right whatsoever to do this. We needed only water and coal. None of us was able to get off to go to Moji and therefore our documents should not have interested the Japanese. However, the captain did not protest. In Vladivostok he had received strict instructions to avoid complications. He restrained himself and remained silent. He only said to us, "Self-control, my friends."

In that anxious year Japanese intelligence lost all sense of proportion in searching for "Comintern agents." China had roused herself and every Soviet citizen headed there was suspected by the imperialists of "subversive" activity. Precisely because of this, the Japanese intelligence agents appeared on board ship and demanded our documents. The Chinese in the hold did not interest them.

In the small first-class lounge three or four Japanese installed themselves unceremoniously like masters at the dining tables on which our passports were already lying. They were markedly contemptuous in their relations with the ship's officers, and they did not even invite us, the passengers, to be seated. Several times I intercepted the fixed gaze of Japanese officers directed at me. At that time I could not understand why I was attracting such obvious attention to myself. Only afterwards was it explained to me. From the viewpoint of our uninvited guests who were seeking Bolshevik contagion on the ship, I appeared to be a "desperate Red" since I had a short, masculine haircut and wore a cap as was the fashion then in Soviet student circles.

The Japanese on whom the banana skin had fallen was pacing up and down the lounge all the while with brisk, nervous strides, glancing at us from time to time. The elder boy entered the lounge. In that very instant, the Japanese sprang at him like a cat and with an unexpected blow knocked off his cap. At the table where the Japanese sat the sharp guttural cry "Taikoo off your khat" resounded. The little fellow bent over and lifted up his "khat." When he straightened up his eyes were filled with tears; he was biting his lip. Having examined the documents presented by the captain, the Japanese evidently understood whose brother the elder of the boys was, and having unloosed his primal wrath on him, now anxiously awaited the appearance of his "insulter." The frightened boy hid in the machine room and didn't want to appear at all, but the Japanese demanded his presence. He had just entered when the enraged samurai advanced on him and struck him in the face with all his might.

Then we exploded. We forgot the captain's warning as we shouted, protested, and raised an uproar. And loudest of all was the "shark of international imperialism" with his gold teeth. In a pure Russian accent he began to shout, "What an outrage!" Almost a year later I met him in South China and learned that of all people it would have been more dangerous for him than anyone else to have fallen into the hands of Japanese intelligence. He was going to take up the post of military adviser to the National-Revolutionary Army of the South Chinese government. He was silent all the way, speaking to no one, but then he could not restrain himself.

Now the conflict took on a general character. The Japanese turned toward us. Raising one arm in the air and holding his hand on the holster of his revolver, he shouted imperiously "Stop!" He let us understand that he was ready to fire. Stunned, we quieted down in an instant. I don't know what might have happened next. We were so agitated that we might have rushed at the Japanese and beaten him. Then he, of course, would have shot at us. Anything was possible at that difficult time when our ambassadors were being killed and our diplomatic mail seized. The diplomatic incident into which we were clearly being goaded (as the pretext for the seizure of a Soviet ship) might have occurred and we might have received no thanks for that in our homeland. We had enough trouble without this. We were stopped by the sight of the usually good-natured face of the fat supercargo, twisted in horror as he made some kind of secret sign to us. The "verification" of passports was renewed. In essence the Japanese subjected all of us to a real interrogation. Of course, our desire "to take a look at Japan" dissolved of itself. The Japanese did not intend to give us permission and we were resolved not to leave the ship in the present circumstances.

Thus did the capitalist world greet us after we had but recently left the territory of our young Soviet motherland. There was nothing surprising in this, but all the same the incident in Moji became an important landmark for me personally. It was precisely from that time that I began a kind of political training which I was to continue afterwards in China and which matured me considerably. Of course, in Vladivostok I had already heard plenty of chilling stories about the terrible times of the Japanese occupation. But I was, probably, more cheerful and carefree than befitted a girl of my age. I had never seen the horrors of war, never held a weapon in my hand, I was studying what I liked and before me lay a bright future which apparently nothing could cloud. Even the past did not affect me at that time. But suddenly it was right there before me.

These people, speaking a guttural Russian, and asking us provocative, insulting questions with a view to establishing our supposed illegal intentions, impudently threatening us, were evidently "specialists on the Russian question." There was no need to entertain doubts as to where they were just three years before. They gave themselves away by their conduct and we knew them for what they were. You can imagine how we felt in those moments.

Towards evening, after taking on coal, the *Hsinp'inghai* turned around and slowly left the unfriendly harbor. A heavy, sullen silence reigned on deck. We passed by the charming, toy-like islands whose vivid greens seemed to grow straight out of the blue sea's waves. The fishermen's and ferrymen's frail boats called to mind the marvelous ancient Japanese prints. What exquisite memories we might have carried away from this blessed place!

Chefoo

Our next stop was Chefoo, a port on the north of the Shantung peninsula. There we were to debark and report to the Soviet consulate. It was situated in the building of the former tsarist consulate right on the shore, and we saw the red flag on its tall flagstaff even before the land on the horizon. How gloriously it flamed in the rays of the hot, southern sun! With what joy we looked at it, at first through our binoculars and then with our naked eyes. It was a welcome and a reassurance from our distant motherland after our experience in Japan.

Before the *Hsinp'inghai* had even lowered its anchor we already understood what important event was taking place in Chefoo. About ten British ships of various tonnages were in the harbor; they looked abandoned and pitiful. No one would load or unload them. It was absolutely clear—a strike! The fevered air of struggle reached us from the Chinese shore.

The harbor workers were striking in reaction to the violence unleashed by the British imperialists against the unarmed demonstrators in Canton on June 23. Pickets were placed on the shore, and they vigilantly ensured the strict enforcement of the strike committee's resolutions. However, no one tried to act counter to them. The population of Chefoo like the whole Chinese people supported the anti-British boycott. In Chefoo not only we but almost all of the Chinese seasonal laborers debarked and they made even more of a tumult and shouted even louder than in Vladivostok.

What a brilliant, beautiful city lay before us. What a mass of greenery, especially pomegranate bushes thickly dotted with red flowers. Evidently this was the favorite decorative plant. Chefoo is a marvelous resort with an excellent climate and beach. Foreigners living in China had already known for a long time about it. Their families went there for summer vacation. We examined the architecture of the Chinese buildings, the decorated shops, their signboards in the form of huge, black boards with golden characters or vertical cloths with sewn-on, varicolored characters. They hung thickly along the whole street.

From every side half-naked rickshaw pullers flew up to us with a cry. We loaded our baggage, which unfortunately was not very elegant for a foreign journey, onto their rickshaws, but we ourselves walked alongside. The pullers were angry with us but we remained resolved in our decision and did not give in to them. An elderly rickshaw man ran by and we listened in horror to his labored breathing. A corpulent European, twice as large as his puller, sprawled at his ease in the rickshaw. Further on we saw a group of men harnessed to a big, two-wheeled dray loaded with a mountain of sacks. The sweat streamed down their naked backs, they were lining out some monotonous refrain, a Chinese worksong. Two others were carrying an enormous pumpkin on a pole at almost a run, and, gasping for breath, cried out in turn, *"aya-kha, aya-kha"* in time to their movement. There he was, among the most numerous in the ranks of the Chinese proletariat—the coolie, "bitter-strength," "the human horse."

Several persons of indeterminate nationality crossed the street; their Chinese clothing contrasted strangely with their evidently non-Chinese features. What kind of a masquerade was this? Why should one combine a red beard with a Chinese skull-cap? Aha, these were the missionaries whose unctuous words for many years already had helped the imperialists to enslave China.

After several minutes we stopped at the consulate's gates. The former tsarist property in China had been returned to the Soviet people by the Sino-Soviet Agreement of May 1924. Over a period of years, the impoverished tsarist diplomats and White emigrés had unofficially controlled it. Thus it was not surprising that the building of the Soviet consulate in Chefoo appeared badly neglected, in places even ramshackle, and definitely crying out for repair. It was a large, old, wooden two-storey house with an imposing exterior. It boasted the highest spire in town, a wide balcony, and a large number of all kinds of carved balusters and decorations.

The wide-open gates with a beautiful wrought-iron grille opened onto a front courtyard with a fountain situated in the midst of weed-choked flower beds which evidently hadn't been tended in years. The enormous garden behind the house also was sadly neglected, as we soon saw; the rosebushes had grown wild, everywhere thick grass sprouted, smothering the cultivated plants, the trees were unpruned, and their branches were intertwined in disorder.

Evidently money had not yet been allocated for repairs on the house. At that time we adhered to a strict regime of economy. Gardens and flower beds were of no importance. The cultivation of flowers seemed like excessive luxury, a useless occupation. It was not even considered necessary to beautify Moscow with greenery. Many trees and gardens were ruthlessly destroyed and in their place denuded squares appeared. Not till several years later did people concern themselves with the beautification of the capitol.

The consul, Comrade Shilo, received us in his office.[8] At the sight of my close-cropped head in a cap he was struck dumb for an instant, then with a suffering tone and wrinkling his brow he said, "My God, just whom are they sending me, just what are they thinking?" By the undefined word "they" the consul evidently meant the administration of our department. He angrily called up and asked to have his wife come down. She gave instructions that a woman's hat be bought for me at once.

But fate had prepared more in the way of new experiences for the consul. Looking hard he suddenly noticed that the well-worn trousers of one of my companions were held together only by a string instead of a belt and he exploded like a bomb. Everything was fuel for his rage; the light-headed young

---

8. One of the first of our diplomatic workers in China, he was an Old Bolshevik who had been an underground worker and political prisoner in tsarist times.

people who went abroad as if on a picnic, not thinking that their irresponsible mode of dress was putting all of Soviet studentdom under a cloud, the leadership of Far Eastern State University which educated the youth poorly, and even the representative of the People's Commissariat for Foreign Affairs in Vladivostok, Fonshteyn, because he was blind to what was going on. The storm raged for a long time. We stood frightened and ashamed, beginning to understand that we had prepared poorly for our foreign assignments. Shilo gave my ill-fated colleague categorical instructions to buy himself a belt at once, and with that he suddenly quieted down. He looked at us and laughed. We immediately cheered up.

The consul warned us about the anti-British strike in the port and said we would have to stay put for a while since English vessels were not sailing, and the ships of other nations were infrequent visitors in Chefoo. Chinese boats were not supposed to carry Europeans who not only never used them but who would not even be sold tickets so firmly established was this custom. "It's better to wait a bit," he said, "the situation will soon be clarified."

Shilo invited us to stay at his house. Cots were placed for us on a spacious, open verandah leading straight onto the garden. A screen separated me from the men. The fragrance of flowering roses and of some kind of sweet grass came in from the garden. An enormous southern moon appeared at night over the old garden. On this first night in China we could not sleep for a long time; we walked in the tall, dewy grass of the garden. We set all the dogs barking and went to sleep only when we heard the crying of the consul's children whom we had awakened.

In the consul's house lived the families of Consul Shilo himself, Solokhin, the representative of the Foreign Trade Commissariat, and the former tsarist consul who had taken out Soviet citizenship and had represented Soviet interests until Shilo's arrival. We did not find him there as he had gone to Harbin on business. The tsarist consul in Chefoo did not want to betray his motherland, and it so happened there were more than a few such persons among the old diplomatic personnel. But he had lived very long abroad and his children didn't know Russia at all. They had grown up and received their education in China and moved only in the "select society" of Chefoo's foreign residents who hated everything Soviet. Their ties and acquaintances were all foreign and hostile to us. They conversed in English with their friends and among themselves, in Chinese with the servant on the order of "give me, bring me." They had almost no occasion to speak Russian. Although their Russian was accent-free one could sense something cold and artificial in it.

"I was in the International Club today," the consul's son, a lad of sixteen, said at dinner, carefully and correctly pronouncing the Russian words. (We had been speaking about Soviet people.) "I said I was a Soviet citizen. They didn't want to believe me." And he laughed in satisfaction at the effect he had produced upon his foreign friends. And we thought, "How right they are, these friends of his." Although he was truly a Russian and had Soviet citizenship he seemed alien to us. It was not a question, of course, of his unusual costume—shorts, which we were seeing for the first time in our lives, and which in our eyes were excessively elegant for a boy. He had a rather pleasant not unintelligent face, and he said nothing to injure our national pride. But we had nothing in common with him. The imperialists' behaviour in China did not bother him; on the contrary, their children were his friends. And he showed no interest in his native land. Obviously, the people at the International Club were much closer to him than we were.

Next to him sat his sister, a seventeen-year-old girl with a fine profile, a sweet, tender face, and curly blond hair. She seemed the embodiment of freshness and purity. But here was Shilo beginning some strange sort of conversation filled with hints which were incomprehensible to us. He was avowing that the girl did not like young people but was attracted only by older men. "Isn't that so?" he said. "Confess! Especially old Greeks. I know one of them. It seems that he has several millions."

The girl listened indifferently. It was all the same to her. But then her mother butted in. With an almost beseeching tone, she asked that this unpleasant conversation be terminated. "You know the young people nowadays, they're not like we were," she said. "My daughter considers that happiness is money. It's not worth talking about. Especially since she's already engaged. There's nothing to be done about it."

The girl somehow indulged in a tactless remark at the expense of one of my companions, V. Novoselov. A participant in the struggle against the Semyonovites, he came to the university directly from his partisan unit, where he had not left the saddle for many months. One could notice this at once by his cavalryman's gait. We were sitting on the balcony of the consul's house when down below our dashing partisan walked by. Evidently feeling the maidenly eyes directed at him he swaggered from side to side in a particularly dandyish manner. At this the consul's daughter snorted and said, "Volodya walks like a tramp." I had to intervene and after that my relationship with her was spoiled.

At that time our diplomatic personnel in Chefoo did not have much work. Our arrival enlivened the old consul's house, and its inhabitants in turn tried to amuse us. We went yachting, we did a lot of shopping, went cycling and dancing. The consul himself took part in all of these amusements and turned out to be not a bad sort at all, on the contrary he was cheerful, sociable like an old friend, and he even showed us how to dance the foxtrot. We heard this word for the first time there.

There was a good library in the consulate which had remained from tsarist days, and Shilo tried to supplement it with new books about China including Soviet editions although there were few such at the time. We had free access to the consul's office, especially since it was often empty, and therefore first one and then another of us would sit on the floor in front of the bookcases, immersed in literature about China. Our enforced stay in Chefoo did not pass idly. Our good-natured consul made sure of this as he daily discussed the latest news with us, trying to "set us on course" as he put it.

At that time China was still a semi-colony where imperialists were the masters. But a great revolution was already in progress. Two governments existed in the country: a revolutionary one in Canton, and a counter-revolutionary one in Peking. The Peking government was the officially recognized one although not only did it not express the interests of the nation, but on the contrary constantly betrayed them. An endless series of coups brought to power the representatives of various military cliques which served as the imperialists' instruments of policy in China. When we arrived in China the office of president was filled by the universally hated Japanophile, Marshal Tuan Ch'i-jui, a former comrade-in-arms of Yüan Shih-k'ai, the executioner of the I Ho T'uan Rebellion (1899-1901) and the Hsinhai Revolution of 1911. Almost every political demonstration in Peking proclaimed, "Down with Tuan Ch'i-jui!"

The government in Canton created by the great Chinese revolutionary Sun Yat-sen enjoyed the sympathy and support of the broad masses. At its head stood the Kuomintang which was a revolutionary party then. In January

1924 at the direction of the Comintern, the Chinese Communist party entered into the Kuomintang for the purpose of creating a national revolutionary united front on the basis of individual membership and the maintenance of organizational and political independence. This served as a dividing line in the development of the Chinese revolution.

We had arrived at an exceedingly tense time. Experienced people asserted that in the very near future one should expect an aggravation of the relations between Marshal Chang Tso-lin, the military dictator of Manchuria and the henchman of Japanese imperialism, and Marshal Feng Yü-hsiang, the commander of the Nationalist armies of the northwest who sympathized with the revolutionary movement and had made contact with the Kuomintang and requested advisers from the USSR. Actually, six months had not passed before war broke out between them.

After the English shot into a peaceful demonstration in Canton on June 23, things which the imperialists had never even dreamed of began happening in China. The Hong Kong-Canton strike became the banner of a national movement, and English goods were boycotted all over China. English trade fell, and the English suffered losses in the millions. Fear and desolation reigned in Hong Kong, the British colony in the south of China, and in Shameen Island, the diplomatic quarter of Canton, as all the Chinese who worked for the foreigners left their jobs. The infuriated colonialists finally dropped their masks of civilization. In July 1925 the governor of Hong Kong, Sir Edward Stubbs, declared that Chinese convicted of agitation during the duration of the boycott would be thrashed with a cat-o'-nine-tails.

The British imperialists ascribed their setbacks in China to our influence and threatened the Soviet Union with war. In the first days of July, the British cabinet discussed the question of breaking diplomatic ties with the USSR and the ministers, including the minister of colonies, Lord Birkenhead, declared themselves in favor of a rupture. Meanwhile, in conjunction with the anxious news in the press a notice of a humorous character appeared. In the English House of Commons a question was raised as to whether the government knew that the Russians in Peking had made an embrasure in the wall between their embassy and the British embassy. Such a bugaboo were the Russian Bolsheviks for the English lords.

In Harbin relations between the Soviet representatives and the Chinese military administration were exacerbated after the directive issued by Ivanov, the manager of the CER, that by June 1, 1925, all persons having neither Chinese nor Soviet citizenship would be relieved of their jobs.[9] The order was directed against the Russian White guards who were entrenched in the CER, but Chang Tso-lin came out in their defense. In the clashes between the Harbin Komsomols and the White emigré youth, the police consistently supported the latter.

But let us return to Chefoo where the strike was still continuing, the first strike which we saw on Chinese soil. Shilo forbade us in the strictest terms from conversing with the pickets in order to avoid any possible diplomatic complications for him. But still we encountered them every day and had a good look at them. Of course, they were a far cry from the pickets of the Canton strike committee who wore paramilitary uniforms, were armed and patrolled the cities like masters. Here one sensed more excitement than a consciousness of power. Yet this was a mass anti-British strike, one of the first and most powerful in North China. As soon as it ended the consul got us three tickets on a British ship to Tientsin.

On the eve of our departure an insignificant incident occurred which, however, affected me and my comrades. As I have already said, our outfits were not distinguished by their elegance. I had only one decent dress and that a dark blue woolen one which was impossible to wear in the heat of Chefoo. My homemade frocks of cheap summer material were old-fashioned and poorly sewn. On the consul's orders I never appeared on the street without my hat, but it fitted poorly on my mannish hairdo, so more often I held it under my arm. In short, I really had to get outfitted quickly. Comrade Shilo and his wife, and the Solokhin couple made no remarks about this to me; I told them I would buy everything I needed when I got to Peking. At that the former consul's wife intervened.

I should say in advance that this woman treated me very warmly and I had no doubts about her sincere desire to help me. Like me she was a Muscovite and we often had long talks about life in Moscow and in Soviet

---

9. A mixed Sino-Soviet administration existed for the CER. Many Soviet citizens worked on the line itself and in its subsidiary enterprises.

Russia in general. I must have been a lousy agitator since, at the end of each talk she would say, "Nevertheless, there is nothing on earth higher than Christian philosophy and morality."

On the eve of our departure she summoned me to her bedroom and started to show me her wardrobe. "We have the custom here," she said as if in passing, "of giving each other dresses. Here, see what a dress the English consul gave me." She took off a hanger something covered from top to bottom with silver sequins. "And here's what the missionary's wife gave me." It was a heavy, black silk falling in wide pleats. "My daughters are so capricious," continued the consul's wife, "you make a nice dress for them, they wear it once and that's all. How many of them are hanging here in the closet unworn. If you would like to take them . . ." She cleared her throat and glanced at me.

I suppose that I was redder than a cooked lobster. What an insult! How dared this woman whom I hardly knew make me such an offer! Here was her Christian philosophy and morality which had no room for human dignity. Now I laugh when I remember that incident, but at that time and in those conditions my indignation was legitimate, and my comrades supported me warmly. It was not easy for students to get by in those days, but we hardly worried about material goods and got accustomed to managing with a minimum of things. Once in Vladivostok I somehow broke the heel off my Moscow shoes, and since I had no money to repair it I broke off the other heel as well and went to school that way knowing that no one would even think to laugh at me. In fact, I was praised for my shrewdness. In short, we often lacked even the essentials, but we were students of Soviet colleges and carefully guarded our self-respect. We would not take a dress as a gift from the English consul or the wife of a missionary. Why should we! This episode clouded our relationship with the family of the former consul and we parted on rather cold terms.

It was several hours from Chefoo to Tientsin. The boat was a small one and the passengers few. There was not a single Chinese, by the way, because of the anti-British boycott. None of our fellow countrymen were abroad and we did not make anyone's acquaintance, especially since our companions at table expressed no interest on that score. In those days, Soviet citizens were boycotted in bourgeois society, and we were very different in appearance from our neighbors at table so that they could not make a mistake. We coped rather successfully with a large number of knives and forks set on both sides of our plates, but we were confounded by a white metal bowl of water served to everyone after dessert. We were cautious in approaching it from fear of some impropriety and we were right. Just a little later, by observing the people around us, we discovered this water was for rinsing the ends of one's fingers after eating. If one of us had trustingly drunk it down it would have been the greatest scandal from the point of view of Western etiquette.

The Tientsin docks swarmed with ragged stevedores—coolies who lived by casual labor and were always half-starved. We gave one of them our sack of sweet crusts in the name of the Russian woman, Aunt Dusha of Vladivostok. Tientsin, an important commercial and industrial center of North China, did not welcome us like the nice quiet town of Chefoo. Consul Ozarnin looked preoccupied. He was a terribly busy man who had no time to deal with us. He quickly loaded us onto a train and we set off on the same night.

This last, shortest section of the trip seemed like the longest. Before us loomed Peking, like the Blue Bird of Happiness, the goal of our student desires. How we had prepared for our encounter with it, with what impatience we had waited. We could no longer think of anything else. The wheels clacked restlessly, the car swayed from side to side. Ahead Peking!

Chapter II

IN PEKING

First Day in the Capital of China

We arrived in Peking about two in the morning, I suppose. The consul in Tientsin had carried out his promise to call the embassy about us. We were met at the station which was a fortunate thing since we ourselves would have been too embarrassed to show up there at such a late hour and would have sat around somewhere until morning. The station was right next to the Legation Quarter and in several minutes we were already there.

From our textbooks we already knew that the diplomatic quarter was surrounded by high fortress-like walls and that foreign soldiers stood guard at the gates. China was forced to agree to this humiliation after the joint forces of the imperialists crushed the anti-imperialist Boxer Rebellion. The gloomy, forbidding gates with their solid iron sections, the guards who stopped the car, and their cold politeness through which one could sense their clear hostility, produced the most oppressive sensation. We remembered the Japanese officers on board the *Hsinp'inghai* and the slap in the face by the samurai.

A two or three-minute ride along the main street of the quarter, half-lit at this late hour, and we were at the gates of the embassy, a stone arch in the classical style with two columns and an iron fence with spear-shaped spikes. Electric lights suspended from iron holders illuminated only a small area in front of the gates. Through the fence could be seen a broad, dark path at the end of which were two lamplights at the entrance to a large white house which was the main building of the embassy. The gate completed the high wall of the fence, over which the tops of trees showed darkly. Stillness, everyone around was sleeping. An old Chinese, the embassy's doorkeeper, with whom we later became very friendly, came out of a white, stone guardhouse and bowed deeply. I and my luggage were entrusted to his care. I was to live in one of the cottages near the main gate, and my comrades were taken further, to a place prepared for them in the military compound.[1]

The hot Peking morning found us in the old, shady park of the embassy. Cicadas chirped deafeningly in the bushes. We thought they were grasshoppers

---

1. The military compound was the area where tsarist Russia placed the embassy garrison.

and were very surprised when we caught a giant fly. It barely fit into a match-box! Before us was the embassy building, a two-storey detached house with a balcony and columns along the facade. At the main entrance two traditional Chinese white stone lions stared with comic fury from under tightly curled manes. On the open verandah instead of chairs there were tile barrels of the most variegated colors. On the other side of the house was the embassy garden in Chinese style. Enormous tripods green from age and standing on stone pedestals caught one's eye. Alas, the long, dried stalks of plants jutted out and spoiled the noble picture of ancient Chinese bronzes. Evidently the tsarist diplomats used these priceless monuments of Chinese antiquity for the most utilitarian purposes—as flower vases.

A rectangular red pedestal was placed on the roof of the building with the angle facing out. The hammer and sickle were depicted on the two forward sides. Over it was a short flagstaff with the state flag of the Soviet Union. The morning breeze fluttered its red folds just as at home, in Moscow or Vladivostok. Subsequently we were told of the triumphant circumstances in which it had first been raised, of the large number of representatives from progressive circles of Chinese society who attended the ceremony, of the crowds which besieged the embassy and the malicious expressions which the imperialists gave vent to on this occasion.

To the left of the main building, in a far corner of the park, was the consulate; along the path to it lived our trade representative N. K. Klyshko in a one-storey Chinese-style house with a terrace decorated with red wooden columns. Next to it, surrounded by ancient trees, stood the tiny embassy church with a tiny belltower. It had been constructed as early as the first quarter of the eighteenth century through special agreement with the Chinese government, and it was an exquisite example of ancient Russian architecture in the style of Naryshinsky Baroque, with columns, carved platbands and all sorts of decorations. It was so small that one could not take it seriously; it was not a church but a little tower from a children's story. I don't know if a dozen people could have fitted into it. However, nothing larger was needed in those times. In former times our embassy to China had few people in it, and the guards which accompanied it prayed in the church of the Russian Orthodox mission in the Peikuan section.

Cottages were strewn around the entire park and diplomatic employees and their families lived in them. Weeds burgeoned from the old flowerbeds;

the lawns were trampled on. This was just the condition in which the embassy grounds were presented to us after they had been managed by the tsarist diplomats. If it had been the present, our hands would have itched to take up shovels and put the park into proper order. But—a characteristic detail—no one even thought of it then, and there were no "fine ladies and gentlemen" among us either. We all lived with thoughts of the great events, and the international scale overshadowed the details of daily life. Flowers, grass! What did they have to do with the world revolution?

On the right of the grounds were attached service quarters and buildings—the military compound, the section for the administration of the Chinese Eastern Railroad, and a connecting section where the TASS bureau, the secretariat, the apartments of the military attaché and the common dining hall were located.[2]

This part of the embassy grounds was separated from the main part by a thick cypress corridor, and high walls which on one end were set against the CER section and on the other led to the outside. This was the service or so to speak rear entrance of the embassy. Communication between the two sections was possible only through the gates which were located in the middle. This corridor left one with a dismal impression. It was through it that almost two years later the soldiers of Chang Tso-lin burst, and our comrades who had been placed under arrest were carried out. But of this we shall speak later.

Like all the foreign embassies in Peking, the Soviet embassy was surrounded by a high, stone wall, and the military compound even had bastions, loop-holes and other archaisms. But in place of the watchman who stood guard for the other embassies there was only an old Chinese man, fat and jolly, dressed in national costume and even with a queue, albeit shamefully hidden by the high collar of his jacket. He knew all the employees and members of their families on sight. His radiant, round face expressed joy and kindness and his high forehead shone in the sun.

He approved of our early stroll and wished us good health. How pleasant to hear one's first *"nin hao"* in Peking![3] We wanted to walk outside the gates but this was not permitted. In front, in the shade of large trees, perhaps fifteen

2. The embassy grounds were much larger in those days than they have been since 1950 when by agreement with the Chinese People's Republic, the Soviet Union voluntarily returned the territory of the military compound, and the former administrative section of the CER.
3. *"Nin hao"* means "hello" in Chinese.

cheerful, white-toothed rickshaw men were sitting without embarrassment right on the sidewalk. Some of them had begun their breakfasts. They rapidly manipulated their chopsticks, holding their bowls at lip-level and joked with one another. All of them rushed towards us and we almost ran back to the embassy in fright to the great surprise of the gatekeeper.

We were astounded. Why were there rickshaws here? Was it possible that the embassy employees used rickshaws like the colonialists? Soon the situation was explained to us. It seemed that in the conditions of the time it was not always possible to act as one wished. An excessive straightforwardness would have caused more harm than good. It was necessary to take the existent order into consideration. The first embassy employees did not want to use rickshaws. The very sight of such exploitation was repugnant to them. But the rickshaw men greeted this decision with hostility. They were being deprived of their wages. The embassy territory had been allotted to them and they demanded work. It almost caused a scandal. Employees coming out of the embassy were grabbed by rickshaw men who shoutingly demanded that they be hired. A delegation appeared at the embassy. The imperialists observed our difficult situation with delight. Thus instructions were given to hire rickshaws.[4]

Soviet citizens behaved toward the rickshaw men in an entirely different manner from the representatives of the imperialist countries. We never disputed the fare and in general were much more generous. But most of all we viewed the rickshaw pullers as men, we never insulted their patriotic feelings or their personal dignity as did some "civilized" representatives of the West who when paying would throw their money on the ground, as if recoiling from handing it over. Almost all of us had a personal rickshaw puller whom we didn't change. By the way, the friendship between one of our comrades and his rickshaw man unfortunately had a tragic ending. Seeing a hammer and sickle tattoo, the rickshaw man himself got tattooed this way. The rickshaw man paid cruelly for his indelible sympathy towards the Soviet Union after the 1927 raid on the embassy.

It was always the same rickshaw pullers who kept watch before the embassy gates. This was not surprising since they were allotted areas of labor by their guilds and associations. It would have gone hard for some who tried to

---

4. From 1949 on employees of Soviet establishments in China again stopped using rickshaws.

get fares in defiance of the established system. It was said, however, that there were spies among the rickshaw pullers at our gate. It could not have been otherwise.

My comrades wanted to show me what kind of a set-up they had so they escorted me to the military compound. It had no outer gates and one could penetrate it only by means of a narrow iron door in the high stone wall which adjoined the embassy mess. Now it performed the most peaceful of functions. The center of social activity and the locus of constant intercourse for the entire embassy community was located in the spacious, one-storey building of the former officers' club. The local Chinese workers' committee and the special circles for Chinese—political literacy, international affairs, Russian and English classes, which were conducted by our students for the most part were all located there. I also joined in this routine work; I taught Russian to the cooks, launderers, and other Chinese servants. My students were all men; the women, lacking confidence in their abilities, did not want to study. They were all illiterate.

The chorus and amateur orchestra sparkled with talent. They performed in both Chinese and Russian. On March 8, 1925, when International Women's Day was celebrated in China for the first time, the Chinese employees of the embassy presented a play about the oppression of women in China. Chinese female students attended the performance as guests.

The jazz orchestra was a huge success among the embassy employees. During these years many people in our country took a great interest in this form of amateur activity. Going to the club for the first time, we found about a dozen persons there who with the aid of the most diverse collection of objects—from a comb wrapped in cigarette paper to an ordinary cast-iron frying pan—were vigorously playing a foxtrot—"Nelly Baby, How Do You Do"—which was popular then. A gramophone was playing in the next room, and one could hear the meowing of the Hawaiian guitar which had recently been "discovered" in the West and was making a triumphant procession around the world.

In the summer of 1925 many Soviet students gathered in Peking. There were representatives from all the centers of Soviet sinology—Moscow, Leningrad, and Vladivostok. The Muscovites V. L. Gamberg, I. M. Oshanin, A. P. Rogachev, and V. I. Melnikov had come earlier and were, so to speak, old-timers. But the recently arrived alumni of the Far Eastern University in Vladivostok were in the majority. In Peking we came across these upperclassmen of FEU: Z. S. Dubasova, T. I. Vladimirova, M. K. Pashkova, F. Bokanenko and their classmates S. A. Vrubel, T. F. Skvortsov, V. Voyloshnikov, N. M. Yakovlev, and B. S. Perlin. Among the Leningraders we met Ye. S. Yolk, S. M. Okoneshnikova, and later P. Ye. Skachkov and E. M. Abramson. Scholars as well as student probationers were visiting Peking. The Leningrad sinologist V. A. Vasilev was there at the time. Soon Nikolsky, a teacher of Chinese in the Frunze Academy and the Institute of Sinology arrived from Moscow, and a year later G. O. Monzeler came from Leningrad University to study Peking's historical monuments.

It is with sadness that I write most of these names, remembering the terrible years of Stalinist repression (the end of the 30s). How many young and talented Chinese specialists perished, men who were loyal to the party and their work, and who laid the foundation of Soviet sinology thereby contributing so much to the cause of Sino-Soviet friendship. Melnikov, Vladimirova, Bokanenko, Voyloshnikov, Yakovlev, Perlin, Yolk, Abramson, Vasilev, Novoselov are no more. Dubasova and Skachkov spent many years in exile.

But at that time they were youth in full bloom, full of hope and enthusiasm. Not long before our arrival, several of them had gone off to work in the Kalgan and Kaifeng missions of our military advisers. Those who had remained in Peking greeted us during the dinner break. We recounted our experiences on board the *Hsinp'inghai* and in the Japanese port of Moji. It seemed that what we had witnessed was not the worst. For example, M. K. Pashkova who arrived via Manchuria related the following:

"At some station on the South Manchurian Railway, two Chinese, one young and the other somewhat older, sat down in my compartment. The older one lay down on the lower berth and fell asleep immediately. He was probably very tired. The younger one took over the upper, but just could not fall asleep. He turned over, got up and lay down again. Obviously, something was bothering him very much.

"It was already late and I had fallen asleep. Shots awoke me. It was all over already. The older man had been killed outright while the younger man lay on the floor and writhed in agony. There was blood everywhere and all my things were spattered with it. Japanese gendarmes, pistols in their hands, stood in the corridor and stared at the dying man. I didn't know who the dead men were; they were removed at once, but one of the passengers said that they probably were Communists."

"That's the Japanese style, brutal work," said one of the guests. "And here's how the British do things." He handed us a pile of English newspapers which were published in China. Thus we became acquainted with the notorious "Dosser Affair" which the reactionary press in China and beyond was foaming about in those days.

This was a provocation organized by British oil companies against representatives of our oil syndicate. The British did not want the Kuomintang to receive oil from the Soviet Union. A. A. Dosser was arrested by British police on a British ship on the way to Canton. He was returned to Shanghai and on the basis of some alleged documents was handed over to the mixed court of the International Settlement on the charge of "undermining public order" in China.[5] One may judge what sort of documents these were if only through the "testimony of Dosser" introduced at the trial.

"Certificate No. 43. The bearer of this, Dosser, Party Card No. 403, is the head of the agitation section of the South China District for Hong Kong and Canton with responsibility for organizing strike committees. All members of the Russian Communist Party are required to support him in the execution of his assigned duties, as attested by the seal of the Agitation Section of the RCP in Shanghai."

These absurd, illiterate falsifications bear witness to the utter stupidity of their composers who were thrown into a panic by the anti-British boycott taking place in China. But nevertheless, on this basis, Dosser was being threatened with death or a twelve-year prison term. Thus were the imperialists accustomed to dealing on Chinese soil with those who appeared dangerous to them.

But the Soviet Union never recognized the foreign imperialists' court in China. Only a Chinese court could sit in judgment of Soviet nationals in China. After our ambassador L. M. Karakhan addressed a note to the diplomatic corps in Peking, Dosser was freed and together with his wife was "exiled" from the territory of the foreign concession in Shanghai. The provocation had failed. Dosser appeared among his fellow-workers at the embassy and laughingly regaled them with his adventures. I was his interpreter for a time and remember

5. This imperialist judicial body existed in China on the basis of the so-called right of extraterritoriality which was granted to the foreigners by the unequal treaties which had been forcibly imposed upon China.

him well. Bearded and shaggy-haired, with a severe face and an unexpectedly cheerful smile, he was a passionate devotee of chess and spent all of his spare time at the chessboard. His wife was his constant partner. Much later in Moscow, I saw a photograph of Dosser in the Museum of the Revolution and learned that he was an Old Bolshevik, an underground worker who had known tsarist penal servitude and life in emigration. His party name was "Woodgoblin." I imagined how his comrades must have joked about his big, curly beard and his tousled hairdo when they gave him this name.

Exchanging the latest news, our friends led us to supper. On the way to the dining hall we met a tiny old man bent with his years, with whom our student companions exchanged greetings in Chinese, pressing their hands to their chests with special respect. This was the teacher Tung whom they had already told us about, "the living tradition of Russian sinology" as someone had called him. For many decades he had worked with Russian students who had come to China for field work as well as with the employees of the Russian embassy. He had prepared quite a few talented Russian sinologists. Tung remembered the old professor Apollinaire Vasilevich Rudakov (whom I introduced to the reader in the beginning of the book), when he was still a youth.

Tung's old, slightly puffy face expressed kindness. His hair was completely white as were the few long hairs on his chin and upper lip. In general he looked very much like the ancient sages whom Chinese artists love to depict even now. He moved slowly and with obvious difficulty; he wore a long robe of a smooth, gray material and a short, black silk jacket with a traditional Chinese design embroidered on it in the shape of decorative, saucer-like circles. A round, black satin skullcap covered his head and he carried the inevitable paper fan dotted with characters in his own remarkable calligraphy. Tung had written on the fan extracts from the Chinese classics which he had revered all his life.

Tung suffered visibly from the heat. Conversing with us he slightly raised the rear panel of his robe. Chinese robes are sewn with cutouts above the knee on both sides. His legs were revealed spread wide in an old man's manner and clad in white cotton trousers fastened at the ankles like our long underwear. Not embarrassed by the presence of girls, Tung placed his "learned" fan in the space opened up under his robe and created a light breeze just below his back. I must confess that we were all somewhat embarrassed although we knew that from the Chinese point of view there was nothing reprehensible in Tung's conduct (later we often witnessed scenes like that on the residential streets of Peking and other cities.) Nevertheless, none of us so much as blinked an eye.

We respected our teacher and did not want to insult him. We were aware of his great learning; that he knew by heart the basic nine Chinese Classics—the Four Books and the Five Classics, which were the basis of Chinese classical education,[6] was not such a rarity in China, but he knew much more besides. But most of all, old Tung was intelligent and very kind especially to his Soviet students. Alas our beloved teacher paid dearly for his friendship with Soviet citizens. On April 6, 1927, at the time of the raid on the embassy, he showed up for his work as always and was seized by the soldiers of Chang Tso-lin who led him off to prison where he died from inhuman beatings.

Tung was overloaded with lessons; therefore we were introduced to Li, a somewhat younger teacher who, however, had worked with Soviet "China Hands" for more than a decade. Li was Russian Orthodox and lived on the territory of the spiritual mission in the Peikuan quarter, but he was a freethinker and couldn't stand priests. "They're all liars and cowards," he said. "During the Boxer Rebellion, the rebels dealt cruelly with those Chinese who had accepted Christianity. And where was our bishop then? He threw over his pastorship and hid behind the walls of the Russian embassy. Why didn't he want to suffer for his faith?"

The Orthodox Mission in Peikuan led a pitiful existence at that time. I went there as a translator with colleagues from the embassy who needed to lithograph or reprint something. Dire need confronted us. The old-fashioned buildings where at one time the famous Russian sinologists, the monks Iakinf (N. Ya. Bichurin) and Pallady (P. I. Kafarov) lived and worked, were in ruins and not being repaired. The equipment of the typography shop was simply archaic. At that time many Russian White emigres lived there, but I did not see them. The Chinese monks spoke with us.

The teacher Li was also an expert in Chinese medicine and he could diagnose all illnesses, including consumption, by taking the pulse. However, he did not practice medicine. He said that to heal people was a holy noble thing, but to heal people for money was bad from the point of view of Chinese

---

6. The Four Books (*ssu shu*) and the Five Classics (*wu ching*) are canonical works expounding the the basic Confucian teachings. In traditional China (before the 1911 Revolution) it was imperative that anyone preparing for an official career know them by heart.

morality. On the first day of our acquaintance he was, at our request, not a teacher but a doctor. With an air of importance he freed his dry, nervous hands from his wide sleeves, and having taken our pulse in six places, he declared that we were all healthy.

The first day in Peking was extraordinarily long and filled with interesting meetings and unforgettable impressions. A walk in the Legation Quarter left us with the strongest impression. Everything that had any connection with the Boxer Uprising produced a special impression on us students of the Eastern Department of FEU. Already in Vladivostok we had, as it were, gotten close to its participants by daily viewing the relics of the uprising in our lecture halls. These were the remains of what had been at one time a vast collection brought out of Peking by an eyewitness of the rebellion, A. V. Rudakov. Civil war and intervention is far from the best time for the preservation of historical relics and Rudakov's collection suffered terribly. Nevertheless, arriving for our lectures, we saw pikes with fringes around the blades, bows and quivers with feathered arrows, old flintlocks, banners with slogans and proclamations by the rebels so it seemed that we breathed the air of that great storm which swept over China a quarter of a century ago.

Almost all of the men among my schoolmates had taken part in the battles with the interventionists in the Far East and knew from personal experience what the struggle against world imperialism was like. The faded and half-faded exhibits, witnesses of the heroic Chinese uprising, were cherished by us. And now, treading on the ground where one of the last battles of the insurgents (which had ended tragically) took place, we were deeply moved.

Before us was a section of the old north wall of the quarter where particularly fierce fighting had taken place. It was riddled with bullets and missiles. The triumphant victors who raised up new fortress walls purposely left it untouched as a warning to the Chinese and a reminder to themselves, with the meaningful inscription "Lest we forget." We were shown the place where the capital state examinations were formerly conducted.[7] In crushing the rebellion, the imperialists not only destroyed the existing structures there, but without

7. In the Chinese empire one had to take an examination in order to acquire an official position to demonstrate one's knowledge of classical Confucian literature. The capital examinations were held every three years. For three days and two nights the candidates were locked up in stone cells where they wrote their compositions. The examinations were done away with in 1905.

standing on ceremony they used the remaining whole bricks for the construction of new fortifications.

We climbed onto the city wall which adjoined the quarter and from which the imperialists had fired into the emperor's palace. The wall remained in their hands. An exemplary order reigned there; there were arbors and benches, soldiers stood on guard duty. Embassy employees strolled with their families enjoying the remarkable view. Chinese were not allowed in of course.

Beyond the north wall, on Hatamen Street, a small very dirty obelisk catches the eye. It was placed by demand of the imperialists on the spot where the German minister Von Ketteler was killed during the siege. No one was interested in the monument any more. It was enough that it had been placed there, and that the Chinese government "admitted its guilt."

The Legation Quarter made a painful impression. Everywhere were walls piled upon walls, behind which the imperialists carried on their base and bloody affairs. From here they exerted pressure on the Chinese government. Here their henchmen confidently hid from the judgment and anger of the Chinese people. After every coup, the representatives of the overturned clique, allied to one or another of the imperialist powers, streamed into the territory of the Legation Quarter. Even the emperor Pu Yi and the princes of the blood found shelter here after the fall of the Manchu dynasty.

There a web of intrigues was woven; provocations against the Chinese people and the Soviet Union were prepared. For example, the provocationist role which the Japanese embassy played in Tuan Ch'i-jui's shooting of student demonstrators on March 18, 1926, is well-known. The imperialists of the Legation Quarter acted even more openly in April 1927, in organizing the raid by Chang Tso-lin's gendarmes on the Soviet embassy.

Such were our neighbors in the Legation Quarter whom we had to live next to and somehow coexist with. They could not control their fury, seeing that the prestige of the Soviet Union was growing from day to day, that the Soviet Union was successfully implementing a policy in China which differed in principle from their colonialist policies and by her actions often causing their plans to go awry.

The imperialists' hatred of Soviet citizens was manifested even in everyday trifles. Everywhere they tried to ruin things for us. Here is a typical example.

Around the walls of the Legation Quarter lay a broad glacis[8] where in accordance with the Protocol[9] it was forbidden to construct any kind of buildings. Only sports grounds and bridle paths were laid out there. When the Soviet embassy took over the buildings of the former tsarist embassy, its employees decided to lay out a soccer field on the part of the glacis adjoining its walls in order to compete with Chinese teams. Seeing that the Soviets were up to something, the Americans at once dug trenches there and busied themselves with military training.

The largest section in the Legation Quarter belonged to the British. It adjoined our embassy on the north side. Only a high, blind stone wall separated us from the British, and this by the way, troubled them not a little. Goodness, what dangerous neighbors!

The former palace of one of the Manchu princes, descendant of the K'anghsi emperor, was located on the grounds of the British embassy and they were quite proud of this. There at one time stood the buildings of the famous Hanlin Academy (the highest institution of learning in old China) and the emperor's carriage house. But the British embassy was not the oldest in China. Russia was the first to enter into treaty relations with China. The first Russian ambassadors had stayed on the former territory of the embassy.

To the right of our embassy stood the United States' embassy where every day the raising and lowering of the Stars and Stripes was held along with the changing of the guard. To the sounds of a military orchestra which the Americans alone possessed, soldiers in colonial uniforms—shorts and cork helmets—loudly marching, triumphantly appeared through the gates and presented arms. The American grounds were small but they had the largest garrison—four hundred fifty men.

Among the soldiers of the French garrison were Annamese—as Vietnamese were then called—small soldiers in basin-like helmets; the British had Indian soldiers, tall, dark and very thin, wearing magnificent turbans on their heads.

---

8. Glacis—an open space in front of a fortress.
9. The Protocol was a one-sided agreement forced on China by the imperialists after the suppression of the Boxer Rebellion in 1901.

The Soviets in Peking

The embassy staff lived on very friendly terms with each other. No one pulled rank. We soon became acquainted with almost everyone on the embassy staff. Everywhere we were received in the best manner. And why should it be otherwise? We were students coming to a foreign country for field work without a penny in our pockets and badly needing help.

We met many remarkable persons in the embassy, among whom we must place Lyov Mikhaylovich Karakhan in the first rank. The grounds for the great influence which he enjoyed in China was, of course, the policy of the Soviet Union—the voluntary renunciation of all privileges and properties which had been acquired by tsarist Russia in the past, but his brilliant oratorical and diplomatic abilities and his broad social activity brought him great personal popularity.

Karakhan was the lone ambassador among the envoys of the diplomatic corps in Peking. The imperialist powers did not consider China worthy of exchanging diplomatic representatives of ambassadorial rank, and they therefore placed themselves in an unfavorable position. The Soviet ambassador, as the highest in rank, was automatically the doyen of the diplomatic corps, and the representatives of the imperialist countries who insanely hated everything Soviet had to show him all the marks of respect which were due to the highest in rank. In the same way, the members of the Peking government, willy-nilly, were forced to recognize the diplomatic priority of Karakhan and pay him higher honors than the representatives of the imperialist powers. All of this created favorable conditions for Karakhan's work and facilitated our policy of supporting the anti-imperialist demands of the leading part of Chinese society.

Many years have passed since then, much has been forgotten, and it is possible that some of my readers will find it difficult to imagine what an enormous, truly international significance Karakhan's speeches in behalf of the oppressed peoples, against colonialism and for the equality of nations had at that time. They would sound quite timely even now. It was impossible to ignore them; they were printed in all the enemy and friendly newspapers; people became engrossed by them, marveling at the iron logic of the Soviet diplomat, his bold polemics against the colonialists, his ability to use any situation to bolster his position. Karakhan did not limit himself to purely diplomatic activity.

He loved to appear at public meetings and large gatherings. One could listen to his lectures at Peking University. Everywhere he went he was greeted enthusiastically.

The foreign imperialist and the Chinese reactionaries were not opposed to settling accounts with Karakhan and his life in China was hardly secure. When he returned from leave in the Soviet Union at the end of 1925 Russian White guards who were plotting against his life were arrested in Harbin. But the masses in Peking gave him a welcome such as no diplomat of any other country had ever been honored with. Karakhan was greeted not only by representatives of the Chinese government but also by delegates from Kuomintang and workers' organizations with banners in their hands.

It was not easy to get to see Karakhan; he worked very hard and was always busy. But the most enterprising of us contrived to meet him frequently. He was a passionate tennis buff and almost every morning was out on the courts. I was embarrassed to display such obvious curiosity and saw Karakhan only three times in all. The first time was at the airport when we were greeting the Soviet fliers who had completed the famous Moscow-Peking flight. He was sitting under a canopy surrounded by representatives of the Chinese authorities, rather far from us. Another time I accidentally bumped into him in the typing office of the embassy and was able to have a good look at him. He had a fine, surprisingly youthful and handsome pale face set off by dark hair. He wore whiskers and a beard, was short and frail in build. His gaze was fiery, straight and very steady.

The last time I saw Karakhan was at the end of August 1925 when he was leaving for vacation in Moscow. His entourage was very large. To the station came those who were bound by etiquette to come—governmental and foreign diplomatic representatives, who grudgingly bowed and scraped before the doyen of the diplomatic corps, and those who sincerely respected Karakhan—representatives of public organizations, basically youth. How many lively, glittering eyes were there, how many dear, youthful faces, frankly expressing curiosity. All the personnel of our embassy also appeared on the platform with their families. I saw Karakhan for just a few moments on the platform of the car when he was taking leave of the people who had come to see him off.

The official interpreter at the embassy was Professor Alexey Ivanovich Ivanov who lived in one of the small cottages with his family. Every day early in the morning we respectfully observed his exercises as he trotted around the house, his solid belly shaking. Alexey Ivanovich accompanied Karakhan on his official duties and in general was very useful due to his wide acquaintances within the diplomatic circles in China acquired in tsarist times. He also carried on much scholarly work; his table was always covered with books and journals in Chinese and European languages; his shelves were filled with Chinese volumes, and he himself sat in state amidst all of this like some god of sinology, severe and inaccessible. On his return from China, Professor Ivanov worked for a time in the Scientific Research Institute on China of Sun Yat-sen University where under the direction of G. S. Kara-Murza he translated Sun Yat-sen's Three People's Principles, and later in the Moscow Institute of Oriental Studies. An enormous scholarly service of the professor was his discovery of a Tangut-Chinese dictionary among some manuscripts brought back from Khara-Khoto by the well-known student of Central Asia, P. K. Kozlov. This made it possible for his student, N. A. Nevsky, to begin the deciphering of the Tangut writing system which had not been understood until then.

Unfortunately, we did not encounter Sergey Mikhaylovich Tretyakov in Peking. He had just returned to the Soviet Union, but people in the embassy remembered him and spoke about him a lot. He was a brilliant representative of Soviet literature, a journalist, writer, dramatist and poet, a friend of Mayakovsky and Meyerhold. Tretyakov taught Soviet literature in Peking University and was a correspondent for *Pravda* at the same time. His "Pis'ma iz Pekina" (Letters from Peking) were impassioned exposures of the crimes of foreign imperialism in China.

Tretyakov's play *Rychi Kitai* (Roar China) was staged with great success in the Meyerhold Theatre in Moscow in the late 20s. It was based upon a true occurrence in the Szechwanese city of Wanhsien where three entirely innocent Chinese fishermen were executed for the accidental death of an Englishman. Tretyakov personally took part in the staging of the play, enriched it with many details from life and even taught the actors certain characteristic gestures and intonations.

Infectiously gay and sharp-witted, Tretyakov was the soul of society in the embassy. After his departure people repeated his jokes and successful turns of phrase for a long time and sang a variant of the popular song "Dunya" (composed by him) which began like this:

Fu-ty nu-ty na fu-fu
Dunya goes to the *o kuo fu*[10]

A special couplet was thought up for almost every one of the embassy
staff. We almost died laughing when we sang this song.

Even more amusing were the nicknames which Tretyakov gave to almost
all of the buildings on the embassy grounds. The house where the very aged
adviser to the embassy, Professor Mikhail Yakovlevich Pergament lived, he
dubbed "Ruins of the Ancient City of Pergamum," the house of the trade
representative Klyshko which was situated directly across from the old embassy
church bore the name of "Nikoly na Klyshkakh," the detached house where
the student sinologues and other young persons lived he called the "Yellow
House"[11] obviously not only because of the color.

After Tretyakov's departure "Letters from China" was written by Professor Alexey Alexeevich Ivin, a well-known sinologue and teacher of Russian
at Peking University. A. A. Ivin made a substantial contribution to the literature
about China and held an honorable place among contemporary Soviet orientalists.
His work on the "Red Spears"—illegal armed peasant organizations of the old
type which still existed then in China—brought him particular renown. Unfortunately, Professor Ivin, a pupil of the Sorbonne and a student of the well-
known French sinologue Chavannes, used the French transcription of Chinese
characters which differed greatly from that which we used and this not infrequently led to a vexatious confusion which caused the students much unpleasantness. I met A. A. Ivin very infrequently in Peking since he lived in the Chinese
part of town and visited the embassy comparatively rarely, but I did work with
him later in the Scientific Research Institute on China of Sun Yat-sen University
in Moscow and I remember him well. Ivin was small in stature and not overly
concerned with his appearance but he was distinguished by his refined politeness and great kindness. He might have become a great scholar but he was
ruined by a passion for drinking which was already in evidence in China and
which later brought about a serious illness.

Since the autumn of 1925 yet another Soviet sinologue, in later life the
well-known historian, the charming and eccentric Pyotr Antonovich Grinevich
taught Russian in Peking higher educational institutions. Grinevich had entered

---

10. Russian Embassy in Chinese.
11. "Yellow House" means a lunatic asylum in Russian: Translator.

the Eastern Institute in Vladivostok as early as 1916 but because of the Civil War and the Intervention he did not graduate until 1924. He lived in Peking together with the Russian sinologist and teacher of Russian, B. I. Pankratov, who had settled there before the revolution. Their home, which was located in one of the most poetic corners of old China, was famed for its hospitality. The site had formerly belonged to some kind of temple, therefore the location of the structure was unusual for a Chinese dwelling. A marvelous garden was situated behind the traditional decorated wall in front of the gates instead of a front courtyard surrounded on all four sides by living quarters. In the event of the hosts' absence, the old doorkeeper with a flurry of bows and not at all worried, left the guests alone although there were no locks anywhere. Two years later when Chang Tso-lin's gendarmes were searching all over Peking for her, F. S. Borodina, the wife of the adviser to the Kuomintang, M. M. Borodin, hid out right here in this modest, isolated Chinese house. Grinevich, to whom she directly owed her salvation, risked his life together with her.

He was silent and gloomy in appearance, but his amazing **goodness** (which by the by people often took advantage of) was irresistible. He treated students in a fatherly way although he was almost our age. He willingly offered his home for student parties and would not sit down but walked up and down with the satisfied look of a hospitable host. Grinevich returned to the motherland in 1928. Until 1938 he worked in the Institute of World Economy and Politics of the Academy of Sciences together with a group of colleagues from the former Scientific Research Institute on China. His profound knowledge of Chinese allowed him to use sources which were accessible to few others. He wrote about Chinese feudalism, the history of Chinese agriculture, about Chinese popular uprisings, and the contemporary situation in China. He left many published and not a few incomplete works which retain their interest up to the present.

My neighbor in the "Ruins of the Ancient City of Pergamum" was the embassy's judicial adviser, Anatoly Yakovlevich Kantorovich. He arrived in China in 1924 on the staff of the trade commission which was headed by the greatest specialist on civil law of the time, M. Ya. Pergament. The interests and activity of Kantorovich, a many-sided talented man, were by no means confined to a single specialty. Serving on the embassy staff, he was at the same time a professor of law at Peking University, special correspondent for the newspapers *Trud* (Labor) and *Ekonomicheskaya Zhizn'* (Economic life) and he also published articles in *Novyi Vostok* (New East) and *Manzhurskyi Vestnik* (Manchurian messenger). Passionately in love with journalism, he never forsook it and in his last years was deputy director of the foreign desk of *Izvestia.* At the same time he carried on an extensive scholarly activity. In 1926 his book *Inostrannyi kapital i zheleznye dorogi Kitaia*(Foreign capital and the railroads of China) appeared. In Moscow, working as a senior fellow of the Institute of World Economy and Politics of the Academy of Sciences, he finished another solid piece of research, *Amerika v bor'be za Kitai* (America in the struggle for China), which became his doctoral dissertation. In all he left more than sixty works.

Kantorovich's name was on everyone's lips in 1927 when the difficult task befell him of defending in Chang Tso-lin's courts the Soviet citizens arrested during the raid on the embassy and F. S. Borodina who had been taken into custody on the ship *Pamyat Lenina.* He fulfilled this task with his customary ability and fortitude.

Lively and inquisitive Anatoly Yakovlevich took part in all our excursions. A passionate lover of literature, he was an enthusiastic devotee of Dickens and exasperated our friends by reciting from heart entire pages from his books in English. A swarthy and dark-haired little boy was born to him in Peking, the general favorite and pet of everyone, who was called the "Little Arab."

Karakhan's personal interpreter, S. Shvarsalon, lived in the "madhouse." Several years together with the China specialist M. Baranovsky he wrote something on the order of a general guide to China under the title of *Chto nuzhno znat' o Kitae* (What you need to know about China), which passed through two editions. Shvarsalon had an excellent command of English. Once, without interrupting his chess game, right there at the table in several minutes and without corrections, he translated and sent off to be typed the text of an urgent note given to him by Karakhan. He was valued highly as there were few good linguists then. Shvarsalon stood out from among the other members of the embassy. He was elegant and somewhat mannered, sometimes he even put on airs and rolled his "r's." At the same time he was sociable and simple, especially with young people, his neighbors in the apartment. It was said that formerly he had served in the tsarist embassy in Peking. It was evident that he kept up his acquaintances among the Peking White emigrés from that time.

The military attaché in the embassy was Aleksandr Ilich Yegorov, a future marshal of the Soviet Union, candidate member of the CC of the All-Union Communist Party (Bolshevik), and chief of the general staff of the Red. Army. In 1918 he was a member of the commission for organization and establishment of the Workers' and Peasants' Red Army and commanded the legendary Ninth Army which destroyed the forces of the White Guard General Krasnov. In 1919 during the decisive days of the struggle against Denikin who was advancing on Moscow, he was appointed commander of the southern front, and in 1920 commanded the southwest front.

At the end of the civil war, Yegorov wrote several military-historical monographs. Aleksandr Ilich was very warm to us young sinologists, personally invited us to his place and gave us advice before our departure for South China. He asked me whether I was happy to be going to Canton and added that he wished he were in my place, so that he might see the Chinese revolution close up and work for it. Aleksandr Ilich was joking, but perhaps he might indeed have wanted to go to Canton. All of us then were very interested in the situation in South China. Upon my return to Moscow I met him more than once while working in the General Staff and I remember his broad, good-natured face, his leisurely speech, heartfelt smile and broad-shouldered, stately figure.

As of September 1926 our military attaché in Peking was Roman Voytsekhovich Longva, a Pole by birth, and a member of the party since 1910. In 1920 the division which Longva commanded stormed the fortress of Brest-Litòvsk, crushed the defending Pilsudskyites, and seized a great many weapons. Roman Voytsekhovich was awarded an order of the Red Banner for this. He came to China with four stars[12] as the head of one of the departments of the General Staff. I saw him several times in Wuhan in January 1927 where he was on assignment. Thin and straight with a fine face, he looked much younger than his thirty-seven years. His comrades loved him for his kindness and modesty. After returning to the USSR he continued to work on the General Staff. His last post was as head of the Department of Communications in the Workers' and Peasants' Red Army.

In Peking we also met some of our military advisers. In Vladivostok we had already read short dispatches in the Chinese and Anglo-American press to the effect that we had military representatives in South China in the Kuomintang

---

12. Marks of distinction for the higher command staff in the Red Army during those years.

armies, and in the north in the Nationalist armies. It was said that in the south, General Chia Lin or Galen (in English transcription) was heading the mission of Soviet military advisers. At that time we had no idea that this was the distorted Russian surname Galin under which Vasily Konstantinovich Blyukher, a hero of the civil war in the Urals, the Crimea and the Far East was working at that time. They also mentioned the chief political adviser of the Kuomintang, Mikhail Markovich Borodin. (His Chinese name was Pao Lo-ting.)

At that time in China there were not a few British, American, Japanese, and even White Guard advisers. These were adventurers, paid agents of the imperialist powers who promoted their own base affairs there and who also received enormous sums of money and valuable gifts from the Chinese as their salaries.

Our military specialists went to China in order to aid the revolution and they received their salaries from Moscow. It was not easy, of course, for the Soviet Union to burden its budget with supplementary expenditures; every rouble had to be accounted for. However, both the South Chinese government and Marshal Feng Yü-hsiang were aided with weapons and money.

Our advisers were the finest cadres of the Red Army. Many had entered the party before the Revolution and had passed through tsarist prisons and exile. Almost all of them had gotten diplomas from the Frunze Military Academy in 1925 or from the highest specialized military academies, and had been decorated with the military order of the Red Banner. Very few persons had been honored with this order—the highest military award then—and very few indeed had been twice decorated with it. In our group of advisers there were even those who were thrice decorated. Their fate was not an easy one. Most of them perished in our motherland's tragic days of 1937-1938. At the time of which I am speaking our advisers had succeeded in expanding their work on a broad scale.

In Peking I saw the head of the Kaifeng mission of advisers, Georgy Borisovich Skalov (Sinani), who for a brief time in the autumn of 1923 had been rector of the Moscow Institute of Oriental Studies.[13] I remember how on the sixth anniversary of the Great October Revolution we students were massed on Armenian Street in front of the splendid building of the former Lazarevsky

---

13. Like the majority of our advisers, Skalov worked in China under a different surname. He continued to use it after his return to the Soviet Union.

Institute of Eastern Languages where we were then located, when our new director appeared—young, tall, dressed in a long Red Army greatcoat which reached to his heels, with the order of the Red Banner on a scarlet silk rosette, in a helmet with a star and three insignia on his shoulder boards signifying a corps commander. Seeing me in Peking, he exchanged greetings warmly. Skalov was blessed with remarkable literary gifts and upon his return to the Soviet Union he wrote a series of interesting articles on China printed in the collection *Kantonskaia Kommuna* (Canton commune) and other places. Later he worked in the Comintern and also in the Institute of World Economy and Politics of the USSR Academy of Sciences. He fell victim to the Stalinist repressions earlier than the others. Nineteen thirty-five was his fatal year.

Soon afterwards I became acquainted with Anatoly Yakovlevich Klimov, an assistant in the political department of the chief of the Kaifeng mission, and a pioneer in our work in Kaifeng. He had arrived there as long ago as October 1924. Anatoly Yakovlevich was an old, leading party worker from the Maritime Region and Siberia, an active participant of the civil war, an underground worker who had more than once been subject to arrest and escaped execution only by a miracle. In addition he had been a member of the revolutionary committee and the district party committee of the Maritime Region and a delegate to the Third Congress of the Comintern. Klimov at that time was already an experienced China specialist. He had studied in the Eastern Institute in Vladivostok in the tsarist period and in 1923 graduated from the Eastern Department of the Military Academy. He traveled to Peking in 1922 with the Ioffe mission. After 1927 Anatoly Yakovlevich worked in the Ministry of Foreign Affairs, the Pacific Ocean Institute of the Academy of Sciences and in the Moscow Institute of Oriental Studies. In 1948 he was unjustly arrested and spent six years in a camp.

I knew Albert Ivanovich Lapin (also from the Kaifeng mission) for a longer time than I knew Skalov and Klimov. At that time he bore the surname Seyfullin. At the end of February 1926 when the Kaifeng mission went out of existence, Lapin was transferred to the post of chief of staff of the Kalgan group and enjoyed the great favor of Marshal Feng Yü-hsiang. Everyone who knew Lapin spoke of him as a highly educated, extremely talented and very fascinating man. He arrived in China with a diploma from the Military Academy and three orders of the Red Banner for service in the civil war.

Lapin, a Latvian by birth, was of above average height, roundfaced and thickset. He shaved his head and seemed to be blond until he sprouted an un-expectedly dark thick beard. Upon his return to the Soviet Union Lapin became the head of the Office of Military Preparedness of the General Staff, a corps commander, and was deputy commander of the Special Red Banner Far East-ern Army under Blyukher (this was his last post). In 1936 when Lapin already had four orders of the Red Banner and the order of Lenin, *Pravda* dedicated a special article to him entitled "Corps Commander with Five Orders." Lapin perished in 1937.

Most frequently we student probationers met these advisers in the General Hotel where we finally had settled. This needs a bit of explanation.

The embassy staff lived in cottages amid the thick greenery of the embassy gardens. New arrivals made whatever arrangements they could—some settled in the military compound, others in hotels. The only hotel in the Legation Quarter was terribly expensive, the aristocratic Wagon-Lits, which belonged to an American tourist agency. We did not favor it, and in general Soviet citizens rarely stayed there. We chose instead the Central Hotel, a Chinese hotel in European style, located immediately beyond the north wall of the Legation Quarter between Le Grand Hotel de Pekin and the telegraph office. Soviet citizens lived there, Russian could be heard along with Russian jokes. The rates were divine, there was no need to dress for breakfast, lunch, or dinner, no one looked archly at us since no one stayed there besides us and the Chinese. The lone deluxe room on the first floor cost 30 yuan a day including meals; the other rooms were priced according to the floor—the higher up the cheaper. A room on the fifth floor cost 90 yuan a month including meals. The kitchen was English—serving small portions of many dishes; the furniture was European but the beds Chinese—a long narrow pillow stretched from one end of the bed to the other, the cotton blanket was in a cover which was colored on top and white underneath.

It was there in the Central Hotel that we became acquainted with the head of the Kalgan advisers' mission, Vitaly Markovich Primakov, a Bolshevik with a pre-revolutionary, underground party record.[14] In China he used the name

---

14. V. M. Primakov joined the party in January 1914 and in 1915 he was sentenced to perpetual exile in Siberia. He was freed by the February Revolution. Primakov participated in the storming of the Winter Palace.

Lin. In the civil war Primakov commanded a corps of Red Cossacks in the Ukraine and, by the way, won renown through two desperate raids to the depths of White territory which ended in the enemy's complete rout.

Vitaly Markovich was awarded two orders of the Red Banner and an honorary golden rifle. After his return from China, Primakov was a corps commander, a military attaché in Japan and Afghanistan, and a deputy commander of the North Caucasus and Leningrad military districts. He was one of the few advisers who had enriched our sinological literature with his memoirs. On his return to the Soviet Union, under the pen name of Lt. Henry Allen, he wrote the book *Zapiski angliiskogo volontera* (Notes of an English volunteer) in which he related his impressions of China. Vitaly Markovich was a lover and connoisseur of literature, himself possessed remarkable literary talent, and even wrote verses. Few of his military comrades could make such a claim.

His adjutant, Boris Ivanovich Kuzmichev, or Wen as he was called in China, accompanied Primakov everywhere. Strong bonds of friendship united them. It was said that Primakov picked up Kuzmichev during the civil war as a lad with neither home nor family, and brought him up to be as desperate a cavalryman as he was himself. They were not at all alike in appearance. Primakov was of above average height, always dressed stylishly, and his face radiated self-confidence. Wen was short, squint-eyed, and very shy. Later he married Vitaly Markovich's sister Vara. Vitaly Markovich Primakov and Boris Ivanovich Kuzmichev were among the first who perished in the latter part of the thirties.

Vitaly Markovich lived in the deluxe room while we students, as befitted our position, lived on the fifth floor. However, notwithstanding such an obvious difference between our positions in this mortal world, Primakov behaved very simply and warmly towards us, and at times even gallantly with the girls. Thus, on my birthday he sent me via Kuzmichev a sumptuous cream cake of staggering beauty and proportions, and also an apology for not being able to call himself. This was no mere excuse; he was really sick in bed and we went to visit him.

In the Central Hotel we also met and became friends with the senior cavalry adviser, Pyotr Zyuk. In China he bore the name of Brode. Zyuk was short, reddish, with widely spaced tobacco-stained teeth which he bared now and then in an aggressive way. He was distinguished for his fearlessness, iron stubbornness, and cold indomitable fury in moments of wrath. Many stories made the rounds among us about his feats in the civil war, to which his two battle orders of the Red Banner attested. At the same time he was an inveterate idler and a tease, qualities which he considered indispensable for any dashing cavalryman. Therefore, Zyuk could not boast of his discipline. He alone of all the advisers got into fights with the White Guards in Peking and even with the British police of the Legation Quarter, so that these latter would hasten to abandon their posts and wait out the threat around the corner when towards evening they saw his somewhat stocky figure with the cavalryman's bowlegged gait for he was a master brawler. Primakov, the head of the mission, punished him more than once but to no effect.

Zyuk was rather unmannerly but no one got angry at him since they knew it was not out of hostility. Still once Professor Ivanov was greatly offended by him and, one must confess, with good cause. It happened at a banquet when Zyuk, unable to make himself understood by some Chinese, simply ordered Alexey Ivanovich "Interpreter, translate for me." When Ivanov made it clear that he was a professor, not an interpreter, Zyuk laughingly said, "I'm glad you're a professor, I'll soon be one myself, but translate anyway." Alexey Ivanovich translated so as to avoid quarreling at an official reception.

Zyuk was easily moved but he never showed his feelings and generally liked to appear as a great cynic which he really wasn't at all. Once in Kalgan it happened that he was given the diary of a White emigrée in which she told how she'd been sold as a concubine to a rich Chinese and asked for help. In the diary were these words "Forgive me dear mama for having fallen so low." On reading these words Zyuk ironically bared his yellow teeth, but I saw that he pitied the girl. After his return from China Zyuk was appointed commander of a cavalry division. He was arrested and perished in 1937.

Nikolay Yulyanovich Petkevich, the senior artillery adviser of the mission, who used the name Dyufren in China, lived for a time in the Central Hotel. His assistant was Alexandr Alexandrovich Argentov whom we knew by the name Marino. Petkevich had been awarded three orders of the Red Banner for service in the civil war. Prior to his tour in China he had commanded an artillery corps and upon his return he was appointed artillery commander of the Moscow military district. He died suddenly in 1936. We knew him as an excellent comrade and specialist and a lover of music.

Our acquaintance with the advisers sealed our fate. Growing accustomed to our company, Primakov offered us work as translators in his mission. There are no words to express how happy we were. Work in our special field, and where? In the Nationalist Army of Feng Yü-hsiang! We were given a small salary and two months to learn military terminology and the general political situation in China.

Sun Yat-sen's Last Journey (According to Comrades' Stories)

Let us go back a bit to our impressions of Peking. Soon after our arrival we visited the famous temple Pi Yün Ssu (Azure cloud temple) in the hamlet of Hsishan some fifteen kilometers from Peking. This temple was the temporary burying place of Sun Yat-sen before the erection of the mausoleum in the Purple Hills in Nanking.

A man who had played an enormous role in the history of the Chinese revolutionary movement, the father of the Chinese revolution as he was called, the founder and permanent leader of the Kuomintang, president of the South Chinese government and first president of the Chinese Republic, Generalissimo Dr. Sun Yat-sen had died in Peking on March 12, 1925, less than four months before our arrival. All of Peking was still talking about this. Sun Yat-sen's funeral turned into a powerful demonstration in which the people openly expressed their hatred of the Peking government and their sympathy and support for the revolutionary government in Canton.

Sun Yat-sen came to Peking at the end of December 1924 for a conference called by Tuan Ch'i-jui. Sun, as the first president of the republic, was shown the highest honors. He was already gravely ill. Sun Yat-sen went from the station to the hotel, the Grand Hotel de Pekin, where he took to bed. His doctors diagnosed cancer of the stomach and the liver.

In view of Sun's illness the meeting contemplated between him and Marshal Feng Yü-hsiang who had recently pulled off a coup d'etat in Peking did not take place. Desiring to discuss with Sun the most important questions of the political situation in China, several times the marshal sent invitations to him to visit his residence in Hsishan, but Sun Yat-sen was no longer able to do this. He lay motionless on his back and could not even turn without aid. His wife, the well-known social activist Soong Ching-ling, M. M. Borodin, adviser to the Kuomintang and Sun's personal friend, and several other trusted persons were constantly by his side.

At first Sun Yat-sen stayed at the American Rockefeller Hospital (considered the best in China[15]), where he was operated on. Public opinion demanded Chinese methods of treatment, so he was removed from there. He spent his last days in the home of the former minister of foreign affairs, Ku Wei-chün (or as he called himself in the English style, Wellington Koo) who had fled Peking after Feng Yü-hsiang's coup. Everything in this house was in the European style with but one exception—Ku had more than twenty wives and concubines each of whom had her own house in the park which surrounded the main building. These houses were distinguished by their luxury, color and pretentious style. They too were empty since the harem had fled with the master.

Sun Yat-sen was treated by a Chinese doctor. Every day the papers printed communiques about the state of his health. Even people who were far from politics looked for news of Sun's condition when they flipped through their newspapers. Sun Yat-sen was a doctor himself and he knew that he was dying. Twenty-four hours before his death he asked that he be laid on a narrow field cot. He wanted to die like a soldier of the Chinese revolutionary army. Sun Yat-sen did not lose consciousness to the very end; he gave his last orders, dictated and signed his testament and a letter to the government of the Soviet Union. He expressed his desire to be buried "like Lenin, close to the masses," that his body be embalmed and transported to Nanking where he had been chosen first president of the Chinese Republic. Not long before his death he sent our embassy a banner with a saying. A banner with an answering inscription was carried behind his coffin. Sun's last words were "Peace, struggle, China's salvation . . ."

Our ambassador, Lyov Mikhaylovich Karakhan, was one of the first persons to express his condolences to Sun Yat-sen's family. The red flag over the embassy building and all Soviet consulates in China was flown at half-mast as it was at all the government buildings. As for the embassies of the imperialist powers, they did this only on the next day, fearing that their unwillingness to honor Sun Yat-sen's memory might provoke a burst of indignation.

---

15. This hospital was built with funds which the Rockefeller Foundation contributed to the Chinese medical department. The U. S. did not have a sphere of influence in China, but fought furiously for one while palming itself off as a "friend of the Chinese people."

The government appropriated 60,000 yuan for the funeral. The universities were closed for three days. Feng Yü-hsiang personally expressed his condolences to Sun Yat-sen's widow. General Hu Ching-i, then commander of the Second Nationalist Army, and several other generals contributed enormous sums towards the funeral. Only Marshal Chang Tso-lin, the Japanese henchman in Manchuria, did not express sympathy. He was happy to be rid of a dangerous opponent who enjoyed such colossal popularity.

The Peking authorities attempted to bury Sun Yat-sen according to the Confucian rites since they feared that the masses would turn the funeral into a protest demonstration which was, in fact, what occurred. But nothing came of Tuan Ch'i-jui's schemes. Sun Yat-sen's body was taken to the hospital for embalming. An altar was erected in the room where he died; every day fresh flowers were placed there. Crowds of people came to honor Sun's memory. A special coffin was sent from the Soviet Union. On March 19 the body of the deceased was carried in a yellow coffin with glass covering the face to one of the pavilions in Central Park, the so-called Temple of Fire for a farewell with the masses. The coffin was covered with the red Kuomintang flag with the blue field in the corner in which is depicted a white sun encircled by twelve rays.

The ceremony of transferring the coffin turned into an unprecedented mass demonstration in which, it was said, more than 100,000 people participated. Members of the Kuomintang CEC carried the coffin. Along the entire route soldiers of the Peking garrison and the police stood lined up. A military band was at the head of the procession. Directly behind the coffin, together with members of the Kuomintang CEC and representatives of various public organizations, followed Karakhan, Gekker (the military attaché), Klyshko (the trade representative) and other leading persons from Soviet establishments in Peking. Other Soviets marched behind in the crowd carrying a red banner with the inscription "Proletarians of all nations, unite!" Members of other foreign missions did not take part in the funeral.

A triple chain of students and Kuomintang members formed around the coffin with their arms linked. Flags were unfurled and anti-imperialist slogans resounded. The coffin with Sun Yat-sen's body lay in state in Central Park for more than a week. During this time more than a half-million persons visited it. The Temple of Fire was heaped with wreaths. On the day when Sun's ashes were carried into the Pi Yün Ssu a crowd of thousands again flooded the streets of the city and the whole length of the road to the Western Hills. Innumerable banners fluttered over the crowd. Young people, fists raised, shouted anti-imperialist slogans. Two five-cornered stars from the Soviet embassy and the government of the USSR were carried over the coffin.

The Pi Yün Ssu is located in an extraordinarily picturesque mountainous location beyond the former Imperial Summer Palace. It is built on the slopes of a rather high mountain. Numerous temples and passages stretch upwards towards the main building in the form of a flat-roofed marble tower on top of which stood several pagodas. Many of the pavilions were partially in ruins. After the temple was converted to a mausoleum, they were not restored but at the bottom of the staircase was a guardpost, a soldier with a rifle, and also an inscription "Visitor, stop here," so that those who were heading towards the coffin of the great man could collect their thoughts and acquire the proper reverential mood.

Borodin was constantly with Sun Yat-sen in the days of his illness. Sun Yat-sen dictated his last testament not only to his wife and party comrade Soong Ching-ling but to Borodin as well. By the time I arrived Borodin was no longer in Peking. Soon after the funeral he went to Canton where I saw him for the first time almost a year later. His wife Fanya Semyonovna and youngest son Norman spent the summer of 1925 in the embassy. Borodin's name was widely known; he was frequently written about in the Chinese and foreign papers as a talented public figure with great influence in the ruling circles of the Kuomintang and therefore it was with great interest that we looked at the plump woman with strong face and head of thick, curly hair who as we knew, was not only his wife, but also private secretary to Borodin, helping him in his work.

The Moscow-Peking Flight

On July 13, 1925, crowds of people gathered at the airport to meet the five Soviet flyers who completed the historic flight from Moscow to Peking.

In our era of cosmic flights it is very hard to imagine what an enormous significance this event had at the time. Now the flight to Peking takes several hours, but then the trip took more than a month. However, this was an outstanding achievement for those times. The Soviet Union was the first to demonstrate not the quality of its aircraft—at that time we could not boast of them—but the ability and courage of its flyers to the dissatisfaction of the powers with pretensions to leadership in aviation.

Later, back in Moscow, the leader of the expedition, O. Yu. Shmidt, in a speech compared our flight to the Italian Rome-Peking flight which preceded it, when only one of the twelve planes reached the goal, and to the American round-the-world flight when only two of four planes finished. Notwithstanding the fact that technical conditions for the Soviet flight were much worse, our planes did not change parts along the way. "Just think," said O. Yu. Shmidt, "the air route to Peking will take seven days." To Peking by air in just a week! It was simply difficult to believe.

The youthful Mikhail Mikhaylovich Gromov, who was to become a famous pilot of Soviet airships, was among the flyers. The non-flying public also took part in the expedition—newspaper correspondents and a cameraman from Proletarian Films who recorded the flight on film. The airport was located fifteen kilometers from the city on the grounds of the aviation school. On the morning of July 13, people began to gather there to welcome the flyers—embassy employees headed by Karakhan, members of the Chinese government, representatives of public organizations. The sun was scorching, a tent had been set up in one corner of the airport. Bands were playing. The well-wishers, dressed in white summer suits, carried flowers, flags, and placards. Everywhere flags flapped in the wind—red Soviet, five-colored government, and red and blue Kuomintang ones.

We had to wait a long time. Finally about one in the afternoon three dots appeared in the sky and quickly drew closer. Everybody at the airport became excited and rushed forward. At once several bands began to play. And there on the yellow field three enormous dragonflies raced along and the flyers were waving their hands. The ovation continued for about fifteen minutes. The noise was such that it was difficult to understand anything. The flyers were strewn with flowers; the planes were covered with red Soviet flags. The official welcome took place at the hangars which were hung with red bunting and posters with anti-imperialist slogans. The head of the aviation school presented traditional Chinese gifts to the participants in the flight—silver vases with their names inscribed. After triumphal speeches the honored guests were seated in automobiles, heaped with flowers and decorated with

Soviet, Kuomintang and Chinese government flags, and taken to Peking. The guests stayed at the Ambassador Hotel.

O. Yu. Shmidt arrived about three hours later in the remaining plane, while the *Pravda*, having met with an accident in the Gobi, was delayed three days. It had to be repaired in unbelievably difficult conditions, but the flyers displayed exceptional tenacity and skill, finishing the repairs with unexpected speed. This did not occur without a provocative incident. On the Kalgan road, the car in which the pilot and the mechanic were riding was attacked and got through to Kalgan only with difficulty. We supposed, not without foundation, that this attack had been organized by White Guards who lived in many parts of China at that time.

The ceremonies honoring the participants in the flight continued for several days in the Chinese capital. There were two banquets—one in the embassy, the other in the grand hall of the Palace of the Chinese Republic in Central Park. The head of the department of aviation and several ministers were in attendance. There was no end to the speeches and congratulations. O. Yu. Shmidt acknowledged these at both banquets.

The air heroes stayed in Peking for almost a month, resting up, becoming acquainted with the national customs and sights of the city, inquiring about the latest political developments in China, visiting the tomb of Sun Yat-sen. The members of the expedition were very popular among the Chinese people, especially O. Yu. Shmidt, who was called *"ta hutz"* (big beard) by the Pekingese because of his beard. The expedition members visited the embassy almost every day. Young and cheerful, they became friends with almost all of the staff and their families. Grisha Rozenblat, a correspondent for *Pravda* who was gathering material for a book and always clicking his camera, was especially sociable.[16] Together with a group of flyers he went to Kalgan to see Feng Yü-hsiang. The marshal entertained them at his staff headquarters at seven in the morning and presented them with gifts—the same traditional vases, and gave to Rozenblat, as a representative of *Pravda*, his portrait as well. Learning that the executive secretary of *Pravda*'s editorial board was Lenin's sister, Maria Ilinichna, Feng Yü-hsiang sent her a vase and an autographed portrait.

---

16. After the Peking flight, G. Rozenblat developed a liking for opening up new air routes. He died in a crash over Kharkov in May 1926. Another participant in the Moscow-Peking flight, the flyer Petrov, died even earlier while trying to pioneer an air route from Verkhneudinsk to Troitskosavsk.

A reception and military parade were held in the flyers' honor. Feng Yü-hsiang introduced the participants in the expedition and then a review of the troops was held. The parade was concluded with a speech in which the marshal unmasked the imperialists. Rozenblat noticed that the soldiers were wearing armbands. Feng Yü-hsiang explained that this was in mourning for the victims shot on May 30 on Nanking Road in Shanghai.

In the middle of August the flyers visited Kaifeng where they met our advisers who were working in the Second Nationalist Army—Klimov, Lapin, Skalov, and others. The reception in Kaifeng was even more enthusiastic. General Yüeh Wei-chün, commanding the Second Nationalist Army and governor of Honan, was flirting with the Kuomintang at the time and making every effort to show himself off as an enlightened, liberal man. He placed no obstacles in the way of popular celebrations to welcome the participants in the flight, and allowed demonstrations and meetings to take place. Our flyers were greeted with ovations; orators called them people from a "fraternal country," delegates from factories and plants presented Shmidt with red banners.

Peking through the Haze of Time

I still have not said anything really about Peking, that wonderful city which we had longed to see and which did not disappoint us. In order to know the real Peking one must live there for quite a few years, and of course my story cannot pretend to depth or thoroughness, but I loved the city with all my heart, and love, they say, is clearsighted. So I have decided to share my impressions of Peking although I lived there for only four months. As soon as we passed beyond the boundaries of the Diplomatic Quarter and its stiff, martial arrogance, the great past of China engulfed us from all sides. History spoke to us with the voice of literally countless monuments. This was a city cum museum, a remarkably well-preserved specimen of a city from the times of classical Chinese feudalism.

The external aspect of Peking inclined one to contemplation, reflection, and quiet labor. Silence and emptiness reigned in the old palaces and temples; in grey, moss-covered stones of the fortress walls grew tall, ancient grasses and shrubs. The slumber of the ancient capital was imperturbable, so it seemed. But this was only a first deceptive impression. In Peking there were almost no

factories and plants; the industrial proletariat was numerically small. But nowhere in China was there such an accumulation of young students. The May
Fourth Movement of 1919 which developed under the influence of the Great
October Revolution and initiated a new phase in the anti-imperialist struggle
in China unfolded first of all in Peking as a movement of the revolutionary
students. Peking also played an important role in the history of the Communist
movement in China. One of the first Communist circles was established here
as early as 1920. Its organizer was the talented, learned, and ardent revolutionary, a professor of Peking University, Li Ta-chao, who later became secretary
of the Northern Bureau of the CCP.

This was one side of the political situation in Peking. But there was
another. Peking was a magnet for all kinds of adventurers. Its seizure held out
the promise of international recognition. Representatives of the various militarist cliques fought endlessly over it. In those years this city which appeared
to be quietly slumbering under the heavy burden of years saw many intrigues,
plots, subornations, and bloody crimes.

Peking had existed for more than a thousand years, and under various
names had served as the capital for more than nine centuries. It became known
in Europe during the thirteenth century under Kublai Khan who constructed
fortress walls around it and called it Khanbalyk, meaning the Khan's headquarters. Beyond the Anting gates I still found relics of this clay wall. Chinese
cities are constructed, as a rule, in the shape of enormous rectangles aligned
according to the earth, i.e., every city has northern, southern, eastern, and
western walls. Peking differs a little from this scheme. It is laid out in the shape
of a square with a rectangle abutting on it to the south, stretching from east
to west. History reveals how this came about.

The present walls of Peking were raised during the Ming dynasty in the
mid-fifteenth century. At that time the poor made hovels for themselves from
the remains of the Mongol walls, thus forming the southern suburbs which a
hundred years later were walled in and joined to the territory of the capital.
Such was the development of the Inner and Outer Cities which stood in opposition to one another as the city of the rich and that of the poor.[17] This
difference was further accentuated when the conquering Manchus settled in

---

17. In Western literature the Inner City is usually called the Tartar or Manchu city and the Outer is
    called the Chinese city.

58

the Inner City and allowed only those of the high Chinese nobility and the Chinese banner troops[18] who had helped them to conquer the country to settle there.

All the tourist guides in Peking affirmed that one had to view the city from the towers of the Ch'ien Men gates in line with the Legation Quarter. These gates were right in the middle of the wall which separated the Inner from the Outer City. Their many-storied rectangular tower is one of the ornaments of Peking to this day. And so we climbed along the *pandus*[19] and staircase to the top storey of the tower. The ascent was not an easy one, but we were amply rewarded by the magnificent view which opened up from there.

Beneath us lay the Inner City enclosed by seventeen-meter-thick walls. From above they looked like broad streets on which two troykas could easily ride. They were framed by big square merlons pierced by loopholes. One could clearly see the massive gates with their characteristic tiered pagoda-like roofs covered with glittering colored tiles. Amid the greenery lay the enormous square of the Imperial City; its rose-colored walls with their towers and loopholes stretched off into the distance. Within was yet another square with reddish walls, the nucleus of the entire layout—the Forbidden or Purple City, the former residence of the emperor and his family where only a small circle of courtiers was allowed in. This most interesting palace complex had been converted at present into a museum under the name of the Ku Kung (Ancient palace). The palaces and temples of the Imperial City were drowning in greenery and surrounded by canals.

In the south of the Inner City towered the blue cupola of the Temple of Heaven crowned by a golden sphere of a distinctive, irregular shape. The broad streets were filled with movement, but the narrow, winding alleys meandering between the silent walls of private homes were quiet and empty. From above one could see what marvelous buildings were hidden behind these grey clay walls. From this vantage a panorama opened up which explained how it was that for so long travelers considered Peking with its enormous square as the most densely populated city on earth whereas in the days we are speaking of

18. Banner troops—Manchu, Chinese, and Mongolian troops who were under the command of the Manchu Ch'ing dynasty and differentiated among themselves by the color of their banners.
19. *Pandus* is an inclined platform for the entrance of carriages and artillery pieces into fortress walls.

it had fewer than a million inhabitants. The largest part of the city was occupied by the palaces, temples, and parks, while the dwellings of the Pekingese
of average means were one-storied with many little courtyards also requiring
much space. Descending from the tower, we then climbed up the fortress
walls of the Inner City and walked along it toward the east.

Now as before, on the upper platform of one of the guard towers of the
eastern wall, under the open sky, the instruments of the old Peking observatory
may be found. A thick green film covers the bronze of the sextants, quadrants,
celestial globes, and other astronomical instruments which were decorated with
dragons. Marble balustrades surrounded each separate instrument. Below we
were shown the building of the observatory in almost contemporary architecture on the spot where, at one time, the first Chinese observatory constructed
by order of Kublai Khan in the thirteenth century had been located. At that
same time the first astronomical equipment had been manufactured. Those
instruments which are now on the tower were made for the most part no
earlier than the seventeenth century but according to old models. In 1900
when the powers plundered Peking in revenge for the anti-imperialist rebellion
of the I Ho T'uan, the Germans took the best of these instruments to Germany
where they used them to decorate the terrace of the palace in Potsdam. By
the Versailles Treaty, vanquished Germany returned them to China.

Late at night we again climbed the tower of Ch'ien Men to look at night-
time Peking. The city lay before us half-illuminated, slumbering. The vague
contours of her monumental buildings and green tracts showed dimly. But
what is that yellow glow? It seems that this is one of the commercial blocks,
located just beyond the Ha Ta Men gates. We descend from the tower, in the
darkness stumbling over the ruts of its ancient staircase. A five-minute walk
through the dark, deserted square brings us to a noisy, vividly lighted world.
It seems to us that we have stumbled across a holiday spectacle; there are so
many people, so much bright light and golden glitter.

The streets are lined with small houses, the bottom floors of which are
occupied by shops which have no fronts; the facade is boarded up at night.
A blinding light floods the wares which fill the counters and overflow freely
outside. Inside and out the shops are notable for a distinctive, exotic beauty;
everywhere is gilt, artistically carved wood, colorful stained glass and artistic
panels.

The street was filled with golden patches of light, vivid colored spots and dark shadows. Garlands of flowers, strings of pennants, enormous lanterns made of greased paper decorated with flowers, dragons, human figures and embellished with long silk tassels hung low over the heads of passers-by. One had the impression of an endless perspective of a gaily decorated enfilade. The mysterious, fairy-tale East had come alive before us, that same East about which Europe, enchanted, had for centuries heard stories from its travelers.

Evening promenades along the commercial quarter were in style among Peking residents. As always one was surrounded by cheerful, laughing crowds of representatives of all classes of Peking society. Elderly persons of learned mien walked unhurriedly holding fans and displaying on their little fingers yellow fingernails several centimeters long. Girl students in the traditional short student haircuts and uniform—a black skirt and bright jacket with a high collar—exchanged smiles with youths in long robes. Maidenly faces with bangs and heavily rouged cheeks—Chinese "camellias"—flashed in the crowd. A melodic sound was heard all the time. These were the rickshaw men calling for the right of way. A surprising thing, even they looked as if transformed here. Their rickshaws began to look like new, they glittered and sparkled with brass decorations, the rags on their shoulders took on a picturesque, theatrical look. But the passengers evidently had lost out. Their postures seemed comically self-important, especially if the passenger was decked out in an expensive satin robe. We always remembered this evening which was so like a living tale of *Scheherazade*.

Perhaps less colorful, but no less interesting for that, was the common, everyday life of Peking. The remarkable variety of traffic in the streets was striking. Heavy peasant carts, harnessed any old way, some in pairs, some in tandem, passed by. Their harnesses joined together the most diverse of traction power, beside a mule a bull would slowly plod, or a gentle little burro mince along. One constantly met up with that same grey little burro, loaded above his ears or carrying a rider who almost scraped his feet on the ground. A lacquered, so-called Peking cart, harnessed to a pair of horses in a splendid frame with silver ornaments and silk tassels went by at a measured pace. This was considered especially chic for horses were scarce in China Proper[20] and

20. China Proper is the territory within the bounds of the Great Wall.

formerly only important mandarins rode that way, but in our time it was possible to hire such carts for a ride. Horn sounding furiously, an auto with soldiers on the running boards swept by and people scurried to the side, yielding the road to some important official or general. Then a caravan of Bactrian camels, bells tinkling, moved slowly along. Peasant carts carrying tubs of excrement went by, spreading a terrible stench. The streets, almost all of which were unpaved, knew no watering but the pitiful sprinkling from the earthenware water-vats at the side of the road. Heavy dust hung in the air.

Beginning in January 1926 trams appeared on several of Peking's main streets, but they did not solve the transit problem. As before, innumerable rickshaw men lined the streets waiting for fares. From time to time, others ran at a dog-trot along the streets—swarthy, half-naked, wet from sweat, with rags or battered straw hats on their heads. They were constantly being overtaken by the so-called private rickshaws in which complacent passengers sat and proudly looked around. These were, so to speak, the "private carriages" of the well-to-do Chinese who had his own rickshaw and hired a coolie by term. He desired to go faster than the others so his puller strived to satisfy his master's absurd whim.

The rickshaw men of the Legation Quarter were aristocrats in their own way. Their rickshaws looked smart and neat; their black lacquer shone and their brass fittings were carefully polished. Their seat-covers were always kept clean. The foreign policemen of the Legation Quarter kept a close watch on this. The rickshaw pullers on the Chinese streets looked much poorer. Only rarely did one of them own his own rickshaw. Special firms leased the rickshaws to them for a fixed sum, irrespective of their actual earnings. Damage to the rickshaw was a catastrophe for the puller since it plunged him into unpayable debt for a long time, perhaps his whole life. And yet there were people, if one can call them people, who allowed themselves to make sport of the rickshaw men. I saw an English sailor in Canton push a rickshaw into a canal; the puller plunged in after it and was drowned.

This was a difficult profession—to run for many kilometers, gasping for breath, in the terrible Peking heat or the bitter cold.[21] The infamous Peking

---

21. Peking is located on a parallel which passes through the Mediterranean Sea but 25 degrees of frost is no rarity there. The hot season lasts from six weeks to two months—July and August, but the heat then is unbearable, reaching 104 degrees in the shade. The dust storms blowing in from Mongolia carry clouds of fine yellow dust and are a torture.

dust wore out the weak. Even the strongest rickshaw men could not long endure. It was not from the hands of a kind fate that the poor Chinese received the slender shafts of the light, two-wheeled vehicle, a vehicle so refined and inoffensive in appearance. If a rickshaw man did not change his profession in time he was doomed. Death overtook him on the run; he fell down and died on the street. This was so common that no one paid it any heed. The passenger in such a case, as the immediate cause of the misfortune, was obligated to give all the money he had on him to the dead man. Such was the custom. God knows how well it was observed.

Rickshaw men at the time were not only the lowest paid but also the most backward category of workers; however, the upsurge of the revolutionary movement in China after the events of May 1925 had an influence even on them. On the eve of our arrival the Peking rickshaw men joined the anti-imperialist struggle and affixed signs to their vehicles reading "No English or Japanese." The rickshaw men of the Legation Quarter actually wrecked this boycott. At that time rickshaw men still had no union, they were organized by native place or into guilds along with the company owners, so that it was easy to split them. Bloody fights among rickshaw men were a common occurrence. It was only in December 1925 that a modern trade union of rickshaw pullers and coolies was established.

Beggars stood, sat and lay along the sides of every street. I saw many of them in China—dirty, half-naked, often blind or with red, suppurating eyes. Trachoma gathered a bountiful harvest. With wild yells they crawled or ran after the passers-by, stretching out a small, saucer-shaped wicker basket or a tin begging cup. I will never forget the first beggar whom I saw in Peking. He had, most likely, been wandering about with his gentle, completely naked little boy and had sat down to rest, but it turned out that the place was reserved by an itinerant barber who came by and began to drive him off. The beggar was so tired that he didn't move and didn't even reply to the torrent of abuse. His begging basket lay before him on the ground. When I walked up the barber fell silent, and the beggar raised his eyes to me. Keeping them fixed on me, with an effort he placed a trembling hand, dry as a stick, on his son's head. Words cannot convey the meaning of this gesture and that look in which despair and a fatal weariness struggled with hope.

A whole army of beggars—about twenty thousand—lived in Peking. Many of them lived in the streets even in winter and during the hard frosts they froze to death beneath the city walls where they tried to seek shelter from the piercing winds. More than three hundred died during the severe winter of 1925-1926.

The beggars had their own union and a leader to whom they paid something like a tax. It was said that he was a man of means. The organization was illegal but the police were well aware of it. In any case, when bearers were needed for a funeral procession or strikebreakers to use against workers, this leader was turned to. The union regulated internal affairs and assigned beats for the collection of alms. Membership was compulsory for all beggars or else their brethren would drive them out of town.

In order to become better acquainted with conversational speech and Chinese popular life some of us, myself included, settled in the Chinese hotel Peiching Kung Yü (Peking hotel). What a marvel of a hotel! Everything there gladdened our hearts—its long courtyard stretched out in the shape of a tent, the big earthenware vats where goggle-eyed Chinese fish with gauzy tails swam, the stone wall covered with drawings in front of the entrance. It was designed especially for defense against evil spirits who fly only in straight lines and would inevitably knock their heads against it after having flown through the gates. At the same time it effectively shielded the interior of the courtyard from outsiders' glances. And the Chinese furniture, the Chinese kitchen and (no small point) the extraordinary cheapness. A big bowl of noodles with meat—*ju ssu mien*—cost twenty cents. It was a real student paradise. Sometimes established people, employees of the embassy, would drop in on us for diversion, especially Abram Izaakovich Khassis, our general favorite. Two years later, as vice-consul in Canton, he died during the defeat of the Canton Commune.

We also had the opportunity of living in a real Chinese private house, built for wealthy persons, which we rented by pooling our resources. It stood in one of the *hutungs* (alleys), an ordinary Peking *hutung* of Hatamen Street, a solid line of blank walls intricately decorated and wide red gates. One house had all the comforts of European civilization, central heating, a bathroom and plumbing, but it preserved in its entirety the appearance of a Chinese dwelling which we loved so much. The rooms opened on a square cobbled courtyard;

the outer walls were windowless. Above the gates jutted a lofty roof made of glittering blue tiles with eaves painted with flowers and amusing figures. And in the courtyard across from the entrance was the same magical wall decorated with a holy lotus. However, there were no kangs in any of the rooms. [A kang is a brick bed under which a heating flue is found. It is an essential piece of furniture in every North China dwelling.]

We hired a story-teller—in Chinese *shuo shu ti*—for practice in conversation. And so in the evenings a little old man in a long robe and round skull-cap shaped like a half melon (which has not been worn for years) began to show up at our house. He would greet us courteously, sit down and launch into his narrative, occasionally sipping fragrant jasmine tea which we served him in a Chinese covered mug on a small figured saucer with an amusing porcelain border.

Later, when I had read the book of medieval tales *Chin ku ch'i kuai*[22] (Amazing stories of past and present), I learned from where he drew his inspiration. But nevertheless he did not slavishly copy his source and often his varieties were even more interesting. Chinese story-tellers, in general, are distinguished by a great creative fantasy. If they make use of an established plot they usually modify it in their own way.

On more than one occasion we ran outside the gates when we heard the sounds of Chinese music from the streets since we knew that a wedding procession was passing by. A colossal red palanquin in which the bride was being carried to the groom's house was lifted above the heads of the numerous bearers. A corps of musicians walked ahead. The red curtains of the palanquin were lowered. According to the custom of North China which was more conservative than the south, no one was supposed to see the bride until the end of the marriage ceremony, not even the groom. Nor was she able to see him. It happened at times that substitutes were married.

Peking funerals were famous for their even greater splendor. The approach of a rich man's funeral procession was announced from a distance by the mournful howling of the three-meter horns[23] alternating with the rolling of

---

22. It was published in Moscow in 1961 in Russian: *Udivitel'nye istorii nashego vremeni i drevnosti.*
23. These horns which are of Mongol origin can be found in Soviet Central Asia where they are used during national celebrations.

drums and the outpourings of flutes. The enormous coffin, suspended from parallel poles, was borne by twenty or thirty men, and swayed back and forth in time to their step.[24] The bearers were dressed in a sort of funeral costume— a loose jacket of dark green material with large white circles, belted at the waist. A corps of professional mourners, usually numbering several hundred, was gathered from among the beggars. Among them or following closely after were the relatives dressed in mourning, that is white costumes or merely white bands around the head. And finally there were throngs of acquaintances and all kinds of hangers-on. The Chinese ascribed greater importance to funerals than to weddings in accordance with the cult of ancestors. All of these magnificent ceremonies were very expensive and only well-to-do persons could afford them, but many poor persons literally ruined themselves financially in order to carry out the prescribed Confucian rites. Only once did I see a poor man's funeral, but it etched itself into my memory forever. It was late in the evening along the road from Canton to Shaho. A peasant was being buried. Four men in peasant jackets open at the breast were carrying a small coffin made of thin, rotten boards. They were moving almost at a run. Two others were escorting a young woman who was covering her face with her hands and wailing in a toneless voice. They slipped past our car which was parked along the road and vanished like shadows beyond the bend.

Peking was famous for its bazaars. Asian conquerors and so-called cultured Europeans had plundered the city many times, but its treasures seemed inexhaustible. Ancient porcelains and bronzes, embroidery and pictures, satin courtiers' costumes, jasper, gold, and silver ornaments—all were offered in abundance to the fanciers. At times, historic valuables were literally sold for a farthing. Most of these were sent abroad.

One of Peking's book markets was located on Liu Li Chang Street. It was always quiet and uncrowded. On its shelves lay old Chinese books in blue cloth covers with bone fasteners shaped like miniature daggers together with contemporary books in Chinese and European languages. With a glance around, Communist editions were offered from under the counter. Ancient sayings

---

24. Wealthy Chinese buried their dead only one or two months after death. Therefore the comparatively small, distinctively shaped coffin made of round logs sawed lengthwise was placed in a large rectangular chest made of thick boards and lacquered inside and out.

written by some well-known calligrapher or by some unknown were offered
for sale, and here one had to look sharp. As passionate lovers of these things
we were often taken in because of inexperience. I didn't escape either. I bought
a so-called *tuitz*, a pair of scrolls made of paper pasted on lengths of silk and
inscribed in the calligraphy of the mighty noble of the Manchu court, the
suppressor of the T'aipings, Li Hung-chang. It was very amusing to see his signature under a quotation from the realm of lofty morality. "The lucid and
bright mind is eternal like the sea, the honest heart shines even at night like a
pearl." Alas, it was all rather skillfully done but a forgery nonetheless. The
Chinese merchants' concept of honesty was a very peculiar one. You could
leave your valuables with them for safekeeping with a calm mind and lend
them money and you would have nothing to fear. But trade was another
matter. Since no one is forcing you to buy, you are doing so of your own
free will and thus you must answer for your own mistakes.

In China calligraphy is a successful rival of painting and Chinese willingly
decorate their homes with examples of it, although often scrolls are kept in
the closet and people take pleasure in them only when showing them off to
guests. Enthusiasts and connossieurs are capable of spending hours discussing
the rules and excellence of execution of this or that particular feature exactly
as lovers of painting in the West discuss the coloring and execution of some
painting.

Often the frequenters of the book markets did not know for sure what
they wanted and the sellers were even less certain as to what they had in stock,
therefore they gave the buyers free rein to burrow about and shake the dust
off their precious wares. We spent long, happy hours at the book markets.

One of Peking's most famous markets was the Tung An Shih Ch'ang on
Wang Fu Ching Street, sort of a covered passageway which brought together
all kinds of stalls, shops, and stores. What couldn't be found there from wide
Chinese wooden beds to goldfish in open-top glass globes? One could hang
these little aquariums in one's room like a bird cage.

In Tung An Shih Ch'ang were sold gold and silver jewelry, paper lanterns
of the most fantastic shapes and colors, various finely carved red lacquer ware,
articles of lattice-work enamel, or splendidly embroidered court costumes
from imperial times. All of this was executed with such talent, with such fine
and faithful traditional national taste, that a visit to the Tung An Shih Ch'ang

differed not at all in essence from a tour of some museum or exhibit of applied arts. It was even possible to buy ancient objects from the collection of some ruined mandarin.

Fortunetellers sat at the entrance. Before them on little tables lay divining tablets with the trigrams depicted on them, the *pa kua*,[25] around the magic sign depicting the male and female principles—the Yin and Yang—in their eternal mutual confluence. These fortunetellers conducted themselves sedately, received clients with dignity, exactly as if they were actually in business. In order to have one's fortune told one had to give one's year and day of birth according to the Chinese cyclical calendar. The fortunetellers checked these in a fat, worn-looking book, gazed at their tables and prophesied. They all wore long robes which was a mark at that time of membership in the intelligentsia. How could it be otherwise! They were literate!

One of the embassy personnel decided to celebrate his birthday in a Chinese restaurant. So we found ourselves at a Chinese banquet for the first time. Now that the Peking Restaurant has opened in Moscow it is difficult to be surprised at an assortment of one's favorite Chinese dishes. Shark's fins, sea cucumbers, swallow nests, and black eggs have ceased being exotic. But I shall try to write of those dishes which I liked most of all, nevertheless.

In China every dish is served in the form of a mound of small, evenly sliced morsels since one eats with chopsticks and doesn't use a knife. Bits of meat or fish are dredged in a special, very tasty flour and fried in fragrant vegetable oil.[26] Sharp, spicy sauces, and pickled vegetables are served as relishes. Bread is not served but bowls with boiled rice are on the table.

Banquets encompass a multiplicity of the most varied dishes commencing with cold hors d'oeuvres and ending with soup. In the intervals between dishes one eats sweets—candied fruit and nuts, lotus seeds in honey, all kinds of pastry which are sometimes unfamiliar to our taste. Spoons are not used and one sips soup from the bowl, using chopsticks to convey the solid matter to one's lips.

---

25. *Pa kua*—a graphic complex of three alternating whole and broken lines. According to legend the mythical emperor Fu Hsi saw them on a tortoise which had crawled out of the Huang Ho and in conformity with them created the Chinese writing system.
26. I am thinking of festive dishes since fragrant oil—*hsiang yu*—and flour are too expensive. Chinese usually prepare their food with ordinary cottonseed oil, tea, or bean oil.

I expected that the restaurant where we were headed—and this was one of the most expensive in Peking—would be as gilded and decorated as the rows of shops. But I was mistaken. In the center of the hall stood a large, round table and Chinese chairs with straight backs and high seats so that when seated not all of us could reach the floor. According to the custom then there were no tablecloths. Out of respect for European customs we were given forks, but we were also supplied with bamboo *k'uaitz,* pairs of chopsticks for eating. There were no plates but instead white porcelain bowls decorated with blue flowers and grasses (blue and white was the most popular color combination in China at the time). On each of the serving plates were several varieties of hors d'oeuvres.

We were barely seated when they began to bring in the food. The high point of the dinner was Peking duck. It was served in mounds of fine slices, cut so that each slice had a layer of meat, fat and reddish crisp skin. With the duck was served a pile of dry pancakes, a plate of green onion and a sharp tomato relish. As it was explained to us one should roll the piece of duck in the pancake and convey it to one's mouth together with onion and relish. Warmed wine was served in pewter pitchers. The wine glasses were shaped like tiny, thimble-sized white porcelain bowls. Fish, flowers, and amusing old men (gods of longevity) with unnaturally swollen foreheads, dragons, land-scapes or Chinese characters with auspicious meanings were painted on them. After the duck what I liked most were the snails fried with eggs and a very hot sauce—*la chiao*—hot pepper in oil. It is very tasty but you can't eat it with-out crying.

We resolved jointly not to touch our forks, but far from all of us knew how to use chopsticks. It was very amusing to watch a comrade, swallowing his saliva, unsuccessfully chase some titbit along the bottom of his bowl. I myself know what a difficult science it is—to control the mischievous *k'uaitz* which laugh at you, twirl in your fingers and have no desire to be obedient. In fact I learned to eat with chopsticks later on when I happened to be travel-ing in the depths of China where forks and spoons were hard to come by.

There were several movies in Peking then, three belonging to foreigners. One of them, a summer theatre, was located on the roof of a tall house under the open sky and was always jammed in hot weather. The wicker chairs were not numbered. Each cost a yuan. There were two screenings daily, the first beginning at nine in the evening.

In one of the best hotels of the city, the Grand Hotel de Pekin, about twice a week there were concerts of symphonic music which we used to attend in a group. Most of the musicians were Russian emigrés. One had to listen to serious music not in a concert hall but in a kind of bar where people sat at tables, ordered alcoholic drinks and were unashamedly noisy. Foreigners were always in the majority there and conducted themselves very freely with an inexpressible feeling of superiority towards the Chinese. Now the building of this hotel, the Pekin, has been expanded and reconstructed.

We were very fond of visiting the Chinese theatre, the ancient Chinese opera. Like true opera buffs we laid in a supply of local delicacies at the entrance and sat at one of the tables which were placed in the pit or the balcony and ordered tea or food. Seats were not reserved. Having bought a ticket you could listen to several operas which went on one after the other from morning till late at night. Artists in vivid, splendidly sewn medieval costumes portrayed the heroes of the ancient Chinese legends. During the performance, in accordance with Chinese custom, we wiped our hands with cloths first dipped in nearly boiling water and then wrung out which were thrown by the strong hands of the *huo chi*[27] and flew like birds over the spectators' heads.

One of our students was especially attracted by Chinese opera. At that time in Peking there was a certain well-known young singer with a good voice and an attractive appearance. Our opera lover was enraptured by her and sent her flowers every time. He was the only European who expressed his admiration for the singer in this way. She herself was evidently flattered by this. But her protector, a famous Chinese general, was disturbed by this and revenged himself in a traditional Chinese way. During a performance he arose and made a cynical gesture in the singer's direction. She was put to shame by this and had to leave the stage. Afterwards, it was said that she became one of the concubines in the harem of this general who took her away from Peking.

Peking's Historical Monuments

A large literature exists in European and eastern languages on Peking's historical monuments. To say something new about them is a difficult task. Still it is impossible not to touch this theme, if only briefly, in speaking of Peking.

---

27. *Huo chi* is a store attendant, in this case a waiter.

We devoted all our days off to excursions to various historical sites; we visited museums, temples, and palaces. Unfortunately, they were very poorly kept up at that time. The dust was probably never removed and a thick layer covered both the holy images in the temples and the priceless examples of ancient applied arts in the palaces and museums. This spoiled the impression quite a bit. Some artificial flower, all gold and precious stones, which at one time adorned the emperor's palace now lay before us, grey, dull, and lifeless. Even the rays of the sun could not penetrate its many layers of dirt.

Chinese almost never visited the palaces and temples, and we were always alone there; no one hindered our enjoyment of the splendid monuments of antiquity. There was something painfully sad in the obvious signs of complete neglect, but at the same time their majestic quiet, undisturbed by the presence of intrusive tourists with their cameras and simulated enjoyment, produced a profound, unforgettable impression.

Naturally, what we visited before anything else was the famous Temple of Heaven, the main temple of Peking and all of China.

Praying to the sky is an echo from the oldest religion of China, the deification of nature's forces, and although Confucianism was considered the official religion, for many hundreds of years the Temple of Heaven was the main sacred place of the Chinese people, and its rulers had to take this into account. Even the Mongol and Manchu dynasties which ruled in China took upon themselves the duty of public worship in the Temple of Heaven insofar as only the emperor himself could perform this and never did any of the votaries of the cults take part.

More than once political adventurers tried out of selfish reasons to make use of the Chinese people's respect and love for this ancient monument of its history. In December 1914, the treacherous President Yüan Shih-k'ai, who dreamed of becoming emperor, performed the public worship like a true "son of heaven." Public opinion ridiculed this comedy and he did not repeat it, but the thought of becoming "son of heaven" did not leave him till his death.

In 1917 General Chang Hsün who attempted to restore the Manchu monarchy occupied the Temple of Heaven with his troops, hoping that the government would not bring itself to infringe upon this territory which the Chinese held sacred. But he was mistaken; the temple was fired upon. Fortunately the structure hardly suffered.

The grounds of the temple are very broad and enclosed by two walls, an outer one five kilometers in circumference and a smaller inner one. Pines and cypresses grow on the grounds. At one time, bulls intended for the sacrifices grazed there. The path to the temple goes through the Palace of Unity where the emperor would spend the night in fasting and prayer before the public worship. This is a typical Chinese building, the roof has turned-down corners of varicolored tile, massive columns of whole timber covered with red lacquer. It is said that a throne and splendid furniture stood there formerly. We found none of it.

I think an entrance ticket cost about ten cents. After handing the gate-keeper our money, our small group entered a rather neglected broad path paved with white tiles which led to the interior of the grounds. We were all very cheerful, laughing and talking, but gradually our mood began to change and soon we were completely silent . . .

We came out onto another, still wider road, also paved with tiles, then turned to the right and there before us was the main structure of the Temple of Heaven, the sacrificial altar. It stood there bathed in the rays of the hot mid-day sun, as if languishing from the heat—a miracle of white marble in the shape of a triple terrace with three tiers of marvelously chiseled balustrades and fantastically decorated staircases at the four corners of the world. Around it in the spacious white plaza enormous bronze braziers, pitted by time, shone darkly. Tall grass grew amid the tiles of the roadway and on the steps of the marble staircases.

All was silence. A deep but not deathly silence, almost a silence of sleep. Our footsteps alone resounded and one could hear the omnipresent chirping of the cicadas. Over our heads glittered the serene blue heaven, that same terrible divinity to whom in the past prayers were offered and blood sacrifices presented. Climbing to the upper platform of the altar, we stopped in the center at the very place where of old the son of heaven prayed. One of us shouted. An unexpectedly loud echo stunned us. We had not known of the amazing secret (as yet unsolved) of the temple's acoustics. We looked around. Was it possible? Not long ago, only fifteen or twenty years distant, these grounds which lay neglected before us were alive and blossoming with the splendid costumes of cruel and selfish parasites by the thousands, who competed with each other in luxury and wealth. Right here, on the path to the altar, fat Chinese dignitaries with long queues, the symbol of national enslavement, and peacock feathers on their mandarin caps, gravely prostrated themselves before the foreign emperor. Living feudalism at the beginning of the twentieth century! Now this was all such distant history. Just like a cloud which had vanished.

In many Chinese and foreign books the ritual of sacrifice in the Temple of Heaven is described, although no outsiders were permitted to enter and no foreigner ever saw the ritual. Preparations for the ceremony went on for months in the imperial palace; its complexities were endlessly rehearsed since it was considered that even the slightest infringement of the prescriptions carried the threat of terrible calamity for the entire country. Several days before the sacrifices the entire grounds of the temple were decorated with yellow imperial standards on which dragons were depicted, lanterns with artistic painting of symbolic significance, and other ritual decorations.

The highest ranks at court and thousands of retainers accompanied the emperor. Persons motionless as idols with fixed, impenetrable faces were carried in innumerable palanquins along the broad avenue which led from the main gates of the palace to the Temple of Heaven. Their costumes, each of which had cost several years of labor by the court embroiderers, did not bend, so dense were the precious embroideries on the tight satin. Famous warriors and innumerable hosts of court servants participated in the procession. The train continued for several hours, movement on the streets ceased, all the inhabitants were ordered not to leave their houses on pain of death, and to close their doors and windows. None of the "unworthy" could see the "son of heaven."

The emperor and his retinue spent the night in the Temple of Heaven, and at dawn the sacrifices were performed. The son of heaven climbed to the upper platform of the altar and stopped in the center. Surrounded at first by concentric circles of marble slabs, with which the plaza was paved, where each circle duplicated the holy number "nine"—symbol of the nine heavens of Chinese mythology—then by the circles of the balustrades of the altar and the line of the distant horizon, he saw himself in the center of the universe where only he, the emperor of the first and only state in the world—the Middle Kingdom (Chung Kuo), could stand, the true son of heaven.

It is not surprising that the rulers of old China were distinguished by an exceptional arrogance. They considered themselves the sovereigns of the whole world, other nations could be their tributary states only. So much more powerful was the blow when at the beginning of the last century the military defeats of feudal China commenced as did its enslavement by foreigners.

The sacrifices in the Temple of Heaven were conducted twice yearly with supplementary ones sometimes in case of natural calamities. A young bullock with a pure one-toned coat without a single blemish was brought as sacrifice. He was killed and burned in a green-tiled stove right there, not far from the altar. In the large bronze brazier offerings of silk and texts read during the sacrificial prayers were burned.

From the top of the altar we saw the building next in importance—the Temple of Prayer for the Harvest. It was erected on a white marble terrace imitating the shape of an altar. It was a round building with a triple roof of blue tile, thirty meters high and topped with something like a golden sphere. Inside it massive columns of whole timber covered with red lacquer were standing. On the ceiling, the walls, and the marble staircases were depicted dragons, the symbol of imperial power.

Along the path to this temple was yet another building, in the same style but of much smaller dimensions. This was the Emperor's Pavilion. There the son of heaven rested after the sacrifice. In the interior where a cool twilight reigned, we saw on a dais a splendid throne carved in relief in the precious red lacquer.[28] Along the round walls were massive columns of whole timbers. The four columns closest to the throne were completely covered with the names of foreign tourists. Various hands, with and without flourishes, distinct or already obliterated, the usual petty vanity of insignificant people who wished to leave behind some trace of their existence.

Next to the Temple of Heaven is the Temple of Agriculture, in Chinese Shen Nung T'ang, that is, Temple in memory of Shen Nung, the mythological emperor who supposedly taught agriculture to the Chinese, and invented the plow and other agricultural implements. Every spring the emperor sacrificed

---

28. Chinese lacquer, usually red, enjoys a worldwide fame, and even Japanese lacquer cannot compare with it. Its preparation was very difficult and time-consuming. Moreover the sap of the lacquer tree burned the hands of the master-workers. Of old, objects were covered with ten layers of lacquer. This took a huge amount of time inasmuch as each layer required a thorough drying. As a result one could carve it quite deeply. It was very expensive.

before the tablet with Shen Nung's name as if thereby showing respect for
the most honorable profession in ancient China, agriculture. Then, dressing
himself in peasant costume, but of yellow imperial color, holding on to a
ribbon tied to a plough, he ploughed three furrows with the help of his
courtiers. Following the emperor his retinue took up the plough. Formerly,
it was said, the imperial plough and the emperor's yellow peasant costume
were on display. But by our time the grounds of the temple had already been
turned into an amusement park, where on weekdays and holidays many people
crowded about, and theatres, movies, and restaurants flourished. A bandstand
had been erected on the altar.

Next in significance was the Temple of Confucius, embodying the official
religion of China. In former times the emperor, and after the 1911 Revolution
official figures of the Chinese Republic, the president and his ministers, twice
yearly, in spring and autumn, visited to bow before Confucius.

The most interesting monument in the temple was the famous drums
of the Chou dynasty, covered with archaic writing about the imperial hunt.
Uncovered in the seventh century, they were valued so highly that eight hundred
years later a special palace was constructed for them in Honan, then the seat
of China's capital. The inscriptions on the drums were inlaid with gold. The
Mongols who conquered China carried them off to Peking, and stripped off
the gold, so that the inscriptions suffered and were now impossible to decipher.
In the neighboring hall three thousand stone slabs with carved classical texts
are gathered. Formerly the emperor would come here, and seated on his
throne, he would interpret the sayings of the sages.

We visited the Lamaist monastery Yün Ho Kung at the end of Hatamen
Street on the north side of the Inner City, in company with our *hsiensheng*[29]
Li who was a very learned Chinese and turned out to be an excellent guide
for historic spots. Fifteen hundred monks lived there at the time of our visit.
Visitors were shown a colossal statue of Buddha (twenty meters high and carved
out of a whole tree) which had been brought from Tibet. But we preferred a
different Buddha in a yellow cap with a walking stick in his hands. We chose
him as our patron when we heard the legend which was told about him.
According to tradition, this figure had been brought from Tibet by a pious
monk two hundred years ago. His road led through Russian territory but he
didn't know Russian. The statue served as his interpreter.

---

29. *Hsiensheng*—teacher.

In the monastery, morning and evening, prayer services were held which anyone at all could attend. This was a very colorful spectacle. The monks in yellow, orange, and brick-red robes knelt around the main celebrant, played on various musical instruments and sang, accompanying all this with body movements which the uninitiated found difficult to understand. Once a year one could see there the famous lamaist devil dance which always attracted a large crowd of spectators. Unfortunately, I didn't get to see it.

At the north wall of the Inner City stands the famous bell tower whose bells were cast by order of the Emperor Yung Lo of the Ming dynasty (who ruled China from 1403 to 1424). Every evening when the city guard was changed the tolling of the bell resounded throughout the city. Our teacher Li assured us that you could hear in the sound the moans of a girl who threw herself into the molten metal, as the legend said, in order to save her father, a master of metallurgy who had failed to cast a good bell and had been threatened with death by the emperor.

In those days the Forbidden City was not yet open for visiting, but a section of it, the halls where the emperor at one time gave audience to his military officials, was already being used as a national art museum. Exhibits had been brought together from various imperial palaces and represented a very great value (the Americans apparently valued it at a hundred million American dollars). Both buildings of the palace set aside as the museum were literally overflowing with these treasures. Lattice-work enamel articles, articles of ancient, so-called carved red lacquer, porcelain, jasper, ivory, a superb collection of very old bronzes, pictures, manuscripts and ancient musical instruments covered with faded snakeskin all were on display. One was struck by the originality and brilliance of China's national art and at the same time perturbed by the carelessness with which the exhibits were maintained.

One of our longest excursions in Peking was a trip to the Shih San Ling (Thirteen tombs)—the burial ground of the Ming dynasty emperors. A marble-arched broad road on both sides of which towered figures of humans and animals twice life-size, led to the tombs which were placed in a semi-circle on the slope of a wooded hill. There stood generals carved of white stone in armor and shoulder plates, each with a sword in hand and a marshal's baton; or civil officials in ancient rectangular head-gear, ankle-length robes with sleeves of unusual length and breadth. Their handsome faces were stern, their eyes downcast. Here were lions, unicorns, camels, and elephants. In the days when the emperor offered sacrifices to his ancestors, splendid processions passed along this avenue. In 1958 one of the tombs was opened. An entire palace filled with countless treasures was found underground. The emperor was buried along with his wives and concubines.

Returning from our out-of-town trip we rode part of the way on asses or in primitive two-wheeled wooden carts without spokes in which one had to sit on the floor with one's legs drawn up beneath one, and which moved only at a walk in view of the unbelievable shaking. Not infrequently the road lay through fields sown with kaoliang, one and a half to two times the height of a man. Even a man on horseback could easily conceal himself in the dense growth. In the thirties during the anti-Japanese War, guerillas often made use of this cover.

The rivers in the Peking area were silt-laden and the water in them was a dark, chocolate color. On the bank of one of them we saw a young peasant woman doing her wash. One can imagine how it came out, but what could she do? There was no other water. We wanted to photograph her, but she got frightened and stood up to run away on her tiny, disfigured feet. Women in North China never wanted to be photographed. Nevertheless, through cunning we did take her picture. In order to calm her, the photographer stood behind and we in front and pretended we were taking our own picture. I still have this picture—a thin woman sitting on her haunches, her bony knees sticking up above her shoulders. She is washing and even in the photo the water came out dark as coffee.

The Situation Becomes Tense

The days of our brief period of probationary work in Peking flashed by and each one brought something new and interesting. We were in a hurry, the term of our stay in Peking had expired, and the situation did not permit of delay.

The summer of 1925 was very tense in China. Towards autumn it had already become clear that the foreign and domestic enemies of the Chinese Revolution were preparing for a new offensive. The shots in Canton had already heralded this. On August 20, the leader of the Kuomintang left, Sun

Yat-sen's successor, Liao Chung-k'ai, who enjoyed exceptional influence and popularity, was assassinated. No one doubted that the British colonialists, enraged by the boycott directed against them, were mixed up in this tragedy. Even the embassy of Great Britain felt the strength of the people's protest.

In the beginning of August a Chinese servant in our embassy informed us that there was a strike in the British embassy. In fact, going out on the street we saw anti-British placards on our neighbor's walls, and at the gates picketing Chinese servants. Of the two hundred odd strikers—clerks, cooks, coolies and other servants—many had served in the embassy for twenty years and enjoyed the absolute confidence of their masters. Now with one voice they demanded a "just resolution of the Shanghai[30] and other conflicts." The English lost their heads completely. On August 17, when the strikers organized a demonstration at the embassy gates, some curious Japanese journalist poked his nose in to see what was happening. He was arrested and severely beaten since he was taken for a Chinese student agitator. The ill-fated Japanese sat in the cellar for several hours. When the misunderstanding was brought to light, the British chargé d'affaires went to the Japanese embassy to apologize to the minister, Yoshizawa.

The British press began to speak of the possibility of military intervention against China. These declarations were enthusiastically greeted by the entrenched British colonialists in China who used to whistle for their Chinese servants as they would for their dogs, and who were convinced that one had "to give the Chinese a periodic thrashing every twenty years" to keep them humble.

At approximately this time, Chang Tso-lin began repressions in Peking where his troops were stationed by agreement with Feng Yü-hsiang. In the middle of August the Peking government, on Chang Tso-lin's request, shut down the Kuomintang's paper *Min Pao*, which by mistake had published a notice of the marshal's death. At night soldiers burst into the apartment of the editor, the well-known Kuomintang activist Ch'en Yu-jen, later foreign minister of the Kuomintang government (Eugene Ch'en), and dragged him right off to prison from his bed, not even letting him get dressed. Ch'en Yu-jen escaped execution only by accident.

No sooner had Chinese reaction raised its head than anti-Soviet provocations began. This time too they couldn't do without them. In Chang Tso-lin's

---

30. This refers to the May 30, 1925 Incident.

patrimony—Manchuria—especially in Harbin, a campaign against the Soviet workers of the Chinese Eastern Railroad began; there were arrests and beatings. The relations between Feng Yü-hsiang and Chang Tso-lin were developing in such a way that one expected the outbreak of armed conflict any day.

All these events were discussed in the pages of the Chinese and foreign press, in student gatherings, and in Communist and Kuomintang circles. The two camps in China—the camp of national revolution and the camp of the Chinese militarists and international imperialism—prepared for a decisive engagement. Hot debates took place in our embassy club at the meetings of the international politics group.

Soviet citizens in Peking celebrated the eighth anniversary of the October Revolution with great enthusiasm. This seemed such a long time then—a full eight years. Enemies of the Soviet Union were prophesying her demise every year, fighting against her and threatening her with war, and yet we were still alive and had lived to see the eighth anniversary. By this time I was already working in Kalgan but I came to Peking for the holiday. Above the stage of a huge hall the large number "8" and the word "years" were hung. A festive gathering was in progress. Besides our Soviet comrades there were members of the Chinese local committee of the embassy, our pupils who were trying to express in Russian their congratulations and good wishes. The jam-packed hall resounded with applause. Then we heard an amateur concert and our favorite band with its combs and frying pans. On the program for the evening was a grandiose fireworks display, but for some reason it did not come off. Instead of flying aloft and burning in the dark Peking sky in an array of colors, the rockets exploded on the ground in the bushes without a single spark but with an unbelievable racket and hissing. We were all chagrined, most of all our young pyrotechnist, Red commander[31] Mikhaylov.

To cap off the disaster, in front of the closed but still illuminated embassy gates (a hammer and sickle on a wreath of electric lights), some disheveled gentleman appeared and breathing heavily began to shout in English

---

31. This is what young officers of the Red Army were called then. There were several Red commanders in the embassy, in Karakhan's bodyguard and in that of the military attaché.

that he wanted to speak with the person in authority at the embassy, that the explosions on our grounds were scaring the neighbors. Comrade Bitner, the first acting secretary of the embassy was, by chance, at the gates, and through the railing heard out the representative of the neighboring power. In view of the lateness of the hour he suggested that he would appear on the following day for discussions. He ordered the fireworks to stop at once. But the British were not satisfied with this. They decided to revenge themselves by turning off our lights. Control over the Legation Quarter's power station was in their hands. The embassy was plunged into darkness, our holiday lights were extinguished, including the hammer and sickle over the gates which was evidently the chief target of our neighbors.

On that day a big meeting was held at Peking University in honor of the Great October Socialist Revolution.

With this I shall end the story of my stay in Peking, that wonderful city which we all loved so well. It is true that much of the Peking of that day remained unknown to us. We dreamed of spending some time in at least one of the famous Peking universities so as to discuss things with our fellow students, to meet Chinese workers, to mix in the ranks of the demonstrators and listen to what they were speaking about, to drop in on a peasant *fangtz* and much more. Alas, it was impossible. Our sincere desire to become acquainted with the Chinese people undoubtedly would have been regarded by the Chinese authorities and imperialist agents in Peking as "subversive activity" which might have led to undesirable political consequences. To this day I cannot recall without bitterness these vexatious limitations which deprived me of many interesting meetings.

I did not get to see the leader of the North China working people, Li Ta-chao, although I would have had this opportunity had I remained in the capital a while longer. After the unrestrained White terror began in April 1926 Li Ta-chao lived for a time on our embassy grounds.

Nevertheless, we remained eternally grateful to Peking for the generous hospitality and cordiality with which it opened up its treasures before us, for the precious help it gave us during our sinological apprenticeship.

Chapter III

ADVISERS IN THE NORTH

Feng Yü-hsiang and the Nationalist Army

At the end of September, I and the other translators received instructions to report for work at the headquarters of the Kalgan mission which, as I have said already, was working with Marshal Feng Yü-hsiang's troops.

Feng Yü-hsiang was one of the most influential figures in the political life of China. Earlier he had belonged to Wu P'ei-fu's Chihli clique which was active in North and central China and was closely tied to British and American imperialism. However, in October 1924, under the influence of the successes of the national revolutionary movement in Kwangtung, Feng Yü-hsiang broke away from the Chihli clique and struck an unexpected blow at Wu P'ei-fu's army. Feng Yü-hsiang occupied Peking and Wu P'ei-fu, deserting his troops, fled to Hankow on a British gunboat. Following this, Feng Yü-hsiang reached an agreement with Chang Tso-lin through which the Mukdenites were allowed to quarter a part of their troops in the capital. From political considerations, Feng Yü-hsiang declined all posts and settled in Hsishan as a private citizen, near Peking, although in fact he continued to hold in his hands the reins of power. The troops which took part in the uprising against Wu P'ei-fu were reorganized by Feng Yü-hsiang into three armies and given the name of the Nationalist Army (Kuominchün). Feng Yü-hsiang knew very well that a fierce struggle for power against the Mukdenites was in the immediate offing. He entered into negotiations with the Kuomintang, decided to reorganize his army and towards this end, following Sun Yat-sen's example, invited the services of Soviet military instructors.

The Kalgan mission of advisers to the Nationalist First Army began work in May 1925. Its first head, for a very brief time, was Vitovt Kazimirovich Putna[1] who was replaced by Vitaly Markovich Primakov (Lin). Still earlier, Anatoly Yakovlevich Klimov had taken up the duties of political

---

1. Putna was a divisional and corps commander in the civil war. After his return from China he served as a military attache in Japan, Finland, Germany, and England. He had been a member of the Communist party since February 1917.

adviser in the headquarters of the second and third Nationalist Armies. However, the group of military advisers was established there only in the second half of June 1925. Georgy Borisovich Skalov served as its head.

Feng Yü-hsiang, the "Christian General" as he was usually called in the imperialist press, was a devout Christian and insisted on the same from his subordinates. He was undoubtedly a remarkable personality, a man of great will power and a progressive cast of mind. There was no doubt about his organizational capabilities nor the force of his personal charm which even several of our comrades did not escape. We used to say, for example, that Primakov "was in love" with Feng Yü-hsiang. But there were comrades who thought different of Feng. They considered that he was too self-assured, let no one in on his plans, could not stand equals and, most importantly, was an inconsistent politician who often wavered and acted contrary to his earlier decisions.

Here are several examples; you may judge for yourself. Towards the end of June 1925, Feng Yü-hsiang issued an anti-imperialist communique about the "events of May 30" in Shanghai for the organ of the British Communist party, *Workers' Weekly*. His soldiers wore black armbands as a sign of mourning and the national flag was flown at half-mast in Feng Yü-hsiang's units. Twice daily the officers lectured the soldiers and the people "in order to create a spirit of unity against the imperialists." In the beginning of June, Feng Yü-hsiang as a Christian protested against the missionaries' silence in regard to the May 30 Incident. He sent out a circular telegram to the Peking government and the local authorities calling for a decisive struggle against the imperialists. But at the end of July, frightened by the charge of Bolshevism, Feng issued a statement to his army in which he refuted the rumors of his closeness to the Communists and stressed his disagreements with them.

Feng Yü-hsiang's closest assistant was his old colleague, the *tupan*[2] of Chahar province, General Chang Chih-chiang. He was a reactionary and hypocrite who never departed from his confessor, an American missionary, a man with very suspicious ties who caused our advisers not a few extremely

---

2. *Tupan* — a general qua governor.

bitter moments. At the same time Feng Yü-hsiang maintained his friendship
with the Kuomintang leftist Hsü Ch'ien who stood on a platform of alliance
with the Communists and conducted a correspondence with first secretary
of the Northern Bureau of the CCP, Li Ta-chao.

In the middle of September, Feng Yü-hsiang again issued public
statements of a very radical character calling for tariff autonomy. In his
speech on the Shanghai events he asserted that the British "were well-
schooled in the business of killing" and he criticized Chinese diplomats for
their silence on the matter. Then he was sending off delegations to Moscow.
But in the beginning of 1926 he was declaring the necessity of struggle
against "ch'ih huo" — the Red peril.

Feng Yü-hsiang's inconsistency bore bitter fruits, especially at sharp
turns in history. But in the final analysis he did enter upon the path of
consistent struggle against the militarists and imperialism. In 1933 in
cooperation with the Communists, Feng organized the United People's
Anti-Japanese Army, and in 1946 while in the United States, he openly
came out against Chiang Kai-shek's reactionary regime and was expelled
from the Kuomintang. In August 1948 while returning to China from the
United States, Feng Yü-hsiang tragically perished during a shipboard fire.

In the year when I was in Kalgan I heard how many persons were
disturbed by the show of democracy which Feng Yü-hsiang affected and by
the devices to which he resorted in order to win popularity. The advisers told
of how when Feng Yü-hsiang's train approached its destination, the marshal
at the preceding station moved from his comfortable car to a heated
baggage car. When the crowd surged forward towards the first-class coach,
feigning surprise he modestly emerged from the baggage car with a knap-
sack of dried crusts on his shoulders; this always produced a great impression.

Feng never let pass an opportunity to declare his negative feelings
towards wealth and luxury; he loved to boast of his democratic background,
to remind people that his father had been a bricklayer, meanwhile not
mentioning that he himself was a big landlord and herd owner. Among his
troops Feng implanted a spirit of peculiar Christian democracy, propa-
gandized the principles of a simple life and Christian morality and severely
punished those who did not live up to them. His illiterate soldiers and

semi-literate generals learned prayers and Biblical legends by heart.
Feng Yü-hsiang himself and his entire staff dressed like ordinary soldiers
and did not even wear marks of rank on their tunics.

In the remote towns of the northwest where his troops were stationed,
the marshal visited the bazaars, dropped into the eatinghouses, chatted with
people, ate with them from the same dish, and enjoyed a great degree of
popularity. Feng Yü-hsiang's striving to get close to the people, in spite
of the completely suspect form which it took at times, was a reflection of
his desire to get support from the masses. One need hardly say that the other
generals in the North, who belonged to the reactionary military factions,
conducted themselves in an entirely different manner.

In 1925 there were already Kuomintang members and even Communists
(illegally) in Feng Yü-hsiang's army, but political work had not yet been
developed. The marshal himself and his generals had expressed their opposition
to it. When in the spring of 1925 Feng was offered a group of our political
advisers he declared that he did not need them, that political work was
already under way in his army. He had in mind partly the talks on anti-
imperialist themes which his officers conducted at one time, but mainly he
referred to bible study.

The notes made by our advisers who were attached to the First
Nationalist Army as early as the spring of 1925 were preserved and describe
what it looked like at that time. "The relations between officers and soldiers
are simple. The soldiers are not oppressed, are not servile, conduct themselves
freely and courteously. Relations between soldiers and generals are another
matter. There is a sharp dividing line: from one side arbitrariness, rudeness,
and cruelty, from the other servile fear. The soldiers are hardy, cool, brave,
and bear wounds with astounding patience. Punishments are cruel, for random
shooting 100 strokes for the soldier and his superior, for visiting a brothel
in wartime imprisonment and 600 strokes. All are very devout Christians.

"In contrast to the second and third Nationalist Armies deserters and
hunghutz are not accepted for service. (Hunghutz are bandits.) The soldiers
are healthy village lads, recruitment in the cities is the exception. Every new
recruit must have his own guarantor. Therefore robbery and violence are
rare.

A majority of the middle-level and senior officers are from the ranks. The generals, also from the ranks, are uneducated and bound to Feng Yü-hsiang by many years of common service in the army. Feng calls them 'my people,' encourages them to lead simple lives, and periodically organizes refresher courses for them, but without special results so far. All this has placed a very special stamp on the First Nationalist Army.

"Weak points are: inaccurate fire, poor supply, absence of arsenals, difficulties in procuring supplies from abroad because of the absence of a safe port and for other reasons as well. A mint in Kalgan has been adapted as an arsenal. There are no warehouses. But the enemy – Wu P'ei-fu, Chang Tso-lin and others—have first-class arsenals in Hanyang, Shanghai, Mukden, Techow, and other cities." It was calculated that even then Feng Yü-hsiang controlled 100,000 regular troops. From the autumn of 1925 this army occupied the provinces of Kansu, Suiyuan, Chahar, and the capital district. In January 1926, Feng's power was extended to the province of Jehol.

In connection with the need to create a counterweight to the strong cavalry of Chang Tso-lin, our advisers raised the question of forming new and reforming old cavalry units. By October 1925 there were already five brigades of cavalry in the First Nationalist Army.By December these were organized into a corps and a supplementary new Sixth Brigade was formed as well. In the spring of 1926, when three Muslim brigades were formed in Kansu, Feng Yü-hsiang's cavalry numbered 12,000. Our advisers did a lot in organizing and instructing the First Nationalist Army. Its political condition noticeably improved; in 1925 revolutionary elements—students and Kuomintang members—entered its ranks. In places, Communists worked in their capacity as Kuomintang members since the Communist party itself was outlawed in the north. The strengthening of Fen Yü-hsiang's ties with the Kuomintang and the Communist party and his future trip to the Soviet Union were direct results of our advisers' influence.

The Kaifeng Mission

The Second and Third Nationalist Armies were formally independent but in fact were numbered among the troops which were obedient to Feng Yü-hsiang. At that time their staff headquarters was in Kaifeng, the main city of Honan province. That is where our advisers' mission was located. I did not work with the Kaifeng mission but I know of it through the stories of my acquaintances and friends, and from the information which reached us regularly from Kaifeng. Of the Kaifeng advisers I knew Klimov, Lapin, and Skalov well, and of the interpreters, Vasilev, Yolk, and Okoneshnikova (from Leningrad), Oshanin (from Moscow) and Skvortsov and Vrubel (from Vladivostok).

Honan is one of the most densely populated provinces of China.[3] It was the nation's granary in years of good harvest and a region of terrible disaster in bad harvest when innumerable crowds of famine victims, paving the roads with the corpses of those who had died of starvation, poured out in every direction. The poverty of the Honanese was proverbial. In Honan where there were no forests, the summer heat and dust were enervating, but the advisers were lucky. They were settled in a marvelous corner of Kaifeng, Nan Yüan park, the former summer residence of Honanese *tupans,* with whimsical stone grottoes, Chinese bridges and arbors amidst a thin woods.

The staff of the Second and Third Nationalist Armies behaved in a friendly manner to the members of the mission and listened attentively to their advice. Nevertheless, our comrades did not achieve any great success in a military sense. It was not easy to transform three-hundred thousand haphazardly armed, ragged, and hungry soldiers into a modern, well-organized, and disciplined army. But they did succeed in exerting a beneficial influence on the overall political situation, creating the conditions for the development of a mass revolutionary movement and the legalization of trade unions, and Kuomintang and Communist organizations. Anatoly Yakovlevich Klimov was particularly active in this regard.

General Hu Ching-i headed the Second Nationalist Army at first and was succeeded by General Yüeh Wei-chün. General Sun Yüeh headed the Third Nationalist Army. The main body of the Second Nationalist Army consisted of Shensi men. They behaved in Honan as if they were in conquered territory: robbery and taxes levied three years in advance were ordinary occurrences. The soldiers plundered because they had not been paid for several months. There were cases of soldiers going off to join the *hunghutz.*

---

3. At that time Honan was thought to have thirty-six million inhabitants.

The *tupan*, Hu Ching-i, unusually fat and extremely imposing in appearance, had taken part in the 1911 Revolution and was an old Kuomintang member. However, soon after the establishment of the republic, he returned to his native province, Shensi, and headed a detachment of the rebellious peasants of the "Union of the White Wolf" — *hunghutz* as they were called then in official government reports. The detachment was defeated and Hu Ching-i spent eight years in prison. According to his story, he was held in the vault of a tower and not even taken out for exercise lest he escape. From that time, Hu was known by the nickname "General of the *Hunghutz.*" He was freed by order of Feng Yü-hsiang who became the military governor of Shensi in 1921 and who took Hu into his service. Klimov related that Hu Ching-i tried to appear a democrat, called himself a revolutionary, and loved to speak about the revolution in Russia and to ask questions about Lenin. Hu proclaimed the freedoms of assembly and association. He played host to Kuomintang activists. His political representative in Peking was a member of the CEC and the Northern Bureau of the Kuomintang, Yü Yu-jen, then a left Kuomintang member. Another member of the Kuomintang CEC, General Li Lieh-chün, worked for him too. During Hu Ching-i's rule, Kuomintang and Communist organizations appeared in the province. He had invited our advisers even earlier than Feng Yü-hsiang.

All the same, Hu Ching-i was rather afraid of the masses and in such cases turned to Klimov for advice. In April when preparations were being made to celebrate May First, he wanted to resort to repressions, saying something to the effect that the workers wanted to strike. Klimov calmed him with difficulty, saying that this was not a strike at all, but an international labor holiday.

In Honan at that time there were many missionaries who followed the situation closely on behalf of their own countries. Hu Ching-i's policies and the appearance of Soviets in Honan seemed dangerous to them. It was decided to remove the *tupan*. An occasion soon presented itself. Hu Ching-i, a passionate mahjong player, once got a splinter in his hand during a game. (Mahjong is a game of chance played with dice.) The wound festered. Doctors in the American missionary hospital proposed to amputate the entire hand and during the operation Hu Ching-i died. This was in April 1925. Hu's death seemed very suspicious to many at the time.

The advisers recounted what an elaborate funeral was held for the *tupan*. According to custom, his body had to be sent to Shensi province, to his native burial ground. The funeral procession passed in state through the whole city to the station. The enormous coffin was carried on a caisson. It was accompanied by vehicles from which resounded the heartrending cries of his wives and professional mourners. A special train waited at the station. A military band played continuously, even foxtrots. The missionaries who gathered on the platform tapped their feet in time to the music.

Klimov, expressing his regret at Hu Ching-i's untimely death said, "He was untouched, virgin soil, a spontaneous, unspoiled nature, not like Feng Yü-hsiang on whom the missionaries, after all, have had an influence. Hu Ching-i might still have accomplished much." A.A. Ivin, who had made a special study of the situation in Honan, supported this viewpoint. In *Pravda* he wrote that Hu Ching-i had established closer ties with the Kuomintang than had Feng Yü-hsiang, that the Second Nationalist Army had a semi-Kuomintang nature. Ivin also had positive things to say about Hu Ching-i's successor, his fellow Shensi man, Yüeh Wei-chün. He asserted that his position in the anti-imperialist movement was the same as Feng Yü-hsiang's, but that unfortunately Yüeh did not understand that it was better to have a small but disciplined army than two to three hundred thousand ill-assorted soldiers, many of whom were outright bandits.

Ivin wrote that for all its shortcomings the regime in Honan compared favorably with those in other provinces, with the exception of Kwangtung. The Honanese intelligentsia, students and workers enjoyed a wide range of political freedoms. The Kuomintang, the Communist party, trade unions, and other public organizations existed legally. Communists were not persecuted and strikes were not outlawed. Our airmen led by Shmidt visited Kaifeng and also noticed the relatively high degree of political freedom which was enjoyed there. In Peking they were not allowed to meet with workers, but in Kaifeng they addressed mass demonstrations, hosted delegations, and attended meetings of workers at the Kaifeng arsenal.

The military advisers whom Hu Ching-i had contracted for arrived in June. Yüeh Wei-chün continued Hu's policies but cautiously. Klimov related how in June 1925 Yüeh was frightened by the protest demonstration

against the May 30 Incident in Shanghai. On the next day, General
Li Lieh-chün, on Yüeh's instructions, held a conference with Klimov which
our advisers christened a "Tilsit conference." Li Lieh-chün summoned
Klimov to a Chinese arbor, situated in Pei Yüan park, on a high rocky hill,
surrounded it with a line of soldiers so that no one could hear anything, and
then eyeball to eyeball, he posed the question to Klimov, "How to proceed
when the masses cry not only 'down with imperialism,' but also 'down with
militarism,' is there not a hint about the *tupan,* General Yüeh Wei-chün?"[4]

The Third Nationalist Army was much smaller than the Second. It had
no more than eighty thousand troops, and its composition was extremely
variegated. The army had no fixed abode; it wandered from place to place.
Its headquarters traveled from Paotingfu (Chihli province) to Kaifeng and
from there to Shensi, then back to Paotingfu, etc. The commander, the aged
General Sun Yüeh, boasted that he could remember when "they still fought
with spears."

My comrades in the Kaifeng mission were not prevented by their duties
from becoming acquainted with the historical monuments for which Honan
is famous as the cradle of the Chinese state and culture. I could only sigh
when I read their rapturous letters describing the famous cave temples of
Lungmen or the "tomb" of the mythical ruler Fu Hsi in the environs of
Chengchow, where according to Chinese legend, Shen Nung, the equally
mythical hero and first Chinese agriculturalist, deified by the Chinese people,
lived at one time. In Honan a number of cities were ancient capitals so there
was something to see. Kaifeng was one of them, but to the disappointment of
our friends, there were few historical monuments in it[5], since the city had
been set on fire more than once, had been subjected to invasion and destruction, and had even been inundated by the yellow, silt-laden waves of the
Hwang Ho, which had justifiably earned the name of "China's Sorrow"
because of its terrible floods. The best preserved monument was the famous
Iron Pagoda which was faced with coloured ceramic.

---

4. In the beginning of the thirties, Yüen Wei-chün, commanding troops of the Nanking government,
took part in operations against Communists in Honan, was taken prisoner and shot.
5. Archaeological excavations had not yet been carried out there.

Once Klimov had pointed out to him a Chinese with an evidently
Jewish profile and was told that about two hundred Jews lived in the city,
a remnant of an ancient community from Babylon where Jews had been
severely persecuted which settled there around the time of Christ. As
recently as two hundred years ago the community had been rich and
numerous, and its members were sharply distinguished in appearance from
the surrounding population.

Our comrades visited the community and conversed with its members.
Assimilation had done its work. Almost all of them looked like typical
Chinese, no one remembered his ancestral language or the prescriptions of
his religion with the exception of the prohibition against pork. Worship was
conducted from ancient, handwritten books, the pitiful remnants of a great
collection of manuscripts which had been brought by the community into
exile. The others had been destroyed in the middle of the seventeenth
century when a great wall of water collapsed upon the city through a breach
in the dike made by order of the popular leader Li Tzu-ch'eng[6] who was
besieging Kaifeng where the government troops were taking refuge. A living
historical monument. This was first time we had come across one.

The Kalgan Mission

Let us now return to our trip to Kalgan which was the starting point of
our service in Feng Yü-hsiang's army.

From Peking to Kalgan is a seven-hour train ride. We entrained early in
the morning and by dinnertime were already there. Spread out before us
were the environs of Kalgan, rather cheerless at this time of the year — yellow
loess looking as if it had been baked by the drought, bare hills, bare branches
on the occasional trees and bushes. One needs time to feel the beauty of this
picture, filled with a peculiar melancholy charm.

Kalgan is a city situated at a pass in the Great Wall of China. There from
time immemorial a great trade route has led from Peking to Urga and
Mongolia. The city is constructed along this route as the endless length of
its main streets attests. At once we sensed the nearness of Mongolia. There
were crowds of people with characteristically prominent cheekbones,

---

6. Li Tzu-ch'eng — leader of a popular rebellion in the seventeenth century which overthrew the Ming
   dynasty.

dressed in Mongol fur hats and boots, and also camel caravans and Mongol wares in the stalls.

The Kalgan advisory mission was located on the outskirts of the city in the former compound of the salt administration. Behind a high brick wall of peculiar design were several dozen small, one-storey buildings around a spacious earthen court. In the largest of them, the one with European windows, the mission headquarters was located; the advisers and translators lived in the Chinese-style houses. In the staff headquarters, in addition to the offices, there were also a dining room and a club where a large portrait of Lenin was hung. In the office of the chief of staff, a thickset, broad-shouldered military man (there could be no doubt about this despite his semi-civilian costume) with luxuriant wheat-colored whiskers rose to greet us with a smile. He was Ivan Korneev (Anders).

A well-trained worker with mainly staff experience, a man of great culture and broadly educated, Korneev was capable and imperturbable. He came to China already possessing a diploma from the Military Academy. There were no details too insignificant for Korneev in his work, everything interested him, and he did everything with the utmost thoroughness. Even the most unimportant of his sketches looked as if it had been printed. He brought back a detailed description of the locality, economy, condition of the population and the local life from every place where he had to travel on official business. He might have become a great researcher, could have written a large, interesting volume about northwest China, but unfortunately, Korneev did not swell the ranks of sinologists. In 1937 when serving as chief of the operational division of the staff of the Belorussian Military District he was arrested and died.

I still like to remember with what comradely concern the chief of staff greeted us. Another person might have behaved more formally towards us. We were student interpreters, civilians, green youth. It might have seemed that all that could be required of us was to translate correctly what we were directed to do. But Korneev wanted to really acquaint us with the work of the mission.

He spoke to us for a long time in his calm, thorough, and convincing way, described the situation in China, explained what were the tasks which confronted our advisers in Feng Yü-hsiang's army, and what the revolutionary sense of their work consisted of. Now, of course, it is difficult to repeat his words verbatim but his talk sounded approximately like this.

"Comrades, you should be proud that you have been entrusted with such a responsible job. I did not make a slip of the tongue, precisely 'responsible.' Our advisers lack interpreters and your job is to fill this breach. Try not to disgrace the lofty name of a Soviet citizen in China. It may happen that in company of the senior comrades you will have to travel to out-of-the-way northwest corners of the country, where the most elementary creature comforts are lacking, you may have to eat unaccustomed foods or else go hungry, to live without medical aid, to fear bandit attacks. But you must overcome all adversity because our work in China demands it. You may ask, why are we here? It is not hard to explain, especially to you sinologists. We are here to help the fraternal Chinese people gain their freedom and independence.

"Who is this Feng Yü-hsiang with whom you shall work? He is playing an important political role in North China. He is popular with the local population, has made contact with the revolutionary Kuomintang government in the South, and has come out against imperialist domination in China, although not very decisively. It is necessary that Feng Yü-hsiang stand in opposition to the reactionaries — Wu P'ei-fu and Chang Tso-lin. You know what kind of people these are; they are the embodiment of blackest reaction in China. Never will they allow any democratic reforms on their territory, never will they refrain from cruel repressions against the masses in response to their demands.

"What will the future bring? It is still too early to judge. Know only that even here in the northwest the Communist party of China is working unobtrusively and soundlessly; its numbers are small now but the future belongs to it. In the north it is still illegal but in the South it is already cooperating with the Kuomintang as a result of which the influence of the Kuomintang government is growing not by the day but by the hour. Of course, it is more interesting to work there, the advisers can clearly see the results of their labours. Things are much harder for us and our successes are not so obvious. However, our task is no less honourable for that and we must fulfill it."

Concluding his talk, Korneev, an enthusiastic equestrian, suggested that we go outside and see how the advisers were practicing, probably nursing the hope of eventually seating us on horses. We saw a small group of horsemen trotting after each other. The instructor gave a loud command and the horsemen changed their gait, practicing the simplest techniques of equestrian vaulting.

After these lessons, those who were younger, for the sheer pleasure of it, set up a donkey race. The long-eared competitors looked absurdly small beneath their tall riders. The onlookers goodnaturedly urged them on with shouts of *"I-i, i-i, tok-tok-tok-tok"* (this is how Chinese drivers urge on their donkeys). One of the advisers, straining forward, could not keep his saddle, his legs touched the ground, the donkey jumped out from under him in a flash, and the unlucky rider crashed to the ground. The laughter went on for several minutes. The advisers looked like healthy, cheerful fellows, dressed each to his own taste. Tunics, field-jackets, jerseys, and coats harmonized with a sportive collection of trousers, shoes, and puttees. It was obvious that they were trying to adapt their clothing for horseback riding.

Our arrival was greeted with animation, especially since many knew us from Peking. We were invited to the dining room, then to the club; the gramophone was cranked up, and they excused themselves in advance for the repertoire. One adviser had been given the job of buying records in Peking, but the others didn't know that he was crazy about Amelita Galli Kurchi so that now — it was enough to make you cry — you had to listen to Amelita because there were no other records.

On that day we got acquainted with almost all the advisers of the mission. These were representatives of the most varied military specialties, including the commissary, men thirty to thirty-five years old and all with civil war experience. The youngest was Vladimir Mikhaylovich Akimov (Petya Silin) who a year and a half later became my husband. He was not quite twenty-four but already there were streaks of gray in his thick, dark slightly curly hair. In fact he grew gray at an early age; by forty his head was entirely white. Akimov had fought in the civil war in Central Asia, and in 1925 had graduated from the Chinese department of the Advanced Course of Oriental Studies of the Workers' and Peasants' Red Army. He worked in

Kalgan without an interpreter and even conducted a study group in Chinese. He received his first Order of the Red Banner in 1927 for his work in China. In 1932 he graduated from the Eastern Department of the Frunze Military Academy. In 1936, Akimov, on instructions from the Comintern, reestablished radio contact with the CC of the CCP which had been broken during the Long March. He almost died carrying out that assignment. In 1937-1938, when China was fighting a difficult war against the Japanese aggressors, he was in Lanchow (northwest China) as the head of the supply-route for providing China with Soviet military technology. By decision of the CC of the CCP, Akimov was awarded the jubilee breastplate "Ten Years of the Nanchang Uprising" — at that time the highest mark of distinction in the Chinese Red Army. In Chinese circles he was called Pei Chia (Petya). During the Great Patriotic War Akimov commanded a division and a corps, and in his last years served as deputy commander of a military district.

I. Koreyvo (Noga), the oldest, was not quite forty and everyone respectfully called him "grandpa." An Old Bolshevik who had been in tsarist prison camps, he often was unwell. Kalgan's severe climate evidently affected his health. He also come to China with a diploma from the Tashkent Advanced Courses in Oriental Studies. He was no great linguist, but he continued to plug away at Chinese.

Konstantin Bronislavich Kalinovsky (Korde), an adviser on armored trains, was already known as a first-class specialist in the Red Army despite his twenty-seven years. He spent the entire civil war on the front and had two Orders of the Red Banner. Kalinovsky came to China after completing the course at the Military Academy. His book *Tanki* had already appeared in 1923, giving him the fame of a Russian Fuller.[7] However, Kalinovsky himself never appeared in print with a criticism of the English general's basic position. Taciturn by nature, Kalinovsky did not take part in the noisy gaiety of the dining table. Everyone who knew him remembered his pensive gaze and his intelligent, quiet smile. In 1931 as head of the Department for Motorization and Mechanization of the Red Army, he died tragically in an air accident.

---

7. Fuller wrote a series of articles and books about mechanization and motorization in modern armies. His basic work was *Tanks in the Great War, 1914-1918*.

Nil Timofeevich Rogov (Ivan Lodzinsky), an adviser on rear areas, came to China in the summer of 1925 with a diploma from the Military-Economics Academy. A worker in Lugan, he volunteered for the Red Army in 1918, but long before the revolution as a sixteen-year-old lad he had taken part in underground work in the Ukraine. In the summer of 1926 Rogov took part in the Northern Expedition.[8]

Balding and snub-nosed, and wearing glasses, he was no beauty in our eyes. But he had a rare physique. Of such people we say "With a chest like a barrel, broad as an ox." It is no wonder that during the Northern Expedition without any real medical aid he survived the Asiatic cholera which was mowing everyone down. Rogov died in the first days of the Great Patriotic War.

On the day of our arrival, a young military man who was known in the mission by the surname Gordon, came up to me. He reminded me that in the spring of 1924 at the apartment of Professor V.S. Kolokolov where students of the Institute of Oriental Studies gathered, he had made a report on the new system which he had invented of classifying Chinese characters by their four corners. I barely recognized him as V.Ye. Gorev, a student of the Eastern Department of the Military Academy. Trying to give himself a more solid image (he was only twenty-six at the time), he let his sideburns grow and fitted himself out with an enormous captain's pipe. However, the cheerful, mischievous expression of his face gave away his age. Dictionaries arranged according to his system are very popular now even within China. (The first of them was put out by the young Leningrad China specialists Kokin and Papayan in the beginning of the thirties.)

Later on, Gorev worked as a military adviser in the south of China under the name Nikitin, took part in the Northern Expedition as senior adviser to the Western Column of the National-Revolutionary Army, and participated in the storming of Wuchang. Upon his return to Moscow he was the military director of the Communist University of the Toilers of the East (CUTE), and later fought in Spain. In 1930 his very interesting book *Kitaiskaia Armiia* (The Chinese Army) was published under the pseudonym V. Vysogorets.

---

8. The Northern Expedition was the military activity of the National-Revolutionary Armies in 1926-1927 against the Chinese militarists of central and North China with the aim of unifying the country on a democratic basis.

One of the advisers, Alexandr Alexandrovich Argentov (Marino), astounded us because he worked without interpreters although he knew no Chinese. In his notebook were written out some fifty or sixty Chinese military terms and he contrived with their aid to get by with the soldiers and officers.

The adviser in military engineering matters was Sergey Sergeevich Chekin (Sergeev) who later became deputy director of the Military Engineering Academy of the Soviet Army.

The adviser A.N. Chernikov (Nikitin) who was called Satrap because of his grand figure and majestic, imperturbable manners, was one of the oldest. In 1926 he went to South China to work in the National-Revolutionary Armies and participated in the Northern Expedition.

The group of comrades whom I saw then in Kalgan was diminished by two in the course of the year. Balk, the blond Hercules, a handsome fellow, got blood poisoning five months later when he hurriedly shaved in some neglected *fangtz* on the front near Tientsin, and died three days later. Later yet another of our advisers died, the very young and cheerful Vikhrev, who worked with armored trains. He was killed by bandits who evidently were sent by the Whites in Mongolia when he was returning from an assignment to Ulan Bator. Attacks on advisers were made frequently, and they knew whose work it was.

There were several Chinese interpreters in the Kalgan mission, mainly Communists, but I remember only the student Hu Hsiao (his Russian name was Pavel Khudyakov). Later I met him in the south in the National-Revolutionary Army. During the Northern Expedition he was an interpreter for the advisers N.I. Konchits, F.I. Olshevsky, and M.F. Kumanin. After the temporary defeat of the Chinese Revolution Hu Hsiao came to Moscow and worked in the Communist University of the Toilers of the East, in the International Lenin School, and the Foreign Workers' Publishing House where he edited Chinese translations of the classics of Marxism-Leninism. A valuable specialist, an excellent, sensitive man, he was arrested and died in 1938.

Among my comrades working in Kalgan were Fyodor Bokanenko (Korf), Venyamin Gamberg (Maysky), Boris Perin, Alexey Petrovich Rogachev — presently holding a chair of Chinese at Moscow State University, and Pyotr Yemelyanovich Skachkov (Krechetov), the well-known bibliographer, historian and Chinese specialist who passed away recently.

In Kalgan for the first time I met another category of persons, albeit very few in number, Russian White emigrès who wanted to make amends for the past and return to the motherland. They worked in the Nationalist Armies as interpreters and military specialists. In those years China was flooded with White emigrès. To say nothing of Manchuria, where even before the October Revolution many Russians resided, all the major cities of central and North China – Peking, Shanghai, Hankow, Tsingtao, Tientsin and others – had large White emigrè populations (as much as 120,000 in toto.) The most reactionary layer among the White emigrès were the officers and Cossacks, a permanent reserve for any sort of anti-Soviet sabotage and provocations on the Soviet border.

It was a mass of goons and strikebreakers ready at any moment to come out against the revolutionary movement in China. As soon as the anti-British boycott began in China the press was filled with notices to the effect that unemployment among the White emigrès in Harbin, Hankow, Tientsin, and Shanghai had disappeared since the British hired them in place of their striking Chinese servants. Hundreds of White emigrès went from Shanghai to Hong Kong to work as waiters in hotels. In Tientsin more than a thousand White Guards were taken into the police academy by the British. Passing through Shanghai I saw a group of Russian policemen in the International Settlement. This was such a repulsive spectacle of moral degradation that to this day I cannot remember it calmly. White emigrès taking shelter in the Russian Orthodox mission also broke the boycott of the British embassy in Peking. A census of the White emigrès was being taken during our stay in Peking. Those without definite occupations were sent out of the city in view of the increasing frequency of robberies in which many of them took part. The White Guards in Peking were always ready to enroll in any anti-Soviet campaign. A list of attacks on our establishments and individual workers as well as other provocations would be long indeed.

The centers of White Guard anti-Soviet activity were Shanghai and Harbin where every sort of White Guard society and brotherhood, Cossack and officers' unions flourished. Besides the legal organizations there were underground ones some of which bore really romantic names. In Harbin there were the Musketeers, unions of the Black Ring, the Green Ring, etc. Some of the organizations were called by their leaders' names — Glebov's unit, Nechaev's unit. All of them, even the religious Epiphany Brotherhood, existed on subsidies from the imperialist powers, chiefly England. In Shanghai there even existed a League for Struggle against the Third International. The imperialists also subsidized the White emigré press.

An entire brigade under the command of Colonel Nechaev (who later became a "general"), and four armoured trains with Russian troops — in all about four thousand White Guards — became members of the Tsinan group, named for the main city of Shantung province, the patrimony of Marshal Chang Tsung-ch'ang. General Merkulov was an adviser to the marshal. A Cossack squadron formed Chang Tsung-ch'ang's personal bodyguard.

Marshal Chang Tsung-ch'ang was an old agent of tsarist imperialism. As early as the Russo-Japanese War he had been a spy and furthermore enjoyed the most cordial relations with Chang Tso-lin, then leader of a band of *hunghutz* who executed the assignments of the Japanese army. They were sworn brothers and evidently worked together on two fronts. After the defeat of the Russian army Chang Tsung-ch'ang was interned. For a time he was in the Russian Far East where he was famous as an inveterate bandit, hunting for Chinese, searching for gold and ginseng (the miracle-working root of life) in the Far Eastern taiga. After the Revolution of 1911, Chang Tso-lin, who had moved from being a *hunghutz* to an officer, took Chang Tsung-ch'ang into his service. From this time, Chang Tsung-ch'ang became an accomplice of Japanese imperialism in China.

Chang Tsung-ch'ang was especially willing to take Russian White guards into his service but the life they led was not easy. According to the Chinese militarist tradition they were not paid their salary for months at a time. People gave way to despair and committed suicide. The recruiters kept on supplying new mercenaries, attracting even adolescents through deceitful practices.

Three thousand White Guards served with Chang Tsung-ch'ang under the command of the Menshikov brothers.

The inveterate White Guard generals, Merkulov, Semyonov, Annenkov, Shilnikov, Glebov, and a good dozen others squabbled among themselves over the leadership of the White Guards in China, since this meant receiving subsidies from world counter-revolution. They were all well-known to us from the civil war in Siberia and the Far East. Some of the advisers knew them "personally" inasmuch as they had fought against them or been imprisoned by their orders.

The White Guards turned out to be quite lacking in military capability. Nechaev's unit, in particular, was routed more than once. It had a bad reputation since it often indulged in pillage. In the spring of 1926 when Feng Yü-hsiang's troops evacuated Tientsin, the administration of the foreign concession organized a special unit of gendarmes to prevent Nechaev's unit from entering the city. In the spring of 1927 it was defeated by the forces of the National-Revolutionary Army in Honan. In the summer of 1925 the imperialist press in China carried articles about a "grand military council" meeting in Paris under the chairmanship of Nicholas II's uncle, the former Grand Prince Nikolay Nikolaevich. This was attended by Generals Vrangel, Denikin, Lukomsky, Kutepov, and others. These reports encouraged the White Guards, and inspired them with the hope that the time was not far off when they would return to their former position in their homeland. In China almost all the White Guards recognized Nikolay Nikolaevich, but there were other tendencies as well, in particular the adherents of the "monarch" – the former Grand Prince Kirill. An emissary from Nikolay Nikolaevich's "military headquarters" in Paris arrived in London in the spring of 1927 to solicit "the provision of subsidies for military activities in South China and Manchuria." In Shanghai Semenov openly declared that the White army which he was establishing would proceed to Siberia after smashing the Cantonites.

On orders of the Japanese the White Guards headed by Semyonov in the spring of 1927 planned to rise in rebellion in the Maritime Province, spread the rebellion to Irkutsk and there await the development of events on the Polish and Rumanian borders. The Japanese were supposed to take part in the intervention. In order to divert attention, it was considered desirable to raise the units in Shanghai rather than Harbin.

Nevertheless, even in this atmosphere of frenzied hatred towards the Soviet Union there were people who were striving to break with the shameful past and earn the right to return to their homeland. I can name three former White generals who were serving as volunteers in the Nationalist Armies — Tonkikh and Shalavin in the Kaifeng mission and Ivanov-Rinov in Kalgan.

The former doings of the White emigrés were not bruited about among the advisers if the former expressed a desire to work on the side of the Chinese revolution. Only in Moscow did I accidentally learn that General Tonkikh had been Ataman Annenkov's chief of staff during the civil war in the Far East, and that Ivanov-Rinov had been minister of war in Kolchak's Omsk government. On the eve of his intended departure for the USSR Tonkikh was arrested together with the embassy employees during Chang Tso-lin's raid in April 1927. In view of his "renegade behaviour" he was treated with particular severity and placed in solitary confinement, but he held out nobly. On learning that the prisoners had started a hunger strike, he quickly joined them. In 1928 Tonkikh came to Moscow where he continued to serve in the military field and married his childhood sweetheart. He died in 1947. Shalavin died in Moscow in 1929. His wife was given a pension. His services to the Chinese revolution were viewed as services to his motherland.

Kalgan and Its Environs

The advisers and interpreters lived in one-storey houses in which the small rooms were all lined up in straight rows. Each of them opened not onto a corridor but directly into the courtyard in the Chinese fashion. The outer wall was only half stone; the upper half was wood with characteristic Chinese pictures and white paper pasted on it. The rooms were light but very cold despite the cast-iron portable stove which was on all the time. The furniture was Chinese. Of course, there was neither running water nor plumbing.

The wind from Mongolia which tormented us even in Peking here showed its true mettle. No sooner had it begun to blow than an ominous reddish darkness descended, the sun sank in a dull cloud of innumerable microscopic grains of sand. They became encrusted on one's teeth, penetrated the houses, and covered everything with a thick layer of yellow dust. Breathing became difficult. There was no salvation from this calamity, the famous Chinese sandstorms.

Kalgan, an important center for the fur, skins and carpet trades, like many Chinese cities of that time, was marked by the features of the not yet vanished medieval period. Her streets made one think of guilds and corporations. The buyer walked between two rows of stalls heaped high with the very same goods. The merchants gathered together in booths and bought out entire streets for themselves.

In the fur shops very comfortable, peculiarly shaped hats with earlaps and tall, fur rims, Chinese fur gowns fur boots, and fur mittens with two fingers were sold. The rug stalls stood out with the amazing beauty and unique craftsmanship of their wares. The marvelous colours gladdened the eye. Many of the rugs were of an incredible denseness and thickness and were very expensive. It was said that they were "eternal," that they would never wear out.

The camels which we saw on the streets looked emaciated and sickly. They were shedding their hair which hung on them in clumps. But in winter they became remarkably beautiful. These large, strong animals have shockingly thin, bird-like voices. Their pale, straw-colored, thick, soft hair — the famous Chahar camel's hair — is world famous. Warm wonderful things are made from it — shawls, blouses, linen, etc.

On one of our days off we took a trip to the Temple of Agriculture, located in the outskirts of the city. The god of agriculture, covered from head to foot in loess dust, was a rather pitiful sight, but in front of him there still stood a censer filled with sand in which were thrust lighted incense sticks which emitted a light, fragrant smoke. Various holy objects (also covered with a thick layer of dust) were arranged on the altar. It probably never occurred to the priest who greeted us with servile bows that it would have done no harm to tidy up the holy place. But he did accept a contribution from us for "temple funds" and even rang the bell in order to draw the god's attention to our generosity.

From the hill where the temple was located we saw the Great Wall of China — the 10,000 li wall, as the Chinese call it. Stretched out it goes for two thousand kilometers, and with its branches its length is doubled. On the outside it is covered with stone and brick, but it is said that in the middle it is reed finished with a special mortar, clay, and earth. Its construction began in the third century B.C., but I remember that they were still singing plaintive songs about it in the village since in the course of its construction over several centuries hundreds of thousands of persons were herded together of whom the majority did not return. It was ruined in many places, but in our time in a number of sections military guards still stood at the gates of the so-called passes through which the ancient trade routes passed.

For hundreds of years the wind-borne sands of the Mongolian desert have scoured it, therefore it is much lower now than it used to be. We were told that its height varies from seven to seventeen meters, and its breadth is six meters. Carts can travel along the top and troops can march. Guard-towers stand at regular intervals, and loopholes may be seen in the square, broad merlons.

The wall unfolded its endless sections before us, now raising its time-corroded back to the ridge of a hill, now sharply falling into a hollow. It made all the surrounding countryside submit to its will. It seemed that the landscape breathed with the same sombre solemnity and became a background for this remarkable monument of Chinese antiquity.

On the way back we passed by a farm and observed the peasants working. The women, hobbling about the courtyard on their tiny stiff feet, threshed and winnowed, and gathered the grain in enormous clay jugs. For women to work in the fields was considered indecent. They were very shy or, perhaps, superstitious and could not endure the gaze of "foreign devils."[9]

The little children, as everywhere in China, were adorable and wholly justified their Chinese name of "barebottomed ones" *(kuang p'i ku ti)*. They all wore the amusing cotton trousers with the slit in back, through which their naked little bodies showed — the traditional costume of little children whom the perpetually busy mothers never had time to fuss over.

Lazar Isaakovich Penn, who had graduated from the Eastern Department of the Military Academy, was the consul in Kalgan. He had arrived in China in 1924 as secretary to the commission for negotiating questions relating to the Chinese Eastern Railway with Chang Tso-lin. The consular staff was small; from among the ranks of China specialists a comrade Marakuev, a specialist in the economy of Manchuria and Inner Mongolia, worked there.

---

9. This is what Chinese called foreigners.

In May 1926 Penn was appointed consul in Changsha, the main city of Hunan. When the Northern Expedition began, the *tupan* of Hunan, fearing that Penn would maintain ties with the enemy, intended to put him in jail. The local underground committee of the CCP which arranged his flight to Hankow, forewarned Lazar Isaakovich of this plan. Not until Kuomintang power had been established in Changsha did Penn return to his duties. In 1937 he was arrested and died in exile.

After spending a short time in Kalgan we received instructions to proceed to Fengchen, a small city on the Peiping-Suiyuan railroad just beyond the Great Wall. Feng Yü-hsiang's cavalry was stationed there and a group of advisers and interpreters (about ten to fifteen people in all) worked there. They were renting a large, wooden, European-style house with a wide, covered verandah. The hall in the center served as a dining room and club. Zyuk, who has already been introduced to the reader, was the chief of mission. When we stumbled into the dining room with our suitcases, Zyuk, anticipating the famous scene from the movie *Chapaev,* was explaining the cavalry's marching order to a fat Chinese general with the aid of spoons, knives, and forks. The Chinese was listening and evidently agreeing as he grunted in assent.

Next to the house was a pen enclosed by a clay wall which served as a stable for one of the cavalry units. Feeding troughs were installed along the walls and down the middle, and there under the open sky stood the horses — the famous Mongolian ponies — fearing neither frost nor snow. Short, shaggy and reddish, with tousled forelocks hanging down over their fierce muzzles, these were beasts, not horses. One merely had to approach one of them and it would start whinnying, baring its teeth, and trying to tear free of its lines. It would be disastrous if it succeeded. It would at once rear up on its hind legs, and begin prancing about its neighbors in that position, trying to bite them. The entire stable would whinny and kick up their heels in answer. It was quite a problem to ride such a horse. The Mongolian ponies were only slightly broken in, and they had the bad habit of trying to snap at their riders' knees, trying to take off their kneecaps. How many times did I see one of the advisers, without letting the reins from his grasp (a cavalryman's honor would not permit this), defending himself against the hooves of his horse which reared up and tried to smash its master's skull.

At first I worked as an interpreter but not for long. In North China women were looked down upon. The officers felt affronted when my services were required. They stared at the adviser's lips trying to figure out for themselves what he was saying. Therefore I was soon assigned to translating documents. There for the first time I felt what a great gap in our Chinese instruction the absence of lessons in grass-writing represented. I guessed the meaning of each document, solving it like a rebus, and spent an awful lot of time on them so that I wasn't able to translate some of the materials.

I returned to Moscow in 1927 with the reputation of being not a bad specialist in Chinese grass-writing, but I achieved this only through long practice. The advisers in Fengchen as in Kalgan quite frequently complained about obstacles in their work. Zyuk would cry with fury "Just what are we? Some kind of medieval mercenaries?" A feeling of dissatisfaction with the results of their activity tormented them as did uneasiness over their loved ones who remained at home. But still the spirit of optimism triumphed. In the evening the walls of the dining room shook from the deafening laughter.

Feng Yü-hsiang in Kalgan

We were in Fengchen for a short time. On November 10 Feng Yü-hsiang declared war against Chang Tso-lin and the cavalry units advanced to the front.

News of the beginning of the war with Chang Tso-lin, which had been a long time coming, sounded like a clap of thunder. This was a campaign against the most reactionary force in China. In a proclamation published at that time by the CC of the CCP it was said, "War against Chang Tso-lin is a war of liberation."[10]

It was already winter when we returned to Kalgan. There was little snow but the frosts were really sharp. The camels which daily passed in endless caravans along the Kalgan route to Ulan Bator had acquired new coats of hair. Their enormous, two-humped figures, weighted with heavy loads, seemed especially huge in contrast to the dark silhouettes of the guides, wrapped in furs, who led them on long lines. On one of these days while

---

10. Battle was not really joined. An agreement was soon reached by which Chang Tso-lin had to withdraw his forces from Chihli to beyond Shanhaikuan.

heading for work at the headquarters, I noticed that a group of Chinese soldiers was standing on the wooden platform which served as a porch. Among them was one rather solid figure with a very familiar face, thick, dark eyebrows and mustache, and full, slightly puffy cheeks. I knew that this was Feng Yü-hsiang. (His picture was often printed in the papers.) I was not surprised by his early visit since I knew that his working day began at six o'clock.

Feng Yü-hsiang said something to his entourage and laughed, showing his teeth which were white as sugar. His advisers stood next to him. Feng Yü-hsiang, according to his habit, was dressed like an ordinary soldier, in quilted cotton trousers and a jacket of the same light-grey material. But he wore an expensive fur hat with earflaps. He carried himself easily, from time to time freely pacing the wooden flooring of the porch with his strong legs which were shod in black cloth slippers and puttees. His Chinese innately youthful appearance concealed his age. He was already forty-five then but looked about ten years younger. The open, simplehearted expression of Feng Yü-hsiang's face pleased me. There was something very attractive about him and I understood why Primakov was so drawn to him. Feng and his advisers were standing right at the doorway and I would have had to pass right through this group of persons who, as I thought, were talking about something very important. I grew timid and turned away. About fifteen minutes later when I again approached the headquarters Feng Yü-hsiang was already gone.

I saw him twice more thereafter but from a distance. Once he rode by in a car, and the other time he was standing on the threshold of a haberdasher's. He was surrounded by a big crowd of people and unceremoniously exchanging smiles with those in the front row — a rather ragged group of people in tattered and frayed winter clothing.

The Revolt of Kuo Sung-ling

We were in Kalgan when the first news arrived of General Kuo Sung-ling's revolt. An old Chinese whom I studied with brought me the news. This orthodox Confucian who from childhood had repeated "Let the ruler be ruler, let the subject be subject" was terribly upset. He maintained that Kuo Sung-ling had stained himself by treachery and black ingratitude in his relations with Chang Tso-lin, his superior. The representatives of the old Chinese intelligentsia whom I had occasion to meet in the North, even our wise teacher Tung, lived by the rules of Confucian morality which were deemed immutable for all ages, and loyalty of the subject was the highest virtue of all for them. You can imagine what a fury reasoning of this sort inspired among the fiery, revolutionary-minded youth. The comrades did not break up until long after dinner. The dulcet-voiced Amelita was silent. A discussion was held on the events which were deeply disturbing us.

Here I want to set forth everything I know from the words of the advisers, the documents which reached us and the press reports of this by now almost forgotten revolt.

Little has been written in our country of Kuo Sung-ling's revolt; however, it exerted a great influence on the political situation in China. News of it was taken by everybody as signifying the end of Chang Tso-lin's power. Even in the reports of the Japanese news service it was said that the revolt was Chang Tso-lin's funeral knell, the complete ruin of his faction.

Kuo Sung-ling, the deputy of Chang Hsüeh-liang, Chang Tso-lin's son, was commander of the Tientsin-Shanhaikuan defense district and was known as the most powerful general in the Mukden army. There were seven divisions, two artillery brigades, and an engineering regiment, more than fifty thousand men in all, that is the larger part of the Mukden army under his command. Moreover, these were crack troops, well-armed and trained. They were being prepared for war against Feng Yü-hsiang. Everyone knew that Kuo Sung-ling was leader of the opposition Young Mukden faction, although its official leader was the twenty-seven year old General Chang Hsüeh-liang. In any case, the Japanese were making advances towards Kuo Sung-ling and showing him marks of respect.

The Young Mukden faction had no political program and was not linked to a mass movement. It was struggling for power and influence with the Mukden militarists of the older generation. However, the patriotic upsurge on a national scale which followed the events of May 30, the rise of the Kuomintang government in Canton, the appearance of the Nationalist armies, and the consolidation of the USSR's international position sharpened the contradictions within the Mukden clique.

Kuo Sung-ling's revolt bore witness in one way or another to the serious ideological differences among the Mukdenites; and the fact that it was directed against Chang Tso-lin, the embodiment of the darkest forces of Chinese reaction and the henchman of the most aggressive feudal-militaristic Japanese imperialism, guaranteed for him the sympathy of progressive circles in China. Kuo Sung-ling's revolt also demonstrated the growth of the Nationalist armies' authority and that of their leader Feng Yü-hsiang.

The link between Kuo Sung-ling and Feng Yü-hsiang was revealed about two weeks before the revolt. Kuo Sung-ling refused to fight against Feng Yü-hsiang when the latter declared war against Chang Tso-lin on November 10. As a result a compromise agreement was concluded in Tientsin on November 12, 1925, through Kuo Sung-ling's mediation. At the same time Kuo Sung-ling concluded a secret treaty with Feng Yü-hsiang. In the text of the agreement were included points about the development of national industry, improvement in the condition of workers and peasants, the creation of a Central People's Government and the reorganization of Manchuria. Kuo Sung-ling demanded the appointment of Chang Hsüeh-liang as ruler of Manchuria and he tried to introduce a point about "the struggle against Bolshevism" but he did not insist upon it. The *tupan* of Chihli, General Li Ching-lin, who was based in Tientsin, was the third person signing the agreement. Agreement was also reached with General K'ang Shao-hsi, the governor of Jehol. Japanese officials gave Kuo Sung-ling assurances of their benevolent neutrality.

Kuo's revolt flared up before the intended day. Chang Tso-lin was informed of the treachery and ordered Chang Hsüeh-liang to shoot his former associate. Getting wind of this, Kuo Sung-ling acted quickly. Earlier a meeting had taken place in Kuo Sung-ling's headquarters in Luanchow on the subject of the forthcoming revolt. The former *tupan* of Anhui, General Chiang Teng-hsüan, considering it his duty to remain faithful to Chang Tso-lin, was terribly upset and spat right in Kuo Sung-ling's face for which he was promptly shot. In the future this fact was brought up time and time again in the reactionary Chinese and imperialist press as an example of Kuo Sung-ling's extreme cruelty which supposedly alienated many of his followers.

On November 23, 1925, Kuo Sung-ling broke the rail link between Luanchow and Shanhaikuan and sent a curt telegram to Chang Tso-lin

demanding that he turn over power to Chang Hsüeh-liang. Simultaneously
his troops were given the name Fourth Nationalist Army, that is, they openly
joined Feng Yü-hsiang's force. General Li Ching-lin also declared his independence. On November 27 Feng Yü-hsiang and Kuo Sung-ling in a joint
declaration finally declared war against Chang Tso-lin. Kuo Sung-ling released
a proclamation in which he declared that he could not look with equanimity
upon the people's suffering, and yielding to their wishes he had risen up
against the cruel, greedy and despotic Mukden usurpers, that he was determined
to give autonomy to Manchuria, that most unhappy part of China where the
population was treated like slaves.

Kuo Sung-ling did not bind himself with any serious political promises.
Moreover, in trying to get the support of the Japanese authorities, he
dissociated himself in every way from the revolutionary movement. His
representative in Tokyo, after a visit with the ministers, publicly declared
that Kuo Sung-ling's task was to effect a reform of Chinese militarism and
to democratize Manchuria, that he was an opponent of communism and was
not allied with Marshal Feng Yü-hsiang.

In Mukden the terror was unleashed. The families of Kuo Sung-ling's
supporters were thrown into jail. All of Kuo Sung-ling's relatives were
beheaded and his father shot. Eighty thousand dollars was offered for Kuo
Sung-ling's head. Chang Hsüeh-liang escaped responsibility for his links with
the mutineers only because he was the marshal's son.

In Peking news of the revolt produced exultation, a massive revolutionary upsurge. The hated regime of Tuan Ch'i-jui was going to pieces.
Demonstrations began under the slogans "Down with the traitors' government!" "China needs a people's democratic government." Here are the
details of one such demonstration which occurred at the end of November.

Several thousand persons came to Tien An Men Square, the regular
place for revolutionary meetings and demonstrations. A declaration of the
Chinese Communist party and the Kuomintang was read aloud and adopted.
It said "The most reactionary military clique which is working for the benefit
of Japan and against the nation is falling to pieces. This disintegration has
been brought about by the struggle of the masses of the people against the
Mukden clique whom the people hate no less than they did the Manchu

dynasty on the eve of the 1911 Revolution. The Nationalist Armies can serve the people only if they join their forces with the national-revolutionary movement." The assembly adopted an appeal to the Chinese nation and Feng Yü-hsiang, suggesting that he overthrow the government of the traitor, the Japanophile Tuan Ch'i-jui. The text of the resignation which the demonstrators wanted to give to Tuan Ch'i-jui for his signature was also approved. With this aim they began to move on the President's Palace. Five thousand soldiers of the First Nationalist Army were on duty there, but they were friendly and fraternization began. The soldiers had orders not to allow the demonstrators to get through, but all the same the crowd broke through the outer cordon to the gates. Tuan Ch'i-jui's personal guard numbered three thousand troops. Skirmishes with them were limited to the opposing sides throwing stones at each other until evening. Finally the commander of the Peking garrison, General Lu Chung-lin, appeared at the gates. He took the text of the resignation for transmission to Tuan Ch'i-jui and promised to return an answer the next day. The demonstrators were told to disperse.

The next day the meeting again assembled and Ku Meng-yü, at that time a Kuomintang leftist and professor at Peking University, spoke. A delegation was despatched to Feng Yü-hsiang with a proposal to organize a National Committee which would convoke a National Assembly for the purpose of forming a People's Government. Demonstrations took place all over the city, the "Internationale" resounded for the first time in the streets of Peking. Soldiers in Nationalist Army uniforms distributed Kuomintang newspapers and brochures from automobiles. In these conditions almost all the ministers submitted their resignations. The government in effect ceased to exist.

The masses sacked the office of the newspaper *Ch'en pao* which was conducting a campaign against the South China government and the Kuomintang. From everywhere came telegrams from public organizations addressed to Feng Yü-hsiang in which the suggestion was made to put an end to the scandalous rule of the Japanese puppet. But still Feng Yü-hsiang wavered and did not resolve on any action. On the contrary, he banned meetings, ordered Lu Chung-lin to safeguard Tuan Ch'i-jui and not permit agitation.

Everything favored Kuo Sung-ling, or so it seemed. On his side were the undoubted sympathy of public opinion, superiority of military force and the unvoiced approval of Japan. Nevertheless, from the first days of the revolt reverses were encountered. In the first place there were the betrayals of his supposedly sympathetic fellow generals.

As soon as Kuo Sung-ling's troops went beyond Shanhaikuan, General Li Ching-lin freed all of Chang Tso-lin's adherents in Tientsin and declared that he would not let any aid through to Kuo Sung-ling. Two days earlier General K'ang Shao-hsi had broken away, creating a threat on the left flank. It was suspected that the Japanese were putting pressure on Li Ching-lin and K'ang Shao-hsi.

According to the plan the First Nationalist Army was not supposed to take part in the battles. Only units of the Second and Third Nationalist Armies were transferred to the Tientsin area. When it turned out that Kuo Sung-ling was cut off from Tientsin and Peking by Li Ching-lin's troops the First Nationalist Army quickly went into action. Battles broke out near Tientsin. Kuo Sung-ling went to Mukden.

The month in which the revolt occurred was a tense one indeed! Success might have signified a change in the political situation in the country, agreement between the North and the South, new conditions for the anti-imperialist struggle. Everyone anxiously followed news of the revolt, both friends and enemies of the Chinese revolution. The papers were filled with sensational reports.

Enthusiasm reigned among the advisers, but alas, what a paradox. With the beginning of the military action came an interruption in their work. Only a few of them were at the front, the rest weren't at their posts. Several of Feng Yü-hsiang's generals tolerated our advisers in time of peace but now tried to get rid of them. War was a convenient opportunity to apply pressure, to procure arms and new soldiers without taking into account the interests of the whole, and the advisers as partisans of strict centralization got in the way.

Because of mistakes in leadership the fighting near Tientsin dragged on, claimed many victims and did not achieve its direct aim. The city was taken by the Nationalist Army only after Kuo Sung-ling's revolt had already been put down.[11]

The Japanese imperialists played a decisive role in putting down the revolt.

After Kuo Sung-ling's victory at Liangshan in the beginning of December no one doubted that Chang Tso-lin's days were numbered. Mukden awaited Kuo Sung-ling as its liberator. The merchants despatched a delegation to greet him triumphantly. He was already just sixty-five kilometers from the city. A general exodus commenced among Chang Tso-lin's supporters. The papers reported that Mukden had been turned into an armed camp; guards were everywhere, the railroads were choked with troop trains. Chang Tso-lin, after distributing four hundred thousand yuan to his supporters, sent his valuables and his family to the Japanese concession, and having withdrawn six million yuan from the Yokohama Specie Bank and half a million from the Chosen Bank[12], fled in an unknown direction (as it turned out later to Talien) and laid low for several days. In Harbin the Mukdenites began to make advances to the Soviet Union. The ban was lifted on a suppressed Soviet newspaper and imprisoned trade union workers were freed. The governor-general of Kirin province, General Chang Tso-hsiang, gave a banquet for our consul and the Soviet section of the Chinese Eastern Railway management.

Suddenly the Japanese imperialists came out on Chang Tso-lin's side. It seemed that by making promises to Kuo Sung-ling they only wanted to increase their pressure on Chang Tso-lin and wrest new privileges from him. Only recently the Japanese minister of war, Ugaki, had received a representative of Kuo Sung-ling and declared to journalists that Kuo Sung-ling was the new leader who could pacify China, and improve its international

---

11. The liberation of Tientsin by troops of the Nationalist Army, although only for a short time, had great revolutionary significance. In this important industrial center, with a population of one million, there were more than a hundred thousand industrial workers but the workers' movement was very undeveloped because of fierce suppression under the previous regime. In Tientsin political prisoners were freed, an order officially recognizing the trade unions was published and they began to operate openly. In a short time the number of organized workers exceeded thirty thousand. A daily workers' paper began to be published. And in the Lenin memorial days of 1926 mass meetings dedicated to Lenin's memory were held in Tientsin and the mining center of T'angshan.

12. The largest Japanese banks having branches in Manchuria.

position, that Chang Tso-lin had lost Japan's favor and she could no longer approve of his ambitious, militarist schemes. But on December 19 the Japanese suddenly forbade Kuo Sung-ling from crossing the South Manchurian Railway line, declaring that they insisted on the neutralization of a zone twenty kilometers wide. In fact this amounted to a prohibition on taking Mukden.

Barbed wire barriers, machineguns, and artillery appeared around the Japanese concession in Mukden. Japanese fliers in Chinese uniforms began to bomb the rebellious troops. There was information that they were even dropping chemical bombs. Japanese instructors and specialists stepped up their work in Chang Tso-lin's units. The transport of troops from Japan commenced. The South Manchurian Railway was filled with troop trains carrying Japanese soldiers. Two brigades of Japanese soldiers were in Chang Tso-lin's active forces. The Japanese took on the responsibility of provisioning Chang's forces.

In China and abroad the Japanese actions were justly regarded as open military intervention. The American magazine *China Weekly Review* later demonstrated that Kuo Sung-ling was defeated because the Japanese administration of the South Manchurian Railway, the real government of South Manchuria, desired it. Chang Tso-lin's defeat would have meant for them the loss of sixty million Manchurian yen on their current account since in the event of Kuo Sung-ling's victory the Manchurian monetary unit would have been devalued.

At that time the Chinese were not masters in their own house. But they did not want to become reconciled to such a situation. Demonstrations got under way in the cities. The Kuomintang delegation in Peking headed by the Kuomintang leftist Hsü Ch'ien and the chairman of the Chinese delegation to the Customs conference[13] the well-known diplomat Wang Cheng-ting who was acting as Kuo Sung-ling's diplomatic representative in Peking, presented a protest to the Japanese minister. But this did not embarrass the Japanese.

---

13. The conference for re-examination of the Customs was held in Peking in October 1925.

On the evening of December 23 the Japanese consul in Hsinmin summoned Kuo Sung-ling, ostensibly for negotiations. He arrived accompanied by a small retinue and was treacherously put to death. When this became known a panicky stampede began in his army. Soon it was disarmed and then almost to a man went over to the side of the Mukdenites.

All the papers featured a picture of Kuo Sung-ling's wife who had been shot. She had intended to flee and therefore changed into ordinary clothes. In the picture the little old lady in a black Chinese headdress was lying flat on her back, her tiny bound feet helplessly jutting out of her broad trousers. In the papers it was reported that she was punished for being involved in politics. It was asserted that she was close to Feng Yü-hsiang's wife[14] and had become the intermediary through whom Feng influenced her husband. Two days later the corpses of Kuo Sung-ling and his wife were exhibited for public viewing in one of Mukden's squares. This was on the road to the temple where Chang Tso-lin bestowed the highest military honors (posthumously) on the remains of the loyal General Chiang Teng-hsüan whose shooting by Kuo Sung-ling in the beginning of the revolt had occasioned such indignation in the reactionary press. Chinese students in Japan organized meetings in memory of Kuo Sung-ling. The largest meeting was held in Tokyo where a resolution was adopted to leave Japan at once in token of protest against the Japanese intervention. Soon we saw in Peking an anti-Japanese demonstration organized by the returned students.

Kuo Sung-ling's defeat was a great blow against Feng Yü-hsiang and several days later he went into retirement.

An Adventure on the Road

At the end of December I traveled from Kalgan to Peking with two friends, an interpreter and a military adviser. The train was late and it was not till past midnight that we arrived at the Hsi Chih Men city gates. A war was in progress. Peking was on a war footing and the city gates were locked at night. We had to spend the night in the suburbs.

---

14. Feng Yü-hsiang's wife. Li Te-ch'uan, presently holds the post of minister of health in the Chinese People's Government.

The frost grew more severe towards night and the wind carried a fine stinging snow mixed with sand. My fellow travelers went off to seek lodging. I remained alone in front of the dark bulk of the many-storied fortress gates which seemed even more gloomy and severe in the darkness. A light dimly glimmered above in the small narrow windows. There was the guard-post, most likely. The huge walls and gates continued to live their medieval lives, locking up the enormous sleeping city. The inn seemed just as distant in time, reminding one of the inns of Liao Chai's time[15] with all their mysteriously sinister atmosphere: a small, dark courtyard, winding back alleys, tiny rooms. The innkeeper lighted the path with a large torch made of yellow oiled paper inscribed with an enormous black character. The place reeked of an unpleasant, peculiar odor — somehere opium was being smoked.

We were led off to a tiny room, really just an enormous clay k'ang which touched the clay walls at three sides and barely left enough room to take off your shoes in front of it or to dangle your feet. We were separated from the corridor by a thin wooden partition the top part of which was fine lattice-work covered with dirty white paper. There was no bedding but we were glad of that. It was better to lie on one's own fur coat than on a public mattress which probably had vermin. We settled down as best we could by the light of a flashlight. After the wintry cold and the blizzard how pleasant it was to stretch out on the hot bricks of a k'ang. We would get a good night's sleep and then set off tomorrrow morning to the Central Hotel. Who else of our friends was staying there? What news would our comrades have for us? . . . We were awakened by rustling in the corridor. Someone was cautiously walking in front of our room. The muffled shuffling of slippers could be heard on the clay floor. Finally a harsh knock at the door gave us to under-stand that they were coming for us. Someone was lighting up the partition from the other side, the broken lines of the latticework formed a pattern on the walls, and in this strange light I saw the sleepy, frightened faces of my traveling companions.

In that troubled time we were defenseless even if just two steps from a guardpost. *Hunghutz,* Chang Tso-lin's agents, White Guards — wasn't it all the

---

15. Liao Chai was the pseudonym of a popular Chinese writer, P'u Sung-lin (1622-1715), who wrote fantastic tales.

same? Our comrades had no idea where we were spending the night and the Chinese police were absolutely indifferent to our fate. As the interpreter I asked in Chinese what was the matter. In pure Russian came the reply, "Open up." We tried to ascertain who our night-time visitors were. The same voice said with an audible jeer, "You can open up, you won't be doing any more sleeping."

Quietly taking counsel, my companions got ready to defend us. One shone the ray of the flashlight on the door, the other aimed the muzzle of his Mauser. They told me to open the door and quickly step aside. The door opened. The beam of our flashlight intersected that of the person coming towards us. There were three elderly men entirely unknown to us. Judging by their sombre faces they were up to no good. However, on seeing us their faces lengthened amusingly. There was a moment of embarrassment and then the one who had threatened us with sleeplessness — we recognized his voice — said slowly "Excuse us, there's been a mistake." Then they were leaving already, brushing against the walls of the passageway which was too tight for their large, broadshouldered bodies. They went away and we stood silently looking at each other.

Putting away the Mauser and getting ready once more for sleep, one of my comrades said as if to himself "They came to settle accounts with some-one." It did not sink in immediately that White Guards had come by with the obvious intention of settling accounts perhaps with one of their number who had decided to return to his homeland, to the Soviet Union.

After the night-time adventure we could not leave the "Liao Chai Hotel" quickly enough. God be with it and its medieval romanticism. Early in the morning an ancient taxi delivered us to the Central Hotel. The weather cleared up as if there had not been a blizzard the night before. In Peking even in winter there is lots of sunshine.

The Tientsin Operation

We arrived in Peking when the fighting in Tientsin was already over. Heated debates were going on in the rooms of the Central Hotel. The advisers who had lived through the defeat of Kuo Sung-ling, the heavy losses suffered by the First Nationalist Army and the fatal delay of the victory at Tientsin were going over the negative factors which had affected the course of military events.

The troops of the Second and Third Nationalist Armies had been unable to offer any real assistance. The First Nationalist Army had carried out an offensive but the work involved in its reorganization and training was still not completed. Feng Yü-hsiang's troops had gone to war with their old habits intact.

At that time the marshal himself was in Kalgan and the Tientsin front was commanded by the Chahar *tupan* Chang Chih-chiang who did not countenance the presence of Soviet instructors. In essence this was the cause of the extended character of the warfare in Tientsin. Without asking the opinion of our advisers Chiang Chih-chiang fought in the old way, displaying his utter operational helplessness. The operations were not completed, the enemy was not pursued, there was a complete absence of intelligence activity. At times the troops moved like puff-pastry; the advance units of the Nationalist Army, the retreating enemy, then again the Nationalist troops. No one harassed the enemy.

"During the operations near Tientsin we were observers sooner than advisers," our comrades said indignantly, "observers who were tolerated but not consulted nor given any information. We ourselves had to question whoever happened by. When we went to the commander, say of a brigade or a division, we had to force ourselves upon them. We were received coldly. Sometimes the relationship was simply humiliating, we were sent to the rear, they avoided us and wanted to get rid of us, abandoned us to fate during the battles, did not provide us with transport, quarters or provisions on the march. What an urge I've got to send that old phoney, *tupan* Chang Chih-chiang, to the devil, but we have to put up with him, the revolution will not permit otherwise."

Amusing stories were passed from mouth to mouth. It was said for example that one of the brigade commanders wanted to let loose one hundred pigs covered with kerosene and set the enemy on fire. He demonstrated that this was a tried method, known in China from the era of the Warring States.[16]

---

16. Fifth to third centuries B.C.

The advisers dissuaded him with difficulty. Another brigade commander wept openly before everyone when his friend, a regimental commander, was killed. We found this quite astonishing then, but later I heard many similar stories. The very same thing was said about Chang Fa-k'uei, the commander of the Twelfth Division of the Fourth Iron Army of the National-Revolutionary Army who cried when the wounded soldiers and officers were carried past him after the unsuccessful storming of Wuhan in the fall of 1926. It is possible that the generals displayed this excessive sensitivity out of demagogic considerations, but the Chinese in general, as a rule, are very impressionable and they don't consider tears as a sign of cowardice.

More and more often the conversation among us turned to the South China mission in Canton. It is true that our advisers commenced work in the North a year or a year and a half later, but it was clear that the main cause of the military failures was not in the military but the political field. Canton was the revolutionary center of the country. There the people were in the vanguard of the anti-imperialist struggle, the soldiers of the National-Revolutionary Army knew what they were fighting for, their commanders, albeit unwillingly, permitted political work to be conducted in the ranks. And the position of the advisers was entirely different there.

Reaction Takes the Offensive. Feng Yü-hsiang Goes into Retirement.

None of us was surprised when in the beginning of January 1926 a report was circulated that Feng Yü-hsiang was going into retirement.

The situation at that time had become extremely complicated. The "Anti-Red Union" of Wu P'ei-fu and Chang Tso-lin, supported by the imperialists, was created in January under the slogan of "struggle against the Bolsheviks" in opposition to the Nationalist armies and the Kuomintang. A new anti-Soviet campaign was organized arising from the notorious "CER Conflict."

It began with the refusal of Chang Tso-lin to pay for the transport of his troops returning via the CER after the suppression of Kuo Sung-ling's revolt. This was accompanied by a series of provocations and interference in the administration of the railroad. Service on the Harbin-Changchun line was interrupted. Ivanov, the manager of the railroad, was placed under arrest and held for three days. Our railroad workers were subjected to repression. Trade unions were closed down and their quarters were sealed. Chang Tso-lin became so brazen that he demanded Karakhan's departure from China, saying that in the event of Peking's being occupied by Mukden troops he would not be responsible for Karakhan's life.

Chang Tso-lin's illegal actions became an occasion for desperate baiting of the USSR in which the entire reactionary press in China — the imperialist, the White Guardist, and the right-wing Chinese — took part. Leafing through the papers in the morning we knew beforehand that we would come across incendiary articles, some of which called openly for war against the Soviet Union. The White Guards already were getting ready for an invasion and conducted themselves with provocative impudence, picking fights with our comrades whenever they encountered them. The Soviet ship *Oleg* with a cargo of arms for Feng Yü-hsiang's army was seized.

The Kuomintang's extreme right wing, the so-called Hsishan faction, also took part in this campaign (this is what all of those who had participated in the right-wing Kuomintang conference at Hsishan in November 1925 were called). They organized an anti-Soviet demonstration in Peking University, but their attempt to organize a meeting of this kind ended in hand-to-hand fighting with the revolutionary-minded students. Generally the Hsishan faction had little success among the Peking students. They were marked by a militant revolutionary spirit, and were under strong Communist influence.

The Kuomintang right-wing faction's papers in Shanghai actively took part in the baiting of the Soviet Union. At the end of January to the bitter disappointment of our ill-wishers the conflict on the CER was resolved but the anti-Soviet campaign continued until May. It was interesting to note the change of slogans in the pages of the Hsishan faction's Shanghai papers. During the conflict they reviled the USSR in every way possible. Afterwards appeared the slogan "With the Soviet Union but against the Communists," then "We are for the Russian Communists but against the Communists in China," and finally "We are not against the Chinese Communists but against their participation in the Kuomintang."

Thus the right wing Kuomintang, not wishing to frighten away the masses and under the influence of the changing situation, softened its demands.

The Red Spear Uprising in Honan

In January 1926 another event occurred which worsened the political situation in China. I have in mind the rout of the Second and Third Nationalist Armies by the rebellious Red Spears.

I have already written about the difficult economic situation in Honan. The ruined population correctly viewed the military oppression as one of the chief causes of its unhappiness. The reader already knows that the Second and Third Nationalist Armies were not distinguished by their exemplary behaviour, and our advisers, despite all their efforts, could do nothing with them. When the rebellion flared up, the advisers were forced to leave Kaifeng quickly in order not to fall prisoner to the enraged insurgents who might not believe that our comrades were blameless in the disasters which had befallen them. By the end of February 1926 the Honan advisers were already living in the Central Hotel in Peking. They had had to travel part of the way on foot since the Red Spears had dismantled the railroad. The head of the mission, Skalov, with two or three advisers, arrived via a circuitous route through Shensi where the remnants of the defeated troops of the Nationalist Army had retreated.

The secret, mystical organizations of peasants of the type which the Red Spears represented still continued to possess great strength although, of course, they were not what they had been in feudal times when the thrones of Chinese emperors trembled and fell under the pressure of their rebellions. After the rout of the Boxers in 1901 their numbers declined sharply.

In the years we are speaking of, in many provinces of China there still existed Red, Yellow, and Black Spears, Leagues of the Large Sword, and Leagues of the Small Sword, Association of the Tightened Belts, Elder Brothers, Union of the Bare Trousers, and many other organizations which were heir to the medieval White Lotus League, Triads, Union of the Red Lantern, etc. At times they took part in the revolutionary movement. In the beginning of the thirties the papers printed amazing reports of Buddhist monks and secret society teachers who, burnt alive on Kuomintang bonfires, cried out that they were Communists.

Honan along with Shantung had for a long time been considered the region where secret societies were most prevalent. The Red Spears, bringing together tens of thousands of peasants, was the most massive of those. Their name derived from their home-made spears which had a scrap of red cloth tied beneath the blade. The Red Spears arose as detachments of peasant self-defense forces. In those dark times the peasants had to defend themselves. Bandits and soldiers robbed without mercy and it was impossible to have recourse to the authorities. In reality these were medieval, semi-religious leagues whose leaders were monks, landlords, and shenshih[17] who exploited the rank and file members.

The Red Spears did not tolerate soldiers and even before the uprising they frequently expelled garrisons from the smaller towns. Klimov told of their attack on a detachment of the Second Nationalist Army which was stationed south of Loyang. It was something in the nature of a psychological attack. The Red Spears sat completely naked on their unsaddled horses, smeared from head to foot with red clay, and on their heads was the kind of headgear which one sees in the depictions of fierce guardians at the entrance of Chinese temples. They believed profoundly in the magical efficacy of their fantastic "uniforms."

The deep superstition of the Red Spears was unshakeable. It was said that having made the prescribed incantations they calmly exposed themselves to fire convinced that bullets would bounce off. Even the death of their comrades before their very eyes could not dispel their delusions. The "teachers" explained this very simply. The dead man had sinned, had not believed in the spirits, or performed the incantations in the wrong way. A battalion commander of the Second Nationalist Army, challenging one such "teacher", shot four of the man's pupils at pointblank range but the "teacher" still calmly faced the gun and was killed on the spot. General Hu Ching-i (whom Klimov had told about this monstrous "bet") ordered the officer shot for undermining the ties between the Second Nationalist Army and the people.

The peasants' dissatisfaction with the Second and Third Nationalist Armies was justified. All the same if work among the peasants had been conducted on a sufficiently broad scale, it would not have been so easy for Wu P'ei-fu's agents to use the detachments of the Red Spears for their own purposes. Only in the one district of Ch'ihsiang where some thirty thousand

---

17. *Shenshih*—the former Manchu bureaucrats tied to the bureaucratic apparatus in the villages and usually landowners.

were united in the peasant leagues of the Red Spears did the Communists succeed in leading the movement. In other districts attempts of a similar nature ended tragically. In the district of Loyang where the Red Spears were especially numerous, out of seven Communists who were sent there during the uprising two were killed, one died in a hospital and the others were seriously wounded.

The uprising of the Red Spears began in the middle of January in western Honan, on the border with Shansi where the remains of Wu P'ei-fu's troops were stationed. His emissaries rode about the district stirring up rebellion. The defeats suffered by the Second and Third Nationalist Armies on the southern and eastern fronts (against Wu P'ei-fu and Chang Tsung-ch'ang) served as the spark which ignited all of Honan like powder. The districts of Hsinyang and Loyang became the centers of the uprising.

Masses of Red Spears joined Wu P'ei-fu's troops and provided them with inestimable aid. They were unsurpassed scouts and guerillas. They merged with the population and couldn't be caught. The rear of the Second Nationalist Army was disorganized. The gates of all the villages along the way of its retreat were closed and the Red Spears guarded the walls.[18] The army was fleeing westward towards the city of Chengchou. Only a few soldiers succeeded in making their way to Shansi. Their accents would give them away and they would be greeted by cries of "death to the Shansi men." Such was the terrible price paid by the Nationalist Armies in Honan because the peasant masses rose up against them.

Wu P'ei-fu easily seized Honan and at once established his own order of things. "In the course of several weeks," wrote one Honan missionary, "control in the province passed from the hands of the radicals into the hands of real conservatives." Public organizations went underground, statements opposing imperialism, strikes and meetings were forbidden. Mass repression was instituted. Wu P'ei-fu promised money to the Red Spears but, of course, he did not keep his word and tried to rescue himself from his dangerous allies. A part of the leadership received military titles, but without monetary

---

18. In Honan and many other provinces of China each village looked like a fortress, was surrounded by high walls, and locked the gates for the night. This was one of the defensive measures against the banditry which was widely prevalent then.

rewards, the rest were disarmed and the most dangerous were executed.

The rout of the Nationalist Armies in Honan crowned Feng Yü-hsiang's military defeats. He decided to leave China for a while. This freed his generals among whom a movement to the right began. The work of the advisers in the North came to a standstill, but they were much needed in the South, therefore many left for Canton.

We Leave for the South

Late one evening, not long before our departure, Kuzmichev (Wen), Primakov's adjutant and constant companion, came to our room on the fifth floor and offered to take us for a ride. The car had been reserved for the night for a trip to Tientsin, but for some reason Primakov was unable to make use of it.

We rode through the half-darkened streets of Peking which were deserted at that hour. The chauffeur was ordered to drive where his fancy directed him and he wheeled along the broad streets and the back alleys without asking for further instructions. The dim outlines of houses, trees, and arches flashed by. Even familiar places took on a strange, fantastic appearance in the night-time darkness. We rode as if in an enchanted city and no one wanted to break the silence. Everyone was somewhat sad. We were saying farewell, perhaps forever, to Peking, a city which we had come to love.

Small, slant-eyed Wen was gloomy. He was suffering over the departure of one of the girl interpreters whom he had fallen in love with and she was trying not to take notice of anything. So we rode without jokes or laughter.

"Come, I'll recite some verses for you," Wen suddenly offered. This was surprising. We knew that Primakov had connections with literary circles in Moscow and that his verses were his hobby. But Wen with his modest, unassuming exterior did not call forth any poetic associations in our minds.

He did not begin to recite love elegies. The remarkable verses of N. Tikhonov resounded in the car — *"Poema o sinem pakete," "Ballada o gvozdiakh"* (Poem of a blue packet), (Ballad about nails), etc. Now it is even difficult for me to convey the impression they made upon me.

Famous poets used to visit the Moscow Institute of Oriental Studies to "exchange experiences" with the students, as the phrase went. At the end of 1923, sitting on the floor in front of the stage of the jammed auditorium,

I heard Yesenin. He did not make any special impression upon us. The boys laughed at his top hat, morning coat and gray-striped trousers which looked so unusual at the time. He recited his famous poem "Everything Living Has Its Own Calling," which I liked very much, and he recited it well, simply and with feeling without the howling that was the style. But all the same we didn't like him. His verses inspired bewilderment, their themes seemed too petty, their fine lyricism somehow inappropriate. Mayakovsky had many more followers among the students.

Tikhonov's verses which we all, it seems, were hearing for the first time on that memorable night, stirred and charmed all of us. All my life I have been grateful to that remarkable poet for what I experienced then. Riding in an old Ford, along Peking's darkened streets that night, we all felt the urge for heroic deeds, readiness for self-sacrifice, pride in our comrades, sadness for those who had fallen for our cause, and yearning for the motherland. At the same time Tikhonov's verses somehow had a sobering effect; false pathos and enthusiasm were foreign to them, they breathed a profound and quiet meditation.

Climbing the stairs to the fifth floor we repeated the lines:
> If you made nails from these people,
> There'd be no stronger nails in the world.

In the beginning of February 1926 we left for the South.

The Difficult Situation in the North

It remains for me to relate the military and political situation in the North after our departure.

The northwest seemed set apart from the broad road of the revolution, whose fundamental problems had been decided in South and central China. There too the attention of the Chinese and international publics was fixed. In the South masses of workers and peasants by the millions had swiftly joined the revolutionary struggle, but the backward northwest was just beginning to stir politically. Naturally, the armies in the northwest were not at all what they were in the South and it was much harder to work there. To the victor are given the glory and rewards. Thus it happened that when many of our advisers returned home they were awarded Orders of the Red Banner, but no one from the Kalgan or Kaifeng missions received such an award since no such brilliant victories as had occurred in the South had occurred there.

Nevertheless, the untiring, painstaking labor which the handful of advisers had performed in Feng Yü-hsiang's armies, so little noticed at first glance, had a great revolutionary significance. In Feng Yü-hsiang's absence our comrades exercised a restraining influence on the capitulationist position of his generals. It is hard to overestimate what they accomplished after Feng Yü-hsiang's return when his army was reconstructed along the Kuomintang model.

The chief of staff of the Kalgan mission, Lapin, in one of his reports upon his arrival in Hankow in the end of June 1927 remarked that our advisers in the northwest, who worked one or two to each unit, sapped the organism of reaction like microbes, slowly but surely. He did not say what selfless labor and self-denial this cost them.

February and March 1926 was a period of great setbacks. The Nationalist Armies lost Honan, Chihli (except for the capital district), and the larger part of Jehol. The enemy advanced simultaneously from three sides. A large part of the Second, a part of the Third and almost all of the Fourth Nationalist Armies were already numbered in the ranks of the militarists. The remains of the Second and Third Nationalist Armies broke through to Shensi. In April they were besieged by troops of the provincial *tupan*, General Liu Chen-hua (of Wu P'ei-fu's faction) in Sian. The siege lasted for eight months. The condition of the troops and the city inhabitants was terrible. Hundreds of persons died daily from starvation. Only at the end of November, after Feng Yü-hsiang's return from the Soviet Union, was Sian liberated by units of the First and Fifth Nationalist Armies.

The imperialists did not pass up an opportunity to intervene in the fighting on their satellite's side. In the middle of March 1926 they presented an ultimatum to the command of the Nationalist Armies in which, citing the final Protocol of 1901, they demanded freedom of navigation between Taku and Tientsin. In reality they were trying to secure the opportunity of aiding Li Ching-lin and threatened to take violent measures if not satisfied. The ultimatum gave rise to a burst of popular indignation which was manifested in the famous "Peking Incident of March 18" — the firing on a demonstration of thousands in front of the presidential palace. Afraid of relying on the masses, the leaders of the Nationalist Army yielded to the imperialists. About March 20 the Nationalist troops evacuated Tientsin.

A campaign against the USSR, the Chinese Communist party, the Nationalist armies, and the Russian advisers continued in the pages of the reactionary press. Chang Tso-lin offered a million yuan for Feng Yü-hsiang's head. Unfortunately, neither during the struggle to support Kuo Sung-ling nor afterwards did the First Nationalist Army appear as a national-revolutionary force. It is sufficient to recall Feng Yü-hsiang's relationship to the government of Tuan Ch'i-jui.

Meanwhile the heat of political passions in Peking continued to increase; the masses entered into the revolutionary movement on a broader scale. March 1926, the last month before Chang Tso-lin's troops occupied the city, was significant in this regard. At the beginning of March, revolutionary-minded students at Peking University beat up the organizers of an anti-Soviet meeting. The memorial days for Sun Yat-sen, March 12-14, shook up the capital. Inasmuch as Sun Yat-sen had been the first president of the republic, the government could not interfere with the outpouring of patriotic feelings, but it was frightened by the scale which the movement assumed and by its militant character. To some degree these days led up to the March 18 demonstrations and the reprisals taken against its participants.

The Sun Yat-sen memorial meeting was organized by the Kuomintang along with the Chinese Communist party and other public organizations in the former reception hall of the imperial palace, the T'aihotien. From early morning till late at night an endless flow of people passed through the hall. Speeches were made. Heaps of flowers lay before a portrait of Sun Yat-sen and all around were innumerable wreaths and banners with inscriptions from the Chinese Communist party, the Kuomintang, the Chinese Komsomol, trade unions, the Kuomintang diplomatic delegation, the Peking government, and private persons. In front of the palace meetings were held where speakers explained the situation in the South. Kuomintang recruitment tables were set up and stacks of Communist and Kuomintang literature were piled on them. Three thousand people joined the Kuomintang in three days.

On the first day official personages, and then crowds of poor people came. On the third day it is estimated that more than a half-million persons passed by Sun Yat-sen's portrait. Two hundred delegates came from the Nationalist armies. Order was perfect. It was maintained by members of the Peking unions and detachments of the self-defense forces of the railroad workers who took pride in the glory of their famous strike of February 1923 and had come specially from Hankow.

Several days later, on March 18, 1926, the masses again took to the streets of Peking, this time to protest the impudent ultimatum of the powers referred to above. The demonstrators, students for the most part, headed towards Tuan Ch'i-jui's palace in order to hand him the text of the protest. The president's personal guard fired at them, killing fifty and wounding seventy. The threads of the crime led to the Japanese embassy. A base role was played by General Chang Chih-chiang who, the evening before, had sent a telegram to Tuan Ch'i-jui in which he complained about the students' lack of discipline and proposed to take measures against the disobedient ones.

In spite of the ban on meetings and demonstrations, they continued with new force, by now in protest against the shootings of March 18. A requiem was held in the National University. Flower-draped portraits of the victims were displayed along with their bloodied clothing. Leaflets calling for revenge were distributed to those in attendance. The police settled down to do their dirty work. Public funerals were forbidden and the arrests began. An order was given for the arrest of the Kuomintang leaders in Peking, Ku Meng-yü, Hsü Ch'ien and others. They had to go into hiding. A purge was also begun in the Nationalist Army. All the Kuomintang political workers were relieved. In open letters about "the education of youth" Chang Chih-chiang and his closest associate, General Li Ming-chung, made a list of reactionary demands.

In May a declaration was published in which the generals of the First Nationalist Army recognized all the unequal treaties with which the imperialists had bound China. By this act the army lost its national-revolutionary character. In fact, not long afterward, it began to call itself simply the Northwest Army. This declaration concerning the unequal treaties was not annulled until Feng Yü-hsiang's return to China in September 1926.

The loss of its political prestige, internal disorders, setbacks on the front, the imperialists' pressure and the forthcoming offensive by the Chihli-Mukden troops made the Nationalist Army's position in Peking very precarious. On April 14, 1926, it began to evacuate Peking. Chang Tso-lin's troops entered the city. A fierce terror began. People were shot without trial. The police rushed to deal with the members of the press. The editors of the newspaper *Ch'en pao* were shot for "sympathy towards the USSR," and of the *She hui jih pao* for an unfavorable reference to Marshal Wu P'ei-fu. The editor of *Shih tzu jih pao* turned up in jail.

By this time Feng Yü-hsiang was outside of China. On the eve of his departure he conversed with Borodin (who had stopped in Peking on his way from Canton to the USSR for vacation), and with Primakov. In answer to Borodin's question of why didn't he want to fulfill the desire of the Chinese people — overthrow Tuan Ch'i-jui's puppet regime and create a provisional government prior to the convocation of a national assembly, the marshal replied that he did not want to be concerned with politics and was going to study in the USSR. "In my country we teach through personal example," he added demogogically, "I will go to the USSR and become a simple worker."

In conversation with Primakov Feng Yü-hsiang expressed himself even more precisely. "I am a revolutionary only by half, otherwise I would have to arrest President Tuan Ch'i-jui. I was a revolutionary in the first year of the republic, what I said I did quickly.[19] I was always attacked because of this. Now I am simply a man retiring into myself."

At the end of April, Feng Yü-hsiang arrived in Verkhneudinsk (now Ulan-Ude) via Ulan Bator and saw the May First holiday. In a press interview while still in Ulan-Bator he declared, "I want to enter the Kuomintang, since I have given myself the goal of following Sun Yat-sen's precepts. I am thinking of spending seven years in the USSR. Right now upon my arrival I will enter a factory and work as an ordinary worker in order to attend basic political school in a worker's atmosphere, to learn about the political and economic conditions in the USSR. A change of conditions is no hardship for me; I am the son of a stone-mason, I have been a worker and a soldier for many years." On the way to Moscow Feng Yü-hsiang made a substantial contribution to the aid fund for the British general strike. A triumphal welcome in which students from the Communist University of the Toilers of the East and from

---

19. He had in mind the first year after the Revolution of 1911 which overturned the monarchy in China.

the Sun Yat-sen University of the Toilers of China took part was arranged for the marshal in Moscow.

In conversation with a *Pravda* correspondent Feng Yü-hsiang declared, "I have come to strengthen the friendship between China and the USSR, to learn about the Soviet state and the building of the Red Army. Along my entire route I have seen a great deal of construction — bridges being fixed, roads being repaired, new houses going up. I am happy to see in your young Russia the image of the future China. On crossing the border I was especially impressed by the excellent condition of the Red Army, especially the Red cavalry. In Verkhneudinsk where I spent May First, I was especially struck by the close ties between the army and the people."

Feng Yü-hsiang's eldest daughter and his son went to study at Sun Yat-sen University. At first the marshal expressed the desire for his son to become "an ordinary worker" and wanted to send him to a management training institute, but this turned out to be impossible since he didn't know Russian. Feng intended to have his younger children raised in a Russian family.

Around the anniversary of the May 30 Incident the marshal made many appearances in Moscow. At one of the meetings he emphasized, "The sole task of the Nationalist armies is to render all possible aid to the popular movement in China. At present the Nationalist armies act together with the Kuomintang army and their goals are identical." Feng Yü-hsiang spent only several months in the USSR. The situation in China demanded his return. His wife and children remained in the USSR.

Feng spent the entire summer in a dacha near Moscow in very modest circumstances. Before his departure he received a representative from *Pravda* and conversed with him for a long time. He said that it was very difficult for the First Nationalist Army to fight against the combined forces of Chang Tso-lin and Wu P'ei-fu since the Second and Third Nationalist armies had actually ceased to exist. Still it continued to fight for half a year. The secret of the First Nationalist Army's strength was that it was bound to the masses and fought for the national cause. The Nationalist Army in union with the National-Revolutionary Army was a great military force.

The Fighting near Nankow

Just how did the First Nationalist Army fight in the half-year that Feng Yü-hsiang was absent? After leaving Peking it based itself beyond the mountain pass of Nankow some sixty kilometers northwest of the city. Its situation was extraordinarily difficult. It occupied a sparsely populated and economically underdeveloped section of Inner Mongolia and northwest China. Its material base had narrowed, but the military activities which had begun demanded supplemental means. Near Nankow the troops of Wu P'ei-fu and Chang Tso-lin tried to break through the strongly fortified positions of the Nationalist Army. The din of the cannonade could be heard in Peking. At the same time fighting developed in the west, in northern Shansi, along the Peking-Suiyuan railroad line where the troops of the Nationalist Army were fighting for possession of the passes of the Great Wall.

In August the situation grew even worse. General Yen Hsi-shan, the *tupan* of Shansi, joined Wu P'ei-fu's and Chang Tso-lin's "Anti-Red Alliance." The Mukden troops began to attack from the direction of Jehol. The Kalgan section of the First Nationalist Army and the troops near Nankow were threatened. The indecisiveness of the leadership and the friction and disagreements among the generals led on August 14 to the Nationalist Army's abandoning Nankow and later Kalgan as well, beginning a retreat to Suiyuan.

The abandonment of the Nankow positions which were considered impregnable occasioned all kinds of second-guesses and commentaries. It was said that it was the result of an agreement between Chang Chih-chiang and Chang Tso-lin with whom the former had always had excellent relations.

On the invitation of Chang Tso-lin, who tried in every way to inflate the significance of his victory at Nankow, foreign experts visited the positions which had been abandoned by the First Nationalist Army and were impressed by their equipment. Three lines of trenches constructed by means of the most up-to-date technology had been erected. An electric current flowed through the barbed wire barricades of the first line. The system of fortifications continued for twenty kilometers along the approaches to the pass. The first line of fortifications was yielded without a struggle. Learning that the positions would be abandoned, the generals, without awaiting orders, began to retreat rapidly, "in order not to remain behind everyone else." The Mukden forces took advantage of this.

Espionage played its role in this too. Chang Chih-chiang's adviser was a Japanese, a privileged person who recognized no limitations, and his confessor was an American missionary who actually was secretly present at all the *tupan's* conversations with our comrades inasmuch as he lived in the next room and knew Chinese. Not long before this the advisers discovered in Kalgan's environs two illegal American wireless sets.

At that time there was no such thing as a military secret in China. News about troop movements and combat losses were printed in all the papers. It became known that the 150,000 man First Nationalist Army had lost more than half its strength. The confusion of the generals and the loss of discipline resulted in the retreat from Nankow turning into a panicky flight. One of our advisers said, "The Nankow mission lost all of its material. Chang Chih-chiang simply took to his heels and left for Suiyuan under a guard of Mauser-bearing troops. The army had no plan of retreat, it fled one by one, on foot, on donkeys, mules and horses seized from the peasants, by train, as in our country during the time of the speculators[20] or during the demobilization of the old army. Engineers were forced to proceed on the red signal. Two crashes occurred and one armored train was lost. The army retreated without its officers who were busy with their own personal affairs. The soldiers robbed the people and fed themselves on their account."

They retreated from Kalgan in order but afterwards even among the Kalgan troops panic set in. Here is what one of our comrades who saw this retreat said. "The withdrawal from Fengchen-Pingtichüan in the second half of August 1926 produced an awful impression. Along the road and for a ten-kilometer strip along it was an unbroken stream of retreating soldiers. The plunder of the people was shameless. There were many senseless shootings. Soldiers seized animals and rode off in all directions. A part of the soldiers and officers rode in the direction of the enemy. The Northwest Army ceased. to exist, it fell apart in a matter of days. The same was true of the units of the Second and Third Nationalist Armies. The interpreter Vasilev saved an old woman whom soldiers had beaten up, demanding flour. Her son had fled, her fourteen-year-old granddaughter had been raped, everything in her house had been pillaged. The peasants had armed themselves and attacked the soldiers."

---

20. This refers to the speculators of the NEP period in Soviet Russia. Translator

A raid had been carried out on the advisers' stables. The soldiers and the officers who tried to seize the horses evidently belonged to the Northwest Army. During the attack General Ivanov-Rinov was wounded. His interpreter Kosachev died from a stomach wound. A Chinese stablehand was also wounded. The advisers were actually thrown to the mercy of fate. A car was provided for the wounded and for dying Kosachev only when the chief of staff of the Kalgan mission, Lapin, firmly presented this problem to Chang Chih-chiang. The adviser Marino reported that he would go on foot.

Retreat to the Northwest

During this difficult time our advisers led lives filled with deprivation and danger, but in return they achieved the long awaited opportunity of dealing directly with the people and the soldiers. They were struck by the fact that in several villages which lay along the line of retreat no one had heard anything about Sun Yat-sen, the Kuomintang, or the revolution in Russia. It turned out that even many officers were completely ignorant. One of them said, for example, that the Kuomintang was an army which Sun Yat-sen's wife commanded after his death. This army was fighting "against all kinds of villains" somewhere in Yunnan. They took the advisers for missionaries.

Some of our comrades kept notes. The extraordinarily interesting diary of Korneev has been preserved in part. Reading it, one is impressed by what a patient, profound, and many-sided researcher Korneev was. His notes along with material which the other advisers collected could have been the basis of a most interesting book. But in those years no one thought of that and by now most of the notes are irrevocably lost and the authors themselves with rare exceptions have left us forever. Few of them survived the repressions of 1937-1938. The war finished off the others.

The advisers traveled with the army through the back districts of interior China. It seemed as if no foreigner had ever set foot there. And yet they met missionaries of every nationality — Americans, Dutch, Spanish, Italian, French. The success of missionary activity was insignificant — one or two families converted a year. But this did not grieve them in the least. Their main goal was by no means the conversion of the heathen.

The mission buildings surrounded by walls reminded one of fortresses. At the same time they were something like landowners' estates with cultivated groves and innumerable outbuildings. The missionaries had much land and rented it out primarily to Christians, luring souls in this way through completely non-spiritual means. At one place the advisers observed a peculiar peasant strike. Driven to desperation, the inhabitants of one village appeared at the district office and handed over to the chief their agricultural tools. Such actions on the part of the population which was bound to pay its taxes and support the authorities was looked upon as mutiny. The district head summoned troops and ordered them to fire upon the "mutineers."

The advisers recorded with sorrow that while service to the National-Revolutionary Army was considered a patriotic duty in the South and coolies undertook it of their own free will, in the Northwest Army they were recruited by force and without any payment. Sometimes they were not even fed, although the bearers and the bargehaulers occasionally were in mortal danger, especially in the gorges of the upper Huang Ho where there were many rapids and waterfalls. Everyone who could tried to run away. Thus did the First Nationalist Army change together with its name.

Finding themselves in the remote northwest districts far from any railways, our comrades felt cut off from the world. Communication among them was extremely difficult, and letters from home took months to arrive. Even the Peking newspapers took several weeks and one could not rely upon the information in the local press which printed the most improbable nonsense. Thus, in April 1927 after Chiang Kai-shek's coup, the Sian paper wrote that Chiang Kai-shek had shot Borodin's wife, nineteen Russian advisers and forty-three Kuomintang leftists. However, the central Chinese press also printed a lot of nonsense then.

The advisers were placed in difficult conditions; they had poor food, walked about in shabby clothes and were deprived of medical attention. They were constantly threatened by the danger of attacks by *t'u fei* who kidnapped people for the sake of ransom and who cruelly tortured their prisoners. An unhealthy situation developed in the army itself. It was located in a poor area while the Second and Third Nationalist Armies located in the more fertile and densely populated province of Shensi did not want to share their provisions with it. The absence of centralized authority rendered the rational exploitation of local resources impossible. The generals fell out among themselves.

The Fifth Nationalist Army

Until now the reader has been acquainted with only the First, Second and Third Nationalist Armies and Kuo Sung-ling's Fourth Nationalist Army. However, in March 1926 the Fifth Nationalist Army under the Honanese General Fang Cheng-wu joined Feng Yü-hsiang's group. Its chief adviser was Korneev.

General Fang Cheng-wu was a Kuomintang member and previously had served with the troops of the South Chinese government. But in the autumn of 1924 during the second Northern Expedition he abandoned his allegiance to Sun Yat-sen and on his own decision went home to Honan.

I heard many curious things about this Kuomintang member who deserted with his troops in the very heat of battle. Here I want to tell about his army and the man himself according to Korneev's description of them.

Korneev noted in Fang Cheng-wu the tendency to decide everything by himself, distrust in his subordinates' initiatives, inability to bind them to himself, despotism. The Fifth Army fought in the old style; they took the enemy by surprise. Sometimes a regimental commander would blindly open fire and be satisfied with that — now the enemy won't show himself, he knows what we've got.

During retreat Fang Cheng-wu's army was also in desperate straits. Not receiving any support it had to "feed on" the locality, although in a number of districts the enemy had already collected taxes for five or six years in advance. He levied a large contribution on the occupied cities and villages; for example, he demanded ten thousand yuan in silver from the little town of Kushih. All night, shouting and cursing, the district chief collected this sum and in fact came up with twelve thousand yuan (and perhaps even more, who knows.)

Things did not stop with official requisitions. The advisers were witnesses to real pillaging and violence against the peaceful population. Korneev saw how the soldiers of the Fifth Nationalist Army robbed the inhabitants of one village, discharging their weapons in the process. Before his eyes a desperate peasant with a young son threw himself into a well.

On the demand of the advisers the leaders of the Fifth Nationalist Army severely punished the guilty soldiers. However, the measures by which Fang Cheng-wu tried to impose military discipline grated not only upon the advisers but on his subordinates as well. For stealing civilian clothing one commander had his ears cut off. This provoked rumblings of discontent in the army. It was said that it would have been better to have shot him. There was a case when the commander hit a brigade commander in front of everyone.

Korneev related how depressed he was by the trial of a company commander who had insulted the chairman of the tribunal which was discussing the question of the theft of civilians' horses by soldiers of his company. The commander servilely fell on his knees, his hands were tied, and he was interrogated in that position. The instruments of punishment were prepared — a stick and a long needle with a pennant inscribed "punishment." He was beaten on the palms with the stick for a long time and the needle was thrust into the external cartilage of his ear.

Squabbles were always in evidence among the generals of the Fifth Nationalist Army; the slightest trifle could lead to a clash. An argument concerning the yamen[21] in the district city Weinan (one commander affixed a paper saying it was occupied, and another came and took it over) took the form of armed conflict. In an instant the huge Chinese sabres flew out of their scabbards as the advisers looked on.

Fang Cheng-wu had the reputation of being a liberal general and a Kuomintang member. He tried to maintain the forms of democracy, only he understood them in his own way. Here are several examples. After occupying the city of Yinghsiang in Shensi, Fang Cheng-wu personally drew up a draft for the organization of a municipal executive committee on the Kuomintang model. The administration was entrusted to a five-man committee, but they were all wealthy men, the poor were not taken into account. In the city of Kushih he didn't want to have an elected district chief for fear that an elected official would not collect the taxes.

---

21. Yamen — an official government office.

Fang Cheng-wu behaved better to the advisers than any other general with the exception of Feng Yü-hsiang, but he was terribly afraid of political activity. Therefore it suffered at his hands. Here are some examples. After returning to China, on the suggestion of his advisers, Feng Yü-hsiang decided to conduct political work in the army and among the people, in the first place to explain the causes of the retreat from Nankow which weighed so heavily on the people's shoulders. The suggestion was to indicate that the main reason was the lack of clarity in the political line of the Nationalist Army at that period, and the resultant lack of mass support. They wanted to explain the necessity for reorganization of the army, organizing the masses and entry into the Kuomintang. However, characteristically, the propaganda campaign in the Fifth Army led to reproaches that "the people had not helped."

The second anniversary of Sun Yat-sen's death (March 12, 1927) which was widely observed all over China, went by almost unmarked in the Fifth Nationalist Army. Only in the staff club did delegates from the units gather and there was not a single common soldier among them. Korneev gave a speech about Sun Yat-sen and his teachings. Here is how the so-called wild generals who belonged to no faction came to join Fang Cheng-wu's army, according to Korneev.

"The regiment of General Ma Lao-chü stationed in the cities of Kushih and Hsiaoyingchen didn't want to fight any more. Negotiations began. They agreed to join us, they opened the gates but allowed no one to enter. Then General Ma himself came and surrendered. They kept their weapons. Fang Cheng-wu entered the city and made a speech to the soldiers. We advisers had to stand in a crowd of soldiers who had just surrendered — eight hundred men armed with rifles and grenades — without the slightest precautions having been taken. Troops armed with Mausers and carrying light machine guns, Fang Cheng-wu's guard, followed him and went to the midst of the crowd. In his speech Fang Cheng-wu said not a word about the national revolution, imperialism, the Kuomintang or submission to the national government."

Such was Fang Cheng-wu, "the general from Canton."

Feng Yü-hsiang's Return. The New Course

Feng Yü-hsiang returned to China at a difficult period in the life of his army. The troops of the Northwest Army were continuing their disorderly retreat. The bulk of them were concentrated in the Paotow-Suiyuan region.

With Feng Yü-hsiang's arrival the situation changed at once. He returned as the representative of the Kuomintang in the northwest, commander of the northwest group of the National-Revolutionary Army and a member of the Kuomintang government. This is how he presented himself at the Supreme Command Headquarters in Wuyüan when he arrived from Ulan Bator. Feng Yü-hsiang called together his comrades-in-arms under the banner of the Kuomintang and proclaimed a "new course." The army again acquired the political orientation which it had lost in his absence.

A large group of Chinese Communists who were returning from Germany via Moscow arrived together with Feng Yü-hsiang.

At the beginning of October the marshal arrived in Paotow where a triumphal reception was arranged for him. Forty thousand soldiers stood lined up along the road. Innumerable delegations from public organizations were there too. There was general exultation. In Paotow enormous activity commenced at once. Communists, Kuomintang members, trade union workers, students, all joined in. They gave speeches to the soldiers and officers about the special features of the Chinese revolution, the tasks of the Kuomintang, the international situation and the alliance between the Kuomintang and the Chinese Communist party. Intensified work on mass organizing began. Feng Yü-hsiang himself spoke at innumerable meetings before soldiers and the civilian population. He enthusiastically related what he had seen in the Soviet Union. His soldiers wore Kuomintang armbands on their sleeves. Throughout the entire territory east of Suiyuan red Kuomintang flags fluttered in place of the former five-colored ones. The October Plenum of the Kuomintang CEC sent Feng Yü-hsiang a welcoming telegram.

Feng Yü-hsiang solved the problem of Kuomintangizing his army very simply: he gave an order for a mass entry into the Kuomintang, and in two or three months he had forty thousand "Kuomintang members" in the army. From among his generals only Chang Chih-chiang failed to declare his allegiance to the Kuomintang. This old hypocrite addressed a petition to

Feng Yü-hsiang asking "to preserve the army's former Christian character."

Corporal punishment was abolished. The troops saluted their officers with the words "We serve the revolution!" The soldiers began to learn the Three People's Principles of Sun Yat-sen. They understood them poorly but they mouthed them diligently as they had the Christian prayers previously.

For the advisers the most responsible period of their stay in Feng Yü-hsiang's army had begun. Their chief task became propaganda for unconditional submission to the national government. The chief of staff of the Kalgan mission, Lapin, worked up a plan for political work in the Nationalist armies, and submitted a proposal to convoke army conferences of Kuomintang members and their sympathizers.

The army's amateur performances became widespread. This method of agitation and propaganda played an especially important role under the conditions of almost total illiteracy. It didn't take long to search for performers. Chinese in general are great theatregoers and there is not a single national holiday without a performance. The troops were lined up in a large rectangle, a stage was set up in the center and the performance began. Men played the women's parts. All kinds of plays were presented concerning everyday life as well as politics. On the stage an imperialist in a top hat shook a stick and threatened a worker or peasant. A young Kuomintang member carrying a banner would come to their aid. A landowner would take away a peasant's entire family for payment of a debt, "women" wailed very convincingly evoking the audience's sympathy. The National-Revolutionary Army arrived and the landlord fled, holding the skirts of his robe. Plays of a genre much loved in China — the pantomime — were also presented.

The reorganization of the army proceeded swiftly, the advisers worked selflessly, and very soon Feng Yü-hsiang had a one-hundred-thousand-man United Nationalist Army (seven corps) which could come to the aid of Sian (as related above).

Our comrades told us what a terrible situation they had found in the city — ruins, desolation, silence, everywhere the corpses of those who had starved to death, stench. The city was enormous but it was as if abandoned. The inhabitants were emaciated and could barely walk. The soldiers too were pale and thin, but the wealthy and the supreme military staff looked as if nothing had happened. During the last two months of the siege, the ones who stayed alive ate the oilcakes from the oil pressing factory. Otherwise the whole population would have died. The dogs and the cats had been eaten long ago.

At the suggestion of the advisers days of donated labor were instituted in Sian in which the generals took part along with the soldiers. The marshal personally lifted a scoop, shovel, and a broom, carted loads of stone and manure and buried the dead. Photos have been preserved depicting Feng Yü-hsiang holding a huge broom.

The imperialist press, impressed by the transformation as it seemed of completely demoralized troops into a strong, battleworthy army, wrote a great deal about the marshal's personal authority and his organizational skills. Feng Yü-hsiang was truly a talented military leader who exerted an enormous influence on his soldiers. However, the remarkable transformation wrought in his army was due in the first instance to the political position which he occupied after his return. It is impossible to forget at what an important historic moment this occurred. The Kuomintang army under whose banner Feng had come was claiming one victory after another in central China. At the beginning of September all of Hunan was liberated and Wuchang was beseiged. Beneath its walls the troops of Feng Yü-hsiang's inveterate enemy, Wu P'ei-fu, were utterly routed. And most of all, the sympathy of all the progressive forces in China was on the side of the National-Revolutionary Army. Hope for liberation from foreign imperialism and emancipation from the survivals of feudal relations were bound up with its victories. The enthusiasm of Feng Yü-hsiang's army which had joined the ranks of the National-Revolutionary troops was quite understandable.

Feng Yü-hsiang conducted himself like a Kuomintang leftist, sent off telegrams about the organization of peasant leagues, called for struggle to raise workers' wages, published a manifesto where the demand for China's national independence was put forth, and guaranteed freedom of speech and of the press. Somewhat later the marshal issued a decree prohibiting soldiers from squeezing money from the population and the army from intervening in civil affairs. In the city of Changwu on the Shensi-Kansu border he executed three commanders from the Third Nationalist Army whose brutality had provoked the Red Spear uprising.

Not everywhere were the new trends taken seriously. The work which had begun for the purpose of organizing peasant leagues was frustrated by local authorities. It is well-known, for example, that in the beginning of January 1927 the head of a district in Sian lashed out at peasants who dared to speak at a peasant meeting. The same man extorted taxes from the population. Chang Chih-chiang who was in the city at the time did not even think of interfering. Fang Cheng-wu, who considered himself the most leftist of the generals, sabotaged Feng Yü-hsiang's orders about the organization of peasant leagues, deeming them dangerous, forbade any discussion on political topics and calmly continued to collect taxes. He could not have acted otherwise since, as before, he didn't receive any money from other sources.

Representatives of the Kuomintang CEC, Generals Li Lieh-chün and Yü Yu-jen, were attached to Feng Yü-hsiang's army.

Despite all its successes Feng Yü-hsiang's army once more had to experience the shame of a disorganized retreat. While preparing for a campaign in central China to link up with the National-Revolutionary Army the leadership slackened its attention on the northeast flank. Taking advantage of this, Yen Hsi-shan struck Feng Yü-hsiang a serious blow. In December 1926-January 1927 the army had to retreat from Paotow and Wuyüan.

What had occurred near Nankow was repeated but on a smaller scale. The senior leadership went ahead providing transport for themselves. Discipline was again forgotten. The soldiers flung the loads from the horses and camels and themselves mounted the animals. The sides of the road were littered with crates of military materials, sanitary supplies, etc. Automobiles were discarded for lack of gasoline, sometimes horses were hitched to them. Fighting leading even to shootings broke out between the soldiers. Even large units like the Second Corps and the Fourth Brigade had to be disarmed. The troops moved through a loess plain, the dust hung in an endless hazy curtain for several kilometers; after half an hour people became literally unrecognizable. Motors could not operate in such dust.

Again there was regrouping and reorganization, and by March 1927 Feng Yü-hsiang's army was again ready to embark on a campaign against the troops of Chang Tso-lin and Wu P'ei-fu, this time in Honan. There Feng Yü-hsiang was supposed to link up with the troops of the South China government which by this time had moved to Wuhan, and to take part in the Northern Expedition. In order to avoid repetition I shall speak of Feng Yü-hsiang's role in this campaign at a different place.

In the autumn of 1927 the Chinese Revolution suffered a temporary setback. From the end of June 1927 a campaign against Communists and Kuomintang leftists began in the northwest. The Northwest Bureau of the Kuomintang and the provincial committees in Shensi, Kansu, and Honan were chosen anew. Everywhere the rightists triumphed. An order to punish Communists in the event of closed or secret meetings was issued. Strict censorship was established over the Communist newspaper in Sian and the editor had to flee because he was threatened with arrest. Unauthorized peasant actions against the landlords and the *shenshih* were forbidden under threat of shooting; the peasant leagues were dissolved.

Still I want to emphasize that in the territory under Feng Yü-hsiang's control there was never a White terror as terrible as that in all the other Chinese provinces. He relieved and expelled Communists but he never sentenced them to death. He did not detain M.M. Borodin who passed through his zone in August 1927 on his way to Moscow although he received an order to do so from Wuhan to which he was subordinate. Feng Yü-hsiang obviously was avoiding a decisive rupture with the Communist party and the Soviet Union. In the summer of 1927 in Shensi the heavy reserves of the revolution – the peasant masses – had already joined the revolutionary movement. But Feng Yü-hsiang could not bring himself to support the agrarian revolution.

At the end of 1927 the Kalgan mission of our advisers ceased to exist.

Chapter IV

TO WORK IN CANTON

On the Road to Shanghai. Nechaevites.

In the beginning of February 1926, I and two other interpreters, A. P. Rogachev and V. I. Melnikov, left Peking for Canton.

As far as Tientsin, just a few hours by rail, the coaches were unreserved and overcrowded. Through the windows the gloomy seasonal landscape stretched out, yellow loess plains, and the same yellow clay *fangtz*. Still the impression produced was much livelier than that in the Kalgan region, primarily because there were many more people here. We were riding through the densely populated North China lowlands.

On the stations there were crowds of men and women dressed in padded jackets and cotton trousers varying in color from dark to light blue depending on the length of service they had seen. Food sellers walked beneath the coach windows; they offered dumplings, chickens cooked with red pepper so that they turned quite orange, and sugared fruit on sticks. Old men and woman, pipes in hand, sat on their haunches against the walls. The pipes with their tiny bowls at the end are good for only one or two puffs after which one has to reach for the tobacco pouch again.

One is struck by the expression of calm dignity on the faces of the smokers. In China old age means that one has a right to be treated with respect. Even the most wretched old beggar, despite his rags, still has something special in his bearing, a kind of solemn sorrow for his undeserved unhappiness.

Having arrived in Tientsin and gotten a room in a hotel, we did not at once notice that something unusual was going on in town. Shouts and some sort of singing began to reach our third floor window. With a glance at the street we understood what the matter was. White Guards were carrying on there, celebrating the forthcoming arrival of Chang Tso-lin. Drunk and dressed in Chang Tso-lin's uniforms, they marched in small groups, shouting out threats and curses against the Soviet Union. "String the Bolsheviks up!" howled one of them.

The frightened attendant came to tell us that it would be better for us not to go out right now. My traveling companions looked worried. I knew that they were primarily troubled by the fact that a woman was with them. Melnikov even said, "Don't be alarmed, in case anything happens we can get away over the roofs." Late in the evening we succeeded in getting through to the consulate. They promised to get us tickets on a boat to Talien so as not to attract any attention.

At one in the morning we were already in a small cabin, for which the calculating management had sold three tickets by counting in a small divan as the third berth. We decided to eat without leaving the cabin. We had not far to go and could be patient.

We arrived in Talien at night. Rain and wind, wet warehouses and a dirty, uncomfortable pier. We spent about a day there but didn't see the town; we weren't up to it. I returned to this region only after twenty years and recalled our quick visit after looking at the familiar facade of the Yamato Hotel.

The only thing remaining in my memory is the hotel's large dining room in which young Japanese girls in national costume worked as waitresses. They all spoke Russian rather well although with thick accents. After all Talien had a large Russian population even before the wave of White emigrés swept over it. After Japan's defeat in 1945 in this same hotel our military personnel heard young Japanese girls, by now dressed in European dresses and speaking without accents, sing such songs as the foxtrot "Uncle Vanya, good and handsome."

We could not wait to leave this city where there were also White Guards celebrating Chang Tso-lin's victories. Therefore we didn't wait to get good tickets, but agreed without hesitation to sail in the hold of a Japanese vessel bound for Shanghai.

Onloading of cargo began late at night. The hold of a Japanese vessel is well adapted for carrying passengers. It is entirely divided into cubicles about six to seven meters square surrounded by a low barrier. The floor is covered with clean mats. The effect is quite cozy. Whole families of Japanese install themselves in these cells. But on that occasion we met few Japanese in the hold. The larger part of it was empty, in some places there were groups of women speaking Russian. These were White emigrés headed for Bulgaria via Shanghai.

We had already settled in to sleep when suddenly, about five minutes before sailing, dozens of feet thundered above our heads, the clamor of many voices resounded, and a crowd of men in motley dress burst into the hold, carrying parcels and suitcases. Several older men in tsarist officer uniforms were giving orders in Russian. It was crystal clear. White Guards.

Their behavior was very free and easy. They quickly took places and put away their things. Except for the commanders, they were all young, beardless youths. One of them reminded me very much of my kid brother in Moscow since his build was about the same. My heart began to ache. I wanted to say "What are you laughing at, why are you so happy? They have deceived you, they are leading you to the slaughter." So it turned out later on. These were reinforcements being sent from Harbin to Tsingtao, comrades-in-arms of Nechaev. A year later the Nechaevites were sent into battle against the troops taking part in the Northern Expedition in Honan. The Chinese soldiers, who always showed contempt and hatred for the White Guards serving in Chang Tsung-ch'ang's army for being hirelings without honour or conscience, treated them mercilessly. They took almost no prisoners and if they took any they mocked them cruelly. Akimov said that about ten prisoners from Nechaev's ranks were brought to him once—they were being led on wire strung through their ears.

Melnikov, a native of Harbin, was the first to feel that he had better go away. He said nothing to me of this and I did not notice his absence right away. Then came Rogachev's turn. I remained alone. I no longer felt like sleeping; I began to look over my new traveling companions.

What impelled them to join up—unemployment, a thirst for adventures, hatred towards the revolutionary movement which innumerable White emigré organizations carefully nurtured? It was clear that they were going willingly, that the anti-Soviet speeches of their superiors fitted their frame of mind. But still . . .

A quarrel flared up in one of the cubicles. A thin, youthful voice sounded off, "You officer's snout . . . " At once the din of voices covered both the juvenile outburst and the coarse swearing which came in reply.

An elderly officer took a seat in the adjoining cubicle where the women were sitting. He had long, hanging mustaches and a thick, apoplectic neck. Clearly, he was no stranger to them.

"What happened?" they asked him.

"Some childish nonsense. He insulted an officer," the military man said in his bass voice, panting from indignation. "What's the use of it? Discipline is the prime thing. No, for such things, overboard with him!"

"What are you saying! How is that possible?" said the women affectedly, flattered that they were entrusted with such important considerations.

"Yes, overboard with him without fail," fumed the officer, but I saw that he was saying this only to show off before the ladies.

"Take us for example, we . . . " he continued wiping his wet bald spot, "you know we are supported by Her Excellency the Empress Maria Fyoderovna. She's worth ten billion. Did you know that? Well, and just look how well we live. Here we are traveling about. Can you call this bad? When we get to Tsingtao if we want to we'll drop into a restaurant. We can do anything . . . "

Chronic need and hopelessness sounded in his desire to convince the ladies and himself too that life wasn't bad for him at all. Such talk sounded especially comical in the hold, designated for passengers of the lowest sort.

He stood up and again turned to his wards. But the women began to bustle about and to whisper; they opened their bundles and took out some kind of rag, hung it up to form a screen and began to undress. When the rag was taken down it was revealed that the youngest had changed her dark dress for a white one made of some sort of cheap, very poorly sewn material. It really made her look ugly and seemed especially absurd at this time of the year, but a happy expression appeared on her worn-out, pitiful face.

I began to get worried at the prolonged absence of my traveling companions. Somewhat later I found them both in the second-class lounge. They did not intend to go below, and they had good reason. "They'll kill me at night and they'll throw me in the water," said Melnikov. "Many of those in the hold know me. How many times have we Komsomols fought with them. How many times have I poked them one in the mug." One of the officers, for no reason at all, began staring at Rogachev. He was smashing drunk and it seemed to him that everyone was spying on him. So he said to Rogachev, "If I see you once more, it's overboard with you."

It was a rough night. Both the officers and the new recruits had all drunk too much. The same kind of drunken, confused day dawned. This one slept, that one bawled out songs, there were several fights. The fat officer visiting the ladies next door again repeated, "overboard with them, overboard." But now, it seemed, even they no longer believed that he had resolved upon so extreme a measure. The air was close and stifling, heavy with the smell of winey exhalations and human sweat. Towards evening I fell asleep and when

I awoke the hold was empty and the engines had stopped. My traveling companions were next to me. We were in Tsingtao.

This city, situated on the southeastern part of Shantung, was known as a superb beach resort and was one of the centers of the Japanese textile industry in China. It was right there that the strike in the Japanese textile mills which later spread to Shanghai and served as the beginning of the May 30 Movement flared up.

Tsingtao was inundated with cheap Japanese goods. The Chinese economy was unable to compete. The Japanese even brought over fruit. My comrades went down to the pier and brought back a small box. Inside were Japanese tangerines not of very good quality but very cheap. Fruit brought from abroad—oranges from Canada, tangerines and apples from Japan—were being sold in China, a country of the most skilled and widespread agriculture.

In Tsingtao we switched to second class. My cabin mates were two Russian emigrés. One of them jabbered away fluently in English; she worked as a sales-lady in a large English store in Shanghai. The other one, a very young girl who lived in Tsingtao, knew only a few words of English although she had just married an Englishman, a naval officer. They hadn't been able to get a separate cabin, and they traveled apart. Therefore he was a frequent visitor to our cabin. It was interesting to observe them together. They looked at each other and said not a word, only she tenderly cooed, "Ro-o." It seems that this was his diminutive name.

Afterwards I was told that the influx of Russian refugees had shaken the family foundations in the foreign settlement in China. A number of people got divorced in order to marry Russians. Some of the emigré women made dazzling careers. But these were exceptional cases. Most of the emigré women descended to the very depths. Work as a bar-maid or a waitress in a bar among drunken, diverse people was not the worst fate which awaited them. Houses of prostitution sprung up like mushrooms and Russians formed the basic contingent within them. In Peking I had already been shown a many-storied building of remarkably monotonous architecture, the walls from top to bottom were densely dotted with small windows each covered by a canvas awning. This was one of the largest pleasure houses where the entrepreneurs extorted enormous sums of money. Some of the women had their families there. And at times when the wife was called away to a separate room, the husband—a musician or waiter—had to serve the gay company.

The International Settlement

At the pier in Shanghai we had trouble making ourselves understood to the driver sitting on his box—Peking dialect turned out to be unsuited there. A passing Englishman noticed our difficulty and came up offering to help us. When we politely thanked him and refused, he said suddenly that white people in this accursed China ought to help each other, that all the cab drivers there were swindlers and one needn't give them much money. The most one should give them was . . . he named a very paltry sum.

When we left Peking someone jokingly told us that we would not get lost in Shanghai since the Russian language had full citizenship rights there, only with the "yat'," theta and the hard sign.[1]

The reader can easily imagine our astonishment when on one of the main streets of the International Settlement we came face to face with an enormous red-bearded Cossack with striped trousers, shoulder straps and tsarist medals all over his chest, rewarded probably for some "pacification." Later on we were no longer surprised; we didn't even glance around when we saw a tsarist general in full dress.

Through inexperience we stayed at the Palace Hotel on Nanking Road which was considered the aristocrat among its confreres by virtue of its respectable age. It was very expensive despite its unattractive exterior, old-fashioned fixtures, and dark, uncomfortable rooms.

Those of us who had lived in the Central Hotel were already familiar with the specialties of local English cuisine. A grand breakfast awaited us in the morning—watery oatmeal, beefsteaks, a two-egg omelette, coffee or tea with sandwiches, and fruit was obligatory. Lunch and dinner would have been very ordinary from our point of view if they hadn't consisted of ten dishes, but just a bite of each one.

We spent a week in Shanghai waiting for a Russian boat. Because of the anti-British boycott English ships were not sailing to Canton and there would have been no sense in going to Hong Kong. We wouldn't even have been sold tickets. The ships of other nations sailed for Canton only rarely and irregularly.

On the first day we dropped by our consulate to see our friends, the student interpreters.

---

1. Russian orthographic signs dropped after the Bolshevik revolution in the linguistic reform. Translator.

Most of the foreign consulates were situated on Huang Pu Street along the banks of the river of the same name. Next to the Japanese consulate and across the street from the Astor House Hotel stood an imposing, four-storey building, completed by the tsarist consul towards the end of the First World War and acquired by us in brand new condition. The windows on the first floor were covered with massive iron grates. This preventative measure came in handy. The Shanghai White Guard community often attacked the building, enjoying the non-interference of the British police. Embassy employees and their families had to drive the attackers off unaided.

Our comrades, the China specialists, promised to introduce us to the Shanghai White emigré youth who had received Soviet passports and even become Komsomol members. We really did get to meet them. Later I saw one of these girls in a big Shanghai department store where she worked as a salesgirl.

The misadventures of one of our students for whom English had never come easy provoked a lot of laughter. Once he was very happy when he saw what from his point of view looked like an extraordinarily democratic sign in a cinema: "No smoking." He took this as a prohibition on coming there in smoking jackets while it meant only that cigarette smoking was not permitted. Another time he had to do some explaining to a policeman when in a café he asked for his favorite ice cream "American girl" but forgot to add the word ice cream and was taken literally.

We were advised in the consulate to move to furnished rooms let by the Russian emigré Tarasov on Bubbling Well Road. No one but our comrades stayed there. This fact was well-known to the police, and there was always some White emigré keeping watch on the opposite corner.

Shanghai looked not at all as it does now. It had only a half-million inhabitants. The Chinese part of the city was ill-constructed, sunk in dirt, and generally struck one in contrast to the foreign settlement. But even then the port of Shanghai was one of the largest in the world. Its enormous roadstead daily sheltered one hundred ocean-going ships. It was divided into numbered quadrangles without which finding the ship one wanted would have been an impossibly difficult matter. The wharves and warehouses stretched out for many kilometers.

After leaving the consulate we walked along the embankment, crossed an iron bridge across the Soochow River and came out on a little public garden. This garden was of the most common sort both in its size and its pitiful facade, but even this, it seemed, was too good for the Chinese. On the fence we read a sign, "Only for foreigners" and next to it another, "No dogs allowed." A nice juxtaposition!

In this district were concentrated the most monumental of the city's buildings, the buildings of the banks and firms whose names were inseparable from the history of China's enslavement by foreign capital. This was the Shanghai equivalent of the City.

The towering, many-storied buildings faced with varicolored marble, glittering with glass and highly polished copper conceitedly rivaled each other in luxury and sullen haughtiness, and demonstrated the strength of foreign metropoles on Chinese soil. The narrow streets between them were dark and deep like wells.

This was the beginning of the main street in the International Settlement—Nanking Road—where the mass demonstrations were most often held and where on May 30, 1925, British imperialism committed a crime which has called forth so many important political events in China.

We strolled about the city for a long time and came across Fukiang Street with its pleasure houses. On the pavement lined up in two rows stood girls in excessively wide trousers and short jackets made of expensive, very thick, bright-colored patterned brocade. Their heads were uncovered, their coiffures were girlish—bangs and braids tightly fastened with colored silk thread on the top of the head and at the ends. They were all young but excessively made-up. Behind each one stood an elderly amah.[2] These girls were songstresses of the lowest ranks. Those of higher rank sat at home and came only on call (there were special papers with their addresses). They also went nowhere without their elderly companions. Usually these were not servants but proprietresses who cruelly exploited the girls. From curiosity we dropped into a Chinese restaurant and choosing a fanciful name from the paper (something like Moon Orchid) told the waiter that we wanted to listen to the girl's singing. She came quickly. She was a small, shy girl accompanied by her inseparable old woman.

---

2. This is the term for female servants in South China.

She was rouged like an operatic heroine, a broad pink stripe went across her cheeks and on her eyelids, her chin and forehead were whitened. She held a stringed instrument in her hands and very sweetly she sang several folk songs and popular operatic arias in her thin, weak voice. We got to talking. Alas, the frail songstress plied not only the musician's trade, she had also to receive guests.

Several days later we discovered an entire Russian city in Shanghai—Avenue Joffre in the French Concession. The sounds of Russian came from every corner, from stores and windows of the houses. Passersby spoke loudly in Russian and on the pavement, cursing in unprintable oaths, lay drunkards just like in the old days in Russia. Here was the center of the White emigrés.

In this part of town films on "Russian" themes were often shown. We wanted to see the picture *From the White Eagle to the Red Banner*, the film version of General Krasnov's novel of the same name which was very popular among the emigrés. However, we were unsuccessful. The management decided to show a newsreel before the film. When Nicholas II appeared on the screen amid the black stripes of "rain" on the old film, something indescribable happened in the hall. The audience howled, stamped its feet and applauded. Someone demanded that the orchestra play the tsarist anthem. The conductor hesitated. Then amid the general uproar an angry young voice was heard, "Why won't you play it? What's the matter?" The audience already began to rise and if we had not stood up at the strains of the anthem, we would probably have been assaulted. We hurriedly left the hall.

The youth who asked for the tsarist anthem to be played was no more than sixteen or seventeen to judge from his voice. In his thirsty desire to hear his national anthem—he knew no other having been taken abroad as a child—resounded a passionate longing for his homeland, the tragedy of a young soul suffocating on foreign soil. Yet he was the most ferocious enemy of his motherland. Young, deceived and enthused with a false understanding of patriotic feeling, he would gladly have enlisted to kill Russians and set our cities and villages to the torch. People like him were ready for any kind of anti-Soviet activity—espionage, sabotage, provocations.

Here is another picture on the same theme. Once on Nanking road we suddenly heard a Russian folk song. A chorus of strong masculine voices pleasantly and gaily was singing, "Soar up falcons, like eagles, enough of grieving." A company recruited from Russian White emigrés for the English police force of the International Settlement was marching along. They were tall, well-built lads with typical Russian faces, dressed in unusually cut khaki uniforms. How painful it was to see features of the Russian character in them, something bold and sweeping. How insulting it was to realize that the imperialists had recruited them for the dirtiest and basest work—arresting Chinese revolutionaries and beating them up, breaking up workers' meetings, shooting demonstrators and engaging in political investigations.

Further Southward

From Shanghai to Canton we sailed on the *Mengkuhai*, a small ship of the Soviet commercial fleet which made regular trips between Vladivostok and Canton.[3] In the future it called on Canton more than once and its crew always paid us a visit. The little ship was permeated with the smell of smoked fish. We were given a small, cramped cabin with six berths. The strong pitching and the stifling smell of fish spoiled all the charm of the passage.

We were not the only persons who were traveling to join the South China mission. On the trip we became acquainted with the aviation mechanic Kobyakov, the air adviser Uger (Remi), the wives of the advisers Gorev (Nikitin) and Remizyuk (Veri). Of them only Uger, who was returning from an assignment, was an old-timer, the others like us had never before been in Canton.

Gorev's wife was traveling with her small son. She was short, with a masculine hairdo, and in her voice and mannerisms there was something unfeminine, coarsely decisive. From conversations with others we learned that Liza Goreva was a remarkable person. During the revolution, while still quite a young girl, she put on a Red Army greatcoat and didn't take it off until the end of the civil war. Conditions beyond the endurance of her sex and her size undermined her health. She was often ill.

On the way our ship stopped at the Fukienese port of Amoy. We went ashore and visited the Soviet consulate. It was the rainy season and Amoy, which is a picturesque nook in sunny weather, seemed raw and gloomy to us.

---

3. This ship had an interesting biography. In 1922 Glebov's White Guard detachment, retreating from Vladivostok, sailed it to Shanghai. Two years later in the presence of the Soviet consul in Shanghai, the ship's crew raised the Soviet flag over it, and returned to the home land.

The wet banana trees sadly rustled their enormous, torn leaves. The mood of the consular employees was sullen, reflecting the weather.

In the region of Shant'ou (Swatow) we crossed the Tropic of Cancer.

Chapter V

IN THE REVOLUTIONARY SOUTH

Sun Yat-sen and Russian Advisers

While our *Mengkuhai* is plunging in the tall, foam-covered waves of the South China Sea, where at this time of the year the weather is always windy and gloomy, I can unhurriedly and calmly tell about the situation which awaited us in Canton. This is all the more necessary since we arrived there during an extremely critical moment, the eve of the well-known March 20, 1926 Incident—Chiang Kai-shek's first attempt to pull off a counter-revolutionary coup. These events stunned us novices who had still not gotten the hang of local affairs. The harsh measures against Communists and members of the strike committee, the purge in the army, the five-hour arrest ordered by Chiang Kai-shek in the offices and homes of our advisers—all this indicated that reaction was raising its head in Canton too. But let us begin from the beginning.

Some two to three weeks before our arrival the Soviet ship *Pamyat Lenina* carried Mikhail Markovich Borodin on a direct route to Tientsin. The high political adviser to the Kuomintang government and the Kuomintang CEC was headed for a rest in the USSR after two and a half years of work in Canton. On the way to Moscow Borodin wanted to meet with Marshal Feng Yü-hsiang. The reader already knows that the meeting took place but without results. Feng Yü-hsiang put down his arms and refused to continue the struggle.

Borodin would hardly have left if he had known what events would come to pass in his absence. But the situation in South China at the beginning of 1926 had become stabilized, the position of the revolution had been strengthened. At the Second Kuomintang Congress which was held in the first half of January the left Kuomintang faction and the Communists gained a great victory.

In Kwangtung the Lenin memorial days were observed for a whole week, the so-called days of the three L's inasmuch as the German revolutionaries Karl Liebknecht and Rosa Luxemburg were also being remembered. Borodin spoke at many meetings and he, the adviser to the government and representative of the lone friendly nation, was warmly greeted by large crowds of people.

The name of Borodin has entered indelibly into the history of the Chinese revolutionary movement. In those years it was well-known on both sides of the struggle which was flaring up in China. Not infrequently it was precisely to him that the enemies of the Chinese revolution ascribed a decisive role in the events which were taking place then in the South.

But how did Borodin come to China, and what was his role in fact? Here we need to turn back a little.

Sun Yat-sen, who from the summer of 1917 headed the South Chinese government in Canton, was able to assess the great significance of our October Revolution. His words are famous: "The October Revolution in Russia is the birth of great hope for humanity" and "From now on only that revolution which follows the path pointed out by Russia will be victorious." In the summer of 1918, shortly after the Peking government, under imperialist pressure, broke off discussions and refused to recognize the new power in Russia, Sun Yat-sen sent a telegram to Lenin in which he greeted him and expressed hope for cooperation between the revolutionary parties of Soviet Russia and China.

However, Sun Yat-sen's position in the South Chinese government was still insecure. Under pressure from reactionary forces he had to leave his post and go to Shanghai where he remained until the end of 1920. In August 1921, replying to a letter from the People's Commissar for Foreign Affairs, G. V. Chicherin, Sun Yat-sen reported that he wanted to establish personal contacts with Soviet representatives. He also wanted to establish ties with representatives of the international Communist movement. In December 1921 during the first Northern Expedition, he received at his headquarters in Kweilin a Comintern functionary, the Dutch Communist Maring and somewhat later in Canton a representative from the Communist Youth International and the Far Eastern Bureau of the Comintern, S. A. Dalin.[1]

Meanwhile, negotiations between the Peking government and Soviet Russia were resumed. In 1922 the new Soviet plenipotentiary, A. A. Ioffe arrived in Peking.

In January 1923, Sun Yat-sen, again driven from Canton by an agent of British imperialism, General Ch'en Chiung-ming, met in Shanghai with Comrade Ioffe. Their final meeting concluded with a joint declaration on January 26,

---

1. S. A. Dalin's trip to China and his discussions with Sun Yat-sen are reflected in his book *V riadakh Kitaiskoi revolutsii* (In the ranks of the Chinese revolution), Moscow 1926.

1923. Two days later, Sun Yat-sen sent his closest aid, Liao Chung-k'ai (already known to the reader) to the Japanese resort city Atami where Ioffe had gone for a while after the Peking government again refused to recognize Soviet Russia. Liao Chung-k'ai was entrusted with holding talks with Ioffe about concrete measures of aid to the Chinese revolution which the first socialist state in the world might extend.

Simultaneously, Sun Yat-sen established contact with the Chinese Communists. In August 1922 he met in Shanghai with the secretary of the Communist Party's Northern Bureau, Li Ta-chao, who was accompanied by Lin Tsu-han and Ch'ü Ch'iu-pai. By this time Sun Yat-sen had already decided upon a reorganization of the Kuomintang and cooperation with the CCP. A month later a conference was held on questions concerning the reorganization at which not only Kuomintang members were present but also representatives of the Communist party (fifty-three persons in all). Soong Ching-ling recalled that there were so many participants that they could not all fit into Sun Yat-sen's apartment and the conference had to be held in the garden.

The place where these meetings took place, a small house in the former French Concession in Shanghai, has been turned into a Sun Yat-sen museum. It was presented to Sun Yat-sen by his admirers, Chinese emigrés, in 1919 during one of the extremely difficult moments of his wandering, danger-filled life.

Thus, by the autumn of 1922 Sun Yat-sen had already adopted a new political course of alliance with the Chinese Communists, alliance with Soviet Russia, and reliance on the revolutionary masses.

Nineteen twenty-three was marked by many important events in China. In February the famous railwaymen's strike occurred on the Peking-Hankow Railway. In May, in reply to an impudent imperialist ultimatum concerning a bandit attack on the Blue Express (a deluxe train traveling between Tientsin and Pukow) the wave of the anti-imperialist movement rose up all over China. The Third CCP Congress which took place in the summer of 1923 in Canton resolved on the entrance of the Chinese Communists into the Kuomintang on the condition of preserving their ideological and organizational independence. These events further strengthened Sun Yat-sen in his resolve to broadly implement his new political course as soon as possible.

As early as February 1923 he sent a delegation to Moscow with instructions to request that the Soviet government dispatch to Canton Soviet workers
from military and civil departments to aid the Kuomintang. In reply to this
request the Comintern activist M. M. Borodin was sent as the chief political
adviser to Canton.

I had occasion to work under him for more than a year in China. Later
I met him in Moscow.

Borodin had the noble look of an old underground Bolshevik; everyone
was involuntarily filled with respect towards him. He looked calmly and with
interest at his interlocutors, barely smiling beneath his drooping mustache
which was the kind Russian workers wore in pre-revolutionary times. His face
had a winning frankness and sincerity of expression. He bore himself with
confidence and great dignity. In those years Borodin was already past forty
but he looked younger. He was tall and wore a tunic and trousers over high
boots, spoke in a resonant, deep bass which was very appropriate to his large
somewhat heavy figure. Mikhail Markovich moved lightly and boldly, leaning
somewhat backwards as he walked. He had black hair (already beginning to
thin) which he parted on the side.

Borodin (Gruzenberg) was born in 1884 in the former Vitebsk province,
to a poor Jewish family, but he spent his childhood and youth in what is now
Latvia. An early political maturation is the destiny of the leading young persons on the eve of and during great political upheavals. At the very beginning
of the 90s Borodin was already working in Latvian Social-Democratic circles
and in 1903, as a nineteen-year-old youth, he decisively defined his party
position by adhering to the Bolsheviks. The difficult life of an underground
revolutionary began—illegal work, secret addresses, police surveillance, emigration.

In 1904 Borodin lived in Switzerland. After the events of January 9,
the Bolshevik organization in Geneva entrusted him with carrying Lenin's
directives into Russia. For almost all of 1905 when the Riga proletariat actively
participated in the revolution and in the beginning of 1906 Borodin worked
in the Riga committee of the RSDLP. As a delegate from the Riga organization,
Borodin took part in the Tammerfors Conference (December 1905) and the
Stockholm Unity Congress (April-May 1906). In the protocol of the congress
Borodin is called Vanyushin. His party name was Kirill.

In 1906 Mikhail Markovich emigrated to London where he carried on active work among the Russian emigrants. From that time he began using the name by which we know him—Borodin. In 1907 he left for the USA.

In later years he said that progressive American social opinion sympathized with the Russian revolution of 1905, treated our political emigrants well, and helped them by means of a specially created League of the Friends of Russian Freedom.

Borodin lived in the large industrial centers of Boston and Chicago as well as in their suburbs, worked in factories and farms, studied in evening schools and took part in the work of the American Socialist party among the Russian political emigrants. Along with other comrades he published the magazine *Amerikanskii Rabochii* (American worker).

At one of the meetings of Russian political emigrants Borodin met a young girl from the Lithuanian city of Vilna. Soon they were married and had children.

In July 1918 Borodin arrived in desolate, famine-ridden Moscow where the Cheka was running its feet off in the process of uncovering one plot after another. The enemies were trying to decapitate the revolution. On August 30 Lenin was wounded.

On August 22 the well-known "Letter to American Workers" was published in *Pravda*. It began like this:

"Comrades! A Russian Bolshevik who took part in the 1905 Revolution and thereafter lived for many years in your country suggested to me that he take upon himself the delivery of my letter to you."[2]

The Russian revolutionary whom Lenin was speaking of was Borodin.[3]

In America the workers knew almost nothing about the October Revolution and the Soviet power in Russia; the false propaganda of the bourgeois press distorted events. It was extremely important that Lenin's voice reach them.

This was no easy assignment. Borodin was known and held under suspicion in the USA. Out of caution while still in Europe Borodin was forced to hand over the precious letter to another Russian Bolshevik who had also

---

2. V.I. Lenin, "Pis'mo k amerikanskim rabochim," *Polnoe sobranie Sochinenii*, 37:48.
3. Ibid., p. 567.

lived in America for a long time, P. I. Slyotov (Travin), a stoker on an American liner, who delivered it. The letter was widely utilized by the American comrades headed by John Reed.

Borodin was a very modest man and never stressed that he had worked with Lenin. Only once, desiring to help me in a translation from the Chinese, Mikhail Markovich told me how at Lenin's request he had translated one of his works. If I am not mistaken it was the pamphlet *Leftwing Communism— An Infantile Disorder*.

"When I came to translate Lenin's pamphlet," said Borodin, "I wanted very much to translate Lenin's text word for word and, of course, my clumsy, literal translation didn't come off well at all. It sounded heavy and even difficult to understand in English. I tortured myself, tried and tried, but to no avail. Several times Lenin asked me how my work was coming, and finally he expressed his surprise. 'What's the matter Comrade Kirill, after all you know English, what's holding you up?' I explained my difficulties to Lenin. He laughed. 'That's entirely unnecessary,' he said. 'You're struggling in vain. Use whatever words you like so long as the original meaning is clear and easily understandable to everyone.'"

A participant in the First Congress of the Communist International, from 1919, Borodin traveled to many countries on Comintern business; for a time he took part in editing the English edition of the journal *Communist International*. In 1922 he was arrested in England and spent half a year in prison where he was subjected to cruel treatment more than once.

In 1923 a new period in Borodin's life began—his work in China.

It has been noted that A. Ya. Klimov whom I have already written of as the political adviser to General Hu Ching-i of the Second Nationalist Army went along with Borodin as his assistant.

At that time Borodin was living in the Comintern dormitory, the Luxe Hotel, on Tversk Street (now Gorky Street). When Klimov showed up there Borodin requested him to point out to him books on China in Russian and English. Klimov collected all the specialized literature he possessed and gave it to Borodin. However, Klimov did not go to China. He received an assignment in Vladivostok.

Borodin's departure from Moscow occurred about July 1923 and by September a second delegation had already arrived from Canton, this time with the task of familiarizing themselves with military affairs in Soviet Russia. The delegation was headed by Chiang Kai-shek who was then considered a member of the Kuomintang left and a partisan of Sun Yat-sen's new political course. He spent a rather long time in Moscow.

Borodin's trip stretched out. On the way he stopped in Mukden where he met with Marshal Chang Tso-lin and discussed with him the still unresolved problem of the Chinese Eastern Railway. His stop in Peking was a longer one. At that time L. M. Karakhan was conducting negotiations (which I wrote about in the first chapters) to re-establish diplomatic relations with China—negotiations which were successfully concluded in the spring of the following year.

Borodin had things to speak about with Karakhan, in their forthcoming activity there was much in common. From various perspectives and through various means, these two—the plenipotentiary of the Soviet land whose foreign policy was dictated by considerations of international proletarian solidarity, and the old Russian Bolshevik who had arrived in China at the call of the revolutionary government and in response to his party's summons—arrived at the same great goal. A free and independent China, eternal friendship between revolutionary China and Soviet Russia—this is what they were thinking of, this is what they saw as the goal of their work.

They established cordial relations from the very first meeting.

Both of them soon became widely known in China and beyond; their names never vanished from the pages of the international press. Who could have known what a cruel, unjust fate awaited them, that they would both become victims of the Stalinist repressions. Borodin was arrested in 1949 and died in imprisonment.

In the beginning of October 1923 Borodin finally arrived in Canton where he was warmly greeted by Sun Yat-sen. Active preparations for the implementation of Sun Yat-sen's plans commenced. In November an extraordinary conference of the Kuomintang was convened in Canton at which representatives of the Communist party were also in attendance. Borodin was appointed as political adviser to the Kuomintang's Provisional Executive Committee. At the conference Sun Yat-sen's new political course was definitely formulated— alliance with the Communists, alliance with Soviet Russia, support for the worker-peasant movements. It was decided that the First Congress of the Kuomintang would convene on January 24, 1924.

More than once in those years Borodin said that it was impossible even to call the Kuomintang a political party. From all points of view—political, organizational, and theoretical—it was something very diffuse and undefined. It had no clear political program. Almost anyone could call himself a Kuomintang member. There were neither party rules, membership dues, or party cards. There was no registration, and no one knew exactly how many members were in the Kuomintang. One could be counted in the party for years and still have no obligations to it. Sun Yat-sen collected the funds for party activity both in China and abroad in the form of contributions.

There were almost no workers or peasants then in the Kuomintang. It included petty bourgeois elements, representatives of the national bourgeoisie, large landowners, and militarist generals. There was not even any question of internal unity, of course. The Kuomintang was constantly riven by internal contradictions which led to armed clashes and revolts by the reactionary generals.

Still all the progressive elements of Chinese society—including the national bourgeoisie which supported the revolution then—warmly sympathized with the Kuomintang, viewing it as a party which was struggling against imperialism and militarism, and for the national independence of the country. Sun Yat-sen's name enjoyed a colossal popularity.

This was a great force which could not but be utilized for revolutionary goals, therefore the Communist party of China upon the recommendation of the Comintern decided to enter the Kuomintang. In January 1924 at the First Congress of the Kuomintang the alliance with the CCP was given organizational form. Nine Communists, among them Li Ta-chao, Chu Ch'iu-pai, T'an P'ing-shan, Lin Tsu-han, and others were chosen as members or candidates of the Kuomintang CEC.

The Congress passed a program and party rules, prepared with the participation of the Chinese Communists and Borodin. Sun Yat-sen's three principles in their new interpretation were placed at the foundation of future Kuomintang policy.[4]

---

4. Sun Yat-sen now defined the contents of his three people's principles as follows: by the first (nationalism) struggle against imperialism was understood, by the second (democracy), the creation of a democratic republic, by the third (people's welfare), improvement in the condition of workers, limitation on capital, and implementation of the slogan "Land to the tillers."

The Congress confirmed the appointment of Borodin as chief political adviser to the CEC of the Kuomintang and to the South Chinese government, and passed a resolution to invite military advisers from the USSR and build armed forces on the model of the Red Army. A commission of six headed by Liao Chung-k'ai was chosen to organize a military-political academy on the island of Whampoa. A congratulatory telegram from the Comintern was sent to the Congress. Sun Yat-sen received greetings from Karakhan.

During one of the sessions the report of Lenin's death was received. Sun Yat-sen interrupted the debates and made a speech in which he called Lenin the great organizer of the revolutionary victories, a genius of revolution, and declared that although Lenin was dead his spirit lived on. After him Borodin spoke about Lenin's life and work. A three-day mourning period was declared, flags were lowered, and the congress did not meet.

Sun Yat-sen treated Borodin with great respect. Personal friendship as well as work united them. Sun Yat-sen said more than once that he had invited Borodin in order to learn from Russian revolutionaries who had great experience in party work, and that he hoped that other members of the Kuomintang would follow his example.

The South Chinese mission of our military advisers was formed in January 1924. The first ones who arrived were V. Polyak, Ya. German, N. Tereshatov, and A. Cherepanov. The work was in full swing when in July a tragic event occurred. In the course of performing his duties, Pavel Andreevich Pavlov, the chief of mission, who had arrived in Canton just two months before, drowned in the East River near the town of Shihlung.

Pavlov was a leading Soviet military commander; during the civil war he commanded corps in the Ukraine and Central Asia, and was awarded two Orders of the Red Banner, a Bokharan Gold Star of the first order, and an honorary gold rifle. His untimely death was a great loss to our armed forces. In a short time he succeeded in doing much for the organization of the revolutionary army of the Kuomintang and he was valued at his worth. Sun Yat-sen arranged a solemn funeral for Pavlov and himself gave a speech in which he paid tribute to his abilities and services. Later Pavlov's ashes were transported to Moscow and buried in the Vagankovsky cemetery.

V. K. Blyukher who, as I have already mentioned, bore the name of Galen while in China, arrived in October to replace P. A. Pavlov. He was accompanied by a large group of advisers including T. A. Beschastnov, Ye. A. Yakovlev, G. I. Gilev, F. G. Matseylik, V. P. Rogachev. M. Chubareva (Sakhnovskaya), Uger (Remi), and P. I. Smirnov arrived somewhat earlier. In the course of the next two years the mission continued to expand especially at the beginning of 1926 with advisers from Kalgan and Kaifeng. When we arrived at Canton there were about forty advisers there.

At first many generals received our comrades who were assigned to them entirely unwillingly, evidently fearing the spread of the "red contagion," the notorious *ch'ih huo*. The advisers did everything to demonstrate their usefulness. Tereshatov related good-humoredly that he acquired his military authority on the horizontal bar.

"I arrived at the exercise ground and took a look. I figured if you don't demonstrate the gymnastics you can't teach the soldiers. I thought I'd let them see how we do it. I took off my jacket and demonstrated. I even did "the sun" for them. So they all shouted from joy; I even became uncomfortable. From then on somehow things went better, they liked me I think."

Six months later the generals were competing for our advisers.

The Whampoa Academy

The reorganization of the Kuomintang, its alliance with the Communist party, and our advisers' appearance called forth alarm on the part of the imperialists, especially in England inasmuch as their colony and chief Far Eastern base, Hong Kong, was located just one hundred-fifty kilometers from Canton. As early as the period of the Opium War England considered Kwangtung province as its sphere of influence, and then suddenly out of nowhere the Russian Bolsheviks were there.

In the imperialist press articles appeared speaking about the Moscow Bolsheviks in Canton and their insidious intrigues. They also wrote about the Whampoa Academy and its "red cadets" as the frightened colonialists expressed it. The red neckties of the students caused the colonialists to tremble. The other military units and some of our advisers wore tricolored red, white, and blue ties.)

The prospectus of the Whampoa Academy contemplated the establishment of a real military academy. For the time being it was a military school whose students received the title of officer only after completing their studies.

However, in view of its enormous significance in the creation of the revolutionary armed forces it is often called an academy in Soviet, Chinese and Western literature.

Chiang Kai-shek, who had just returned from Moscow, was appointed the commandant of the academy. At that time the Kuomintang lacked an adequate financial basis and the government was forced to resort to loans in commercial circles. At the end of February 1924 a loan of sixty thousand Canton dollars was received in order to found the academy but this sum was insufficient. Chiang Kai-shek had a fit of hysterics and left for Shanghai. He even demonstratively and without Sun Yat-sen's knowledge declared the academy closed and gave out severance pay to the instructors who had been recruited by that time. In Chiang Kai-shek's absence money was found, the buildings were repaired, the instructional program was prepared, and teachers were hired.

Studies began unofficially on May 1, 1924, but it was on June 16 that the triumphal opening of the academy occurred in the presence of Sun Yat-sen, the members of the government and the Kuomintang CEC, Commissar Liao Chung-k'ai, Chiang Kai-shek, and our advisers as well. In a speech about the tasks of the academy, Sun Yat-sen said, among other things, that it was necessary to assimilate the lessons of the revolution in Russia, to create a revolutionary army, for which the present students of the academy would serve as the backbone, that without a good army the Chinese revolution would be doomed to eternal failure.

The army which was being forged in Whampoa was to become a national one; Sun Yat-sen was striving for the liberation of all China. Therefore cadets were recruited from every province and instruction was in Peking dialect, the official language of China. Our advisers taught the basic subjects.

At first it was intended that the Whampoa Academy have six hundred cadets, but already by the end of 1924, when the second class was admitted, a thousand persons were studying there. Thereafter its registration varied between one thousand and twenty-five hundred cadets. About twenty per cent were Communists and Komsomols on assignment from the CCP. The students were representatives of the democratic strata in Chinese society, but there were few workers and peasants among them—in those years the Chinese toilers were almost all illiterate. The students from the first graduating class became officers of the first two Whampoa infantry regiments which served as the foundation for the establishment of the Whampoa corps. In June 1925 this received the title of First Army of the National-Revolutionary Army.

In several units at that time military schools of the type of the Whampoa Academy were created or actual branches of the academy itself. On the eve of the Northern Expedition when Kwangsi officially united with Kwangtung and the Seventh Kwangsi Army was formed, a branch was opened in it.

The academy existed for three and a half years. It would be difficult to overestimate its military and political significance. It was not only the forge of new military cadres but also the reliable support of the revolution. It is not surprising that whenever reaction raised its head in Canton its first blow was reserved for the Whampoa Academy.

In the stormy years of 1924-1925 the cadets left their books to throw themselves into battle as our Red cadets had done before them. So they experienced a militant, revolutionary tempering. More than once the academy played the role of chief military support for the revolutionary power. In October 1924 during the uprising of the "paper tigers"[5] the government took shelter on Whampoa Island, within the walls of the academy which became the center for mobilizing the forces of the revolution. The rebels were basically crushed by the cadets of the first class. The revolutionary masses from the city and the suburbs also took an active part in the battles.

In 1925 the troops of the British agent Ch'en Chiung-ming were smashed to bits twice in the East River region and a rebellion of the Yunnan and Kwangsi militarists in the Canton area was suppressed. Again the two Whampoa regiments and several companies of academy cadets played the decisive role.

Fraternal relations existed between the Whampoa cadets and the local population. During the military campaigns the advisers reported from the front that peasants were volunteering as bearers, serving as scouts, and providing important intelligence information. Peasant self-defense units took part in the engagements. Everywhere enthusiastic welcomes awaited the soldiers of the

---

5. An ironical name which the Chinese people gave the Cantonese merchants' self-defense forces which revolted in October 1924 under their leader, the English agent Ch'en Lien-po. This was a counter-revolutionary uprising under the slogan "Save the Kuomintang and Canton from the Bolsheviks."

revolutionary army. Our comrades saw not a single closed door, the soldiers were completely trusted, whereas previously life in the villages came to a standstill with the appearance of troops.

The Haifeng and Lufeng districts were at that time already an area of intensive peasant struggles. The Communist P'eng P'ai, called "the king of the Hailufeng peasants," was their leader. Peasant women held their children aloft so that they might look at him and remember. The Communists' influence was also strong in the towns as witness the following fact. In the district town Haifeng there were four Lenin Streets and one named after Karl Marx. Naturally, the revolutionary troops got especially broad support in this part of the province.

The common people loved the Whampoa cadets, these ardent, patriotically inclined youth, so unlike the militarists. Previously in China it was said "You don't make nails from good iron, good men don't become soldiers," but now the saying was outmoded. The Whampoa students faithfully took part in every mass undertaking—meetings, demonstrations, etc. They carried on extensive political activity, and were linked to all the public organizations in town. Their activity among the masses was especially intense when the Hong Kong-Canton strike flared up.

During maneuvers and field studies the cadets fraternized with the peasants, brought them revolutionary handbills and proclamations, carried on propaganda work, and supported the peasants in their struggles against the landlords' self-defense forces. Their faithfulness to the cause of revolution and their gravitation towards the masses of the people was inculcated in them primarily by the Communists.

From the very beginning the Communist party occupied a strong position in the Whampoa Academy. The head of the political division was the secretary of the Kwangtung Committee of the CCP, Chou En-lai. Yün Tai-ying, who later became head of the Central Military-Political Academy in Wuhan, worked in the political division. Yün Tai-ying did not live to see the Kuomintang defeated, he fell victim to the White terror. Lin Tsu-han, head of the political department in the Sixth Army, taught at the academy. Among the teachers and students there were not a few active members of the CCP. The Kuomintang leftists led by such devoted revolutionaries as Liao Chung-k'ai and General Teng Yen-ta also played an important role.

164

The Whampoa Academy ceased to exist in the beginning of August 1927
right after the Nanchang Uprising when it became known that the troops of
the Communist generals Ho Lung and Yeh T'ing were moving south. Not
without reason the reactionaries feared that the revolutionary insurgents would
find support among the students of the academy since despite the "purge" it
continued to remain a seedbed for revolutionary ideas. After an appropriate
check-up its personal staff was transferred to Nanking where on this foundation Chiang Kai-shek's clique formed a new military academy which, of course,
was completely alien to the former glorious traditions of the Whampoa
Academy.

Chiang Kai-shek Appears on the Stage

The military victories of the regiments and cadets of the Whampoa
Academy which demonstrated that at last the Kuomintang government had
given birth to its own revolutionary army had another aspect—they greatly
strengthened the position of Chiang Kai-shek. At that time no one had delved
particularly into the details of his biography. Many leading Kuomintang
figures, the military in particular, could not boast of an irreproachable past.

Chiang Kai-shek grew up in Chekiang province, in the family of a salt
merchant, that is to say he belonged to the most reactionary layer of the
Chinese merchant class, the tax-farmers who were closely bound to the
rotten Manchu state apparatus. He was trained for a military career. He studied
for a year at the Paoting Military Academy in North China and spent four years
in Japan studying military affairs. Returning to his homeland during the 1911
Revolution Chiang Kai-shek with his family's funds and using their connections
recruited a whole brigade of Shanghai gangsters and members of the famous
underground lumpen-proletarian organization, the Ch'ing-Hung pang,[6] becoming a "general" in this fashion. One can imagine what kind of an army this was.
Chiang Kai-shek did not succeed in becoming famous although his brigade
took part in the battles near Shanghai on the revolutionary side.

6. A common name for two organizations of the same type—Ch'ing pang (Green Gang) and the Hung
   pang (Red Gang). These were feudalistic, underground, mystical associations of the urban poor
   spread along the coast and in the Yangstze Valley. They were frequently led by various criminals
   and rogues who used them for their own ends. Chiang Kai-shek was a member of the Ch'ing-Hung
   pang.

Since his military career had been less than a success at the time, Chiang Kai-shek decided to play the market in league with his Shanghai and Chekiang friends, the big-shots of the urban stock exchange. This was a gang of thieves which traded in the shares of non-existing enterprises, mercilessly causing the ruin of thousands of people while raking in colossal profits without any risk to themselves. Chiang Kai-shek quickly became rich. There on the Shanghai stock market he acquired useful connections which he used against the revolution in the future. He became acquainted with Tai Chi-t'ao, the future ideologist of the Kuomintang right, with Ch'en Kuo-fu, the elder of the Ch'en brothers, future leaders of the Blueshirts, Yü Ch'ia-ching, future chairman of the Shanghai Chamber of Commerce, with the great Shanghai capitalist Chang Ching-chiang whom he advanced to leading positions in the Kuomintang after the March 20, 1926 Incident.

During the post-war depression the stock market got steadily worse and Chiang Kai-shek decided to take up political activity. He "sacrificed" a rather large sum on the Kuomintang's revolutionary enterprises. In February 1923 he came to Canton from Shanghai with Sun Yat-sen. A shameless demagogue, Chiang Kai-shek everywhere proclaimed himself as a Kuomintang leftist, a resolute supporter of Sun Yat-sen's new course, although as became known later, he secretly mocked it. He got what he wanted. Sun Yat-sen appointed him to head the military mission sent to Moscow in the autumn of 1923. In view of the fact that Chiang Kai-shek had become acquainted with the principles of the Red Army, upon his return he was entrusted with a responsible role in the creation of a new revolutionary army at the head of the Whampoa Academy.

In China where various military cliques are often formed on the basis of ties formed during the period of instruction in one or another of the military academies, this meant that Chiang Kai-shek would enjoy influence among the new cadres of the Kuomintang army, but Chiang Kai-shek's authority was so insignificant in those years that no one even thought of such considerations. The Kuomintang tried to build up his reputation as a counterweight to the other generals of a purely military type.

As the head of the academy and commander of the Whampoa corps, Chiang Kai-shek was appointed as commander of the First and Second Eastern Expeditions, but he did not play an autonomous role in the leadership of these operations, but merely confirmed the plans which had been drawn up by the advisers, a large group of whom personally took part in the battles. However, without embarrassment, he ascribed the success to himself.

Now known as the liberator of Canton, Chiang Kai-shek's fame spread far. Marshal Wu P'ei-fu, the Anglo-American henchman, reflecting the fury of his transoceanic masters, declared that "In China there are two evil men: Ch'en Tu-hsiu and Chiang Kai-shek." For him as for the majority at the time, these two names were the embodiment of the Communist party of China and the army of the revolutionary Kuomintang.

Chiang Kai-shek continued to rise. In June 1925 after the defeat of the counter-revolutionary uprising of the Yunnan and Kwangsi militarists by the Whampoa army and cadets, he became garrison commander in Canton and brought his Second Division into the city. He was appointed chief inspector of the National-Revolutionary Army which had been officially established in June 1925 and a member of the Military Council.

Our comrades labored under no delusions concerning the personality of Chiang Kai-shek. Among themselves they said he was a real lazy-bones, not very able in military affairs, lost his head in difficult circumstances, unable to resolutely make operational decisions, inclined to panic and hasty conclusions, ready at critical moments to throw in everything on the turn of fate and to go into retirement or simply disappear so that later on he would be asked to return. His favorite ploy in such cases was "I am tired and going to Shanghai." At that time he was already a power-loving, envious, stubborn, terribly mistrustful person.

The advisers used to joke that Chiang Kai-shek thought of himself as Napoleon and so he really did. Books about Napoleon were his favorite reading matter, and he often declared, hinting at himself, that the Chinese revolution needed its Napoleon. It was said that at the Kremlin in Moscow in 1923 the first thing he did was to ask where was the spot on the Kremlin wall from which Napoleon looked at the Moscow fire.

The first signs of discord between Chiang Kai-shek and the Kuomintang leftists, the Communists, and our advisers were evident as early as the latter half of 1925 in connection with the centralization of finances in general and expenses for the army in particular.

We must examine this question in somewhat greater detail. In June 1925 after the victories which had been registered, important reforms were conducted in Canton. The government began to be called national, and the National-Revolutionary Army consisting of six armies was formed. Chiang Kai-shek was appointed as commander of the First Army.

Life in the army remained as before. Soldiers received ten or twelve yuan a month, fed and clothed themselves on their own account, and lived according to collective principles in companies. The soldiers' pay was distributed via the commanders who ordinarily kept a part of it for themselves. The provisioning of the army was also done in the old Chinese way. Money was disbursed without a plan, more to one general less to another depending on personal ties. Graft flourished. In his capacity as chief inspector, Chiang Kai-shek took for himself the lion's share of the funds disbursed for the army's needs—seven to eight hundred thousand yuan per month—while to the other armies he gave one hundred to two hundred thousand. He collected all the weapons, let them rot in the storehouses, and exaggerated the number of his troops. His relations with the other generals became exacerbated.

The Russian advisers insisted on centralized army administration and an equitable division of funds. N. V. Kuybyshev, who was head of the South China mission after V. K. Blyukher's departure for the USSR in the summer of 1925, posed this question in an especially sharp form. At the sessions of the Military Council he was actively supported by V. P. Rogachev, then adviser to the chief of staff of the National-Revolutionary Army, and by I. Ya. Razgon (Olgin), Kuybyshev's deputy in the political department. Wang Ching-wei, who was the head of government, chairman of the Military Council and the Politburo of the Kuomintang, and commissar of all six armies of the National-Revolutionary Army, agreed with this point of view.

After the tragic death of Liao Chung-k'ai, Wang Ching-wei was the "most leftist of the Kuomintang people" and he was considered as Sun Yat-sen's successor. In those years it never even occurred to anyone that he might turn towards treason and become the head of a pro-Japanese puppet government. Everyone knew that a hidden struggle for power was going on between Chiang Kai-shek and Wang Ching-wei, that on one side was political prestige and on the other was military force. Since Chiang Kai-shek with remarkable shamelessness was misappropriating money designed for the building of the National-

Revolutionary Army, Kuybyshev ignored him and dealt with Wang Ching-wei on all military matters. Chiang Kai-shek came to hate him.

However, the chief cause of the counter-revolutionary activities of the rightists headed by Chiang Kai-shek was different. The Kuomintang government was moving increasingly toward the left and this frightened the hypocritical "followers" of Sun Yat-sen.

The Hsishan Faction. Society for the Study of Sun Yat-senism.

The shift of reaction to the attack was natural and inevitable. It was called forth by the changing relationship of forces in the leadership of the Kuomintang and by the general political situation. The scope of the revolutionary movement and the growth of the influence of the Communist party frightened the rightists in Canton. At the same time they joyfully learned that in the north, on the other side of the front, forces were forming which they could rely upon.

The schism in the Kuomintang had come to a head as early as the summer of 1924 when Sun Yat-sen removed from the leadership several rightist leaders including his son Sun Fo who tried to oppose the new course. However, during Sun Yat-sen's lifetime, the rightists were humble and did not resolve upon an open struggle against the "patriarch of the Kuomintang."

Therefore, the news of Sun Yat-sen's death caused many to suppose that now the schism in the Kuomintang was unavoidable. The newspapers wrote about this, some anxiously, some with malicious joy.

Foreseeing the outcome of Sun Yat-sen's serious illness, several days before his death the rightists created a club in Peking which played the role of an organizational center up until their congress at the end of March 1926 in Shanghai. They participated in the conference called by President Tuan Ch'i-jui although Sun Yat-sen himself had refused to do so, discerning its anti-democratic essence.

Profiting from the fact that they were all Kuomintang members with a long party history and that many of them had worked with Sun Yat-sen from before the 1911 Revolution, the rightists called themselves his "true followers." They were representatives of the old Chinese intelligentsia and bureaucracy or former military figures. Not infrequently they were persons of substance, with ties to militarists, the landlords and the big bourgeoisie. In the years of emigration many of them lived abroad, received their education there, assimilated European culture, and always preserved a pro-imperialist orientation. Their slogans rather accurately reflected the imperialists' desires in China. They demanded a rupture with the USSR, the removal of Borodin and the military advisers, the exclusion of Communists from the Kuomintang, the limiting of the national-revolutionary movement, and rapprochement with foreign capital.

During the May 30 Incident in Shanghai the rightists did not blush to come out openly against public opinion. The blood on Nanking Road had not dried before rightists' organizations in Peking and Shanghai had published declarations directed against the Communists and the USSR. In the midst of a universal anti-British boycott they addressed Prime Minister Snowden through their representatives in London with a request "to support them in their struggle against the Comintern."

The tense situation created in the North in connection with Kuo Sung-ling's rebellion when, as was written in the papers, all the nationalist forces of China joined together in a struggle against the Mukden clique, hastened the split in the Kuomintang. Fearing that in the event the rebellion succeeded the power of the South China government would grow still stronger, the rightists hastened to hold the so-called Hsishan conference. At the end of November 1925 they gathered at Sun Yat-sen's tomb in the Pi Yün Ssu in the Western Hills near Peking and proclaimed themselves to be the Fourth Plenum of the Kuomintang CEC; that is, in fact they placed themselves outside of the party. Decisions were taken to liquidate the Politburo of the CEC in Canton, to expel Wang Ching-wei from the party, to get rid of Borodin, to transfer the CEC to Peking, to convoke the Second Kuomintang Congress there, to get rid of the Communists in the party, etc.

By this time the rightists had provincial as well as municipal committees. They were already a rather unified organization. A third of the members of the Kuomintang's CEC supported them, they had sources of money and strong links abroad. Their main slogan was "Down with the alliance with the CCP and the USSR!" When a congress of rightists was held in Shanghai in March 1926 the very same slogan was put forth in the manifesto they published. The head of the rightists in Shanghai was the Kuomintang veteran Chang Chi.

The union of the rightists in Canton took place in veiled form, but the resultant struggle became more and more fierce. It was precisely there that the rightists resorted to methods of political terror, and there too the infamous Society for the Study of Sun Yat-senism arose from which the rightists received their ideological weapon—Tai Chi-t'ao's brochures *Philosophical Foundations of Sun Yat-senism* and *The Kuomintang and the National Revolution.* Little has been written in our country about this, but the role of this society and of Tai Chi-t'ao himself in the March 20, 1926 Incident admits of no doubt. More than once I heard that from the autumn of 1925 Chiang Kai-shek was under the strong influence of the society, and that on March 20 he appeared only as the executor of its will, but that the ideological leader was Tai Chi-t'ao. Several people put it this way—Chiang Kai-shek was an armed Tai Chi-t'ao.

I have mentioned above the enormous contribution the Whampoa Academy brought to the cause of the Chinese revolution. However, at the same time within its walls, among Chiang Kai-shek's Chekiangese fellow provincials—he always took pains to ensure that there was a goodly number of them—there appeared an organization which caused a great deal of harm to the revolutionary movement in China.

The Society for the Study of Sun Yat-senism arose among the former cadets of the first class of the Whampoa Academy during the First Eastern Expedition (February 1925). Sun Yat-sen was still alive, but was already in Peking. The organizers of the society, who maintained that it was created to struggle for the purity of Sun Yat-sen's teachings, succeeded in deluding many Kuomintang leftists.

Every month the government disbursed three thousand yuan to them "for the purpose of learning Sun Yat-senism." Wang Ching-wei aided the society, not knowing that soon they would demand his removal from the post of chairman of the Kuomintang's Politburo.

Such influential persons as Chiang Kai-shek, Sun Fo, and the deputy commander of the Whampoa army, General Ho Ying-ch'in, had ties with the society. The Kuomintang rightist Ts'ai Kuang-ch'u was its leader.

By resolution of the Kwangtung committee of the CCP several Communists joined the society, but they obviously were unable to alter its course. Subsequently they were reproached for placing themselves in sharp opposition to the society rather than working from within. This reproach was also directed at the Union of Young Soldiers which the Communists created within the Kuomintang army as early as 1924. It had many members in the Whampoa Academy and among the troops and was known as a very steadfast organization devoted to the revolution. It distinguished itself particularly during the Paper Dragon Rebellion.

The enthusiasm generated by the successes of the First Eastern Expedition did not permit the society to commence its anti-Communist activity at that time. Everyone knew very well that its successes were ensured by the alliance between the Kuomintang and the Communist party and that it was dangerous in such circumstances to come out against the Communists.

In the South the rightists switched to the offensive only in the autumn of 1925. From that time on the society began to grow rapidly, to spread beyond the confines of the Whampoa Academy and the First Army. Its branches appeared in other military units, among the young students of the Sun Yat-sen Central University and in the missionary schools. Later there were even attempts to create branches in Moscow within Sun Yat-sen University.

The society was organized on the model of the Kuomintang—periodic congresses, a CEC and its departments, provincial and municipal committees. The strongest branches were in Shanghai and Swatow. In Shanghai they published the weekly *Kuo min ko ming,* in Swatow the *Shih kuo min pao.*

From the autumn of 1925 the most dyed-in-the-wool rightists like the chief of police Wu T'ieh-ch'eng, the mayor of Canton Wu Ch'ao-shu, and the minister of finance Sun Fo were in the leadership of the society which was already clearly divided into two wings, a moderate and an extreme.

Sun Fo was an extremely picturesque character. Shielding himself with Sun Yat-sen he acted in ways which others could not have gotten away with. Borodin said that many times he robbed the departments he headed, the Ministry of Finance, the Ministry of Communications, the municipal administration, etc. This was always hushed up out of respect for Sun Yat-sen although he, after learning of his son's shameful deeds, more than once offered to bring him to court. Already a multi-millionaire in those years, Sun Fo had ties with Hong Kong and the Hong Kong compradors and he was not shy of enriching himself by this means as well. Sun Yat-sen's new policy did not suit him. He secretly attended the Western Hills conference and never concealed his relationship with the Society for the Study of Sun Yat-senism. Thus in April 1926, exiled from Canton and secretly arrived in Shanghai, he requested the authorities of the International Settlement to guard the society's headquarters which was located on their territory.

Chiang Kai-shek was linked with the leaders of the society in Canton and Swatow. He also had contact with the rightists in Shanghai.

Tai Chi-t'ao did not officially control the Society for the Study of Sun Yat-senism. He avoided leading any organization openly, even those which followed his political dogmas. He did not attend the Western Hills conference and at the congress of rightists he even made the pretense that some disagreements separated them from him. However, everyone knew that the preparation for the conference and the congress proceeded under his slogans and that he himself was in Hsishan and Shanghai while they met although he did not attend the sessions. He adhered to the same tactics with respect to the society.

Tai Chi-t'ao's teachings were not distinguished by their originality. They were a variant of the usual bourgeois theory of denying the class structure of society. Trying to play on the national feelings of the Chinese, Tai Chi-t'ao called them "Chinese," and affirmed that their roots lay in ancient Chinese history, in Confucianism, etc. He demonstrated that in general there were no classes, that this was an insidious invention of the Communists who were trying to dismember the nation. There existed only conscious and unconscious persons, the first ruled, the latter submitted. Sun Yat-senism was radically different from communism: the Communists had the dictatorship of a class, Sun Yat-sen had the dictatorship of the revolution, the construction of a society by state power. China needed not the Comintern but the international of oppressed peoples. Tai Chi-t'ao demanded the exclusion of the Communists from the Kuomintang. Later on he went so far as to advance the slogan "Use the right hand against communism, and the left hand against imperialism." That is, he found communism to be a more dangerous enemy than imperialism.

The Communist party of China, naturally, could not ignore the appearance of a theory which distorted the revolutionary essence of Sun Yat-senism and attempted to slander communism. In July 1925 the Communists began a struggle against Tai Chi-t'ao; the Second Plenum of the CCP CC in September of the same year already put forward this task.

The Second Congress of the Kuomintang

The defeat of Kuo Sung-ling's uprising, Feng Yü-hsiang's temporary withdrawal from the political arena, and the strengthened pressure of the imperialist forces inspired and encouraged the rightists. In these circumstances they accepted the victory of the leftists and the Communists at the Second Kuomintang Congress as an open challenge.

The Second Congress of the Kuomintang took place in difficult circumstances. On August 20, 1925, while getting out of his car in front of the headquarters of the Kuomintang CEC, Liao Chung-k'ai, chairman of the Politburo of the Kuomintang, was mortally wounded. He passed away after several minutes on the way to the hospital. One of his assassins was shot on the spot, one was arrested, and three succeeded in getting away. Soon the Communist Ch'en Ch'ü-lin, editor of the Kuomintang newspaper, became the next victim. The assassin, who was seized, confessed that the Hong Kong compradors and British imperialists who had hired him were plotting a whole series of terrorist acts. It became clear that a militant group of rightists was operating out of Hong Kong territory.

Wang Ching-wei was of the opinion that bribe-takers had killed Liao Chung-k'ai. In fact, the reactionaries objected furiously to the centralization of finances. This got in the way of their freely dipping their paws into the government treasury. Liao Chung-k'ai, the minister of finance, who energetically implemented the measures which were recommended by our advisers was like a sore in the eyes for them. But this, of course, was not the main thing. More generally, Liao Chung-k'ai stood in the way of reaction. He actively struggled for the betterment of the lot of the workers and peasants, and was a faithful partisan of the Kuomintang alliance with the Communist party and the Soviet Union. It is understandable why he was first on the list of victims.

Several days later the troops of the minister of war, General Hsü Ch'ung-chih, were disarmed since the threads of the crime led to him.

In the course of the investigations it was learned that Hu Ying-sheng, a Kuomintang veteran and brother of the rightists' leader in the Kuomintang who occupied a high place in the Kuomintang leadership, was mixed up in the assassination. It is enough to remark that Hu Han-min had substituted for Sun Yat-sen during the latter's last visit to Peking as commander-in-chief of the armed forces, and later became minister of foreign affairs and mayor of

Canton. The rightists guilty of the assassination were arrested. Hu Han-min was removed from office and sent away from Canton. Characteristically, this was done in the guise of an assignment to Moscow as a delegate from the Kuomintang.

Preparations for the Second Congress of the Kuomintang began in the midst of general indignation against the rightists who had taken the path of political assassinations. For the first time in the life of the party such an important event had to be conducted without Sun Yat-sen. The Second Congress had to evaluate the work of the Kuomintang after the death of the permanent chairman and to defend the party from the rightist onslaught.

The rightists attempted to undermine the work of the congress. On the eve of its opening the Society for the Study of Sun Yat-senism, supposedly in honor of its official opening, arranged a demonstration in which about a thousand persons took part. However, the slogans against the Russian Communists and in support of the Western Hills group had to be removed on the spot since they provoked general indignation. It turned out in fact that the demonstrators did greet the congress. On the day of its opening, January 1, 1925, another demonstration was held—this one a revolutionary one—organized by the Communists and the Kuomintang members.

At the beginning of January when the Second Congress was getting down to work, a letter from Sun Fo and other rightists was received from Shanghai which contained a proposal to delay the congress and call a conference to liquidate disagreements. This proposal was rejected. The exasperated Sun Fo arrived only at the very end of the congress.

The congress continued until January 19. Three days were spent on greetings. A large military parade in which ten thousand troops participated was staged. More than two hundred thousand demonstrators passed by the building where the congress met. Like all Kuomintang meetings, the congress began with three low bows before a portrait of Sun Yat-sen and the Kuomintang banners after which Sun Yat-sen's testament was read aloud.

The report on the political situation was made by Wang Ching-wei, that on the military situation by Chiang Kai-shek, and on the worker-peasant movement by Ch'en Kung-po who was a Kuomintang leftist at that time. Liao Chung-k'ai's widow gave a speech calling for the continuation of the cause for which her husband died. The third session of the congress was held on the hill Huang Hua Kang (Hill of yellow flowers), the graveyard of the seventy-two heroes[7] near Tungshan where Liao Chung-k'ai and the victims of the shootings of June 23, 1925, were buried as well.

The congress adopted a whole series of declarations in defense of oppressed peoples, against Japanese intervention in Manchuria, in support of the Nationalist Army in North China, etc. Before the close of the congress one of the members of the presidium unfurled a red banner with a gold inscription "Oppressed peoples of the world unite and throw off the yoke of imperialism"—a gift from the Third International. The ovation continued for several minutes.

The congress became a triumph for the revolutionary section of the Kuomintang. Communists and Komsomols constituted one-third of the two hundred seventy delegates. Only fifty delegates were rightists and only ten of these conducted themselves aggressively. Four participants in the Western Hills conference, including Tsou Lu, rector of the Sun Yat-sen Central University in Canton, were expelled from the party (two temporarily for one year). More than ten rightists received punishment.

The congress underlined the necessity for an alliance with the Communist party of China and the USSR. Wang Ching-wei was even more "left" than the Communists. Instead of the two Communists whom the Communist party had proposed for the Kuomintang's thirty-six member CEC seven were chosen on his suggestion, and of the rightists only Sun Fo, Tai Chi-t'ao and Wu Ch'ao-shu. T'an P'ing-shan and Lin Tsu-han (candidate member) were chosen for the Kuomintang Politburo. The routed rightists kept their silence.

Sun Yat-sen's widow, Soong Ching-ling, attended the congress and was chosen for the presidium. She came specially from Shanghai. An enormous crowd led by representatives of the government and public organization went down to the pier to meet her.

After the congress almost all the departments of the Kuomintang CEC were in the hands of the Communists and the Kuomintang leftists. Their work developed on a broad scale.

But the rightists did not give up their arms, they prepared for revenge. It was decided to make use of Chiang Kai-shek. This was spoken of as early as

---

7. The seventy-two heroes were members of the T'ungmenghui (forerunner of the Kuomintang), participants in the unsuccessful uprising in Canton on April 28, 1911.

the Western Hills conference. Aware of Chiang Kai-shek's remarkable touchiness and suspiciousness the rightists very ably set about cultivating him. They began whispering to him that the Russian advisers were behaving badly towards him, that they wanted to get rid of him. Borodin's departure and his upcoming conversations with Feng Yü-hsiang were depicted as an intention to transfer the center of activity of the Russian advisers to the northwest and to strengthen Feng Yü-hsiang as a counterweight to Chiang Kai-shek. They even assured him that the Russians wanted to kidnap him and forcibly carry him off to Moscow.

These seeds fell upon ready soil. As early as the middle of February Chiang Kai-shek had already become extremely agitated and constantly complained that the Russians did not trust him.

The situation grew more and more tense. The Kwangtung Communists requested the CC to strengthen the local party organization by sending to it the eldest son of the CCP's general secretary, the talented young organizer, Ch'en Yen-nien. He was later chosen as the secretary of the Kwangtung-Kwangsi party committee.

Such was the situation in Kwangtung at the time when our group of student interpreters who had long dreamed of seeing with their own eyes the accomplishments of the revolution in the South was about to arrive. It didn't occur to any of us that there too the danger of a counter-revolutionary coup was present.

Tungshan—the Residence of the Advisers

Our ship went by a direct route without stopping at Hong Kong. Before the Hong Kong-Canton strike this was almost impossible. All foreign vessels dropped anchor in Hong Kong bay and one had to proceed further on a different boat of smaller tonnage. The question of dredging the harbor in Canton was raised many times, of putting it in condition so that at least during high tide large ocean-going ships could dock there. But the Chinese lacked the means for this and all their appeals to the imperialists for loans were without results. England as before monopolized Canton's ocean transport and trade.

The strike brought its corrective. Any vessels which stopped in Hong Kong would not be allowed into Canton. Such was the rule, and it was enforced vigorously. Ships rode at anchor either across from the city embankment, somewhat west of Shameen island, in White Goose Bay, or in the inner harbor

near Whampoa island. These were vessels of medium tonnage, loaded in
Shanghai or other Chinese ports.

Now Canton carried on its trade independently. Vessels with foreign flags
passed by us. Every day Hong Kong lost two hundred fifty thousand pounds
sterling, that is four million yuan. Its imports and exports were reduced by
sixty per cent. The British were selling off their ships.

There already existed a regular service between Vladivostok and Canton.
The Soviet ships *Simferopol, Astrakhan, Tomsk, Yerevan, Pamyat Lenina* and
our *Mengkuhai* plied back and forth bringing oil, weapons, and even dis-
assembled airplanes.

The imperialists launched attacks on our vessels. In one of them—on the
Tomsk—in the vicinity of the Portuguese colony of Macao, the local river
police, White Guards, British and Chinese pirates took part.

On February 28, 1926, after a five-day journey from Shanghai, we finally
entered the many-branched delta of the Pearl River, broad as the sea, and for
a long time traveled upon its far from pearl-like waters, turbid with red silt.
Finally the engines stopped and the anchor chain creaked.

Before us were gently sloping hills, sparse trees, and a few one-storey
buildings. This was Whampoa—harbor, fort, and location of the Military-
Political Academy. From the pier came the sounds of discordant martial
music. Representatives of the National-Revolutionary Army were greeting
the aviation adviser Uger who had arrived with us (he had gotten on somewhere
en route). At that time he was temporarily discharging the duties of chief of
aviation. The planes were a gift from the Soviet Union. I remember that one
of them bore Sun Yat-sen's name—Chung Shan.

February is a gloomy month in Canton, and I must confess that our first
impressions were not very good—humidity, stuffy air, dull, opaque colors.
The scenery disenchanted us. We were waiting to see something exotic although
we ourselves didn't know just what. Only later did we understand that one had
to look for Kwangtung's tropical beauty in the interior of the province; the
coastal areas had long been treeless.

Dozens of sampans streamed towards the ship, along the shore lay hundreds
of others four or five deep, their small humped roofs closely pressing against
each other. They all looked very poor and were of a dirty, rotten color. Whole
families took shelter in them, and little kids craned their tiny heads in our

direction with interest. The young ones were fastened by the leg with a rope or wore on their backs a peculiar life belt—a dry log. Chickens pecked for food with loops around their feet. The loud, high-pitched voices of the boat people, trying to outshout one another, sounded sharply and penetratingly with their characteristic South Chinese inflection.

Nowhere in China was there such a collection of boat people. The other cities could not even begin to compare in this respect. We saw boat people in Shanghai and Amoy but it was not the same at all. It was said that there were more than two hundred thousand of them in Canton and its environs.

There were people to meet us and after several minutes the launch *Pavlov* belonging to the South China mission brought all the newcomers to the eastern suburb Tungshan (Eastern Hills). Had we been alone we would have risked getting lost as once happened to the advisers Ye. V. Teslenko (Tereshchenko) and V. N. Panyukov (Komi), who, unable to make themselves understood to the rickshaw pullers, were taken to the White Emigré dive, the Moulin Rouge, instead of to the headquarters of the South China mission. One can imagine how confused our comrades were. They had to shift and feign in order to get away. It was a very dangerous adventure although while telling it they both almost died laughing.

Now no trace remains of the Tungshan of that era. It was destroyed in 1938 during the anti-Japanese War and then rebuilt. Witnesses to the historic events of 1924-1927 will orient themselves only with difficulty in the new Tungshan. In those years this picturesque spot was something in the order of a summer residence for the local aristocracy. Chiang Kai-shek's villa was there as was the country house of General Chang Fa-k'uei, etc.

Our advisers lived to the south of the railroad branch line, close to the canal. There were some five or six small streets and alleys with stone houses in both European and Chinese style, for the most part detached houses with small gardens. Three such houses completely identical and enclosed by a common fence were occupied by the staff of the South China mission and its club. We thought of this as the main street. The advisers settled around it.

From the launch we went straight to the club and the first thing that struck us were the flowering camellia bushes which set off the stone slabs of the garden paths. We put down our suitcases, touched the stiff leaves, and sniffed the tight, wax-white flowers.

The manager of the dining hall, Maria Mikhaylovna, a pretty young woman with long gypsy earrings (wife of the adviser G. I. Gilev) met us joyfully. Despite the earliness of the hour we were fed at once. The dining room was a model one, but Maria Mikhaylovna was running her feet off. Not knowing the local customs and the language it was difficult for her to deal with the cooks and provisioners who often cheated her.

On the first floor of the club were the lobby, the dining and reception rooms, and also a small photographic darkroom; upstairs was a billiard room and a library. In the drawing room hung a large picture of P. A. Pavlov in a black frame.

The furniture in the club was quite modest, but still there was a piano. The wives of the advisers S. B. Matseylik, A. Ya. Beschastnova, V. F. Yakovleva, M. M. Gileva, and others expended no little effort in making the club a real place for rest, study and socializing for the Soviet population of Tungshan. Meetings, club activities, amateur performances, ceremonial receptions and leavetakings were held there. On the lobby wall newspapers were hung and each fresh issue attracted a large crowd of persons. They were very interesting because of their timeliness and were noted for their genuine humor. They included items concerning the political situation and the internal affairs of the mission. Almost all of the notices were accompanied by amusing drawings and very life-like, good-natured cartoons. It is a pity that not a single copy has been preserved.

Right there in the club we were advised on how to get settled. I was put up temporarily by one of the interpreters, the talented China specialist Ye. Yolk who had left Peking before us. He was married to the interpreter T. I. Vladimirova and occupied a small, three-room apartment on the second floor of a small house. Below lived Madame Antoinette, a Negro woman who operated a sewing shop and who did the sewing for all Soviet women in Tungshan. Madame Antoinette was married to a Chinese and spoke only French and the local Chinese dialect. God knows how she got to China from some French colony in Africa.

Chinese homes in the South are not at all like those in Peking. They are built with verandahs and open balconies on the roof. It was in just such a house that I settled. It was a genuine Chinese house to which the bath—a large clay tub conical in shape and waist-deep—bore witness.

I was warned that I'd really suffer at night unless I bought a mosquito net, since the local gnats and mosquitoes were renowned for their numbers and bloodthirstiness. A mosquito net was an expensive item, it cost as much as three or four good pairs of shoes, and was sewn of thick tulle of which an awful lot was needed since Chinese beds are almost square. I was also advised to buy incense candles the odor of which mosquitoes fear. At night the master of the house Zhenya Yolk demonstrated how to use them. On the desk in front of him he placed half a dozen snake-green coils, twisted into a spiral shape with a raised head, exactly like a miniature rattlesnake ready to strike, then he lit them all at once. The coils began to glow and a fragrant, astringent odor began to spread through the room. With a triumphant look Yolk sat down to his books. Soon, however, he threw down his studies—the coils had smoked him out along with the mosquitoes.

Finally all the fussing was over. I lay beneath the opaque white shade of my mosquito net. Beyond the window could be heard the unfamiliar, song-like speech and the clatter of the local wooden footwear which are held on only by a diagonal strip of leather across the toes. In the city this noise accompanies the street traffic like the gay, cheerful sound of castanets. Here it was hollower and less frequent.

I awoke at dawn. Beneath the window someone's voice was insistently and monotonously repeating some short Chinese phrase. Armed only with a knowledge of Peking dialect I could not understand what was being said, and I poked my head outside from curiosity.

Nothing special, just an ordinary fish peddler. He stood near the house and looked up at me. A large, round woven hat hung over his shoulders. His trousers, rolled up above his knees and the jacket, open on his bare chest had evidently been dark blue at one time, but were faded now to a light gray. He wore wooden-soled sandals on his feet.

A warm, predawn haze hung in the air and it seemed that the entire plant world was eagerly drinking in its generous life-giving moisture. Something softly chattered and gurgled, as if the plants were hurrying to push up out of the warm moist earth to unfold their buds and to develop new leaves. Then something burst loudly. This was a banana leaf unfolding. Everything was thrusting upwards, storing juices, thirstily seeking life, giving off a fresh, juicy smell.

The peddler still stood there and looked at me inquiringly, then he moved on and his monotonous cries became more and more distant.

Then suddenly something burst and unfolded within myself. The beauty of this still unknown region opened up before me. I fell in love with it passionately and forever. How could it have displeased me the evening before, by seeming gray, sullen, and boring? This old city of Canton, the new hope of China, was beautiful in any weather.

To this day the fresh spring morning, the drawn-out call of the peddler, and the sensation of tense life force pouring out from everywhere, are inseparable in my mind from my memories of Canton.

The South China Mission

In the next few days we became acquainted in the dining room and the club with almost all of the advisers in the South China mission.

As in the North these were very interesting people and despite their comparative youth were excellent specialists. Many of them had held high positions during the civil war and subsequently, after returning from China, again held responsible positions in the Red Army, commanded divisions and corps, and worked in military academies and departments of the general staff.

The majority wore civvies but those who were directly involved with the troops or were coming from the field wore the smart uniforms of the National-Revolutionary Army made of thin khaki gabardine with Chinese-style brown buttons, a fur cap or cork helmet.

Almost all the advisers had sent for their families. The wives, even those with small children were without exception working in the headquarters of the mission, in the dining hall, the club, the library, or the kindergarten. Several of them used to go into town to give Russian lessons to Chinese youths who were planning to go to Moscow on assignment to Sun Yat-sen University. Life in the Soviet colony in Tungshan was in full swing.

There were many children, especially little ones. Several were even born there, for example, to F. G. Matseylik, Mira Sakhnovskaya, I. Zilbert, and I. K. Mamaev. Now they always astonish passport officers when writing down their places of birth.

In my time, Mira Sakhnovskaya was the chief of staff of the mission and a teacher at the Whampoa Academy. She came with her husband who was also a military adviser. An active participant in the civil war (at first in Bubnov's propaganda train and then in the First Cavalry) she was the lone woman in the Soviet Union who had finished the basic course at the Frunze Academy. Her masculine profession and the habit of wearing men's clothes placed an indelible stamp upon her. She spoke in a low voice, smoked a good deal, and walked with large strides. Woman's clothing sat strangely on her and it was clear that she was annoyed when she had to wear it. After returning to Moscow she went back to her usual gymnastics, riding breeches and boots which, one must confess, fitted her tall lean figure much better. Her bobbed golden hair was thick and curly. During her infrequent smiles it was clear that she was missing a good many teeth. In response to my question she said that during the civil war her teeth often ached, but there was no time to treat them, so she simply had them extracted. Everyone who knew her at the front said that she was really remarkable, but was contemptuous of anything that smacked of femininity. This was no rarity then. In Tungshan there was yet another such heroine of the civil war whom I have already mentioned, Liza Goreva. Both of them, Mira Sakhnovskaya and Liza Goreva, were arrested without cause in 1937 and perished.

The comrades all good-naturedly bantered with Sakhnovskaya when, on maternity leave, in the characteristic peculiarity of her position, she lectured at Whampoa Academy, which perhaps seemed rather strange, but her students just viewed it as superfluous evidence of the equality of women in the Soviet Union.

Sakhnovskaya was a very tender mother to her two children. Only she lacked the time to show them all of her love. I remember one scene: beneath the headquarters' windows the amah walked indecisively with the infant Pavel Sakhnovsky in her arms. From time to time she went up to the window and said in a supplicating voice, "Mississi, beby wanchee chao chao," which meant in pidgin English "Madam the baby wants to eat." Mira stuck out her head and ordered the amah to leave; she was busy.

One day on the porch of the club I bumped into an adviser whose face seemed quite familiar to me. He smiled and flashed his gold teeth. I gasped loudly, having recognized "the shark of international imperialism." It was I. Ya. Zenek (Zebrovsky), adviser to the Second Army of the National-Revolutionary Army.

Afterwards I often dropped in on Zenek and his wife Nina Mikhaylovna; they were my neighbors. Several times I found Chinese Communists at their place, political officers of the army, and their wives who were also Communists. One of them once gave a talk in the club on the women's movement in China. She spoke in French and Nina Mikhaylovna translated.

When I arrived at Canton the chief of the South China mission was Nikolay Vladimirovich Kuybyshev, a corps commander in the civil war, and brother of the prominent Soviet political figure Valerian Vladimirovich Kuybyshev.[8] His assistant in the political section was Razgon, his chief of staff, Sakhnovskaya, his staff commissar was Ter (Teruni, Tayrov), a prominent political worker from civil war days. I remember him particularly well; he was a small, lame Caucasian with glittering eyes, remarkably active and energetic. After Kuybyshev's departure, when Blyukher returned, Ter became his assistant for political affairs.

Some of our advisers temporarily held command positions in the National-Revolutionary Army until the recruitment of the requisite candidates from among the Chinese. Thus Uger discharged the duties of the chief of aviation, P. I. Smirnov headed the Naval Bureau, and V. P. Rogachev was chief of the General Staff.

Chiang Kai-shek's adviser in the First Army was A. I. Cherepanov, a former participant in the battles around Pskov in February 1918 when our Red Army was born. He came to China after completing the basic course at the Frunze Academy. At that time the First Army was the strongest and most battleworthy since from the very beginning it was given special attention in the areas of military preparedness, equipment, staffing, and political work. The chief of the political division, almost all of the political workers, and many of the commanders were Communists. But Chiang Kai-shek's deputy and chief of staff was General Ho Ying-ch'in, a wealthy capitalist, a crafty, secretive man of reactionary bent.

As already mentioned above, Iosif Zenek was the adviser to General T'an Yen-k'ai's Second Army. General T'an Yen-k'ai, the son of the imperial viceroy of Hukuang (the provinces of Hupeh and Hunan), and himself just recently the military governor of Hunan from which he had been driven out by another

---

8. N. V. Kuybyshev was unjustly subjected to repression in 1937.

militarist, was only nominally numbered among the corps commanders. He was considered one of the most learned representatives of the Chinese intelligentsia,[9] but he had no military education at all. Naturally, he spent little time on the military affairs of the corps, preferring to exercise "general leadership." Moreover, he was busy with other affairs as the chairman of the Kwangtung provincial government. In reality, the Second Army was commanded by General Lu Ti-p'ing. It was said of T'an Yen-k'ai that he was weakwilled and lacking in character. He looked like a typical Mandarin bureaucrat. Obese, slow-moving, with a broad face and a flat nose, he reminded me very much of a hippopotamus.

General Chu P'ei-te's adviser in the Third Army was F. G. Matseylik, a man of excellent education who spoke English and German fluently. Later he became chief of the Division of Foreign Exchanges of the General Staff of the Workers' and Peasants' Red Army.

V. Gorev was adviser to General Li Chi-shen of the Fourth Army who was at that time the chief of staff of the National-Revolutionary Army. Li Chi-shen committed not a few crimes against the Chinese Revolution, but in the end he was able to find the right path, headed the Kuomintang Revolutionary Committee and died as a deputy chairman of the CPR government. In the period I am writing of he treated the Communists with patience. In his army was a regiment commanded by the Communist Yeh T'ing; in our literature it is now called "the Communist regiment." General Chang Fa-k'uei commanded the army's Twelfth Division. It was said of him that he was the "best divisional commander of the best division of the Fourth Army." An energetic man, he was, in fact, deputy army commander. With the exception of Teng Yen-ta he was considered the most leftist of the generals. He developed very good relations with the Russian advisers. Many political workers and commanders in his division were Communists. Chang Fa-k'uei was about thirty years old then. He was known for his hot, fiery temperament; Gorev said that he lacked self-control and composure. Chang Fa-k'uei retained his ties with the Communists longer than any other of the Kuomintang generals and was one of the last to desert to the side of reaction.

---

9. Under the Manchus, T'an Yen-k'ai passed the capital examination, and received his *chin shih* degree. For a time he was a member of the Hanlin Academy in Peking.

General Li Fu-lin, commander of the Fifth Army (whose adviser was Lunev) had been a Kuomintang member since 1912, although in the past he had commanded almost all of the Kwangtung pirates and his corps was recruited from his former subordinates. After entering Sun Yat-sen's army, he took upon himself the obligation of controlling the entire mass of sea pirates who teemed along the sea coast and in the estuaries of the Kwangtung rivers. The pirates feared him and even paid him tribute. Li Fu-lin was the lone army commander of the National-Revolutionary Army who did not hold a high post in the Kuomintang party apparatus. He was considered a rightist and was a representative of the so-called Kwangtung clique which included all his friends, natives of Kwangtung province linked to the local landlords and bourgeoisie and men of reactionary bent (such as Wu T'ieh-ch'eng, Sun Fo, Hu Han-min, and others).

The Sixth Army was headed by General Ch'eng Ch'ien (or Ch'in Ch'im as the southerners called him), a Kuomintang veteran and personal friend of Sun Yat-sen, whose war minister he had been for a time. He developed very strained relations with Chiang Kai-shek, who evidently feared him and therefore particularly oppressed his corps, giving him neither money nor weapons. N. I. Konchits, a brigade commander in the civil war, was the adviser to the Sixth Army. The chief of the political department was Lin Tsu-han, then already a leading figure in the Communist party and a candidate member of the Politburo of the Kuomintang's CEC. He and Konchits were linked by friendship as well as their mutual work.

I had seen N. I. Konchits in Peking, but I did not know him then. He lived in the Ambassador Hotel, where the participants in the Moscow-Peking flight were staying. In Canton I recognized him at once—he had a very remarkable appearance: a young, sunburned face (he was about thirty-five then), blue eyes, and completely grey hair. He was very good-looking—tall, lithe, well-proportioned, always smart-looking and collected. The Chinese military uniform fitted him as it fitted no one else. He worked accurately and in an organized way, he wrote detailed military reports in the field and he kept a daily diary.[10]

As I have already noted, the commissar for all six armies was Wang Ching-wei.

---

10. The diary of N. I. Konchits, now a retired major-general, was published in part in the collection *Sovietskie dobrovol'tsy v Kitae v 1923-1927 godakh* (Soviet volunteers in China, 1923-1927; Moscow 1961).

Later, on the eve of the Northern Expedition, two more corps were added to these basic corps of the National-Revolutionary Army—the Seventh Army of General Li Tsung-jen's Kwangsi clique to which I. K. Mamaev was appointed adviser, and General T'ang Sheng-chih's Eighth Hunan Army whose adviser was F. I. Olshevsky (Voynich).

The military engineer Yevgeny Andreevich Yakovlev, who was past forty, was the oldest in the South China mission. A superb specialist, he was the friend of D. M. Karbyshev, his fellow student at the Military Engineering Academy in Petersburg under whose leadership he worked during the Soviet period. As a former colonel in the tsarist army, Yakovlev was a brilliant representative of the old military cadres, who after the revolution joined the side of the revolutionary peoples. During the civil war Yakovlev held responsible positions in the front-line staffs. He came to China in the fall of 1924 together with Blyukher. He took part in the Eastern Expedition, stormed the Weichow fortress, and for a time gave lectures on fortifications in the Whampoa Academy.

He was arrested in 1931 on an unjust accusation and spent three years in the stockades. There was no trial. Yakovlev was freed, rehabilitated, and appointed an instructor in the Military Engineering Academy. He fought at the front during the Patriotic War; he left besieged Sevastopol on the last submarine. He died in 1951 as a major-general, doctor of technical sciences, departmental chairman at the academy, and the author of many scholarly works.

Timofey Andreevich Beschastnov, the senior artillery adviser, came to Canton together with Yakovlev. He gave lectures at the Whampoa Academy and worked in the Kwangtung arsenals (Large and Small). After returning to the Soviet Union he was the head of artillery in a military district, dean of faculty at the Artillery Academy and chief of the higher artillery courses for advanced commanders. His last military title was colonel-general of artillery. Beschastnov was a participant in the Great Patriotic War. He passed away in 1947.

I also met a group of our pilots in Tungshan. Theirs was an especially hard lot as they had to fly over unfamiliar routes and in rather poor crafts. I well remember the pilots Dzh. Talberg, V. Sergeev, Remizyuk, and A. M. Kravtsov, and the flight mechanics Bazenau and Kobyakov. We used to call them "our heroes." They received well-deserved decorations for their work in China, but 1937-1938 were fatal years for many of them too. Talberg, Remizyuk, Uger, and Bazenau were arrested and died.

I went to work on the day after my arrival. I was taken on as an interpreter by the intelligence division of the staff of the South China mission. The head of the division was V. M. Akimov, who had recently arrived from Kalgan; his deputy was yet another pupil of the Higher Military Course of Orientology in Tashkent, N. Miller (Meyer). Miller soon took sick and had to leave China.

Like almost all of the advisers Akimov worked at the Whampoa Academy at the same time. For a long time I kept the splendid, yard-long proclamation of his appointment as an adviser at the academy. It was printed in huge, blue characters on Chinese silk paper with a beautiful red border and the seal of the General Staff of the National-Revolutionary Army. Below were the huge, eye-catching square seals. Printed in India ink was Akimov's Chinese name— Hsilin—very poetic characters with the meaning of "western forest" were chosen for him. During the Patriotic War, while evacuating from Moscow, I burned superfluous papers and unfortunately, in my hurry, I destroyed this curious document.

In Canton in the spring of 1926 preparations for the Northern Expedition were going ahead full steam. Having learned that Akimov had begun the civil war as a machine-gunner, the chief of the mission, Kuybyshev, entrusted him with teaching this specialty to the cadets of the academy. The instructional machine guns were of poor quality and often jammed, and Akimov had often to take them apart on the spot and eliminate the problem. Each time when the machine gun he was holding began to work again, loud shouts of approval from the students rang out: *"hao, hao"* (good). The comrades good-naturedly teased Akimov who was sorry that he could not get any "real" work (he wanted to give lectures in Chinese on tactics as he had done in Kalgan) and they called him "our machine gunner." This humorous nickname stuck with him even in Moscow.

During the Northern Expedition, Akimov was appointed adviser to the Second Division of the First Army—Chiang Kai-shek's favorite division. Meeting Akimov at the front, every time Chiang Kai-shek would smile broadly, raise his thumb high as a token of approval, and say in Chinese: "The second division is the best division." In fact it was one of the most battleworthy divisions of the National-Revolutionary Army. Like the other divisions of the First Army it was staffed and armed better than the rest, but most important, Chinese Communists worked effectively within it. Our comrades too contributed not a little to its effectiveness. It is true that on the very first day of the March 20, 1926 Incident Chiang Kai-shek ordered the arrest or relief of all its commissars and commanders, members of the Communist party, and ordered the division to take part in the roundups and arrests. It was the soldiers of this very Second Division who stood guard in front of the offices and private apartments of our advisers in Tungshan, but they were ashamed to look us in the eye.

Chiang Kai-shek did not succeed in destroying the revolutionary spirit within the Second Division. By the beginning of the Northern Expedition its Communist stratum had already been strengthened again. The division performed well on the front.

My work in the Intelligence Division was uncomplicated. Perusing the Chinese press on required subjects and translating handwritten materials were among my duties. The English press was examined by Poroshin (a White emigré). I don't know how he came into our midst but he was well treated. In 1927 he went to Moscow with us, but he didn't like the way things were (after all things were not easy then) and Poroshin could not bear up. He went away to the Far East, supposedly for a job, and then returned to Harbin.

At the entrance of the Intelligence Division and near the mission headquarters a guard of two or three soldiers stood next to each building. The majority of them were Communists; we developed friendly relations with them. They lived and ate right there on the lower floor of the intelligence division. When they prepared their food, the thick smoke of bean oil entered the open windows of our press bureau, alternating with the sharp aroma of flowering magnolia trees from a neighboring garden.

Canton

Within the next few days we were taken to see the city. It was decided that we go to the "narrow streets" where the artistic crafts were represented for which Canton was famous. (There was no modern industry in Canton at that time.) We rented a pair of antediluvian cars in a small garage whose walls and roof were made of matting and we set off. The cars carried us rather swiftly past the cemetery of the seventy-two heroes, through the railroad right-of-way, and soon we were on a broad highway. Fields where peasants were working lay on the sides. Several minutes later we entered Canton through the Eastern Gates which survived from the old fortress walls. We were in the very heart of the city.

Canton was over two thousand years old. It had traded with ancient Rome, and later with the Arabs; the mosque erected by them remained. In the sixteenth century the Portuguese arrived, then the Spaniards, and in the seventeenth century the British, who two hundred years later initiated the shameful Opium War. After its conclusion, the island of Shameen in the very center of the city was divided between the two allies: two-thirds was reserved for the English, one-third for the French. Thus the foreign concessions developed in Canton. The legendary cheap labor of the coolie turned this small island into a flowering garden covered with beautiful buildings.

The province of Kwangtung is situated far from the capital and always enjoyed a significant measure of autonomy. This placed a stamp on the character of its inhabitants who for a long time have been distinguished by their love of freedom and their striving for independence, their curiosity, and their bent for innovations. In China there is a saying "Everything new comes from Canton," and the development of the revolutionary movement in the years when I was in China confirmed this.

The majority of the Chinese emigrants, hundreds of thousands of whom yearly went in search of a living to the USA, Australia, the Philippines, Indonesia, Malaya, etc., were natives of Kwangtung and the neighboring province of Fukien. From this stemmed the close ties of the inhabitants of Canton with their fellow countrymen abroad, the material aid which the overseas Chinese gave them, and the lively interest with which they followed political life in South China.

Canton was previously known the world over for its unusually narrow streets. S. A. Dalin, who was in Canton in 1922, reported that it was a typical medieval city, no wide streets, no auto roads, no large European houses, no bus transport. We already encountered an entirely different situation. It is true that there were still rather few buses, and those which existed were very tiny, while trams were entirely lacking. I was told that the rickshaw pullers were energetically protesting against the enlargement of the urban transit system, and that the city administration was not crossing them.

Now we came to the Hsikuan section, a remnant of old Canton. We rode along European streets, and a large gay crowd bustled about us.

In that time the city already numbered more than a million inhabitants. It was obvious that people wanted to escape from the heat. The second stories of the houses protruded over the sidewalks, and the pedestrians walked in deep shade, behind massive columns which separated them from the road-way. Windows opened onto closed verandahs. Matting hung everywhere. In Canton 104 degrees in the shade was no rarity. Heat and sunstroke felled even the Chinese who were accustomed to the locality. After all they had to work in the blazing heat for long hours and the least carelessness could lead to disaster. In our headquarters there was an order forbidding us to appear on the street during the day without headgear.

There were not a few monuments of antiquity in Canton, but this was primarily a port city. At that time its appearance was defined by the embank-ment with its large, beautiful modern buildings among which stood out two department stores, six and nine stories high—Sincere and Sun Company. On the embankment all was animation and bustling, and in the port the whistles of launches and the honking of ships could be heard. The water lapped at the sides of countless sampans.

In our literature the Chinese sampan dwellers are sometimes depicted as vicitims of exceptional exploitation and social inequality. It is said that no room remained for them on dry land. To a certain degree this was historically correct. It is well-known that the boat people were given equal rights after the 1911 Revolution. But subsequently the difference between the worker or peasant on dry land and the sampan dweller on the water was only a difference of profession. Life on the water was only one of the local peculiarities of China like, shall we say, the canals in place of streets in Amsterdam or Venice.

On the sampans one encountered women more often than men. It was said that the sampan dwellers exploited their wives and did nothing themselves. But it was not entirely so. The men sometimes worked on dry land at harder labor and they were not discriminated against.

To live on the water and to know that only two or three rotten boards separated you all the time from the unfaithful surface might frighten persons who were accustomed to feeling firm soil beneath their feet. But this did not in the least bother the sampan dwellers who on their own flat-bottomed boats felt like fish in water. They even lowered their dead onto the bottom as if to their native element. The sampan dwellers looked better than the factory workers; their work was not as hard, and life in the open air was better for their health. Subsequently I saw more than once how the laboring population of Kwangtung lived and worked; therefore the sampan dweller never seemed the most unfortunate to me.

The sampan dwellers transported passengers and goods, and helped to unload ships. But there were also shady characters among them who were occupied with unlawful activities. At that time there were still picturesque sea pirates along the South China coast, as one of our advisers who lost his suitcase on board a ship which was attacked assured us. There was a ramified net of agents among the sampan dwellers who let them know when and which ships were about to depart. Contraband runners also used the sampan dwellers in trying to smuggle in British goods during the boycott. The criminal element also found refuge among them, to say nothing of the fact that their boats could be rented at any time by devotees of opium-smoking, cards, and low-class love. Controlling the uncounted number of sampans was no easy problem.

Our cars slowly moved along the crowded streets. In contrast to other Chinese ports, especially Shanghai, where one can meet representatives of all races and nations, the street crowd consisted solely of Chinese. After the strike foreigners were afraid to appear in the city. Everywhere we were recognized and greeted with friendly smiles. The mood was one of elation, the people were gay and bore themselves with dignity and even a certain degree of self-satisfaction as befitted victors. This is how they felt in their struggle against imperialism.

Political life was in full swing. All the open places on walls and columns were plastered with placards and handbills, flags were hung from poles fastened above the heads of the passersby, narrow strips of material covered with slogans were stretched across the streets. A detachment of Pioneers in khaki dress, white panama hats and red bandannas passed by. A trumpet sounded hoarsely and a picket of the strike committee appeared. The pickets were dressed in semi-military uniform and armbands and were armed with rifles. On their service caps were twelve-rayed Kuomintang stars, but everyone knew that the strike committee was under Communist influence and it was even jokingly called "the second CCP municipal committee." The picket walked out of his headquarters in the embankment, the famous Tungyuan, where previously the worst gambling dens in the city which the national government closed down had been located. A long line of rickshaw pullers with empty rickshaws moved slowly past—a demonstration against a projected new tax on members of their profession.

Sweet-looking girls, lively and agile, skipped across the street. What a contrast with Northern and especially central China, where the larger part of the women from among the so-called common people hobbled about on tiny feet disfigured by the awful custom of foot-binding. In Kwangtung this custom never held sway, women moved lightly and quickly. They carried their infants on their backs. We never observed this in the North and it was quite understandable. How could a mother carry a baby on her back when she had constantly to think about how to keep her own balance!

I asked for the car to stop since I wanted to take a few pictures. Instantly we were surrounded by a gay, curious crowd. They silently watched us with friendly attention.

I chose my subject right there—a young girl in local costume: half-length trousers of black, shiny, wrinkle-resistant material with a pattern of barely visible tiny holes, and a jacket of snow-white semi-transparent ramie cloth which cooled the skin pleasantly. Her partly open collar left her neck bare. The girl had shiny lacquered hair. Alas, again that acrid, sticky pomade which causes Chinese women to grow bald by the age of forty. Some sort of white tropical flower was stuck behind her ear. This detail struck me especially. Nowhere in the North had I seen anything like it, and not every young Chinese girl adorns herself with flowers and, from our European point of view, looks like a charming Chinese Carmen. The girl gladly allowed herself to be photographed, whereas a Northern girl would undoubtedly have run away.

There were many, many children on the streets; they ran after us stretching out their little hands and repeating "cumshaw, cumshaw" (a distorted word of Portuguese origin, meaning money for a commission, fees). The adults also didn't take their eyes off us and followed us in droves to all the shops. They had time to spare. As in the North, there was not enough work.

We saw that all the stores and shops were filled with shop assistants who had really nothing to do at all. We were told that these were usually the owner's country relatives whom he exploited literally for a farthing or sometimes for a bowl of rice.

The "narrow streets" as we called the Hsikuan quarter, the ancient port district, were in the western part of Canton. Our road lay along the embankment close by the warships which stood in the roadstead flying foreign flags, past the island of Shameen which protruded like a splinter in the living body of the city. It lay before us, hushed, on guard, separated from the embankment by a small artificial canal and the wall of hatred and anger of the Chinese people. Some sort of sawhorse-like barrier draped with barbed wire stood on the bridge with its heavy cast-iron gates, leaving only a narrow passageway into the place of residence of all the foreign consulates (with the exception of the Soviet which was right within the city, along the embankment). The building of the former tsarist consulate on the island of Shameen had been seized by the British. Negotiations for its return had been conducted without result since 1924. The imperialists did not recognize the Kuomintang government as the de jure government. They refused to recognize the Soviet consulate in Canton because it was a consulate accredited to an unlawful government. Our representative was not even a member of the consular corps.

Two British soldiers in colonial uniforms—cork helmet, short khaki pants, rifle in hand and a broad sword at the belt—were pacing evenly up and down by the barrier on the bridge. Not a sound was heard from the other side. It was as if the island were dead. In fact, very few inhabitants remained there. Even the missionaries who had fled from the mainland had gone away.

I have written above that on the very eve of our departure from Vladivostok (June 23, 1925), right across from Shameen island on the Shakee embankment, shots were fired into a massive anti-imperialist demonstration in which representatives of all strata of Canton's population were taking part—schoolchildren, students, strike pickets, Whampoa Academy cadets, workers, and employees. Fifty-two corpses lay on the roadway and one hundred seventy-eight demonstrators were seriously wounded. Many school children and students were among the victims. The firing continued for twenty minutes. Even medical orderlies who were trying to remove the wounded were fired upon. The nature of the wounds revealed that the imperialists were using exploding dum-dum bullets. An English naval officer, who ordered the firing to begin, was raised in rank after two weeks.

These events provoked unprecedented indignation. The strike grew so that in the next few days life in Hong Kong and Shameen island seemed paralyzed since all the Chinese workers and employees, including servants, went away. British entrepreneurs lost millions.

After getting a grip on themselves, the imperialists began to spread about an absurd slander to the effect that the first shots were fired by the Russian Communists. The English news agency Reuters reported "A conversation between two Russians was overheard in Canton. One of them said: 'I myself fired the second shot at Shameen, Ivanovich fired the first. It took two weeks to receive the money from Borodin.'" The authors of this dirty lie evidently didn't know that Ivanovich is not a Russian surname but a patronymic.

The inhabitants of Shameen almost never appeared on the streets in the city. Only twice did I happen to see these "islanders." Once in one of the "narrow streets," I came across two haughty young people in stylish suits who were looking straight ahead and walking with even steps, like robots; both held their left hands in their pockets. This was the fashion then. Another time a Shameen islander was riding in a rickshaw past the car in which I was sitting and he looked me over curiously without lowering his eyes. At that time all kinds of absurdities were being written in the imperialist press about Soviet citizens. In May 1925 during the counter-revolutionary mutiny of the Yunnan and Kwangsi troops, some of the advisers' wives went to Hong Kong; it was still possible then. Sofya Bronislavna Matseylik told me how many "civilized" men and women came to the hotel dining room where they were eating, to take a look at "the wild Russians." They were not ashamed to express their surprise aloud: Well, wasn't it strange, Soviet women looked quite decent.

When I arrived it was already impossible for us to visit Shameen, but from rumors I heard that the island was in a very neglected state, and did not at all resemble the clean, comfortable little city, which it had been before the strike.

Along the embankment I was shown the place where the blood of the demonstrators had been spilled. A small obelisk stood there with the inscription, "Do not forget this day." Several years later, Chiang Kai-shek, currying favor with the imperialists, ordered it removed.

The anti-British boycott was strictly observed. Not only the strike pickets who walked the streets with clubs and rifles, but the broad masses of the people jealously enforced it so that their enemy—British imperialism—suffered material losses. I was able to observe an example of this that very same day. In one of the shops someone remarked to us that one of our women was holding a pack of British cigarettes (Camels) in her hand. I must confess that we were all very embarrassed and the guilty party in the incident—she had just arrived and had still not gotten her bearings—discarded the cigarettes at once.

"The Narrow Streets"

"The narrow streets" which once we visited with so much pleasure are no more. They were gradually replaced both before and after the revolution. No modern city could put up with such a large part of itself serving as a museum of feudal architecture and trade. "The narrow streets" were very picturesque but completely impractical. The existence of these countless tiny stores and workshops which simultaneously served as living space, like the sampan for the boat dweller, had long since ceased to be justified.

Many of the streets were so narrow that the passerby could easily touch the walls on both sides. Two rickshaws could not pass each other in them and two palanquins could pass only with difficulty. But there were also somewhat wider streets where alongside the small stalls which glittered only because of their marvelous goods one also encountered luxury stores decorated with gilt and colored glass panels, with counters made of precious wood—stores whose owners looked dandyish in their expensive brocade gowns. They, of course, found it crowded in "the narrow streets."

Every craft was represented by one or several side streets. We walked along one street after another specializing in items of ivory, amber, mother-of-pearl, tortoise-shell, porcelain, precious wood, jasper and silver, streets of embroidered pictures, embroidered slippers, famous Kwangtung shawls, robes and pajamas adorned with vivid embroidery, ramie goods, handmade lace, beaded embroideries, painted fans made of white chicken feathers. There lacked only lattice-enamel and red lacquerware which Peking had had in abundance.

We went enthusiastically from store to store, delighting in the marvelous products of popular arts. It seemed that time had stopped for us. And only after we were already rather tired did we finally ask ourselves, where are the people whose hands have labored lovingly over everything which has delighted us so?

We didn't have to look far. They were right there before us. Before the eyes of the pedestrians, in the depths of their cramped, cluttered workshops they were bent over their work. There were many of them and all were men: youths, adults, and the very aged. They were sawing, hewing, drawing, glueing, sharpening, painting, and embroidering. From time to time the older ones would straighten their stooped backs and look at us with tired, reddened eyes, but the young people were cheerful and laughter-loving. They lived right there, breathed in the industrial dust, and slept on old boards right on the ground. This was not the worst of it. In one of the back alleys of the narrow streets I turned my attention to a strange structure—a long, wooden trunk resting on high props. Torn matting and rags protruded through the cracks. This trunk served as a home for three persons—two adults and a baby—or rather as a lodging for the night, because one could only lie down in it. The trunk was elevated because at night packs of rats ran about, and during the tropical monsoons, ten inches of water and sometimes more would flood the streets in minutes.

Heavy labor, terrible working conditions, beggarly wages, such was the common lot of Chinese workingmen at that time, and Canton was no exception. There for the first time the Chinese worker raised his head and the government recognized his rights, proclaiming a worker-peasant policy as one of the bases of its program, and beginning a series of measures to improve the life of the masses. This was already a good deal, but victory was still far off.

Later we visited "the narrow streets" many times. I remember well how they looked at that time.

Imagine yourself in Canton in the mid-twenties. Let us enter a tiny shop where amber goods are sold. Under a glass counter lie strings of large and small beads made of amber of every color from opaline to dark red. Seals and cigarette holders are displayed and figurines of people and animals stand on tapered stands of black wood. These are all cheap wares made from melted bits of amber. But if you enquire they will show you velvet cases with expensive necklaces. In the center of the individual beads you will see fragments of earth or wood preserved in an amber case for thousands of years. This is genuine amber found in whole pieces.

Here is a store selling embroidered shoes, typical Chinese slippers with upturned toes. They are sewn of cheap satin of every color and embroidered with the traditional dragons and phoenixes, symbols of the emperor and empress. The sole is leather and the lining of cotton. A pair of such slippers costs a dollar eighty-five in local currency (the Kwangtung dollar was worth sixty kopecks then). If you figure in the cost of the satin, the silk thread, the soles, inner-soles, lining and the middleman's profit, what remained for the poor embroideress who so diligently covered the whole surface of the uppers with even, patient stitches?

The most difficult embroidery (that of pictures) was done by men. Many Chinese provinces had developed this art and each was known for its own style. In Hunan, for example, it was close embroidery on white and colored satin, in Kwangtung they embroidered on white semi-transparent silk cloth, with light airy stitches. There were no dragons in the pictures but there were phoenixes. Basically birds and flowers were depicted. Even prosaic chickens and ducks were awarded the artist's attention. However, most often, a pair of storks, symbols of connubial faith and longevity were embroidered on the pictures, and behind them a large, glowing sun. There too were sold the black wooden frames for these embroideries.

Here are the world-famous Kwangtung shawls. They are made from very beautiful sturdy Kwangtung silk crepe and decorated with long heavy fringes of twisted silk. They come in all colors and sizes, and it is difficult to choose just one. If you settle, let us say, for one of peach color with multicolored embroidery in the shape of pagodas and houses amid mountains and trees, at once you start wanting a black one covered with pale crimson and dark purple roses. Right then the salesmen will unfold a huge, cream-colored one with a monochrome embroidery depicting a scene from a Chinese novel. And so on without end. The average price of a shawl did not exceed sixty yuan in Kwangtung currency, but the cream-colored one I have mentioned was twice as dear. These goods were for export; Chinese women did not wear shawls, and shawls in general were of foreign origin. It is said that Spaniards brought them a very long time ago. The Chinese adopted the craft and far excelled their instructors. The embroidery of shawls was done by women.

At the mother-of-pearl stores they sold large pairs of hinged shells covered with scenes from ancient legends, mother-of-pearl necklaces and every sort of small wares.

Small fans made of white chicken feathers glued to a horn frame sold very cheaply. But they were so gracefully made and painted with such talent that they seemed like expensive trinkets.

You walk along the street of porcelain wares, calculated to please every taste and purse. Next to expensive vases brought from the center of the China industry, the city of Chingtechen in northern Kiangsi where the imperial factories were constructed many centuries ago, are cheaper goods. Only be wary of blindly trusting the trade mark on the bottom which the salesman will obligingly show you. It may happen that Chingtechen has no relation to the given item and the indicated marks of the imperial administration also do not correspond to reality.

Ivory carving has existed in China for hundreds of years. There is a wide assortment of articles made from it ranging from small household articles— combs, powder-cases, cigarette-holders, cigarette-cases, rings, etc.—to massive depictions of every kind of god and table ornaments carved from whole tusks. The Chinese ivory spheres in which the outer shell encloses several revolving globes covered with fine patterns are famous. The chess-sets are very fine. The pieces are made in the shape of little figures beginning with the simple, feudal pawn and ending with the emperor himself. The rooks are shaped like elephants.

On one of the "narrow streets" are sold the straw mats for which Kwangtung is famous. Here are simple, unadorned ones a meter and a half long as well as luxurious room-length carpets decorated with enormous, bright flowers. All of them are handmade with the help of only the most primitive equipment. Mats are a necessary household article in South China where they serve as both mattress and sheet. In such weather even a pillow is replaced by a porcelain block.

Not far away expensive period furniture which forms one of Kwangtung's most important export items is sold. The seats and backs are made of marble of every color framed with artfully carved precious dark woods.

On one of the streets you are offered pictures on an unusually heavy, brittle paper. The effect of watercolors on the blindingly white background is striking. There are Chinese landscapes, flowers, fish, scenes from folk life, depictions of artists in colorful, ancient costumes. The pictures are placed in series according to the theme in small glass-lidded boxes, with patterned material pasted on the sides.

There too are sold postcards on which the artists had drawn only the heads, arms and legs of people in ink and watercolor while their clothing and the surrounding objects were depicted with the aid of cutouts from Chinese postage stamps of every color.

The streets where edibles were sold presented a vivid picture of the generous abundance of Kwangtung's soil. Imagine a narrow passageway between two rows of stalls covered with torn matting. The blinding tropical sun falls in slanted rays or rounded patches on the produce spread in the heavy, brown shade. There are mountains of exotic fruits: round bunches of bananas, the hairy heads of coconuts, orange mangoes, small lichees in green, prickly skin looking just like unripe chestnuts, pineapples with green-feathered sharp-ended leaves. Further on are vegetables, also unusual in appearance. Long narrow cucumbers twist about like snakes; the radishes are thick and long like our horseradish, and horseradish is of an unusual violet color. Here are Chinese cabbage growing tall, not wide, tomatoes wonderful in color and taste, sugar cane, lotus roots. And all of this is thrown generously on the stalls in great heaps.

The fish stalls are a real icthyological museum. The small octopi remind one of starfish with their elegant tentacles marked by two rows of suckers. Next to them is a silver swordfish and some kind of flat monster in the shape of a distorted square with a long, narrow tail. Tubs of tiny ocean lobsters. Frogs jump about in wire cages and snakes writhe. The only thing I did not see was the famous sea cucumbers with their bluish-black skin dotted with funny little spines; evidently it was too expensive a delicacy for the market.

The meat stalls with their Rembrandt-like lighting were very picturesque. The portly shopkeeper in his shorts and open jacket looked especially striking amid the pigs' carcasses hanging by their feet. His fat, naked belly shines and harmonizes remarkably in color and form with the contents of his stall.

And the buyers? Their eyes must swim from all this splendor. One wants to load oneself down and carry home as much as one can.

But all these riches of Kwangtung's bountiful nature, despite their seeming cheapness, are not so accessible to the population. There a woman stops at a stall and wants to buy something. She has a bunch of hooks on a ring—that serves like a net bag. On each hook a purchase is fastened: a frog dangles from one, a chicken foot from another, from a third a bunch of some sort of greens. This woman cannot allow herself very much . . . What kind of a soup can you make from a chicken's foot!

By the way a few words on the theme of south Chinese frogs. It turns out that this is an amazing thing, it reminds one of very tender chicken meat. We often teased new arrivals, dining them and afterwards showing them the frog legs. In the first minute the guest's eyes bulged and he prepared to disgorge the frog, but the next time he himself would order a frog ragout.

Not far from the city market were found the cheap eating places and the expensive restaurants. Kwangtung cuisine is no less famous in China than is French cuisine in Europe. Kwangtung men were known as great gourmands. They supposed that everything in nature is clean and can be used as food as long as it does not harm the health. Even such apparently repulsive creatures as poisonous snakes are considered a delicacy, not to mention the dogs which are specially fed. Those who have tasted their flesh cannot praise it sufficiently. An old Chinese anecdote tells how once a European ate two portions of a dish he liked very much, and not knowing Chinese he began to quack, in this way asking the waiter whether this wasn't duck. In reply the waiter barked at him.

There was a large selection of snakes at any restaurant in town. You definitely had to buy them alive or else you could be poisoned. You were taken to a wire cage and you saw a whole tangle of these disgusting creatures which twisted and writhed about, large ones and small ones of every color. Holding a special fork, the chef stands near you and asks which one you want. Suppressing your revulsion you quickly point out any one of them, it's all the same which one it is, but the real gourmand makes his choice without rushing, with appetite; he's a connoisseur of this dish: after all there are different kinds of snakes and each has its own taste. Only once did I eat snake meat and it seemed to me that I was chewing rubber, but they say there are snakes with tender, juicy flesh, reminiscent of perch but even more tender and tasty.

Barely opening the cage, with lightning-like speed, the chef seizes your chosen one, instantly cuts off its head and just as quickly skins it. After this the cooking commences. One makes soup from snake, boils them in butter, etc.

On the following Sunday we visited both of the city's department stores—the Sincere and the Sun Company. These were quite modern commercial enterprises comparing favorably with the British stores in Shanghai. In one of them a remarkably beautiful salesgirl was pointed out to me and it was explained that she was one of the representatives of the families of mixed blood. The foreign businessmen in Hong Kong and on Shameen island often left their families behind at home and acquired new ones there. It happens that they would become attached to them, provided for them financially, fathered children who as a rule were exceptionally beautiful and capable and well-educated, but they never recognized them officially.

Settling down in Tungshan

For us daily life in Tungshan was unusual and in its own way also not without interest.

I arrived in early spring. The heat had not yet set in but the humidity was terrible. In the closets and under the bed everything was covered with a green coating. In view of the unsanitary condition of the locality certain precautionary measures were prescribed for us. No one looked after the sources of water supply in Canton, there was neither sewerage nor filters, therefore we drank only carefully boiled water, poured boiling water on our fruits and vegetables and added a spoonful of lysol to our bath water so that we soon fairly reeked of it. The inhabitants of Tungshan were often sick since they used water straight from the canal where all sorts of dirt flowed. Every year in Kwangtung there were two or three outbreaks of epidemics (typhus, typhoid fever, amoebic dysentery and even cholera). The real scourge of the Chinese people was tuberculosis and Kwangtung was no exception.

Our comrades often fell ill. Iraida Petrovna, the wife of the adviser I. P. Shuvano, almost died from typhoid fever. Ye. V. Teslenko suffered for almost a year from malaria and tuberculosis and was crippled for the rest of her life. We all suffered from skin and stomach disorders.

The majority of the advisers lived in four houses which we called "the boxes." They stood in a row on the canal bank, behind them the rice fields stretched out. Still further off, on Tashat'ou Island, stood the airport where from time to time the planes piloted by our flyers took off with what seemed to us like a mighty roar. "The boxes" were completely identical, three-storey

European-style buildings with massive stone verandahs in front, a three-room apartment on each floor with all the tropical conveniences down to window screens for protection against mosquitoes and ceiling fans shaped like large propellers. The flat roofs were enclosed by balustrades. In front of the boxes, behind the stone grillwork of the wall with its iron gates, was a small common garden with enormous trees on which almost all year round small pungent white flowers thickly blossomed, distantly reminiscent of our jasmine. The paths were covered with paving stones and lined with camellia bushes. In general in Kwangtung there were many evergreen bushes and trees with stiff, lacquer-like leaves and pulpy odoriferous flowers.

Artur Golicher, the progressive German journalist, visited Canton a month before our arrival, lived in Tungshan at the German consul's, and was received by Borodin. He was sympathetic to the Chinese revolution and spoke respect-fully of our advisers. But still he was unable to abandon the characteristic bourgeois journalists' love for sensationalism, the striving to shock the reader. It is also possible that to Golicher, a man of Western culture, the posi-tion of the handful of our advisers who dared to appear unarmed in Canton and submit themselves and their near ones to the arbitrariness of political passions and unexpected events seemed truly dangerous. In any case he wrote that our boxes produced a sinister impression upon him, that supposedly we kept soldiers and military vehicles there and that the iron gate to the garden was always locked. However, I lived in Tungshan almost contemporaneously with him and I never saw a single soldier before our advisers' homes. Only in front of the staff headquarters of the mission were sentries posted, but this was more of a guard of honor than a real guard and in general we soon refused it.

Day and night sampans plied the narrow canal. The sampan dwellers with uplifted heads stared at the verandahs of the houses where the Russian advisers lived. Sometimes ancient boats with unfurled sails passed ever so slowly along the canal, boats just like those in the drawings in Chinese historical novels. They had paintings on the prow of open-jawed dragons and enormous high carved sterns with several rows of small windows. They literally hung over the bank so closely did the vessels fit within the canal. The time-blackened wood and the archaic form bespoke many years of sailing full of romanticism and fascinating adventures, as it seemed to us.

At first we were unable to sleep because of the small Chinese horns—
these were the sampans calling to each other in order to avoid collisions in
the dark. Their plaintive outpourings, now drawing closer, now fading into the
distance, sounded like an exotic musical composition against the background
of the tropical night. But at dawn we were awakened by a more than prosaic
cause. A long line of sampans carrying excrement for the fields passed by at
this hour; long before its appearance the sharp odor awakened us.

Enormous bluish-black, almost hairless water-buffaloes, knee-deep in
liquid mud lazily pulled eternal plows on the other side of the canal. Their
terrible, three-edged horns, twisted like yataghans and often more than a
meter in length, almost lay on their backs. We were told that in the jungles
of southwest China where water buffaloes still exist in the wild, they are very
fierce and will attack man, but it was difficult to believe this on observing
their phlegmatic disposition. They crawl into the water right up to their
nostrils and stand that way for hours on end without moving. Boy buffalo
herders ride on their backs without any fear.

After plowing the square inundated fields, dozens of peasants in broad,
conical hats appeared and bending over, they planted the seedlings. The sun
blazed mercilessly, and the chocolate-brown water, hot and thick, gave off
a heavy vapor. At this time we were very much afraid of the Kwangtung snakes
which we had heard so many stories about, and we thought with horror that
perhaps death threatened the people at every step taken in the rice fields.
How could one see what was beneath ones feet in the turbid water! Later we
never even thought of snakes. In Tungshan there was only one case when the
wife of the adviser Ter stepped on a snake right on the street in front of her
house. The disgusting creature instantly coiled itself around her leg, but the
woman managed to get it off.

But our comrades who fought on Hainan island against the troops of
the militarist General Teng Pen-yin said that there were huge numbers of
poisonous snakes there. When the soldiers dug trenches these were filled with
snakes by the next morning. It was dangerous to walk in the forest thickets;
tree snakes which jumped on a man from above lived there.

Together we hired an amah who lived in the small servant's room. She
was a woman no longer young and with three children in the village, but she
took good care of her appearance. We sometimes found her in the company

of her friend, another amah, who arranged her complicated hairdo, wound her hair on some sort of device and thickly smeared it with a sticky substance from which her head took on a lacquered appearance. The amah sat with a satisfied look, convinced that such a hairdo became her very well and she was, by the way, not mistaken. A final touch—a flower behind the ear—made her almost pretty. Naturally such a hairdo was not something for just a day, the amah preserved it for a whole week.

Unfortunately we soon had to part with our amah. We were simply unable to make ourselves understood to her. No matter how we explained things to her, she always replied with a crushed look "no sabe" which means in pidgin English, "I don't know." We didn't speak Cantonese. She went away to her village and we hired another. She was a girl of about sixteen, cheerful and lively. We became very attached to her. With the onset of the torrid season, we noticed that at night without undressing, she would go to sleep right on the stone slabs of the antechamber. Then one of the interpreters departed and we settled our amah in his room with the "propeller."[11] When we left for the North we made her a present of all our furniture. She cried bitterly when we parted.

The heat was a trying experience for all of us. Those who bore it worst were the ones who drank too many fruit-flavored drinks. When a gloomy day came along, we said to each other in astonishment "Just think, it is never hotter in Moscow than it is right now, but we never even realized what bliss it is!" We also became acquainted with tropical downpours. Suddenly clouds appeared and after several minutes the streets were turned into rivers. A downpour might begin any time or place and there was no chance of foreseeing it. Once it overtook me in the narrow streets. I had to rent a palanquin and travel in that mandarin manner, while the bearers made their way through nearly knee-deep water. After a downpour the water quickly ran off. In an hour the streets were almost dry.

At school you may learn that moonlit tropical nights are bewitchingly beautiful, but you learn this truth anew in Canton. For a long time we couldn't get accustomed to the enormous yellow moon right above our heads. It looks into your very soul, and you cannot escape it. Someone cannot restrain himself and suggests that everyone go out for a stroll. Might as well, you can't sleep, there is such a commotion in your head.

---

11. i.e. ceiling fan. Translator.

You walk in an enchanted lunar kingdom where everything is black and white. Enormous trees dotted with flowers scatter a sharp, unsettling aroma, their short, coal-black shadows are cast onto the brilliantly illuminated ground. A light mist rises from the canal and the rice fields. Warm, moist air caresses your cheeks. And there is an evening concert no less. A chorus of frogs sings in self-oblivion, cicadas whirr deafeningly.

But it wasn't the moon so much as the heat which hindered our sleep. In South China the people often sleep on the street in summer on folding cots. We could not allow ourselves such luxury, but we often walked about at night. Sometimes you went out and heard that there was singing at the club. You go there. From the wide-open, brightly lighted windows a voice floats out, "Amid the crowded ball, accidentally . . . " At the gates is a silent group of poorly dressed Chinese. They part to let you pass. At your suggestion that they enter one of them is quietly embarrassed and the others make a characteristic, negative gesture.

In the small living room are quiet young people together with their superiors, the older people. Pavlov looks sternly from the wall and, it seems, does not take his eyes from you. Our most mischievous Komsomolka, the typist Nadya Tsorn (later the wife of the adviser N. T. Rogov) is seated at the piano. She was horseback riding and hasn't changed her clothes. The masculine Junkers jacket was tight on her full, strong figure. Next to her was our lyric tenor the topographer Styopa Protasov who was small and undersized. But now no one even noticed his unassuming appearance. He bore himself with assurance, his pale face had taken on color. He sang and how he sang! We were afraid to go in lest we break the spell. Then the adviser Korneev, the name-sake of I. Korneev who worked in the North, sang the gypsy song "Be gone, don't look at me," and at the words "money have I none, only the cross on my chest," he flung open his shirt with a tragic gesture. The effect was unexpected; since he wore no cross everyone began to laugh.

We loved to sing Russian folk and revolutionary songs in chorus, not forgetting either the famous "Dunya" but adapting it to our Tungshan reality.

Almost every evening we went riding by taxi to get a breath of fresh air after a wearying day of labor. This was inexpensive; many of us crowded into the car and the price was just a dollar an hour in local currency. We settled the account at the beginning of the month when we received our salaries. Our route was always the same, past the cemetery of the seventy-two heroes and further to the village of Shaho.

I have one amusing recollection connected with the hot season. Suddenly Nadya Tsorn, Sonya Okoneshnikova, and I began losing our hair. Our hair was fashionably short then and after considering it briefly, we tore out our girlish beauty by the roots. You can imagine how we looked, but we weren't embarrassed, we were even somewhat proud of our action and were inclined to view it as a revolutionary gesture, the denial of feminine inequality. Many of our girls at that time wanted to be like men! Sonya Okoneshnikova even wore riding breeches in our native land and I tried to speak in a deep voice and sang the "Internationale" in a bass.

It never even occurred to us that our shaven tops might call forth any particular reaction. On the street we often met almost completely bald-headed Chinese old women, while Buddhist nuns we knew generally were completely shaved. Moreover, short bobbed hair was considered a mark of freethinking in China then, and this was already a big change for the better in popular customs.

My colleagues only teased me slightly for the change which had occurred to me. Borodin, seeing a shaven boy in a dress in place of his interpreter, kept a delicate silence, although he set off at once for his wife and advised her to take a peek at how I looked. Blyukher, who was visiting Borodin that day, and gave me a lift to Tungshan in his car, expressed a categorical protest with his whole face—he could do this very well—but he also said nothing. But the Chinese population reacted to my shaven head as to some sort of challenge to their aesthetic and even moral ideas. "To our way of thinking it's no good, it's shameful for a girl," Chinese explained to me later. And I understood. After all in Russia too at a time not so long ago, to crop a girl's hair meant to shame her.

This is what happened. Our fellow workers decided to set off for town, to go to the Bluebeard, a Chinese café with an English name which we often visited to have ice cream. I joined them. Evening came on. At that time a black prickly growth was just beginning to appear on my uncovered head. Suddenly as we entered the city my rickshaw puller began to summon his countrymen with loud cries to turn their attention to me. "Look what sort of a foreign devil I'm pulling," he shouted. My companions did not understand Chinese but still they could not help but notice the general mirth which my appearance was provoking. People threw down their work, ran to me as fast as they could, laughed, shouted, and pointed their fingers at me. A whole crowd of squealing children ran behind my rickshaw. The friendship of my companions could not withstand such an experience, and they declared that they could not go anywhere with me until my hair grew out or I began to wear some kind of proper headgear.

I remember an excursion to the White Cloud Mountain (Po yün shan) where an ancient Buddhist monastery was located. The locality was considered one of the most picturesque in the vicinity of Canton. The gently sloping although rather high, grass-covered hills alternated with gentle hollows and valleys. A line of flagstones like the steps of an endless staircase led up and then down. It was evident that at one time the monastery had been much frequented, the flagstones were deeply worn by pilgrims' feet, but in our time most of the enormous monastery was abandoned and only in the center of it did monks still live. They greeted us rather coolly, and we didn't bother them, but we carefully inspected all the courts and the twisting staircases which joined them in the abandoned part of the monastery. This nook was very poetic, a living embodiment of the fading Chinese past, and might have served as an excellent set for plays on themes from the ancient Chinese novels. At one time the beauty Ying Ying walked on such staircases as these, and White Jasper knocked at such narrow doors in order to become a monk and bury his broken heart forever.[12]

In Tungshan we also had an "enemy"—the owner of a primitive little factory for making lime from heated seashells. It is difficult to describe the suffocating stench which emanated from this enterprise and hung over the entire part of Tungshan where our Soviet colony was located. The factory worked at night, evidently the owner figured that in their dreams people would not bother about what sort of air they were breathing. In fact as soon as the ovens were fired and their inexpressible, unbearable stench began to diffuse, everyone woke up and rushed to shut the windows. Still, a repulsive loathsome odor penetrated through the cracks and we languished without sleep, pacing from corner to corner. The doctor found symptoms of poisoning in some of us. The factory worked sporadically about twice a week, otherwise

---

12. Ying Ying is the heroine of the famous drama by Wang Shih-fu, *The Spilled Cup*. White Jasper (sic) is the name of the hero of Ts'ao Hsüeh-ching's novel, *Dream of the Red Chamber*.

we simply could not have endured it. Negotiations with the owner including an offer to buy his factory produced no results. We had to turn to the authorities and they somehow made him see reason.

The leaders of the mission provided us with free foreign language instruction, and we studied almost daily. English was taught by an elderly American lady, the wife of a Chinese professor who had received his education in the USA. She was very homesick for her country and was completely unable to get adjusted to Canton although she had lived there more than ten years. The eternal knocking of the wooden sandals irritated her. "Why didn't you stay in America?" we asked her. She replied "Chinese can receive an education in America but they can't receive the right to settle permanently. They are taught so that they will become purveyors of American influence in China."

Evenings I gave Russian lessons to the director of the Kowloon Railroad who came every other day and studied very diligently. Once he invited me and another comrade to his house for tea. His villa was not far from our boxes, on the other side of the railroad right of way. We expected to see a colorful Chinese way of life, but we were mistaken. Everything in the house was on the Western model, the whole family was dressed in the latest American styles. It turned out that he had lived in the USA for a long time and, evidently, had grown unaccustomed to his homeland. The children even spoke their native language poorly.

On March 8, 1926, China marked International Women's Day for the second time. During the day we watched a demonstration in which, the press reported, ten thousand women took part, and we read articles in the papers dedicated to the holiday. In the evening at the special invitation of the Kuomintang CEC's Women's Work Department we took part in an amateur night arranged by various Chinese institutions. I also had to perform. I seem to recall that it was held in Sun Yat-sen University but I wouldn't swear to it. Only the stage was illuminated, the hall was plunged into semi-darkness. There was a really huge crowd. The thunder of applause greeted us.

Our number consisted of several revolutionary songs, including the "Internationale," unfortunately without musical accompaniment because it turned out at the last moment that the piano on the stage was so out of tune that literally not a single note was correct. Special success was enjoyed by a living tableau depicting the countries of the world in the form of women wearing national costumes. They surrounded Soviet Russia—the wife of the adviser Rogachev in a sarafan and a *kokoshnik*[13] holding a red banner. I was made up as a Chinese woman—dressed in pajamas embroidered with dragons and shod in ancient satin men's slippers on high wooden soles. My head swam in a jet-black wig, parted in the middle, with a bang and long braids, fastened from both sides near the ears; the hairdo was not in the least Chinese. I portrayed awakened China and stretched out my hands towards Soviet Russia. No matter how surprising it may seem, the Chinese recognized themselves in me and applauded deafeningly. However, I also made a hit with our own people. They said that Chinese dress was just my style.

Several days later an entire week was devoted in Canton to the anniversary of Sun Yat-sen's death. Our advisers spoke at memorial meetings.

At the same time in Nanking there occurred the solemn ceremony of laying the foundation stone for the memorial to Sun Yat-sen on the Purple Mountain in the presence of Soong Ching-ling and many delegations. At large meetings orators called for unity in the struggle for Sun Yat-sen's ideas, and against imperialism and militarism. At one of the meetings the USSR's vice-consul in Shanghai, Solomon Lazarevich Vilde, who had come specially for the ceremony gave a speech. Afterwards he paid a visit to Soong Ching-ling.

Chiang Kai-shek Throws Down His Mask

In the middle of March I was summoned to serve as interpreter for the head of the South China mission, N. V. Kuybyshev. In his office sat a man whom I recognized at once since I had seen his picture in the papers more than once. It was Wang Ching-wei, the leader of the Kuomintang leftists.

He looked very efficient in a European suit and smoothly combed haircut in the contemporary style. His hair glittered from brilliantine. One sensed that he really looked after his appearance and knew about his reputation as a humbler of female hearts. He was already past forty, but he seemed much younger.

I confess that seeing one of the leaders of the Chinese revolutionary movement I really stared at him then.

It was no accident that Wang Ching-wei came to be head of the Kuomintang leadership. His "leftist" views it seemed permitted of no doubts. It was not for nothing that the imperialists considered him a "Red" and the Kuomintang rightists demanded his expulsion from the party and even made

---

13. A type of old Russian woman's headdress. Translator.

attempts on his life. The best orator and publicist in the Kuomintang, one of Sun Yat-sen's earliest collaborators who had taken part in the organizational meeting of the T'ungmenghui in 1905, a member of the executive committee, Wang Ching-wei seemed a natural successor to Sun Yat-sen after the death of Liao Chung-k'ai. That he had violated Sun Yat-sen's will in 1910 by organizing an attempt on the prince regent, for which he was imprisoned, was indulgently forgiven him. After all he was so young then!

However, it soon became clear that Wang Ching-wei was a cowardly, unprincipled politician and had never been a real revolutionary.

There existed a legend that Wang Ching-wei escaped execution because he had caught the fancy of one of the Manchu princesses. In fact he was freed by the 1911 Revolution. However, a rubber princess if not a Manchu had the most direct relationship to him. He was married to a surprisingly ugly but very rich Chinese woman from the island of Penang in the Straits of Malacca where she had spacious rubber plantations. It was said jokingly then that all Shanghai wore rubber shoes made from her raw materials. She was terribly jealous, and what was most important, exerted a baneful influence on her husband. At one time she had with Wang Ching-wei made an attempt on the life of a Manchu prince, and now she had turned into a violent enemy of the revolution.

During the conversation which I translated not a word was said about any kind of danger from Chiang Kai-shek. N. V. Kuybyshev, stubborn and with a broad forehead, was sitting across from Wang Ching-wei and coolly looking at him with his big blue eyes. Meanwhile there were just a few days until the March 20 Incident.

Just about this time, Chiang Kai-shek demanded that the advisers who were living across from his country villa in Tungshan move. It stood far off and was in no way subject to observation. Nevertheless, despite our comrades' protests they were simply evicted. This is a characteristic fact which indicates the degree to which Chiang Kai-shek's suspicions were excited with respect to the Russian advisers.

On March 20 Chiang Kai-shek committed his first counterrevolutionary act; reaction succeeded in crowding the CCP from its former positions.

Just prior to it without the knowledge of the advisers he carried out a massive transfer of Whampoa senior cadets from the First Army to the other units, thereby weakening the revolutionary cadres. In addition, he resorted to provocations. As an excuse for his actions Chiang Kai-shek cited the appearance of the gunboat *Chung Shan* on March 19 near the Whampoa Academy, although he himself had issued the order to the commander, a communist. Accusing the gunboat's officers of intending to pull off a coup and to arrest him personally, Chiang Kai-shek issued an order to take the commander and the commissar into custody.

On March 20-21 he expelled the commissars and the Communists from the Whampoa Academy and the First Army, arrested many of them and dispatched troops to Tungshan in order to surround the staff headquarters of the advisers and place a guard around their homes.

At the same time the strike committee in the city was surrounded, and the strike leaders (mostly Communists) were arrested. Chiang Kai-shek abolished the Military Council, having declared himself the commander-in-chief of the National-Revolutionary Army.

On March 21, we employees of the Intelligence Division showed up for work as usual. The news of what was happening had already reached Tungshan. Some of us wanted to question the Chinese interpreters in our press bureau, but the chief strictly ordered us to "stop conversations" and get on with our work.

None of us thought that the actions undertaken by Chiang Kai-shek would in any measure affect the advisers who never interfered in the internal affairs of the Kuomintang. But still it was plain that he was up to no good and this disturbed us.

We had not succeeded in getting immersed in our translations when on our floor chairs began to be pushed about and doors slammed. The Chinese interpreters stormed along the corridor and locked themselves in the bathroom. Some sort of commotion had broken out in the courtyard in the front of the building. We heard the clang of rifles, military commands rang out in Chinese and Mira Sakhnovskaya, the mission's chief of staff raised her excited voice. "Interpreter, tell them immediately to return at once the Mausers they have taken from the sentries."

I ran down the staircase and jumped out onto the porch. The garden in front of the staff headquarters and the Intelligence Division was occupied by a detachment of soldiers. The disarmed sentinels stood forlornly on the side.

One of them, just a young lad, was almost crying. A Kuomintang officer stood in front of Sakhnovskaya and it was evident that her rebuff had produced an effect on him. He excused himself and said he was following orders. He returned the Mausers but led the sentries off somewhere.[14] A strengthened guard—about twenty, sullen, stern and rifle-bearing soldiers—was placed around the staff headquarters and the Intelligence Division.

Going back upstairs I ran right into the chief who severely reprimanded me for lack of restraint and improper curiosity, and ordered me to return to my place and not go out anywhere without instructions.

In the headquarters of the mission a delegation was formed at once to hold conversations with Chiang Kai-shek. It included Mira Sakhnovskaya and some others. Yolk went along as interpreter. Chiang Kai-shek did not want to see Kuybyshev.

At two o'clock we set off for the dining hall. The soldiers let us through on orders of the commander who limited himself to asking us where we were going. We ate without any appetite.

A Soviet delegation headed by A. S. Bubnov (Ivanovsky) was in Canton from March 13 through March 24. It included a representative from the All-Union Central Council of Trade Unions I. I. Lepse and the chairman of the Far Eastern Bureau of the All-Union Communist Party (Bolshevik) N. A. Kubyak. They were supposed to attend a meeting of the Politburo of the Kuomintang CEC at which Bubnov was scheduled to give a speech. They were living in Tungshan and on March 21 Chiang Kai-shek did not blush to place a guard at their door as well although he knew the high positions they occupied in the Soviet Union. Bubnov called up the staff headquarters of the mission and asked what was up, why wasn't he being allowed to leave his house.

Our delegates returned from Chiang Kai-shek only after dinner. It became known that he was demanding the departure immediately of Kuybyshev, Rogachev, and Razgon, and the return of Blyukher.

Wang Ching-wei fled Canton. A report appeared in the press that he had gone abroad. Later on he was removed in absentia from all of his posts but not expelled from the party. The commander of the Second Hunan Army, General T'an Yen k'ai, became chairman of the Nationalist government and Chang Ching-chiang—the big Shanghai capitalist, in the past Chiang Kai-shek's

14. The following day the guard around our establishment was restored but soon we ourselves refused it.

partner in the Shanghai stock market—became chairman of the Kuomintang CEC. This old man—broken by paralysis (he was carried everywhere in a chair)—was able to generate incredible energy in the struggle with leftists and Communits. But all of this happened later. Right now all of the many posts which Wang Ching-wei had abandoned remained vacant. Everyone was convinced that he would return. No one even thought that "Sun Yat-sen's successor" would turn out to be such a coward. Wang Ching-wei's disappearance provoked hysteria in the ranks of the Kuomintang leftists who did not understand the actions of their leader and didn't know what to do. On the evening of March 24, A. S. Bubnov's delegation departed for the Soviet Union on the steamship *Pamyat Lenina.* He was supposed to have had a final meeting with Wang Ching-wei before departing but it did not take place, nor did his speech to the Politburo of the Kuomintang CEC. Kuybyshev, Rogachev, and Razgon departed on the very same ship. T'an Yen-k'ai and Sung Tzu-wen saw them off from the government.[15] Chiang Kai-shek did not show up at the send-off.

The Tungshan colony said a warm farewell to its comrades. Standing on the threshold of the dining hall and lobby where tables had been set up, N. V. Kuybyshev gave a farewell speech and wished us success in our work. The others who were leaving spoke and then it was the turn of those who remained. Everyone was depressed by their knowledge that the situation had grown more complicated and that it would not be easy to work.

The incident led to exultation, of course, in imperialist circles. What kind of absurdities were not printed in the papers! In April the Shanghai *North China Herald* reported that Chiang Kai-shek had "arrested sixty Moscow agents, ten of whom, including Rukachev, had escaped" (this was how Rogachev's name had been garbled). *The Peking and Tientsin Times* maintained that "all the Russians in the Kuomintang army received advice to depart, almost all of the forty-seven advisers had been in prison."

It is possible that Chiang Kai-shek, who was inclined to hysteria, had acted in a fit of passion. He very quickly came to his senses and began to beat a retreat. His action was clearly directed against Sun Yat-sen's new course, at a time when the majority in the Kuomintang understood that the preservation

---

15. Sung Tzu-wen, Soong Ching-ling's brother, was director of the Central Bank in Kwangtung and minister of finance in the Kuomintang government, and was considered a leftist then. Subsequently he was the head of one of the four families which controlled the national economy during the period of the Kuomintang regime.

of the alliance with the CCP and friendly relations with the Soviet Union, as well as support of the mass popular movement were completely indispensable for the further development of the national-revolutionary movement. The arrest of Communists and revolutionary workers continued for only two days, and the troops remained in Tungshan for only five hours. Subsequently Chiang Kai-shek generally denied the facts concerning the surrounding of the strike committee and the homes of the advisers.

The majority of the Kuomintang generals did not desire Chiang Kai-shek's elevation, his dictatorship did not suit them. The leftists, Teng Yen-ta and Li Chi-shen, for example, openly expressed their indignation. Li Chi-shen as chief of staff of the National-Revolutionary Army, personally came to Tungshan to apologize and said that he would have it out with Chiang Kai-shek. Similar declarations were made by several rightist-oriented generals. There is even information that at the end of March the rightists were preparing a blow against him. In the first days after the March 20 Incident, the Kwangtung clique made advances to our advisers. Sun Fo held a banquet in their honor. The commander of the Fifth Army, Li Fu-lin, paid a visit to Tungshan for the first time and gave a dinner in honor of his adviser Lunev.

Chiang Kai-shek also lost prestige among the workers of Canton. He had not only surrounded the strike committee and carried out arrests there, but also placed the provocateur Ch'en Sen at the head of the Kwangtung Workers' Federation.[16] The latter was well-known for his statements in favor of ending the Hong Kong—Canton strike and it was said of him that he had been suborned by the Society for the Study of Sun Yat-senism which was trying to lead the Kwangtung proletariat.

A strong faction in the Whampoa Academy demanded Wang Ching-wei's return and the transfer of political leadership in the army to the Kuomintang. The same mood prevailed in the ranks. Chiang Kai-shek could count only on the support of the First Corps but it was very much weakened by the recent transfers.

---

16. The Kwangtung Workers' Federation was one of three trade union organizations in Kwangtung at the time. It was supported by Kuomintag rightists as a counterweight to the revolutionary Council of Workers' Deputies, and was under the influence of bourgeois elements. It joined together artisans for the most part.

In a word, Chiang Kai-shek's position after March 20 was extremely shaky. Therefore Wang Ching-wei's behavior provoked even more astonishment; he did not even make an attempt to censure Chiang Kai-shek in public.

Sensing danger, Chiang Kai-shek lost his head for the first time. He began to repent, to cry and to threaten suicide, he declared that he would retire immediately, and he began trying to arrange a meeting with Wang Ching-wei. The latter stubbornly remained in hiding and maintained contact through his wife who told everyone that her husband had suffered a heart attack and could see no one. Getting nowhere, Chiang Kai-shek left Canton on March 26, leaving a letter saying that he would not return until Wang Ching-wei returned to work.

In the first days of April a letter arrived from Wang Ching-wei in Swatow. He wrote that he was shaken by the fact that Chiang Kai-shek, his lone hope, had betrayed the revolution—as if to say that he, Wang Ching-wei, had fought while there was still hope. Now he could no longer take responsibility for the future and was going home.

Chiang Kai-shek, satisfied that his chief rival was opening the way so easily for him, still pretended that he was very disturbed. "What am I, a counter-revolutionary?" he exclaimed. "I have never been one and am ready to prove it."

At the end of April he penned a circular telegram in which he came out sharply against the participants in the March conference of the Kuomintang rightists in Shanghai. He pretended that he was really struggling against them.

"It is necessary to deal with the rightists," he said in one of his official statements during this period. "I have decided to dissolve the Society for the Study of Sun Yat-senism but at the same time the Union of Young Soldiers will also be dispersed.[17] It is necessary to get rid of the chief of police General Wu T'ieh-ch'eng, let him go to Shanghai. It is necessary to work with the Communists, but once we have dealt with the rightists it will be necessary to display severity towards the Communists too. The Communists should have their own party, but should work together with the Kuomintang. The

17. The Society for the Study of Sun Yat-senism was in fact declared dissolved at a Kuomintang CEC plenum in March 1926, but in fact it continued to exist under the new name of Society of Young Chinese Comrades headed by Yü Chih-huan. The Union of Young Soldiers dissolved itself and was not re-established.

revolution can triumph only with the two parties—the Kuomintang and the Communists."

The May holidays came at that time. The spring rains had stopped some time ago, everything shone, and sparkled in the blinding rays of the tropical sun. The stiff leaves of the evergreen plants exuded the heavy scent of their warm flowers, glittering as if polished. The May First demonstration turned into a vivid unforgettable spectacle. The participants marched in broad hats woven of palm leaves on which patriotic slogans were inscribed in red, white, and black paint. Trade union banners were carried in front of the columns. Dragons danced, fierce fantastic beasts opened their jaws. Humorists recited verses on political and everyday themes. Their comic singing and funny grimaces provoked deafening laughter in the crowd. The model of a boat sailed by amid the marching columns carried by people representing passengers. Cunningly contrived effigies of Chinese militarists, missionaries, compradores, and imperialists, swayed above the crowd. The deafening roar of Chinese fire-crackers resounded. The orators grew hoarse and perspired on their platforms.

On that day the Third All-Chinese Trade Union Congress and the Second Congress of Kwangtung Peasant Unions opened in Canton. The delegates took part in the demonstration and made an excursion to the Whampoa Academy in sampans decorated with paper flowers. They visited all the departments and the divisions of the academy.

As before Canton continued to march in the vanguard of the anti-imperialist struggle; all-China congresses met there, preparations for the forthcoming Northern Expedition went on. But the former correlation of forces within the Kuomintang had been destroyed.

Right up until the May plenum of the CEC[18] when Chiang Kai-shek finally received the official support of the Kuomintang, he wavered, and rushed from side to side. "I am not for the rightists and not for the leftists," he declared, "I am for Sun Yat-sen's testament." He sent his delegates to Moscow and wrote to the general secretary of the CCP in Shanghai, Ch'en Tu-hsiu, suggesting that he come to Kwangtung and settle everything. When in a conversation with him Sun Fo tried to slander the Communists, Chiang Kai-shek replied that he advised him not to trust in gossip, that it didn't matter to him whether a person

---

18. The plenum opened on May 15, 1926.

was a Communist or not so long as he worked for the revolution. He criticized the Kuomintang rightists Wu Ch'ao-shu and Wu T'ieh-ch'eng and expelled from Canton Sun Fo and Hu Han-min who had just returned from Moscow and who tried to unite with several rightists against Chiang Kai-shek.

At the same time Chiang Kai-shek hastened the calling of the Kuomintang CEC plenum in the expectation of consolidating his victory at it and beginning his general offensive against the Communists.

On the eve of the plenum the situation in Canton was tense. Fearing disorders Chiang Kai-shek declared martial law in the city. On his instructions an accelerated cultivation of public opinion was carried on everywhere. The plenum opened in an atmosphere of pressure and intimidation.

Chiang Kai-shek was supported by his fellow Chekiangese, and some of the teachers and former students of the Whampoa Academy who now occupied important posts in the Kuomintang, the government and the army. The Communists did not come out against Chiang Kai-shek because the right opportunist Ch'en Tu-hsiu insisted on retreat. The Kuomintang leftists lost their heads and cravenly threw themselves on the mercy of the victor.

The plenum obediently submitted to the usurper's will. The Communists were forced to accept the notorious "eight limitations" by which they were forbidden to occupy more than a third of the places in the Kuomintang CEC, to head its departments, to occupy responsible positions in the Kuomintang, etc. The plenum adopted a resolution to establish a liaison commission of five Kuomintang and three Communist members to resolve the problem of mutual relations between the Communist party and the Kuomintang with the representative of the ECCI in the capacity of adviser.[19] Such a commission was in fact established. Its adviser, G. N. Voytinsky, arrived in Canton in the middle of June. His bright red-thatched head appeared in the streets of Tungshan.

As always the measures against the Communist party brought in their train measures against the revolutionary movement in general. At the plenum the Kuomintang rightist and leader of the Kwangsi militarist clique, Li Tsung-jen, made a proposal to limit the worker-peasant movement. He was supported by the commanders of the Third and Fourth armies, Generals Chu P'ei-te and Li Chi-shen. The proposal was adopted.

---

19. The decision concerning a liaison commission had been already taken at the Second Kuomintang Congress but then it was supposed that it would discuss a wide number of questions, and not only the question about the two parties' mutual relations.

Having secured the official support of the Kuomintang leadership, Chiang Kai-shek, dizzy with success, hurried to settle accounts with several of his rivals, Kuomintang rightists who had pretensions to power after March 20. He ordered the arrest of Wu T'ieh-ch'eng, on the charge of embezzling public funds and expelled the mayor of Canton, Wu Ch'ao-shu, and a number of other rightists.

Simultaneously he tried to weaken the position of the leftists. General, Teng Yen-ta was removed from his position as head of the political department at the Whampoa Academy. Ch'en Kung-po, the new rector of Sun Yat-sen University who four months before had replaced the Western Hills adherent, Tsou Lu, now was himself replaced by Tai Chi-t'ao, the ideological leader of the rightists. Kan Nai-kuang, then one of the leftist leaders in the Kuomintang, was removed as candidate member of the Politburo, displaced from his posts as head of the Youth Department of the CEC and secretary of the Kuomintang cell in Sun Yat-sen University. This wave of removals was felt throughout the entire Kuomintang organization.

Chiang Kai-shek began to speak more boldly and openly about the Communists, saying that hegemony in the leadership of the Chinese revolution should belong to the Kuomintang, and that there was nothing for the Communists to do in the Kuomintang. Here is one of his post-plenum speeches:

"The Chinese national revolution requires the unitary leadership of the Kuomintang and the world revolution the unitary leadership of the Third International. It would be better for the Communists in the Kuomintang to leave the Communist party. The Kuomintang can directly join the Third International or create its own Fourth International."

A month had not passed when Chiang Kai-shek was chosen for the post of chairman of the CEC at a Kuomintang conference on June 4, 1926. On July 7, when Chiang Kai-shek already held not only military but also political power, he gave his famous speech at the Whampoa Academy concerning the Communists, speaking in a frankly hostile tone. Of course he would never have dared to do this were it not for the deterioration of the revolutionary situation in North China in the spring of 1926.

Ch'en Tu-hsiu, who considered that it was time for the Communists to leave the Kuomintang, in essence adhered to the same viewpoint as the Kuomintang rightists. But leaving meant handing over to the power of the reactionaries an organization of three hundred fifty thousand members at a time when the Communists had not more than twelve thousand. The correct line triumphed among the Communists and in accordance with the Comintern directive they remained in the Kuomintang.

At that time Chiang Kai-shek had still not resolved to make a final break with the hated Communists. He knew that without their aid he could not get along. He needed the support of the masses; the Northern Expedition was in the offing. This was the source of his hesitation and his contradictory statements and actions.

We in Tungshan were also looking forward to the Northern Expedition. The advisers were convinced that the forthcoming difficulties in the struggle with the powerful militarists of central China and the unavoidable clashes with the imperialists in the Yangtse Valley would compel Chiang Kai-shek to make concessions. So it was at first, but subsequently Chiang Kai-shek's new, decisive rightward movement ensued.

Right up till the expedition discussions were held in the club and we young people did not pass up an opportunity to listen if not to dispute. The question of the Northern Expedition, said the advisers, was the following: who would beat whom? For the Communists and Kuomintang leftists it was an opportunity to establish contact with world reaction and to seize power. Struggle, vigilance, accurate calculations, and a correct general line would decide to whom the victory.

Many spoke of Tai Chi-t'aoism and the agrarian revolution. The political adviser, M. Volin, who worked for Borodin on problems of the peasant movement in China gave a report at the club in which he declared that in the immediate future the Kuomintang leftists in the struggle against the new militarists of Chiang Kai-shek's type would have to rely upon the peasant masses and for this they would have to give the peasants land. I remember how the adviser Gorev said, "But how can this be done? All I have to do is hint about this to the 'boss' and he drives me away immediately." His "boss" was General Li Chi-shen. The adviser Lysov who had just arrived from the Kalgan mission where he had observed a good deal of peasant activities like that of the Red Spears raised the question of the very existence of a conscious peasant movement in China. "What kind of an agrarian revolution is this?" he asked. "There has always been such a revolution. It is not a revolution but a belly." He clapped himself on the stomach. Very soon the events which unfolded in Hunan showed how mistaken he had been.

The Return of Borodin and Blyukher

Borodin returned at the end of April, a little more than two months before the beginning of the Northern Expedition. Chiang Kai-shek raised no objections. He remembered that earlier Borodin had supported strengthening the Whampoa Academy and the First Army by all means at the expense of the other units and he mistakenly supposed that in the new conditions, after the establishment of the National-Revolutionary Army in June 1925, Borodin would hold the same opinion. He conceived a hatred for Borodin as he had for Kuybyshev but much later.

The news of what had happened on March 20 caught up with Borodin in Peking on his way to the Soviet Union where he was going on leave with his wife and youngest son. He turned back at once.

His eldest son was in Canton at this time. He was born and had grown up in America and spoke English better than Russian. Within the family he was called Fred in the American fashion. He was sixteen then, some five or six years younger than us, but he was drawn into our student group and was often in Tungshan. Once Fred joyfully informed us that his father had arrived and was returning to work. We still knew nothing about this. Borodin's return was being kept secret and this was not a superfluous precaution.

On May 1, Borodin's wife, Fanya Semyonovna, came to Tungshan with Fred to attend the May First celebration in our club. She was dressed in a traditional Chinese costume—a long, black gown fastened on the right side, slit on the sides, and with a high, standing collar. I had already seen her in Peking and recognized her at once. When I entered the club she had just been prevailed upon to dance some Russian dances and she did not refuse. Later F. S. Borodina was chosen as chairman of the wives' council and she was often present. I never once saw Borodin himself in Tungshan.

While the festivities were proceeding in the club Fred suggested going out for a drive. We drove to the city. It was not so late but already dark. An absolutely black, velvet sky dotted with large bright stars hung right above our heads. Fred was at the wheel. On the road we were hailed by soldiers of the garrison and strike pickets. To the question of who goes there Fred replied

"*Saiyang, saiyang*"[20] but Borodin's car was probably known everywhere. We were allowed to pass.

The car stalled on the embankment. While Fred tinkered with the motor, we got out but came back at once; the embankment was swarming with rats, they ran by squeaking repulsively, and it seemed they were not afraid of people in the least.

With Borodin's arrival his staff began to work again. He needed interpreters and I entered his service. Borodin's residence looked rather gloomy. It was a dark-gray, two-storey building of typical tropical design with verandahs and a flat roof, almost without supporting walls inside, but only light partitions which didn't reach up to the ceiling so that there was always a draft in the house. On top there was an open area enclosed by a balustrade. Across the street was a group of northern style houses. There even the windows were latticed and covered with white paper. It looked as if this had been at one time the palace of some important mandarin sent from Peking to govern and to make his fortune. The buildings were surrounded by a wall with a Chinese arch at the entrance. This was the location of the Kuomintang CEC. I was often sent there to the Workers' and Peasants' Departments for materials. The pass for Borodin and the CEC was an enamel badge on a gold chain which hung in the button-hole of one's jacket or pinned on the breast. It was a white Kuomintang sun with twelve spreading rays on a blue field. A guard stood at Borodin's house and the CEC quarters. At the drawnout command "*Chi-ik chok!*" the two soldiers raised their rifles in greeting to the visitors.

Behind Borodin's house was an enormous parade ground—a place for meetings, parades, and, rarely, military instruction. Criminals were executed there and from the verandah one could see this gloomy scene which always attracted a group of curious persons. The man was made to kneel with his hands tied behind his back. All of his offences were written on a strip of paper or scrap of cloth pasted to a long, wooden board which stuck out behind his head. A soldier with a Mauser approached and shot him in the back of the head.

On the top floor lived Borodin and his family, two Red commanders assigned to him as aides, a house orderly with his wife, and a Russian typist. The larger part of his staff worked there as well. Every day a Russian summary

---

20. "*Saiyang*" (in Peking pronunciation *hsi jen*) means western people. This was what foreigners were called in Kwangtung.

of the Chinese and English press was prepared. Material without urgent significance was sent downstairs where about ten Chinese translated articles from the Chinese press and documents from the sessions of the Kuomintang CEC into English. From here emerged the hefty typewritten volumes of the protocols of the plenums and congresses—the pride of Borodin's archives.

Under Borodin a group of comrades worked on problems of the workers' and peasants' movement in Kwangtung and Kwangsi. M. Volin, Ye. Yolk, and O. Tarkhanov were in the peasant group.[21] Volin and Yolk published a lithographic edition of a large opus *Agrarnye otnosheniia v provintsii Guandun* (Agrarian relations in Kwangtung province).[22] The same kind of work was supposed to appear on Kwangsi. Tarkhanov had already collected the necessary materials, but did not succeed in publishing it at that time. G. Sinani who arrived from the North in the summer of 1926 worked on the workers' question.

In Borodin's lithography shop was published the journal *Kanton* (Canton), the organ of our Soviet colony in a very small edition of about one hundred copies.[23] I remember the issue of March 1926, when I first began reading it. Problems of the forthcoming Northern Expedition, in particular the organization of power in the liberated territory, were discussed in it. The adviser Pallo described the military order which our advisers found in the old forts of Kwangtung including Humen (Bocca Tigris) and Whampoa. According to the old custom the garrison there consisted of the watchman and his family. The art of using the pieces of ordnance was considered a family secret and passed on from father to son. One can imagine the age of this technology!

There was a very interesting article in the journal by F. G. Matseylik: *"Generaly Guandun i ikh armii"* (The Kwangtung generals and their armies)—a review of the period beginning with the 1911 Revolution.

On the pages of *Canton* were printed materials from discussions on the problems of the Chinese revolution. Everyday matters were also discussed.

The journal enjoyed great popularity. People read it and wrote for it very willingly. Many of the articles have not lost their interest up till now. *Canton* continued to be published in Hankow in 1927 under its old name.

---

21. Later on O. Tarkhanov under the name of Erdberg published a collection of Chinese novellas in Moscow (reissued in 1959).
22. This work was destroyed during Li Chi-shen's coup of April 1927.
23. At first it was called *Bolshevik v Kantone* (Bolshevik in Canton); six issues were published under this title.

Vasily Konstantinovich Blyukher, the chief military adviser to the National-Revolutionary Army, arrived in Canton in the beginning of May, two weeks after Borodin. V. A. Stepanov temporarily headed the mission until his arrival. This was Blyukher's second assignment in China. After the events of March 20 the Soviet government considered his candidacy the most appropriate in the given situation.

V. K. Blyukher was the son of a peasant and was himself an experienced metallurgy worker. From 1910 on he took an active part in the revolutionary movement, was arrested and served three years in prison. He fought in the First World War as a line and non-commissioned officer and was awarded crosses of St. George. After a serious wound he returned to the factory in 1916, and at the age of twenty-seven joined the party. Beginning in February 1917 when he was chosen as a member of the Revolutionary-Military Committee in Samara, Blyukher worked in responsible party military positions. He was commissar of a Red Guard detachment sent to aid the workers of Chelyabinsk and he commanded Red Guard units in battles against General Dutov. Under his command the South Ural partisan army broke through encirclement and linked up with the Red Army after forty days of uninterrupted fighting. For this he was the first in the Soviet republic to be awarded an Order of the Red Banner. Later he commanded a division in the fighting against Kolchak and fought on the Kakhovsky beachhead and near Perekop.

By 1921-1922 Blyukher was already commander-in-chief, war minister and chairman of the Military Council of the Far Eastern Republic. After the civil war he commanded a corps and was head of the Leningrad fortified district from which he left for China for the first time. He already had three Orders of the Red Banner; he received a fourth for his work in China.

In his last years Blyukher commanded the forces of the Special Red Banner Far Eastern Army, was twice decorated with an Order of Lenin, and received his fifth Order of the Red Banner. From 1934 he was a candidate member of the CC of the RCP (B).[24] He died tragically in 1938.

Blyukher's name is linked to the victories of the National-Revolutionary Army in the main stages of the revolutionary movement of those years. The rout of the Paper Tigers in November 1924, the victories of the first Eastern Expedition, and most important, the successes of the Northern Expedition,

---

24. Russian Communist Party (Bolshevik). Translator.

compelled people to speak not only of China's new revolutionary army, but of the man as well, who had given so much of his strength and vigor in rebuilding and instructing it, and who had personally taken part in its battles.

Blyukher was of medium height, broad-shouldered, well-built and evidently very strong. His bearing was remarkable. He held his head high and because of this he looked somewhat haughty. His hair was darkish red and thick. Like all military men he wore his hair rather short and sported a short mustache.

Kwangtung's tropical climate adversely affected Blyukher; the comrades said that he was often ill. The wounds which he had received in the First World War and the civil war told upon him. His body was covered with terrible scars.

Blyukher lived with the rest of us in Tungshan. He and his family occupied a small detached house behind the mission headquarters. There too were his offices and the reception room where he received the leading political and military figures of the South Chinese government. Chiang Kai-shek often stopped by to see him.

Blyukher's name was well-known in China, but he was especially popular with the masses of Kwangtung. He spoke at gatherings and mass meetings to which he was often invited and received an enthusiastic welcome everywhere. Eyewitness notes to this effect have been preserved. I will cite one of them about a meeting in Sun Yat-sen University on the occasion of the first anniversary of Lenin's death. The day of Lenin's death was considered a general day of mourning. On that day the Chinese railroad workers executed by Wu P'ei-fu in 1923, the seventy-two heroes, Karl Liebknecht and Rosa Luxemburg were all commemorated. Blyukher was accompanied by other advisers, and was chosen for the presidium along with the leading figures of the Kuomintang. Opening the meeting, according to tradition, everyone bowed first to a portrait of Sun Yat-sen, and then to a portrait of Lenin. Liao Chung-k'ai opened the assembly, then Blyukher said a few words. He was roundly applauded. Ten varicolored paper wreaths from the railroad workers and local peasants were brought to the presidium. Portraits of Lenin, Liebknecht and Luxemburg, the text of the "Internationale," proclamations, and slogans were distributed. In his speech the Kuomintang rightist Hu Han-min declared publicly that the Soviet system was the single appropriate system for China.

Blyukher got along well in Chinese surroundings. After his return to the USSR he intended, together with a group of advisers, to publish a book about China.

In Borodin's House

Members of the government and the Kuomintang CEC, and generals of the National-Revolutionary Army including Chiang Kai-shek visited Borodin's house, or as the Chinese called it, Pao kung kuan (Borodin's establishment). I remember the frequent visits of the chairman of the government, General T'an Yen-k'ai, and the chairman of the Kuomintang CEC, Chang Ching-chiang. The appearance of the latter always caused a commotion because he could not walk and had to be carried upstairs. An infrequent visitor was the Kuomintang leftist Ku Meng-yü, a former professor at Peking University, who was considered a revolutionary since President Tuan Ch'i-jui had wanted to arrest him after the shooting of the student demonstrators on March 18, 1926. He had to flee to save himself. He always fawned upon Borodin in every possible way and appeared in the company of his wife in an effort to impart a familial character to his visits. Later Ku Meng-yü became one of the most bitter enemies of the Communist party of China and played no small part in the temporary betrayal of Feng Yü-hsiang with whom he had longstanding ties. Another "leftist" also came, Kan Nai-kuang. From among the rightists at Borodin's, I met Sun Fo, of whom I have one amusing recollection.

On Borodin's instructions, I once went as an interpreter to the commercial representative of our Soviet consulate. He had learned from local merchants that a large lot of lumber was being held up at one of the custom points. Since the owners had neither paid the likin tax[25] nor given bribes, the goods were sold at auction to fictitious persons. This was quite common at that time. However, our commercial representative, a person new to China, was indignant to the depths of his soul. He hastened to inform Sun Fo, not knowing that the majority of officials of the Ministry of Finance with the minister himself at the head engaged in all kinds of machinations, that the illegal sale of the lumber

---

25. Likin tax is an internal customs levy which has been collected since feudal times in China on the borders of the provinces or even separate districts.

could not have occurred without Sun Fo's knowledge and that he had already profited from it.

Evidently having learned the purpose of our visit from the merchants, Sun Fo did not even rise to greet us. Small, fat, very pompous, wearing round horn-rimmed glasses, he sat at his desk and looked at us with irritation. After listening to the commercial representative's observations about the baneful influence of the likin system on the country's internal and external trade, he asked emphatically why the Soviet trade representative was defending Chinese merchants. We left empty-handed.

I saw Chiang Kai-shek at Borodin's place about two times and only from a distance. He came accompanied by several bodyguards whom he stationed on the staircase. Narrowchested and puny, he wore a Chinese military outfit and Russian boots. He walked past us, clumsily stooping, into the reception room where Borodin's large figure rose to greet him.

I also met CCP figures there—Su Chao-cheng, Teng Chung-hsia, Ch'en Yen-nien, Chou En-lai, and others.

Borodin had especially close relations with Chang T'ai-lei, candidate member of the CCP CC. Beginning in 1925 he was attached to Borodin as an aide and from that time they never parted, even living in the same house. Borodin entrusted only him with translating his speeches, went to the sessions of the Politburo of the Kuomintang CEC with him,[26] and invited him to his meetings with members of the Kuomintang government. Chang T'ai-lei was Borodin's secretary, consultant, and personal interpreter. They loved each other very much despite their difference in age. Borodin's family treated Chang T'ai-lei like a close relative.

Young and tall with long brushed back hair, Chang T'ai-lei looked at people boldly with a firm intelligent gaze. He often flashed a broad, white-toothed smile and lived and dressed very modestly, usually wearing a light gray Chinese robe. In December 1927, at the age of twenty-nine, he was killed during the uprising in Canton which he was heading because Su Chao-cheng, the Politburo member who, according to the decision of the CCP CC was supposed to lead it, was unable to make his way to the city. The Chinese people honor Chang T'ai-lei as a hero of the revolution; the Sixth Comintern Congress rose and stood in respect to his memory.

---

26. Chang T'ai-lei was technical secretary of the Politburo of the Kuomintang CEC.

Chang T'ai-lei was one of the pioneers of the Communist movement in China. In 1920, a full year before the First Congress of the CCP he had already become a member of one of the Communist circles. He was a participant in the May Fourth Movement, a representative of the Chinese Communists to the Third Congress of the Comintern in 1921, organizer of the Chinese Komsomol, secretary of the Shanghai Municipal Committee of the CCP in 1922, and one of the active builders of the united front between the Communist party and the Kuomintang in the following years. His work with Borodin demanded much time, but Chang T'ai-lei was still able to head the Agitprop Department of the Kwangtung CCP committee, to edit the journal *Narodnyi ezhenedel'nik* (People's weekly), and in general to carry on an active party career.

Chang T'ai-lei and his wife lived on the first floor of Borodin's house in a large, bright, modestly furnished room whose windows faced the parade ground. Chang T'ai-lei worked at a simple, unadorned table heaped with books, newspapers, and manuscripts in Chinese square-hatched paper. Close by too stood his square Chinese bed beneath a snow-white mosquito net. No matter when you entered he was always immersed in work.

After the March 20 Incident, Ch'en Yen-nien, the eldest son of the general secretary of the CCP, Professor Ch'en Tu-hsiu, was chosen as secretary of the Kwangtung Committee of the CCP. I saw Ch'en Yen-nien several times, but had occasion to speak with him only once. It was in the autumn of 1926, in the headquarters of the Kwangtung-Kwangsi Committee,[27] where the adviser Sinani invited me in my capacity as interpreter.

Four members of the committee and Ch'en Yen-nien sat at a table. He was a young man of twenty-eight with a very intelligent, pleasant face. He resembled his father but at the same time he looked entirely different from him. Ch'en Tu-hsiu had a typical professor's face, his refined, subtle appearance bespoke his belonging to the higher Chinese intelligentsia. Glancing at Ch'en Yen-nien one could say at once, notwithstanding his undoubted intelligence, that he was a representative of the proletariat. He dressed very modestly, almost shabbily, like all workers at that time, and like them he shaved his head. To distinguish him from his father, he was often called Little Ch'en.

---

27. The Kwangtung-Kwangsi Committee was established in May 1926 after Kwangsi joined Kwangtung.

During the First World War Ch'en Yen-nien went to study in France. The son of well-to-do parents, he could have quietly studied in the Sorbonne like other Chinese youths. However, Ch'en Yen-nien began by working as an agricultural laborer in a French village. Later he settled in Paris where he worked and studied at the university at the same time. He wanted to be with the common people, to live their life, to experience their adversities. In Paris he entered a Communist group.

In 1923 Ch'en Yen-nien went to Moscow where he entered the Communist University of the Toilers of the East, but soon afterwards the great events began in China, and after a year he was called back to his native land. There he emerged at once as one of the able and popular leaders of the working class. Ch'en Yen-nien was inseparably linked to the proletariat, he fought shoulder to shoulder with it and died for its cause. He did not live to the time when his father was removed from leadership, but he came out more than once against the line of the then CC CCP.

In the spring of 1927, after the Fifth Congress of the CCP, at which he was chosen as a member of the CC, Ch'en Yen-nien went to Shanghai where he was appointed first secretary of the Kiangsu-Chekiang CCP Committee. During Chiang Kai-shek's coup in April 1927 the local leading party group committed not a few opportunistic errors. Ch'en Yen-nien's candidacy was recognized as the most appropriate for rectifying the situation, and in fact he succeeded in accomplishing a good deal. However, soon the White terror began in Shanghai. At the end of June, General Yang Hu whom Chiang Kai-shek had sent to deal with the Communist and Kuomintang leftists arrived in the city. Eleven executioners with large, double-edged swords accompanied him from the station. The Kiangsu-Chekiang Committee was crushed. Along with the other members, Ch'en Yen-nien was arrested and executed. I was in Shanghai at the time and I remember what a depressing feeling this news produced.

Fate granted me a much closer encounter in Borodin's house with yet another of the remarkable people living then in Canton. This was the Vietnamese Li. We jokingly called him Li An-nam. (Annam was the name of the French colony in Indochina). He was thirty-six years old. He was unimpressive in appearance; there was something wrong with his lungs.

I can remember vividly his small, spare figure in a white linen suit of European cut, which hung loosely on him, his attentive somewhat sad gaze and the walk of a very tired or sick man. He spoke French, English, and Cantonese well, and knew Russian. I took Vietnamese lessons from him and this pleased him and he willingly taught me. He was friendly towards us but reserved and he never told us what his work was and what he had done in the past. We knew nothing about him except that for his capture the French imperialists had offered a great sum of money and that the Kuomintang government had given him political asylum. He was quite at home in Borodin's house.

After three or four months, Li disappeared. For a long time I had no news of him. Much later, in Moscow, I was told that Li had been sentenced to death in absentia by the French colonialists in 1929, that thereafter he was arrested in 1931 in Hong Kong and spent two years in prison. Happily, the English police did not consider the pursuit of Vietnamese Communists as part of their job. But the Chinese Communists with whom he had been arrested paid with their lives.

In the spring of 1934 I met Li on the staircase of the Institute of World Politics and Economy in Moscow. We hurriedly exchanged addresses, but I did not get to meet with him. Li was very busy and almost every day I returned home way past midnight.

Soon I learned that he had been present at the Seventh Comintern Congress. From that time I finally lost track of him completely.

Only much later did I learn from F. S. Borodina that our Li An-nam was none other than Ho Chi Minh.

Even in peaceful times the lives of our advisers were far from safe. This was confirmed in the aftermath of the murder of Liao Chung-k'ai when it became clear that any Chinese Communist or Kuomintang leftist or any of our advisers might die from a hireling's bullet. Borodin rode to the sessions of the Politburo of the Kuomintang CEC, right across the street, in a car with Mauser-bearing Chinese soldiers on the running-board. After all, it was right at the gates of this building that the killers of Liao Chung-k'ai had lain in wait for him. Borodin did not go to the movies; films were brought to his house. But he went to meetings constantly. He spoke in English and Liao Chung-k'ai translated.

The People of Canton

When I remember Canton now I think of endless meetings and demonstrations. According to the Chinese custom, many revolutionary holidays and memorial days were celebrated at that time for a whole week. This was an enthusiastic revolutionary period and the masses animatedly participated in the revolutionary movement. Canton remained the lone place where all-Chinese congresses of various revolutionary organizations could meet without fear of repression, and each time this was an occasion for demonstrations and welcomes.

We were never among the demonstrators, we lived according to the same rules that we had in Peking, but at one meeting, to my surprise, I took an indirect part. I can't say exactly when or for what reason it had been called. It seems that they were marking the beginning of the Northern Expedition.

From morning on drums began to thunder, bare feet slapped along the roadway, wooden sandals knocked. From every direction columns of demonstrators preceded by drums and banners poured into the parade ground behind Borodin's house. Hundreds of trade union and peasants' banners floated by along with hundreds of red posters. I was afraid there would be a terrible crush, but this did not occur. The columns calmly took their places in front of the platform made of bamboo poles and matting.

From the flat roof of Borodin's house where I was standing there was a good view of the entire square, a yellow sea of woven hats. The mighty discordant din of voices was punctuated by sharp, distinct cries. *"Wan sui!"* the square thundered. Suddenly it became quiet, the orators' speeches were beginning. I was always struck by the exceptional discipline of the mass meetings in Canton.

Borodin spoke from one of the rostrums; Chang T'ai-lei translated his speech. I ran downstairs and went out into the square. I wanted to listen. But on the way I was caught by someone's sun-blackened hands and forced to climb onto another of the rostrums to give the crowd greetings from Soviet women.

I don't know how much the peasants who surrounded the rostrum understood of what I said; I was speaking in Mandarin, but they applauded thunderously. The next day in the *Kwangchou min kuo jih pao*, the semi-official organ of the Kuomintang, there appeared a notice that "some Russian girl named Wen (this is how the Chinese pronounced my name) greeted the

Kwangtung peasants in the name of Soviet women and spoke with great feeling."

The following real-life scene had a great success. The adviser Naumov's three-year-old daughter appeared on the platform hand-in-hand with her Chinese friend of the same age. Both of them walked to the edge of the rostrum and kissed. This touching symbol of Soviet-Chinese friendship provoked general laughter from everyone and unrestrained applause.

The meeting was filmed by Soviet cameramen. I saw the film clip later and even recognized myself on the screen.

As an interpreter I had occasion to be present at Kuomintang meetings. The premises were very modestly furnished, decorated with slogan-bearing placards and paper garlands. A portrait of Sun Yat-sen hung between two crossed Kuomintang banners, next to them were portraits of Lenin and Marx looking not infrequently like real Chinese. In a glass-covered frame was the "testament" which was recited before the opening of the meeting. The ritual required three bows preceding and three minutes of reverential silence following this obligatory introduction to every meeting.

However, like my colleagues, I rarely came into contact with the people.

It was recommended that we not do this in order to avoid any kind of idle talk and accusations to the effect that we were spreading Red propaganda. Our comrades appeared at gatherings and meetings only upon official invitations and avoided personal ties with the Chinese.

One need hardly say that we regretted this very much. We wanted to get to know China and its remarkable people more deeply.

Take even the strike committee which was leading an historic strike. What did we know of it? Only from afar, walking along the embankment, did we glance into the wide courtyard with its few structures, the former Tung Yuan where the strike committee was located. We knew that the members of the CCP CC, Su Chao-cheng, Teng Chung-hsia, Teng Fa, and others headed the committee, but we saw them only when they walked past us into Borodin's office. On the streets we often met groups of strike pickets dressed in their dark blue uniforms with armbands on their sleeves; sometimes they were armed. Their well-formed, smart figures flashed by, they had become an integral feature of city life. This is all that we witnessed. What a pity it was, don't you think?

Meanwhile, the strike committee was an important factor in the life of Canton, defining its course to a certain degree. The presence of a delegate from the strike committee at all gatherings and meetings in the city was a tradition; without its representatives not a single question in municipal administration could be decided upon. The strike committee was very close to the Communist organization of the city, it was often called the "CCP's second municipal committee."

Fifty thousand of the one hundred fifty thousand strikers who arrived from Hong Kong and Shameen remained in Canton. There were many workers among them from large industrial enterprises such as did not exist in Kwangtung at the time.

It was no accident that their appearance exerted a profound influence on the political situation in the city.

Life was not easy for them. They and their families huddled together in overpacked, ill-constructed barracks, slept right on the earth and received a daily pittance. The daily budget of the strike committee was just six thousand dollars in local currency. The government contributed part of the money, the rest came in the form of contributions from all over China and from abroad. The strikers performed picket duty, and public municipal work, but still there were many unemployed among them. The committee organized courses for propaganda workers and groups in international politics and literacy for the strikers.

Many of the strikers entered the ranks of the Communist party. They were the most progressive, revolutionary section of the Kwangtung proletariat.

Upon its return to Moscow the Soviet trade union delegation headed by I. I. Lepse which visited Canton in the summer of 1925 highly praised the activity of the strike committee, noting that it was excellently organized, manifested an exceptional political sensitivity and consciousness, and had its own guards and tribunal to judge strikebreakers and traitors.

In those years modern enterprises did not exist in Kwangtung with the exception of several electric stations and two arsenals, but there were many tiny factories and workshops. These were for the most part sugar-makers, oil-mills, spinning mills, textile industry, rice-cleaning and silk-cleaning enterprises, bottle-making for artificial mineral water, etc. There were even more handicraft, artisan, and merchant businesses. It is clear from this what kind of proletariat was found in Canton then. Along with the rickshaw pullers there were tens of thousands of so-called coolies in the city. There was also the river population, the "transport workers" so to speak; I have already written of them.

Arising amid the disintegration of guilds and corporations, the workers' organizations in Kwangtung were distinguished by their atomization. In Canton, for example, there were twenty-two transport workers' unions, twenty-three shop assistants' unions, sixteen carpenters' unions, fifteen tailors' unions, etc. The struggle between parallel unions, especially between real unions and yellow unions, not infrequently led to fighting.

Once I observed a clash between rickshaw pullers, evidently belonging to different local associations. Approaching by car while still some distance away, I heard some sort of shouting and howling. Suddenly a crowd of half-naked men appeared from around the corner carrying sticks and wet ropes; another crowd appeared from the opposite direction. A violent melee ensued.

The most progressive and strong of trade union organizations—the Council of Workers' Deputies, directly linked to the Labor Department of the Kuomintang CEC—had joined the Profintern; there were not a few Communists among its leaders. Still even it had one hundred seventy-six unions for its one hundred seventy-thousand members.

The Kwangtung Workers' Federation which, for the most part, covered handicraft workers, not infrequently along with their bosses enjoyed the support of the Kuomintang rightists. Its leader, Ch'en Sen, already known to the reader, protected the entrepreneurs, conducted a splittist policy, and opposed the organization of workers on industrial lines.

The third largest trade union organization in Canton—the reactionary Mechanics' Union—united about nine thousand skilled workers from electric stations, railroads, and arsenals. Their wages were several times higher than the ordinary (thirty to seventy-five dollars, whereas the ordinary worker received six to twelve dollars). This was the so-called labor aristocracy, jealously protecting its ranks against the incursions of its lower paid brethren. The Mechanics' Union encompassed six unions. It possessed strong armed units and always came out on the side of reaction.

The working day in Canton, like everywhere in China, stretched from eleven to fifteen hours; wages were only a little higher than the general Chinese level. Teng Chung-hsia, member of the CC of the CCP and a leading trade union activist, wrote in 1926 that the wages of more than ninety per cent of Canton's workers fell below a living minimum wage.

Yet the proletariat there lived far better than in other Chinese cities. In Canton they had at least some sort of social legislation and political rights, the imperialists could not insult them with impunity, they had acquired a sense of their own dignity and of national consciousness, they saw before them a bright future and this gave them the strength to endure economic difficulties.

Beginning in 1924 the Communists and Kuomintang leftists carried on active work among the peasants of Kwangtung province. In May 1925 the peasant unions in the province which already numbered two hundred fifty thousand members held their first congress. After six months this membership figure had increased to half a million.

At that time peasant demands were very moderate: a decrease in rent to twenty-five per cent of the crop, a prohibition on taking land for debts, annulment of mortgages, removal of extraordinary taxes, abolition of the landlords' armed units (*min t'uan*), increase in agricultural laborers' pay, etc. Sun Yat-sen's slogan "To the tiller his own land" was not then on the order of the day. But the landlords gave a hostile reception even to these minimum demands. In the villages of the province there were continuous clashes between the peasants' self-defense forces and the *min t'uan*. The landlords even resorted to primitive artillery. They sat behind the walls of their fortified compounds and it was not easy to defeat them. There were cases when troops were sent to suppress the *min t'uan*.

After the March 20 Incident the situation in the villages became even more exacerbated, the landlords' lawlessness and arbitrary behavior increased. The *min t'uan* along with the bandits killed peasants and dispersed their organizations. Landlords received rifles from Hong Kong and Macao and the local organs of power were on their side.

Let me say a few words about the student movement in Canton.

In the North we had become accustomed to consider the students as the leading patriotically-inclined section of the population. At that time almost all the Peking students were under Communist influence. The situation was different in Canton. Until 1926 the student union there was headed by

Kuomintang rightists, and this inevitably had an effect on the course of the student movement which lagged behind that of Peking in many respects. Also responsible in this regard was the unhealthy, stifling atmosphere which existed for a long time in the central higher educational institution in Canton— Sun Yat-sen University. Until January 1926 its rector was the Kuomintang rightist Tsou Lu who was expelled from the party at the Second Congress as a member of the Western Hills clique. Tsou Lu had the reputation of being a man without conscience or honor. Everyone knew that he had bought a home in Peking for one hundred fifty thousand dollars which the government had given him for university expenses. He encouraged nepotism and toadyism, and could not abide well-educated teachers. While humiliating his subordinates, Tsou Lu was very ingratiating and servile to everyone whose position was higher than his own. He had about two hundred supporters from among the students. When the reorganization and financial auditing of the organs of the national educational system was undertaken in July 1924, he came out against the government in support of the university's complete autonomy, but even after this he remained at his post until his expulsion from the Kuomintang.

After the university reorganization a bitter struggle flared up between the reactionary Student Union and the newly established revolutionary Society of New Students. In the autumn of 1925 there also emerged a Society for the Study of Sun Yat-senism. After the March 20 Incident it was temporarily closed upon Chiang Kai-shek's instructions, but at the same time the Society for New Students was banned and many Communists and Kuomintang leftists were expelled from the university.

As for the national bourgeoisie, it participated in the anti-imperialist struggle, supplied the Kuomintang government with material means, and actively supported its revolutionary undertakings. Of the representatives of the big bourgeoisie the most persevering were the owners of the well-known tobacco company Nanyang founded in Indonesia by a Chinese emigrant who had become wealthy by playing on the patriotic feelings of his fellow country-men in Indonesia who preferred his product because it was Chinese. The company was linked to the Kuomintang from before the 1911 Revolution. Its main enterprises were in Hong Kong and Canton.

At that time the company was going through a period of prosperity. One need not be surprised that it sympathized with the Kuomintang leftists.

Formerly it had encountered competition in all the markets from the oldest company in China, the all-powerful Anglo-American Company which occupied a commanding position everywhere. Now that the anti-British boycott was in effect, Nanyang could not keep pace with the demand of its unbelievably expanded clientele. There were many Kuomintang leftists and even Communists among the workers and personnel of the company so that the management did not interfere with their political activity in the factories. Of Chang Yü-ching, one of the main shareholders of the company, it was said that "he supported the Communists."

One should not think, of course, that all the bourgeoisie supported the Kuomintang. Above we have already referred to the compradors and middle-men who were in the service of the imperialists. These people did not only not take part in the anti-imperialist struggle, but actively struggled against the revolution.

The commercial and industrial bourgeoisie of China was organized into chambers of commerce. There were four of them in Canton, the largest—the so-called General Chamber of Commerce—linked seventy-two guilds including the richest one, the silk guild. The millionaire Ch'en Lien-po, one of the com-pradors of the Hong Kong–Shanghai Banking Corporation, was the chairman of the silk guild and of the General Chamber of Commerce until he fled to Hong Kong after the defeat of the Paper Tiger Uprising which he had instigated.

The word "comprador" is of Portuguese derivation. The Chinese do not use it. To express this meaning they have the Chinese word "maipan" which they pronounce with anger and contempt as a synonym for a traitor to the motherland.

The compradors were a powerful stratum of the Chinese bourgeoisie. Some of them were fantastically wealthy, their influence in the Chinese economy was great. The imperialists, who did not even consider Chinese as human beings, showered their compradors with honor and attention, and created a high social position for them.

If at that time you picked up the well-known handbook published in Shanghai by the American journal *China Weekly Review* under the name *Who Is Who in China* containing the biographies of the most important Chinese personalities (from the point of view of the imperialists) your attention prob-ably would be attracted by a superb picture of a graying gentleman in a rich, brocade gown of ancient cut with a high, standing collar. Barely screwing up his eyes, like a man who knows the power of his own money, he looks out at you calmly and his mocking look serves as an answer in advance to any who might try to call forth in his conscience a feeling of patriotism. No wonder! Do you know who this is? The famous Hong Kong comprador Sir Robert Hotung (Ho Tung in Chinese). Why "sir"? Because he had legal rights to this title. The English king himself, George V, elevated him to knighthood. He is the largest shareholder of the British Hong Kong–Shanghai Bank, the shipbuilding works, the Hong Kong–Whampoa Dock Company and others, director of the Hong Kong electric company, Hong Kong tram company, Hong Kong Land Bank, Hong Kong Company for Marsh Land Reclamation, Hong Kong–Canton–Macao Water Transport Company, the Hong Kong Insurance Company, etc. His activity extended right up to "industrial interests in North China and Manchuria."

He was a convinced, embittered enemy. Along with the imperialists, he supplied weapons to the Paper Tigers, did not spare his resources to wreck the Hong Kong-Canton strike, and later during the thirties was the organizer of the so-called A-B t'uan (Anti-Bolshevik Alliance).

Such was the disposition of forces in Canton on the eve of the Northern Expedition.

The Northern Expedition

After the completion of the second Eastern Expedition in November 1925 and the decisive defeat of the militarist units on Hainan Island in the beginning of 1926 Kwangtung province was finally rid of reactionary troops. Neighboring Kwangsi united with it; in this way the basis was created for the Northern Expedition bequeathed by Sun Yat-sen. There were strategic considerations as well why it could not be avoided. In the beginning of 1926 Wu P'ei-fu began to prepare an offensive against the Kuomintang government in the South. The British and American imperialists promised him two million pounds sterling for military expenses. He received a loan of five million Chinese dollars from the Anglo-American Tobacco Company. It was absolutely necessary to forestall Wu P'ei-fu's attack.

The Northern Expedition began under the following conditions. In March 1926, T'ang Sheng-chih, one of the Hunanese generals, betrayed Wu P'ei-fu, went over to the Kuomintang government and became commander of the Eighth Army of the National-Revolutionary Army. The Hunanese *tupan* Chao Heng-t'i fled. The Independent Regiment of the Fourth Army under the command of the Communist Yeh T'ing went to T'ang Sheng-chih's aid on May 19. On June 11 the main forces of the army moved north. The troops of the Fourth Army, lingering at the beginning of the movement, did not pass Shaokuan until June 30. This was the final point of the then incomplete railroad line to Changsha. For the time being T'ang Sheng-chih avoided a decisive engagement with Wu P'ei-fu's troops and only the Independent Regiment entered the fray.

At the same time the Northern Expedition was officially proclaimed in Canton. All the armies (with the exception of the Fifth) were sent to the front—more than sixty-five thousand troops. In response to a call from the strike committee seven thousand strikers voluntarily enrolled as bearers for the army transport.

Our Tungshan colony thinned out considerably. The advisers were at the front; their families returned home. Mikhail Georgevich Yefremov (Abnold)[28] stayed behind as the head of the mission in Canton. He was also adviser to General Li Chi-shen, commander of the Fourth Army who stayed in Canton as chief of the armed forces. In reality the army was commanded at the front by General Chang Fa-k'uei but in place of his signature he placed Li Chi-shen's seal.

During the campaigning in the northern part of Kwangtung and in southern Hunan there was an outbreak of cholera. There was no anti-cholera vaccine in the army and generally speaking its sanitary condition was on the lowest level. The advisers recounted that in some units there were doctors who had no medical education but had received their position through influence. The Second Army which lost half of its bearers and more than a thousand soldiers suffered most of all. The local authorities took no measures against the epidemic. In order to expel the "evil spirits" they organized firecracker processions for which money collected for battling cholera was spent.

---

28. Yefremov was a member of the party from 1919. He was a brigade commander during the civil war and a corps commander before his assignment to China. After returning from China he commanded military districts. During the Patriotic War he commanded an army. Not wishing to be taken prisoner he shot himself on April 19, 1942, and posthumously received the title "Hero of the Soviet Union." A monument to him was erected in Vyazma.

The military actions commenced. The National-Revolutionary Army aimed its first blow against Wu P'ei-fu's troops in Hunan.[29] The powerful Marshal Sun Ch'uan-fang—the Master" of four provinces—Kiangsi, Anhui, Kiangsu and Chekiang—was in a de facto alliance with Wu P'ei-fu and therefore one might expect his appearance at any moment.

Everywhere the National-Revolutionary Army was greeted ecstatically. Its soldiers and officers behaved in model fashion, its enemies too acknowledged this. Even the Western press wrote that the Southerners presented a striking contrast to the shameful tyranny of the Northern militarists, that China up till this time had not seen an army which the population reacted to in this way and which was so disciplined. In truth the inhabitants of villages and towns from many kilometers away came to greet them, arranged real welcomes for them replete with colored lanterns, music and singing. The welcomes turned into mass meetings at which political workers from the National-Revolutionary Army spoke. They furnished the people with placards and leaflets.

The old administrative apparatus was subject to reorganization in the newly liberated territory. The command headquarters appointed new district chiefs upon the recommendation of local public organizations and attached inspectors to them from among the army's political cadres. The former rural militia was disbanded, the five-colored flag was replaced by that of the Kuomintang. Lessons on Sun Yat-senism and the national-revolutionary movement were introduced into the schools.

War is war and under any conditions it weighs heavily upon the people's shoulders. After warm greetings, the enthusiasm waned somewhat; the revolutionary troops demanded the fulfillment of various duties which were at times extremely burdensome. Therefore political work among the people acquired an especially important significance. The people had to know that their defenders who wanted to emancipate them from injustice and poverty had come. The troops marched on, leaving persons to work in organizing the masses and creating new organs of power.

The fulfillment of this task was possible because during the Northern Expedition, many commanders did not interfere in the return to work of the

---

29. Wu P'ei-fu's troops occupied three provinces—Hunan, Hupeh, and Honan.

240

Communists and Kuomintang leftists in the army from which they had been expelled after the March 20 Incident. Chiang Kai-shek himself again introduced the system of company commissars and did not object to Communists or Kuomintang leftists filling these posts. By the way, the promotion of T'ang Sheng-chih, whom he saw as his rival, to commander of the Eighth Army strongly influenced his position.

At one time T'ang Sheng-chih had been a monk in a Buddhist monastery and he continued to be a fiery supporter of Buddhism. He carried with him everywhere an image of the Buddha, lit lamps before it, and said that he intended to erect a Buddhist temple. There were many Buddhists among his subordinates.

At that time, T'ang Sheng-chih was seeking a rapprochement with the Kuomintang leftists and the Communists, putting forth leftist slogans, demanding democratic reforms, and calling himself an adherent of Sun Yat-senism. Only he understood Sun Yat-senism in his own way. He said that the teachings of Sun Yat-sen were a path to the practical realization of the goal indicated by Buddha, therefore there were no contradictions between Sun Yat-senism and Buddhism. Political work in his army was carried on in this spirit. He was a large landlord and capitalist; he owned his own ship, a factory and three houses in Changsha.

T'ang Sheng-chih hastened to liberate "his" province without considering the operational plan and directives of the command headquarters. In his speeches he demonstratively avoided any references to the national movement or the commander-in-chief Chiang Kai-shek.

Chiang Kai-shek was in a difficult position. His First Army, the Whampoa Army as it was still called sometimes, had lost its former importance. In essence it had been ruined by Chiang Kai-shek himself who removed its best cadres on March 20. During the Northern Expedition the army was divided in two. The best divisions, the First and the Second, Chiang Kai-shek took with him to Hunan and Kiangsi and guarded them jealously; the Third and the Fourteenth Division of the Fifth Army which had been appended to it was located in Fukien.[30] The victories in Hunan strengthened the position of T'ang Sheng-chih. Chiang Kai-shek arrived in Changsha after T'ang Sheng-chih was in control of the city, and he regarded this victory as a mandate to

30. A. I. Cherepanov was the adviser attached to it.

rule the entire province. At this time Chiang Kai-shek felt so unsure of himself that he didn't dare contradict him in anything.

On T'ang Sheng-chih's side were the Paotingites, as those who had graduated from the Paoting Military Academy in North China were called at the time. The command of the Fourth, Seventh, and Eighth armies belonged to them. They tried to compel Chiang Kai-shek to fight against Sun Ch'uan-fang in Kiangsi so that they themselves might move against Wu P'ei-fu in Hunan and Hupeh. Chiang Kai-shek understood that this was disadvantageous for him. Sun Ch'uan-fang was stronger by far than Wu P'ei-fu; the fight against him would drag out and victory be in doubt while at the same time the Paotingites would be strengthening their position in Hunan and Hupeh and controlling the Hanyang arsenal. Chiang Kai-shek at once quieted down, began again to speak in an extremely "left" spirit, asked aid from the Communists, repeatedly expressed his repentance for what he had done on March 20, and finally even humbled himself to the point of secretly ordering Teng Yen-ta, the chief of the Political Department of the National-Revolutionary Army, to request the Communists and the Russian advisers to spare his First Army in battle so that he would not become a general without an army. This fully justified our advisers' suppositions that in the event of war with the Northern militarists Chiang Kai-shek would make concessions which would be used for revolutionary purposes.

Our advisers came out in favor of beating the enemy one by one, beginning with Wu P'ei-fu. The military situation demanded this.

Both the rivals, Chiang Kai-shek and T'ang Sheng-chih, vied with each other in depicting themselves as the most leftist of the generals and not only made no attempt to limit the revolutionary movement in the liberated territory, but themselves signed decrees for various revolutionary measures. The Communists could work freely among the masses of the people of Hunan where a mighty revolutionary movement was under way. Even Kwangtung did not know such a tempo and scale. By the end of 1926 there were two million peasant league members in Hunan, twice as many as in Kwangtung. The trade unions in the cities numbered a hundred and seventy thousand industrial workers.

Our comrades selflessly worked and fought at the front. From time to time we in Tungshan received their letters which had been delivered from the front. We learned that the adviser on provisions, N. T. Rogov and his interpreter, a Chinese Communist just arrived from the USSR whom we knew by the name of Yanovsky, were sick with cholera. The adviser on medical services, Nikolay Alexandrovich Sokolov (Orlov) could not himself stay with the stricken, but he tried to direct their recovery as far as possible. Rogov gave directions to his orderly, a simple Chinese soldier, on how to take care of the sick, he forbade him to allow them to be treated by local quacks who "healed" cholera by placing iron shavings beneath the tongue. A crate of cognac was left as the main medicine. The orderly faithfully looked after both of them. Rogov's Herculean strength and the cognac overcame the cholera but Yanovsky succumbed. At that time his wife lived in my apartment in "the boxes." Two Chinese Communist women came to inform her of the sad news. Yanovsky's wife soon left for the Soviet Union.

Then came a report that the pilot Remizyuk and the mechanic Kobyakov had been taken prisoner during a forced landing in Kiangsi and were sitting in prison in Kanchow. They were not freed until September 1926 in Nanchang. The news of another air accident, this time in Hunan, became known to us. However, the pilot wasn't injured.

From Akimov's letters we learned that his "boss," the commander of the Second Army, was carried about in a palanquin and that the same sort of palanquin had been prepared for him too. However, he categorically refused to use it and until he procured a horse he walked on foot with the soldiers. Moreover, it turned out that from the Chinese point of view he ate too much. "Sometimes there are no provisions," Akimov described his mis-adventures, "my colleagues tear off some sort of grass, chew it and are full. What can I say? That I want to eat it?"

The adviser Konchits reported that he began coughing up blood on the front near Changsha (he suffered from tuberculosis contracted during World War I) and he related how his boss, General Ch'eng Ch'ien, treated him. On the general's orders the Chinese army physician gave him an injection, the instruments were not sterilized and the wound festered for a long time, but the spitting up of blood ceased. Konchits did not know what sort of medicine it was but from that time he wasn't sick again.

The most important military operations in the first stage of the Northern Expedition were those of Wuhan and Nanchang. I will try to recreate what

I was told by my husband and the other advisers who personally took part in them.

The Kuomintang troops advanced to the north in two columns, a western and an eastern. The commander of the former one was T'ang Sheng-chih whose chief adviser was V. Gorev. It consisted of the Fourth, Sixth, Seventh and Eighth armies and the Second Division of the First Army. The eastern column consisted of the Second and Third armies, the First and Third Divisions of the First Army and the Fourteenth Division of the Fifth Army. It was commanded by Chiang Kai-shek whose adviser was V. K. Blyukher.

In a month the enormous province of Hunan with its thirty million people was freed of Wu P'ei-fu's troops. The question arose of the liberation of the neighboring province of Hupeh with its Wuhan tri-cities (Wuchang, Hanyang, Hankow) where the unlucky marshal had retreated and intended to wage a decisive battle.

On August 12 at a meeting of the army commanders on the Hunan front in Changsha it was decided to attack Wuhan. The first blow was aimed against Wuchang which from time immemorial had been considered the key to the mastery of central China from which came its proud name.[31]

The general offensive commenced on August 17. In fact only the Fourth Army, the so-called Iron Army, attacked. In essence it bore the entire weight of the war in Hunan on its shoulders. Yeh T'ing's Independent Regiment played the main role in all the battles. The Seventh and Eighth Armies consciously avoided battle, the Sixth Army was held in reserve.

The approaches to Wuchang were unusually difficult. The troops marched between lakes along a narrow neck of land which was no wider than five kilometers and near Wuchang narrowed to one to two kilometers. In these extremely unfavorable conditions, the National-Revolutionary Army utterly smashed the enemy. After two fierce battles on August 27 and 30 near Tingssuch'iao and Hoshengch'iao the road to Wuchang was opened. Wu P'ei-fu fled from Hoshengch'iao a half hour before the victors arrived. He was in a fury; he shot some of his generals and instituted a fierce regime in Hanyang and Hankow. The executions there of Kuomintang members and Communists began.

---

31. The city of military might.

On August 31, the Fourth Army approached Wuchang. The city could have been taken right away since the enemy had fled in panic and did not intend to defend it.

However, through the fault of the commander of the Tenth Division, General Ch'en Ming-shu, the moment was allowed to pass. He was ordered to storm into Wuchang at 4 or 5 o'clock but he decided not to act alone. At dawn Chang Fa-k'uei's Twelfth Division arrived and about 10 o'clock in the morning the Second Division of the First Army, the so-called Second Whampoa Division, arrived, but it was too late already, the enemy had succeeded in bringing his troops into the city.

The failure to execute this order led to great losses; fifteen hundred soldiers of the National-Revolutionary Army and many tens of thousands of peaceful inhabitants died.

The remnants of the Hupeh troops headed by the *tupan*, Ch'en Chia-mo, barricaded themselves in Wuchang. General Kou Ying-tzu was the head of the garrison. There were no more than six to eight thousand troops in the city, but subsequently the enemy succeeded in bringing in as many more. Accurate information on the size of the garrison became known only after the surrender of Wuchang. No matter how our advisers tried, intelligence work remained on a low level.

Wuchang was shaped like an irregular square. It looked out on all sides of the world through its narrow gates. One of them, opening westwards in the direction of the Yangtse, was especially tall. This was the famous Golden Falcon Tower, landmark and observation tower from which one could look out over the surrounding territory for some distance. The ditch around the city was almost dry, but from the northern and southern sides there ran a rather deep canal from one lake to another. A chain of hills, the so-called Snake Mountains, lay across Wuchang, with their batteries from which one could also observe the enemy. There were two lakes within the city, the source of drinking water in case of a siege. In places the fortress walls were fifteen meters high but on the average did not exceed ten. Strictly speaking it was not even a wall but a high earthen bank faced with stone on the outer side.

At the meeting on September 1, it was decided to storm Wuchang. No one imagined how difficult this would be. Still fresh in everyone's mind was the taking of the fortress of Waichow during the Second Eastern Expedition when this city, famed for its impregnability, was taken in the course of several hours.

Beneath Wuchang were stationed the Fourth and Seventh Armies and the Second Division of the First Army.

The operation was fixed for September 3. The plan was to storm the south wall with the forces of the Seventh Army (adviser Mamaev), the eastern wall with the Tenth Division (adviser Ter), and the north with the Second Whampoa Division (adviser Akimov). The Tenth Division was to strike the decisive blow. It was decided to take Wuchang in the following way. Volunteer Mauser troops would ascend the scaling ladders and start throwing hand grenades. It was impossible to destroy the walls by firepower; artillery of the requisite calibre was lacking.

However, all the plans were ruined. Instead of one hundred ladders only twenty were made, the Seventh Army began the attack at 4:30 instead of 3 o'clock and the Fourth Army at 5 o'clock when it was already light. Lacking ladders the Seventh Army did a bit of firing but "could not cross the river," as it was put in the commander's report, and stopped firing. The Second Division which had succeeded in preparing ladders tried to advance to the wall but was driven back. Units of the Tenth Division approached the wall without ladders. Soldiers stood ten to twenty paces from it and exchanged curses with the enemy, waited for ladders, but wound up by not getting any and were called back in the morning. In essence there was no attack, nonetheless the Tenth and Second Divisions lost between 200-250 men.

On the same day V. K. Blyukher, Chiang Kai-shek, and T'ang Sheng-chih arrived at the front near Wuchang. In the evening a meeting of the supreme command took place. Blyukher pointed out that the reasons for the failure were poor intelligence and poor preparations in general, the absence of precise tasks and the violation of schedules.

A decision was taken to storm Wuchang for the second time at 3 o'clock on the morning of September 5, along the whole line of the front. The command duties were placed upon T'ang Sheng-chih.

As always before the decisive battles, Communists in the ranks held meetings at which they took oaths to advance forward and to show an example.

Before the assault Chiang Kai-shek himself inspected units of the Second and Tenth Divisions. At 3 o'clock battle was joined.

It was not easy to direct the assault, there was no radio and in effect no telephones either at the front. Communications were maintained by messengers and were not always reliable. Here is an example. At 7 o'clock in the morning the Sixth Regiment of the Second Division rushed into the city through the Wusheng Men (Gate of military victory) and requested assistance. The adviser Akimov informed the senior adviser Gorev of this in writing. After an hour another note from him arrived saying there were no communications with the Sixth Regiment, that the divisional commander had lost control of himself and was not directing the battle. Akimov asked what to do. Gorev wrote that in any case he should not retreat from the wall and informed him that there were fires in the city in the region of the wall within the sector of the Second Division. This directive did not reach Akimov and was returned to Gorev with a note in English on the other side "Comrade Nikitin (Gorev was known by this name in the National-Revolutionary Army) it is impossible to deliver your message." The messenger evidently could not find the division's location or else was afraid to pass through the dangerous sector of the front.

The Sixth Regiment did not enter the city. It only passed through the outer gates. Beyond them, as was common in China, was an enclosed space shaped like a great semi-circle and then more gates. Those who penetrated this far were in a trap. The Sixth Regiment had to retreat.

Later Gorev related how the assault had proceeded. The Seventh Army had not been in battle for an hour when it retreated without permission. The Thirty-Sixth Regiment of the Tenth Division trying to "reconnoiter the locality" got stuck in the ditch and could do nothing. Yeh T'ing's Independent Regiment which fought better than all the others was forced to retreat because of heavy losses. The Twelfth Division lost about 500 men if not more. The Tenth Division fought indecisively. Gorev praised the Second Division saying that it attacked well, suffered small losses, and that the soldiers' and officers' morale was good. The division even intended to repeat the assault at 5 P.M.

Blyukher's assistant for political affairs, Ter, personally took part in the attack. The adviser on military medicine, N. A. Sokolov, told me about this. Here is his story as I remember it. "At the second storming of Wuchang I was with Blyukher beneath the walls of the city. We arrived before the assault had begun, it was rather dark, but the threatening fortifications were still clearly visible. The troops advanced in the ominous silence, soldiers ran by with long bamboo ladders. Blyukher walked slowly along the road, binoculars in his hand. Suddenly the air shuddered from the terrible shouts of the attackers and the besieged. The soldiers flung themselves across the ditch, set up the ladders and clambered up the walls; they were pushed off, hot pitch and boiling water were poured upon them. With heart-rending shouts they broke through and fell into the thick, stinking mud which was in motion from the many wounded and the dying who floundered about in it and whom there was no chance of rescuing.

"It seemed that feudal times had returned. Blyukher observed the assault through binoculars. Suddenly he summoned Ter and ordered him to join the assault at the head of several score Mauser troops from his personal guard. Blyukher's guard consisted of reliable men. The unit headed by Ter threw itself towards the wall but was driven back and almost entirely destroyed. Filthy and covered with scratches, Ter stood before Blyukher in his torn clothing and could not say a word except for frenzied curses."

After two unsuccessful attempts to take Wuchang the advisers suggested that the assault on the city be abandoned. But without their knowledge the command had ordered a third assault. Gorev later wrote, "Only the Second Division which, it may be said, seriously wanted to fulfill the orders, approached the wall at exactly 5 o'clock. A graveyard silence reigned on all the other sectors. The division began firing but from prudence did not climb onto the walls and retreated without loss."

The siege of Wuchang lasted for more than a month. In the city with its half-million people famine set in, and cholera flared up. The ungathered corpses poisoned the air with their stench. Here and there fires blazed.

The city was bombed twice daily. At the appearance of the airplanes the garrison scattered in panic. As before the military flights were the responsibility of our advisers. The planes carried out an enormous responsibility in the areas of communications, intelligence and bombardment, making several flights a day. The pilots took great risks in descending to 60 meters during the attacks. Many times they had to land with bomb loads at unfamiliar airports. They showed their worn-out machines to their comrades and said, "Look at what we're flying in, these are coffins." Kravtsov and Sergeev, whose spotters were Talberg and Bazenau, flew the most often.

At first the city still had links across the Yangtse to the other side from whence came reinforcement and supplies. Later the besiegers began to sink all the sampans and junks on this side and to dig tunnels. The soldiers were afraid to work underground so the excavation was done by volunteers—the Pinghsiang miners. The enemy destroyed one of the underground tunnels and ten patriots were suffocated. .

Negotiations for the surrender of Wuchang began even before the third assault. On September 7, the commander of the Sixth Regiment tried to reach an agreement with the commander of a battalion stationed at the Wu Sheng gates, but without success. Subsequently, such separate negotiations continued more than once, the besiegers sat beneath the walls waiting for an agreed upon signal but without results.

A constant exchange of gunfire was going on within the city between the partisans and the opponents of capitulation.

Negotiations in the name of the fortress commanders were carried out by missionaries and other foreigners in Wuchang with the command of the Kuomintang troops in Hankow thanks to the telephone link between the two cities which functioned flawlessly during the siege. The besieged tried to obtain the condition that they be allowed out with their arms. Knowing that the enemy beneath Wuchang's walls would never agree to such a condition, Generals Ch'en Chia-mo and Kou Ying-tzu tried to reach an agreement with the "fellow traveler," the commander of the Fifteenth Army of the National-Revolutionary Army, General Lu Tso-lung.[32]

While the defeated generals tried to bargain for better terms Wuchang was taken. It happened like this. One of the commanders of the regiment on the southern wall of the fortress agreed to open the gates (he was promised promotion to brigade commander). At 3 o'clock on the morning of October 10, the enemy really did begin to leave the fortress, but the gates were not opened. The soldiers of the National-Revolutionary Army had to clamber up the wall on ladders. There were barricades on the streets of the city since the evening before those loyal to Wu P'ei-fu had suppressed an uprising of soldiers who wanted to capitulate. Units patrolling the streets put up the first resistance.

---

32. During the Northern Expedition, many so-called fellow travelers joined the ranks of the National-Revolutionary Army and the number of armies grew.

Fighting flared up, the result of which was that the enemy was surrounded in the northern part of the city and forced to surrender. Gorev later used to say that he didn't know what to call this operation. To consider that Wuchang was taken by storm was impossible, to say that it had surrendered was also impossible. General Ch'en Ming-shu was appointed garrison commander in Wuchang. Almost all the prisoners joined the southern army.

The garrison commander, General Kou Ying-tzu, who had stayed faithful to the end to Wu P'ei-fu, was taken prisoner and put in the pillory with a dunce's cap on his head. A photo of him in this position made the rounds of all the newspapers. Subsequently when he was brought up before a public show trial in Hankow he said in his defense that "I am a soldier and must fulfill my duty. I will never betray my superior." The inhabitants of Wuchang viewed him as the cause of their sorrows and listened to his self-justifications in a fury. In the days immediately following the surrender of Wuchang a decision was taken by the municipal organs of self-government created by the new power that the city would never again be subjected to a famine siege. It was decided to level the walls. Thousands of people came out on a sort of holiday and swarmed over the walls like ants, destroying them in great bitterness.

The fate of the former governor-general of Hupeh, Ch'en Chia-mo, turned out differently. Although Wuchang had been taken basically by the units of the Fourth Army, T'ang Sheng-chih declared that the captured Ch'en Chia-mo was his prisoner, refused to hand him over to the supreme command, and took him away to Changsha as much because he figured on receiving a rich ransom as from considerations of prestige.

As early as September 7, T'ang Sheng-chih without any special commotion took Hanyang and Hankow, which he had secretly prepared to do for some time. This victory raised his authority even more and dealt a strong blow to Chiang Kai-shek. T'ang Sheng-chih ignored his rival, insulted him, and chased him off to Kiangsi to fight Sun Ch'uan-fang. It was right at this time that he made the remark "If the commander-in-chief is tired let him go to Hankow and I will take Wuchang."

In fact, as usual, Chiang Kai-shek complained about tiredness and threatened to abandon everything and go off to Shanghai. And this at the moment when the fate of the Northern Expedition was being decided at Wuchang! Only in the middle of November, after the victory at Nanchang, did Chiang Kai-shek again raise his head.

The military operations against Sun Ch'uan-fang actually unfolded in the second half of September. Around this time, T'ang Sheng-chih's troops were advancing north along the Peking-Hankow Railroad and taking the mountain pass Wushengkuan on the border with Honan thereby blocking the path of Wu P'ei-fu's troops out of this province. In the middle of September, first the Seventh Kwangsi Army and then the Second Whampoa Division were sent from the vicinity of Wuchang to Kiangsi. Now Akimov was often together with Blyukher who demanded from his advisers, especially the young ones, a smart appearance and discipline. Akimov related that to ride horseback together with Blyukher was real punishment; he ordered the young advisers to ride ahead and he observed closely so that they would hold themselves correctly and maintain a proper carriage.

Blyukher was accompanied everywhere by his personal interpreter, Emmanuel Moyseevich Abramson, who subsequently became the scientific secretary of the Scientific Research Institute on China at Sun Yat-sen University in Moscow. Chinese, which he had known from childhood since he had been born in Harbin, he knew superbly. Now the main battles developed for Sun Ch'uan-fang's headquarters—the administrative center of Kiangsi—Nanchang. This enormous city with its quarter million population was famous for its impregnability. Nine centuries ago it was surrounded by thirty-kilometer-long ramparts and from that time had not been taken once, even the Taipings' strength was broken on its mighty battlements.

I cannot tell about Nanchang in detail since I was there for only one day almost two months after its liberation. I remember the ruins of the buildings destroyed during the siege, a large, oddly shaped lake in the center of the city, the magnificent towers of the rampart gates, and on them black signboards with gold inscriptions of splendid titles, "Gates of Eternal Harmony," "Gates of Victory Achieved," etc. The city, it seemed, had forgotten its adversity and had settled down to a peaceful life.

The first assault on Nanchang took place on September 19. The city was taken by the Sixth Army, but after four days it was yielded again. In this unsuccessful operation, the army lost almost half its strength, and the First Whampoa Division which took part in the battles lost even more. The decision to take Nanchang was made without the knowledge of the High Command and its chief adviser V. K. Blyukher. But in any case the situation would have been different had the commander of the Third Army, Chu P'ei-te, responded to the Sixth Army's request for aid. Like a typical Chinese militarist he decided that the success of the Sixth Army was not in his interest and with a light heart, and perhaps, joyfully, he allowed his neighbor and ally to be defeated.

The Kuomintang forces went away to Hupeh and towards the western borders of Kiangsi. Chiang Kai-shek arrived at the front in the first days of October. Nanchang was taken on October 20 and once again yielded. The troops of the National-Revolutionary Army retreated some sixty to seventy kilometers toward the west. Great exhaustion after almost two months of fighting and the shortage of weapons and military supplies were taking their toll.

The fighting near Nanchang cost many lives, not only those of the soldiers on both sides. After returning to Nanchang, Sun Ch'uan-fang took reprisals against the peaceful inhabitants who hated him and impatiently awaited the arrival of the revolutionary army. More than two thousand persons perished without trial, including the rector and two professors of Nanchang University. The chief of the Department of Education in the provincial government was thrown into prison. The corpses lay scattered about right on the streets spreading a terrible stench. All the stores in the city were looted. Several dozens of students were decapitated at Kiukiang in the beginning of October. Subsequently, Sun Ch'uan-fang ordered the execution of four hundred more students.

The period before the decisive victory at Nanchang was a most trying one for Chiang Kai-shek. His spirits fell once more and he again pretended that he was trying to satisfy the revolutionary aspirations of the masses.

Characteristically, upon receiving a letter from the Western Hills group calling upon him to break with the USSR and the Communist party, Chiang Kai-shek did not give them an official answer but sent his envoy to Shanghai and informed them that he would do just that after the conclusion of the military actions.

The final assault on Nanchang which took place in the beginning of November was directed by Blyukher from Chiang Kai-shek's headquarters in Kaoan, some thirty kilometers to the southwest of Nanchang. Subsequently, Blyukher related that Chiang Kai-shek was very nervous, understanding that the forthcoming operation was crucial for him. Failure would put an end to his whole career. Several times Chiang put on a real show of hysterics in front of his chief military adviser, wrung his hands, cried, shouted "It's all over" and promised to shoot himself. Each time Blyukher with difficulty succeeded in calming the weak-nerved commander-in-chief. After the victory Chiang Kai-shek immediately began giving himself airs.

The city was taken on November 8. The Nanchang contingent of Sun Ch'uan-fang's troops were surrounded, forty thousand prisoners and an enormous amount of captured material was seized. One of Sun Ch'uan-fang's best divisions, the Chekiang Division, went over in its entirety to the side of the National-Revolutionary Army. The overjoyed Chiang Kai-shek ordered a couple of dozen splendid gold watches, intending to give them to his advisers, but none of them accepted the gifts—this was strictly prohibited among us—and Chiang Kai-shek demonstratively distributed the watches to his staff officers. The First, Second, Third and Sixth Armies played decisive roles in the battles. All of them suffered great losses and after the victory numbered in toto only about thirty-five thousand men.

The Situation in Canton

Important events were taking place in Canton during the Northern Expedition. At the beginning of September the government of Great Britain declared in the press that it would consider the river pickets of the Hong Kong strike committee as pirates with all the attendant consequences. The British imperialists, rushing to the routed Wu P'ei-fu's aid, intended in this fashion to frighten the Kuomintang government whose troops were at the front.

On September 4, the British naval forces began military operations against the launches of the strike committee on the Pearl River near Canton. A landing party from a gunboat descended onto one of the private British wharves and removed the picketers by force. The British undertook the same actions in the vicinity of Swatow. A burst of indignation was the response to these new provocations. Meetings and demonstrations were held all over Canton. A protest note was dispatched to the British consul-general in Shameen.

The consular corps in Canton which consisted of four consuls-general (England, USA, Japan, and Germany) and seven consuls (France, Italy, Portugal, Sweden, Denmark, Holland, and Switzerland) began discussions with the minister of foreign affairs for the Kuomintang government who at that time was the European-educated, extremely erudite and able diplomat, the Kuomintang leftist Ch'en Yu-jen (Eugene Ch'en). The discussions, however, led nowhere. The gunboat was stationed right next to the embankment for several days. We rode over to take a look at it.

I did not get to see the beginning of the Hong Kong–Canton strike but I did see the end of it. It need hardly be said that the cessation of the strike in October 1926 was necessary. Truly, at a time when the revolution had reached the Yangtse there was no sense in exacerbating relations with the British imperialists in the South. But the enfeeblement of the strike committee—the advance guard of the workers' movement in Canton—strengthened the position of the rightists and eased the way for the counter-revolutionary coup in April 1927.

The victories at the front inspired a general upsurge in Canton; in all layers of the population there was a movement to the left. The Kuomintang leftists and the Communists now constituted more than eighty per cent of the cadets at the Whampoa Academy. In the Western press even Sun Yat-sen University began to be called nothing less than "the breeding ground of the red contagion." The leftward movement also affected the Kuomintang leadership.

On October 15 the plenum of the Kuomintang CEC convened in Canton and turned out in its resolutions to be more radical than the First and Second Congresses. It adopted an extensive resolution on the workers' and peasants' movement, decided to struggle implacably against those who violated party discipline, and expelled one group of Western Hills adherents. A declaration on the immediate tasks of the Kuomintang was published. It included points about the abolition of the unequal treaties, the return of foreign concessions, and prohibition on the operation of foreign banks in China. There was also mention in it of factory legislation, agrarian reform, pensions for the wounded and families of deceased soldiers, feminine equality, popular election of provincial governors, etc. The plenum sent a telegram to Wang Ching-wei requesting that he return to work and one to Feng Yü-hsiang congratulating him on the occasion of his return from the Soviet Union.

Chiang Kai-shek sent a telegram in which he informed them that he was unable to come but accepted in advance all the decisions of the plenum. The advisers said that he cried in rage when composing the text. The situation in Kiangsi was very tense and Chiang Kai-shek feared defeat; therefore he curried favor with the plenum.

Skipping forward I will say that the fate of the plenum was like that of the Second Congress. Just as on that occasion the victory of the leftists turned out to be of brief duration.

Prior to the Northern Expedition it had been decided that after the victory the government's new location would be Hankow. With the liberation of Nanchang the center of the revolutionary movement was shifted to the Yangtse Valley. It became necessary to transfer the capital of the government which there was no longer any reason for calling South Chinese.

The last week prior to the departure to the north of the first group of government leaders[33] was passed in noisy celebrations. The ninth anniversary of the Great October Revolution was marked with unprecedented enthusiasm. A governmental committee in which representatives of all public organizations took part was formed to conduct the festivities. November 7 was declared a holiday. The evening before gatherings and meetings were held everywhere. On outdoor stages members of amateur groups, many made up as Russian workers, peasants, bourgeoisie and White Guards performed sketches from the history of our civil war. The whole city was decked out with Soviet flags, portraits of Lenin and of Sun Yat-sen. A banquet was given in honor of the Soviet colony at which T'ang Sheng-chih and other members of the government declared that the alliance with the USSR would be an enduring one and that the USSR was the lodestar for the liberation of the world's oppressed peoples.

On the morning of the following day a grandiose demonstration began. Orators addressed the crowds from scores of platforms which had been erected on the streets. Detachments of uniformed pioneers carrying sticks preserved order. Borodin and the Kuomintang leftist Hsü Ch'ien spoke at the main meeting. The papers carried articles dedicated to the significance of the Great October Revolution; many brochures and leaflets appeared on this theme.

Soon came the news of the liberation of Nanchang signifying the successful conclusion of the first stage of the Northern Expedition. It is impossible to convey the ecstasy which gripped Canton. November 12, Sun Yat-sen's birthday, was observed in a condition of national exultation. It is estimated

---

33. This was sometimes called the Preparatory Commission.

that no less than half a million persons took part in demonstrations. In the evening a colorful torchlight parade was held in the city. The festivities went on long past midnight.

Before the departure of the government to the North a special conference was held on questions relating to the education of China's revolutionary youth in the Soviet Union. A Society for Aiding Sun Yat-sen University in Moscow was established with the participation of Soong Ching-ling, T'an Yen-k'ai, Sun Fo, and Tai Chi-t'ao. The latter was chosen on the formal consideration that he was rector of Sun Yat-sen University in Canton. After the departure of the other members of the committee for Wuhan, Tai Chi-t'ao took upon himself the selection of candidates for study in the USSR. The results of this activity became apparent later on when an underground Chiang Kai-shek organization—the Chekiang Brotherhood—arose in Sun Yat-sen University in Moscow.

On November 15 we saw off the first contingent of government members—the minister of finance Sun Fo, the minister of justice Hsü Ch'ien, the director of the Central Bank Sung Tzu-wen, the minister of foreign affairs Ch'en Yu-jen and others. M. M. Borodin, Chang T'ai-lei and others set out with them, and also the military adviser M. F. Kumanin, the financial adviser V. M. Shteyn, the Canton representative of Moscow's Sun Yat-sen University and special correspondent for *Pravda* S. A. Dalin, Ye. Yolk, O. Tarkhanov, and someone from the Soviet consular staff.

The sea route via Shanghai and then up the Yangtse was cut so they had to go by land. This route was known in Western literature as the Ambassador's Road along which the English embassy of Lord McCartney had journeyed from Canton to Peking at the end of the eighteenth century, and the embassy of Lord Amherst had returned from Peking at the beginning of the nineteenth century. It had not been used for a long time and on certain sections of it palanquins and junks had to be resorted to as the means of transport. The junks were towed by bargehaulers or propelled by boat coolies who pushed their poles along the river bottom.

Three weeks later a second contingent of government members set out by the same route—Chang Ching-chiang who in Chiang Kai-shek's absence was the chairman of the Kuomintang CEC, T'an Yen-k'ai, chairman of the government, Ho Hsiang-ning, the widow of Liao Chung-k'ai with her daughters, and still others. Borodin's wife and youngest son, along with the remainder of the personnel in Canton including myself, traveled with them.

No matter how eager we were to follow the advancing revolution, no matter how much we desired to reach quickly the banks of the Yangtse where the victorious banners of the Northern Expedition flew, it was not easy for us to depart from Canton.

On the eve of our departure we went to the city for the last time. We rode along all the main streets and the embankment. Tung-yuan remained behind. The strike committee had not been disbanded, the pickets kept order in the city, but the former animation had vanished, the struggle was over.

The car stopped next to the photographic studio *A Fong* where all of the Soviet colony at Tungshan went to have their pictures taken. We proceeded further on foot. In front of us were our beloved "narrow streets" where we were greeted like old acquaintances. For the last time we bought the excellent products of the Kwangtung craftsmen.

The government members had not succeeded in leaving Canton before the rightists' offensive commenced there. On orders from Li Chi-shen, commander of the armed forces in Kwangtung, the provincial government entered the struggle against the strike committee, allowed the *min t'uan* to smash the peasant unions, published new regulations concerning the trade union movement which prohibited strikes and the possession of arms by the workers.

This sharp turn to the right was made easier by the fact that in Canton the leaders of the Kuomintang left betrayed the revolution. Here I must say a few words about Kan Nai-kuang.

Kan Nai-kuang was chosen as a member of the Kuomintang CEC at the First Congress and he headed the Youth Department. He also worked in the political department of the Whampoa Academy together with the Communists and Kuomintang leftists, was secretary of the Kuomintang cell in Sun Yat-sen University, edited the newspaper of the Kwangtung Provincial Committee of the Kuomintang, and was head of the State Auditing Bureau. At the Second Congress of the Kuomintang he was chosen as a candidate member of the Politburo.

He was considered a staunch leftist, but after the March 20 Incident many of the leftists wavered and moved to the right. The July conference of the Kuomintang reinforced their changed positions. Among the "switchers" was Kan Nai-kuang.

Beginning with the autumn of 1926, Kan Nai-kuang who was managing the Peasant Department of the Kuomintang CEC began to treat the Communists and the Russian advisers noticeably more coldly. Formerly, when coming to see Borodin, he would greet all of us courteously, now he was aloof and sullen.

At that time he had already worked out his theory of "using the rightists to struggle against the Communists," although he had not yet steered into an open alliance with the rightists.

Before the government's departure for the North there were several leading figures among the leftists in Kwangtung. After their departure he became the acknowledged leader of the leftists, but he led them not to the left but to the right.

In his time Tai Chi-t'ao had developed a theory which "served as a foundation" for rightist activity. Kan Nai-kuang did the same for the "leftists." His pamphlet *The Peasantry as the Kuomintang's Class Base* was distributed during the summer of 1926 in an unprecedented edition for that time of 50,000 copies. The class basis of the Kuomintang, Kan Nai-kuang said, is the peasantry—go work in the villages, do not hand the peasants over to other parties (meaning the CCP). Soon he declared that the Communist party was the enemy of the Kuomintang and was robbing it of its mass base.

The program which Kan Nai-kuang set forth in his pamphlet was distinguished by its extreme opportunism. He issued it during a period of sharp conflict between the peasants of Kwangtung and the landlords, and he found no other way out than the suggestion "to alleviate conflicts" and "to send troops in case of need."

At the beginning of December Kan Nai-kuang created a secret organization within the Kuomintang called the Leftist League which, according to his intentions, was to replace the Society for the Study of Sun Yat-senism since the latter had suffered a defeat, as he saw it. Kan Nai-kuang openly became the bearer of the rightists' cause. The league's program approved of the changes which followed after the March 20 Incident. In its regulations was a clause that the divulging of organizational secrets was punishable by death. Members of the league included such well-known leftists as Ku Meng-yü and the minister of justice, Hsü Ch'ien. It was active in Hunan as well where it had the most motley membership.

Soon the bloc of Kuomintang leftists and rightists was put together and this had an immediate effect on the political situation. Notwithstanding their majority and their leading positions in the provincial party apparatus, the leftists were led about by the rightists. In January 1927 a provincial conference of the Kuomintang took place at which the anti-Communist bloc of leftists and rightists was given organizational form.

The April Coup

On April 13, 1927, General Li Chi-shen pulled a counter-revolutionary coup in Canton on the pretext that the Communists along with the peasant detachments and Whampoa cadets were preparing to seize political power. After the coup the imperialist press triumphantly reported that "Canton now is the whitest place in the territory of China. The Society for the Study of Sun Yat-senism, disbanded a year ago, is open again and has issued a declaration against the Communists. Sun Yat-sen University was the breeding ground of the Reds, but now a White rector has been appointed there. Three hundred cadets of the Whampoa Academy are under arrest and are being held on board ship under the guard of the gunboats *Chungshan* and *Chiangtu*."

Alas, all this was the naked truth. Only that part of the revolutionary-minded teachers of the Whampoa Academy who fled to Hong Kong by cutter were not on the floating prisons on the Pearl River.

A Soviet trade union delegation headed by S. A. Lozovsky[34] arrived in Canton on April 14, 1927. It was to attend the Pacific Trade Union Conference which was due to open soon. It found itself in the thick of events. At the end of July 1927 Lozovsky returned to the USSR on the same ship as my husband and I, and he told us about those tragic days in Canton.

"On the day of our arrival," Lozovsky said, "there were already mass arrests going on, and many trade unions were surrounded. The railroad workers resisted and there were many victims among them. On the following day, the city which was usually so lively, seemed silent and deserted. Only the sounds of military trumpets could be heard. Bound workers were led along the street under convoy. Canton was occupied by troops and police, arrests and round-ups did not cease. More than two thousand persons were arrested and several

---

34. At that time he was the general secretary of the Executive Committee of the Profintern.

hundred Communists were shot. A wave of arrests also occurred in Sun Yat-sen University. The Whampoa Academy was destroyed.

Even several members of the provincial government and the provincial committee of the Kuomintang who were suspected of belonging to the Communist party were thrown into prison and the leftist editors of Kuomintang newspapers were purged. A "reorganization" of the unions began. The reactionary Mechanics' Union and the Kwangtung Trade Union Federation took part in the coup.

Just as on March 20, 1926, troops were sent into Tungshan and surrounded the apartments and offices of our advisers who were still working in the Whampoa Academy. Posters were hung in the city with the slogans "Down with the Chinese Communist Party!" "Down with the Wuhan Government!" "Long Live Chiang Kai-shek!" The assassins of Liao Chung-k'ai were freed and the Paper Tigers Organization was again allowed to operate.

At the same time a cruel suppression of the peasant movement was underway, to which the peasants replied with mass insurrections. A very serious situation was created in the villages. In the Chung Shan district, for example, a ten-thousand man peasant defense force even threatened the cities.

In such a situation there could be no question of the conference meeting in Canton. Our letter to the Kwangtung Section of the All-China Federation of Labor (Council of Workers' Deputies) was opened and returned to us. It turned out that the addressee no longer existed. Also we were not allowed to get in touch with the Soviet colony. Then the delegation left for Wuhan. As is known, not all of us succeeded in getting there, but the conference was held all the same.

Despite the cruel repression, the revolutionary struggles in Canton did not cease. The whole spring and summer of 1927 the papers reported the actions of the masses and the cruel persecution of the city's revolutionaries.

In Canton by the end of June even the anti-imperialist movement was considered illegal. On the eve of June 23, the second anniversary of the bloody shootings on the Shakee embankment, martial law was declared in the city. Still a demonstration was held and leaflets denouncing Chiang Kai-shek and Li Chi-shen were passed out. This evoked new persecution. From three o'clock in the morning of June 28 Canton was again under martial law. All the troops and police in the city were mobilized, traffic in the city and the suburbs was halted. Searches and arrests began in the unions. The workers (primarily from the railroad) resisted but were disarmed. Fifty workers' organizations were smashed and one hundred fifty men (the majority of them strikers) were arrested, much illegal literature and weapons were seized. In the government report it was said that these measures were taken in response to the "acceleration of Red activities."

Crushed and bleeding, Canton continued to fight on.

CHAPTER VI

IN WUHAN

Journey of the Government Members

I well remember that day in the first week of December 1926 when the second contingent of government leaders left for Wuhan. The weather was cool and overcast, people were wearing their summer coats. But almost all the trees were wildly blossoming. The tall trees lining the streets and roads were especially flower-laden. They reminded one of white acacia only their flowers were yellow. Many plants from the temperate zone grew to gigantic proportions in Kwantung's tropical climate. Our modest shrub — the Far Eastern marsh tea which in early spring adorns the yet bare copses — turns into huge trees in Kwangtung. They stand just like enormous bouquets of violet flowers.

Running quickly down the winding staircase of our "box" I looked up for the last time at the tear-stained face of our amah who was hunched over the banister.

At the station a crowd of people was seeing us off, representatives from public and governmental organizations, relatives and acquaintances. Almost all of our sorely depleted Tungshan collective gathered on the platform.

The as yet uncompleted Canton-Changsha railroad was in poor repair; accidents were a frequent occurrence. The comrades who saw us off teased us and tried to frighten us with talk about the forthcoming catastrophe. The mood was one of elation. The brilliant successes at the front were no joke! But by this time the reactionaries in Canton were already preparing to struggle against the revolutionary masses.

The official train consisted of several ordinary cars and one salon car with appropriate furnishings. Only the most important people rode in the latter.

We arrived at Shaokuan, the final point on the railroad, towards evening. A triumphal reception had been prepared and a banquet was held. A wind ensemble of students from a missionary school under the direction of a White emigré performed. When the "Internationale" — the Soviet anthem at that time — was played, the director turned and bowed in our direction.

On the same evening a long line of palanquins deposited the members of the government on the shore of the Tanshui, the left fork of the North River. From here there was the prospect of a trip by barge upriver to the city of Nanhsiung which lay en route to the Meiling Pass, on the high road to Kiangsi. Along the deck of the large, thatch-covered barges ran a plank walk with cross-cut boards fastened to it so that the boatsmen could support their legs and propel the boat by pushing their boathooks along the river-bottom.

Each barge could hold several dozen people. Canvas cots, tables, and stools were set up. The departure time was set for the following morning, but the members of the government had already claimed their places the night before.

I was awakened in the morning by the motion of the barge. Bare feet slapped alongside behind a thin partition, something heavy was carried past, then a heavy splash was heard. Suddenly a human howling such as I had never heard before began to ring out in the air. Simultaneously, the nasty, grating call of a jackdaw was heard.

The Tanshui River was very shallow and the barges were constantly scraping their bottoms. They almost had to be portaged along. Six boatsmen, three on each side, strained at their bargepoles, painfully dragging themselves along, their noses to the stern, pushing the barge forward in this manner. The banks echoed with their shouts which were unbearable to the unaccustomed ear. They started with a cry which expressed the maximum tension of human effort and ended with a drawn-out moan. It seemed that their voices would crack at once and the men would fall into the water exhausted.

The thought that you are serving as an additional burden to this unfortunate boatsman is completely unendurable. Therefore I happily joined a small company of Chinese youth and several Soviet comrades who were walking along the bank. We proceeded in this way until we were placed on large barges with sails at the prow; these were later hitched to a small steamer.

On the whole our barge contained young persons. I especially remember Liao Chung-k'ai's daughter and her friend who had just returned from Moscow where she had studied at Sun Yat-sen University. For this reason she wore the same sort of man's cap which had brought so much censure upon me during the first days after my arrival in China. Liao Chung-k'ai's daughter, sad and quiet, was still feeling the loss of her father. Her friend, a pretty, cheerful girl, was an enthusiastic partisan of traveling on foot.

The Tanshui River was very picturesque. It wound between green banks, and babbled over shoals and sandbars. At first we walked along the narrow path made by Chinese bargemen at the water's edge, but later we began to take shortcuts and often got far ahead. So we had a chance to look into the villages and the markets.

In the fields I saw thickets of sugarcane for the first time. It was even denser and taller than the kaoliang in North China and probably also caused not a few worries to the Japanese troops in their struggles with the guerillas at the end of the thirties. Sugarcane is the favorite delicacy of Kwangtung youngsters. We also gnawed quite a bit of it during our journey.

In one village we saw an eating-place — actually several long tables sunken into the ground beneath a mat canopy held up by poles. In the middle, as if on the second floor, reached by a short ladder, was something like a plank closet. Evidently the owner lived there and kept his cashbox there as well because when we left the traditional cry of "bring the box" rang out. This was so that everyone would know we had left a tip. Until the thirties, on Tsvetny Boulevard in Moscow there were many Chinese eating-places, and this cry always accompanied the departure of the lively customers.

I confess that the condition of the village eating-place did not inspire my appetite. When I saw the dirty tubs of water where the dishes were washed and the wet, stinking cloth used to dry them, I felt not quite myself and said that I wasn't hungry. But noodles with meat, the famous *ju ssu mien* which we used to gorge ourselves on in Peking, were placed on the table. The marvelous aroma of my favorite dish had its effect. I hurried to join my comrades.

In this way we traveled for some three or four days to Nanhsiung. There another triumphal welcome and a banquet awaited us. In the morning it was revealed that some of the palanquin bearers who had been hired the night before had run off because the government members whom they were supposed to carry across the mountain, over the pass, seemed too heavy to them.

Early in the morning several dozen bearers crowded in front of the house where the members of the government were staying. Southerners in

China are an expansive people. When the travelers came out to get seated an uproar such as one hears at a bazaar arose. The bearers, gesticulating furiously, their faces distorted with anger, cursed each other paying no attention to us. "The arms of the law" had to spend quite some time with the help of smacks and shouts before they were able to restore calm. Lifting up their passengers the palanquin bearers moved out along the road one after another.

The road ahead was not a short one. Arrival at Tayu (Nanan) in the south of Kiangsi was scheduled for late in the evening. The road was a difficult one. The ascent, rather gentle at first, became steeper and steeper. The palanquin bearers in trying to get the lighter passengers had not quarreled over nothing.

From the morning on a hard rain fell making the road muddy and slippery, but the bearers, encouraging each other, stubbornly carried on. They were lightly dressed — conical straw hats, trousers cut short at the knee, and jackets of cotton homespun. They were soon soaked to the skin. Inside the palanquin it was dark and damp, a clay pot with hot coals was at one's feet. By raising a corner of the cloth which hung in front one could see the narrow road covered with paving stones, the wet trees and the endless sheets of rain.

Once or twice the caravan stopped at inns for a rest. The rain did not let up. Steep mountains rose before us. Finally, there it was, the Meiling Pass.

The bearers quickened their pace. On the left a magnificent old temple floated by, its ancient red columns supported a decorated roof that seemed to come out of a fine, austere painting. We hurried past a guardhouse, and splendid, old fortress gates which guarded the pass. They were open and soldiers stood rigidly at attention before them.

Then began the descent to Kiangsi.

It is well-known that the traveler who has passed through the Baidar Gates on the road to Sevastopol after traveling through the yellow, sun-baked plains is suddenly struck when he sees before him the glittering, blue sea and the lush, subtropical vegetation. Meiling produces roughly the same impression. Beyond the gates at the summit of the pass a new world opens up entirely unlike the one which lies to the south. Even the speech of the people changes

There is no trace of that Kwangtung dialect which drove us students to despair.

Beyond the pass the descent is very steep. In essence this is something like a *pandus* formed of great slabs of stone. For the inexperienced traveler, especially in the rain, it is downright dangerous. A chasm yawns to the right. But the broad panorama which unfolds below is amazing.

The palanquin carrying my thin self was the lightest and the bearers carried me almost at a run. Soon we were far in front of the others. Night drew nigh, the road could barely be seen in the darkness, but the bearers still hurried along its wet, slippery rocks, speaking softly to each other. I had already begun dreaming of bandits, and I was prepared to stop my "kidnapers" and demand to be returned. But light glittered in the distance, and one could hear voices. In another few minutes the palanquin listed to one side and was put down on the ground.

Someone raised the curtain and shone a lantern on me. "Is this Borodin's wife?" they asked in chorus (thank God I again understood Chinese speech). "No, this is a girl in her suite," one of the bearers replied, wiping his damp neck. The welcomers were disappointed but not for long. I started speaking Chinese and at once acquired many friends. I was again seated in the palanquin and carried to the old yamen, designated as the dwelling place for the arriving government members. This was the large district town of Tayu.

On the following day we were seated in barges as in Shaokuan and again the heart-rending cries of the boatsmen were heard along the river. From early morning we again walked out onto the bank and marched forward, outdistancing the floating caravan.

A month had not yet passed since the revolutionary troops had cleansed Kiangsi of the Northern militarists. The province was experiencing an unprecedented revolutionary upsurge. Communist and Kuomintang organizations, workers and peasants unions and student and women's societies were being formed in all the districts.

Our path lay along the main water-transport route in the province, the Kan River. The villages through which we passed were well-informed about the most important political events. Specifically everyone knew that the Kuomintang government was being transferred to the North. Everywhere along the shores our caravan was greeted by peasants carrying the unfurled banners of their unions. Delegations from public organizations crowded about on the piers, music rumbled, firecrackers exploded, people cried *"wan sui."* T'an Yen-k'ai who at first gave speeches rather willingly soon got tired of the outpourings of popular enthusiasm and tried to shirk this duty. He was particularly angry when disturbed during meal time. It happened that delegations waited in vain for the appearance of one of the government members and had to settle for someone of lesser stature.

The people also knew that the Soviets were their friends. Everywhere the most cordial welcome awaited us.

Entering one of the villages we saw a simple, blue palanquin with a lowered curtain on the main square in front of the ancestral temple. People walked up to it, pushed the curtain aside and looked in. It didn't even occur to me that this was a matrimonial palanquin. I knew that red, the color of joy, predominates at Chinese weddings. In Canton and Peking brides were carried in spacious decorated palanquins and accompanied by large retinues. Here was the most ordinary gloomy colored palanquin, without any decoration, standing alone as if abandoned.

We also lifted the curtain and saw a peasant girl dressed in a new woolen gown despite the hot, sunny weather. Her tiny, bound feet were shod in embroidered slippers of bright satin shaped like lotus buds. A dark, simple kerchief of cotton cloth covered her face. Something was knotted into each corner. I learned later that these were salt, rice, chopsticks, and an onion — the symbol of a prosperous life. We were told that she had been sitting there since early morning. It was already about two in the afternoon.

The relatives of the young couple came up to us and invited us to the temple for the wedding. There we saw the groom. He was also in a winter fur gown, but he wore a European-style summer straw hat. The fur is certainly an important part of the dowry if it is worn even in hot weather. The bride and groom were placed at the very threshold facing the exit and then the marriage ceremony began.

A small, poorly dressed, funny old man accompanied by a cheerful youth approached the young couple. He smiled sweetly with his toothless mouth. His bare, dark, absolutely hairless crown glittered in the sun as if it were polished. On seeing him everyone clasped his hands in great respect and began to bow, repeating in singsong voices *"Lao yeh, lao yeh."*[1] We did the same. He was the eldest of the clan coming to join the conjugal pair with the bands of the ancestors.

The old man turned around, and the person accompanying him quickly handed him a live rooster and something which looked like a large chopping-knife such as we use for chopping kindling. With a groan the old man placed the rooster's head on the threshold and began to chop at its neck. The rooster screamed wildly. Seeing that the head of the clan was having trouble, the youth attending him took the cleaver and cut off the rooster's head with one swing, after which he thrust its feet into the old man's hands. The old man solemnly raised the rooster over his head and sprinkled the young couple with its blood. After this he was given another rooster, already plucked and decorated behind with a large, pretty feather. Then he gave a speech, but he mumbled and lisped so that I understood almost nothing. I only made out that he suggested that the wife obey her husband and present him with as many sons as possible.

Then innumerable obeisances by the young pair to the relatives began, some on the knees, some at the waist, depending on their age and degree of kinship.

And finally came the wedding feast. It was held in the same temple where the ancestral tablets of the whole village were placed and where now tables with modest fare for the many guests were set up. We were invited too and sampled the matrimonial viands. According to custom we presented gifts to the young ones; someone handed us the red wrapping paper. Caught unprepared I could not think of what to give the bride and with a pain in my heart I wrapped up in a bit of red paper a museum piece — one of those dollars which Sun Yat-sen had minted during the brief period of his presidency in 1912.

It was comparatively warm in the south of Kiangsi but it got colder further to the north. Snow fell in the vicinity of Chian. True it melted right away but because of it I bought for myself the same sort of sheepskin coat in which the Chinese bride was married, only a somewhat more expensive one. The long, thick white hair was very soft and fine and parted into separate coils, curling into tiny ringlets.

---

1. "Father, father"

After Chian we disembarked only at the stops in the larger towns. The enthusiastic welcomes for the official caravan continued right on up to Nanchang, Chiang Kai-shek's headquarters where many of our advisers including V.K. Blyukher were living.

We arrived in Nanchang on December 31, 1926. A splendid reception was organized on the pier. Red and blue banners fluttered, firecrackers exploded, and cries of welcome were heard. In the evening a banquet was held in the headquarters of the General Staff, and this served simultaneously as a greeting to the New Year.

The tables were arranged in the shape of the letter π ; Chiang Kai-shek and Blyukher sat in the center along with the newly arrived members of the government. Borodin's co-workers headed by Fanya Semyonovna sat at the table to the right.

Chiang Kai-shek was very animated, smiled all the time and played the host's role with a satisfied air. He was dressed in uniform with a tri-colored tie and a squeaky, new leather belt which further accentuated his hollow chest and stooped shoulders. Before the banquet Chiang Kai-shek went up to Borodina and with my assistance asked her how she had stood up under the journey and whether she had news from her husband. He bared his large, horse-like teeth and seemed about to neigh from pleasure that the success of the Northern Expedition had turned into a personal success for him. This was the first and last time that I saw Chiang Kai-shek from so close.

Speeches were made and toasts offered. I did not perceive any hidden meaning in them. In fact at that time a hidden struggle was already under way between the Wuhan government and the commander-in-chief Chiang Kai-shek.

Chiang Kai-shek tried to detain as many leading government figures as possible in Nanchang. When the first government contingent arrived in Nanchang the famous Kuling conference was held. Representatives of the highest military and political circles of the Kuomintang gathered in this famous Chinese resort, high up in the mountains. It seemed that the rightists had conceded at this meeting. A decision was taken to summon Wang Ching-wei from abroad and to shift the location of the government not to Nanchang, Chiang Kai-shek's headquarters where he felt himself complete master of the situation, but to Wuhan under the protection of the revolutionary masses.

Hoping to reopen this question Chiang Kai-shek detained the entire second contingent in Nanchang. Only F.S. Borodina and her traveling companions proceeded to Wuhan on the following day. Chiang Kai-shek's wife, a tall, stately Chinese woman in her middle years, came to see them off. Wanting to conceal the fact that her feet were disfigured by binding she did not wear cloth slippers but ordinary leather shoes, only of a very small child's size. Still her gait (she stepped on her heels) gave away her secret. She was in a depressed mood although she tried to smile amiably. She evidently sensed that Chiang Kai-shek, who never appeared together with her and was ashamed of her old-fashioned appearance and her inability to hold her own in society, would soon abandon her. Chiang Kai-shek was looking for a foreign-educated wife with ties to imperialist circles. A year later in December 1927 he married Soong Mei-ling, the sister of Sung Tzu-wen. He became a Christian upon her insistence.

Borodina and her comrades were ferried to the left bank of the Kan River where there was a railroad station. A special train waited at the platform. We traveled to Kiukiang, a port on the Yangtse, from where we were to proceed by boat to Hankow.

After two or three hours we arrived at Kiukiang. It was intended that we spend the night there and sail for Wuhan in the morning.

Kiukiang is a small city, but here too the British imperialists had contrived to snatch a concession. There were a multitude of porcelain shops in town, evidently because Kingtechen with its famous porcelain factories was not far distant.

A women's delegation came to the hotel where we were staying to welcome Borodin's wife. I remember the sweet young faces full of unfeigned enthusiasm.

Wuhan—the Tri-cities. Provisional Residence of the Government Members.

The first contingent of government officials arrived in Wuhan on December 12, 1926.

The great significance of the transfer of the capital of revolutionary China was understood both in China and abroad. The British imperialists who regarded the Yangtse Valley as their sphere of influence did not hesitate to express their views on this matter. The little river steamer on which the government officials were traveling was decorated with paper flags and scarlet banners with greetings in honor of the Kuomintang, our advisers, and M.M. Borodin personally and slogans against foreign imperialism. When it was not far from Hankow the following incident occurred.

A dock belonging to the American Standard Oil Company which had large concessions and about two ships in China was located there. Several gunboats and light cruisers, among them the English cruiser *Cockchafer* which not long before this had taken part in the shooting of the peaceful population of Wanhsien were laid up at the pier.[2]

Allowing the steamship to pass the *Cockchafer* overtook it from the left and after cutting it off stopped at the shore. Everyone was indignant. But just at this time there appeared on the scene three planes of the National-Revolutionary Army which had flown in from Wuhan to salute the government. They circled menacingly over the cruiser to the general satisfaction of the passengers.

A launch was sent out from Wuhan to meet the government; escorted by it the steamship set out for Wuchang. General T'ang Sheng-chih and the members of the Hupeh committee of the Kuomintang and of the local administration came to the pier in Wuchang to greet the government. Those present shouted "Long live the alliance with the USSR," "Long live Borodin," "Down with British imperialism," "Long live the national revolution," and even "Long live the dictatorship of the proletariat," evidently barely understanding what that was since such a goal, of course, was not on the agenda for the present stage of the Chinese revolution. The air shuddered from the deafening roar of firecrackers and drums. The city had a holiday air. The walls of the houses were inscribed with slogans and covered with posters. A Chinese shaking the hand of a Russian was depicted on one of them.

In the evening a meeting was held at which the government was presented to the people. The square was divided into four sections — for workers,

---

2. The Chinese authorities in Wanhsien were holding the two English commercial vessels which had sunk three Chinese junks resulting in the drowning of fifty-four Chinese. On September 5, 1926, in response to this British war vessels laid down an artillery bombardment on the town. A thousand persons were killed and twelve streets were turned into ruins.

soldiers, students, and merchants — each section had its own platform. More than three hundred thousand persons came to the meeting. Members of the government and of the Kuomintang CEC, including Soong Ching-ling who had joined them along the way, spoke.

Beginning on January 1, 1927, celebrations began again in Wuhan in honor of the arrival of the second contingent of government leaders. This time the center of festivities was in Hankow.

By a decree of January 1, 1927, Wuchang, Hanyang, and Hankow were united as Wuhan — the capital of the National Government of China.

As long ago as 300 B.C., Wuchang (the center of Hupeh province) was the capital of the ancient principality of Ch'u. Surrounded by walls of purely Chinese dimensions, it was a genuine, old Chinese city untouched by Western influence, consisting of one-storey houses without any conveniences; at night it was almost unilluminated. An animated crowd of people among whom archaic palanquins slowly threaded their way, shoved and shouted in its narrow streets paved with broad stone slabs. The city was peopled with merchants, craftsmen, and coolies.

The rather high Snake Mountain divides Wuchang in two and formerly was quite a bar to communications. Only after the 1911 Revolution was a tunnel constructed. The governor-general under the Manchus would not permit this fearing the revenge of the enormous snake which supposedly was concealed in the depths of the mountain.

Soon after the liberation of Wuchang by Kuomintang troops the Central Military-Political Academy in which our advisers worked was opened there. Despite the brief span of its existence, like the Whampoa Academy it played a great role in the fate of the Chinese revolution.

Wuchang was located on the right bank of the Yangtse while Hanyang and Hankow are on the left bank. The cities stretched out towards each other across two kilometers of angry, yellow waves which rushed headlong to the ocean whose name the great Yangtse (Son of ocean) bore. The crossing was difficult and dangerous. Not infrequently the frail craft went to the bottom, having collided with steamships or with each other. No matter how broad the Yangtse was it was too crowded for the countless vessels and boats which furrowed its waters at this place. It happened in windy weather that they were flooded with water. People perished but the municipal authorities wasted little grief. No one could even imagine building a bridge then. Such a grandiose task was beyond the power of backward China. A bridge was constructed only in 1957 according to the plans of Soviet specialists and with their aid.

Hanyang, separated from Hankow by the estuary of the Han River, a tributary of the Yangtse, was considered one of the largest centers of Chinese heavy industry. It was famous for its arsenal and its steel mills constructed at the end of the last century by Krupp engineers. As it had been done in China from time immemorial, the factory sites were chosen by shamans who calculated the influence of *"feng-shui"*— wind and water. As a result they were far from the sources of raw materials and fuel.

By the twenties the equipment of the mills and arsenals was already very much obsolete. The arsenal was the subject of the ardent longings of the militarists. Mausers, revolvers, rifles, machineguns, and artillery shells were manufactured there. The workers (numbering four hundred thousand) received the most diverse wages — the old masters up to one hundred twenty yuan a month which was rather a lot according to the prices of that time; the unskilled workers received six yuan. With the arrival of the Kuomintang their economic position deteriorated. The National-Revolutionary Army was preparing to continue the Northern Expedition and so the working day was lengthened. Real wages actually dropped due to the high prices which were brought about by the imperialist blockade of Wuhan and the merchants' sabotage. Despite the fact that there were dissatisfied persons among them, the arsenal workers considered themselves the leading, most reliable workers.[3] Half of them were already in unions by the beginning of 1927 and the trade union organizers said that in the near future everyone would be organized.

General Teng Yen-tzu, the former chief of staff of the Fourth Army and the brother-in-law of General Teng Yen-ta, became the new director of the arsenal.

Hankow was the most modern city of the three. It had a large foreign population of which, as in Shanghai, the majority were Russian White emigrés.

---

3. In August 1927 when a fierce White terror began in Wuhan the arsenal workers were branded as Reds and many of them were exterminated. The arsenal was temporarily closed.

From the middle of the last century when the imperialists installed themselves by force in these areas they turned Hankow into an important base for their colonial activity. The British based themselves there first; in general the Yangtse Valley became their sphere of influence. It was not surprising that the British were especially hated there.

The enormous imperialist concessions where their consulates, banks, and commerical-industrial enterprises were located were found in the best parts of the city occupying almost the entire embankment. A boulevard on which an iron chain about the thickness of a hand was stretched out ran the length of it while here and there ancient artillery pieces served as decorations. Our comrades who arrived in Hankow in September 1926 still found the shameful legend on the benches of the embankment "Only for foreigners."

Wuhan is the city where the 1911 Revolution was first victorious. This revolution overthrew the Manchu dynasty and proclaimed the republic whose president was Sun Yat-Sen.

The troops of the National-Revolutionary Army occupied Hanyang and Hankow on September 6-7, 1926. The people greeted them ecstatically; this was acknowledged even by their enemies. The British paper *Hankow Herald* reported "The troops of the Southerners who have campaigned on foot from Kwangtung to the Yangtse in uninterrupted battles had a tired appearance, however, smiles played on the sun-scorched faces of the warriors. And the people smiled with them. A continuous ribbon of troops crept along the streets of the city and thousands of workers, employees, coolies and merchants moved along with them. For the first time we heard cries of welcome and applause in honor of troops occupying a city. An enormous number of workers gathered at the train station, they conversed with the soldiers and the Whampoa cadets. The Southerners paid in cash in the shops while the retreating troops of Wu P'ei-fui had plundered the city a few days before. There were no triumphal arches, no special welcoming committees, but the people themselves greeted the victors with mighty shouts."

Under Wu P'ei-fu the Kuomintang, the trade unions and other mass organizations, to say nothing of the CCP, had been banned. Now they came out from underground and began to grow rapidly. The entire apparatus of the provincial administration in Hupeh was reorganized, the former rural militia bound to the landlords and *shen shih* was disbanded, the peasant

masses took part in the organization of the new militia. A new subject —
Sun Yat-senism — entered the curriculum of the schools.

Having become the center of the revolution, Wuhan began to live a full,
impetuous life. Here and there meetings and demonstrations arose sponta-
neously. The people responded warmly to the political measures of the
government, for example, to the campaign for mobilizing volunteers into
the National-Revolutionary Army and the celebration of the fifteenth
anniversary of the Hsin Hai Revolution of 1911. They also responded with
understanding to the campaign of explanation of the new taxes levied in
order to continue the Northern Expedition, the more so since the taxation
primarily affected the well-to-do.

With the transfer of the government a new, extremely tense and dramatic
phase of the revolution began in Wuhan. Even now, many years later, it is
impossible to remember the Wuhan of 1927, its struggle and defeat, without
pain and bitterness.

The entire second contingent of leading members of the Kuomintang
CEC and members of the government was detained at Nanchang upon the
initiative of Chiang Kai-shek who was not pleased by the decision to transfer
the capital to Wuhan.

This was still not known in Wuhan. The city prepared for a triumphal
welcome. Businesses were closed, beginning on January 1 meetings and
demonstrations were held in all three cities. The streets were festively
decorated; two characters dominated the city: *"huan-ying"* — "welcome."
They were everywhere, including the display windows of the shops.

We arrived in Hankow only towards evening. Darkness, cold, the damp
exhalations of the enormous, agitated river — these were our first impressions
when we landed on the deserted embankment. Although warmly dressed, we
still began to shiver immediately. Foreigners called Hankow "the Gates of
Hell" because of its hot, suffocating summers, but it was still desirable to
have a winter coat there.

Borodin was waiting for us in the house where the members of the
government who had arrived first were settled. The house was located on
Hsin Ma Lu, the main street of the Chinese part of the city and belonged to
the well-known tobacco company Nanyang Kung Ssu. Large, four-storied,
in European style, equipped with every convenience including even an

elevator and hot water, it was obviously superior to all the other houses of this district. At the entrance stood a sentry who greeted us with the same familiar cry *"Chi-ik chok."*

There were neither trolleys nor buses in Hankow. An attempt to introduce bus transport into the city provoked such a violent reaction from the rickshaw men that the idea was dropped. Automobiles almost never appeared in the Chinese part of town. So much the more noticeable then were the official cars, including that of Borodin which belonged formerly, it was said, to Wu P'ei-fu himself.

The curious constantly crowded in front of the Nanyang building. It was made available by the company free of charge for an indeterminate period. Borodin occupied several rooms on the third floor. Next to him the minister of foreign affairs, Ch'en Yu-jen, was settled with his family. During the Wuhan period of the revolution he, Soong Ching-ling and General Teng Yen-ta represented the extreme left tendency in the Kuomintang and this earned him the furious enmity of the imperialist press which accused him of Bolshevism and personal friendship with Borodin.

Ch'en Yu-jen's children, two sons and two daughters, had been educated in England, had English names and spoke English as their native language. They also didn't look Chinese. Ch'en Yu-jen, who had been born on the island of Trinidad, was married to a Negro woman. He never brought his wife to China and spent almost his entire life apart from her. He knew that the upper circles of Chinese society in which he moved were poisoned with racial prejudices. At that time the younger of the sisters (Iolanta) was about twelve years old. Now Iolanta Ch'en is a well-known Soviet cameraman. The older one, Sylvia, was already a ballerina. Many years later, on the eve of the Second World War, she came on tour to Moscow and the Soviet theatre-goers greeted her warmly.

Other members of the government and their service personnel were located on the lower floors. It was natural that we Soviet workers felt constrained living in such close quarters with such highly placed personages. Therefore on the next day we went off in search of our comrades who were already in Hankow. We wanted them to help us get settled.

On that day we were able to admire to our heart's content the festive streets of the still unknown city, the gay crowds dressed in their simple cotton gowns who overflowed the streets. It seemed that the entire Chinese population of Hankow was out-of-doors. We made our way with difficulty along the edge of the sidewalk. One demonstration after another passed close by. Everyone was discordantly shouting something; we could not always make out just what it was in the general uproar and noise of the exploding firecrackers. Among the demonstrators one could see mummers — imperialists, their agents, the Chinese compradors and militarists. There was a dragon dancing. His terrible head with the wide-open mouth and protruding eyes soared over the crowd, bending right and left. A red sphere representing the sun which he was hunting was carried before him on a pole. The drums rolled in a characteristic dance rhythm. The musicians walked in pairs. The first carried a large drum fastened to his back by a strap, the second, walking behind, drummed away in self-oblivion. A genuine gaiety reigned in the streets. The effect was something like that of a carnival.

The workers' pickets in their blue semi-military uniforms with a red, five-cornered star on their caps stamped with the character *"kung"* (labor) in the center were distinguished by their severity and smart appearance. Upon command, raising their clenched fists they snappily chanted slogans. Their ranks bristled with sticks as tall as a man and a couple of inches thick which they carried in token of their serving as upholders of revolutionary order. These workers' militia appeared right after the liberation of the city following the emergence of the trade unions from underground, as strikes were begun by workers demanding wage boosts and improved working conditions. They evolved from strikers' self-defense forces to detachments for preserving order in the city at large.

I had not been able to outfit myself in European style and was dressed in a Chinese woolen coat and shoes with heavy, felt soles which gave me such good service during the journey. I don't know what I was taken for, perhaps a missionary; of the foreigners only missionaries wore Chinese dress then. In any case one of the demonstrators rather unceremoniously seized me by the sleeves and demanded that I express my opinion as to what was happening. I hastened to say in Chinese "Down with foreign imperialism!" and earned stormy approval.

The carefree appearance of the demonstrators, their laughter and good-hearted jokes misled us. On this very same evening these gay youth with their red banners became involved in fighting with armed soldiers on the border of the English concession, and yet it had seemed to us that they were simply overjoyed at the arrival of the revolutionary government. We returned home without the slightest foreboding of what would occur on the morrow.

The Seizure of the English Concession

Many and various accounts have been written about what took place on January 4. The following version circulated among us.

On the evening of the 3rd, the last day of celebrating the transfer of the government to Wuhan, there was supposed to be a large fireworks display on the Yangtse not far from the English concession. A large crowd of persons gathered to see the show. The meeting began, orators called upon people to struggle against the imperialists and the Chinese militarists. More people kept on arriving. The latecomers pushed against the early arrivals, and willy-nilly many crossed the "forbidden" line of the border. The marine guards began to drive away the transgressors and wounded several persons with their bayonets. No sooner had the cries of the wounded rung out than the already aroused crowd was gripped by rage. Angry shouts and threats were heard, the pressure on the marines was increased and some of them became the targets of rocks. If they had not retreated things would have gone badly for them.

At this time a meeting of the Kuomintang Politburo was in session. Delegates from the meeting rushed into the hall and reported the incident. The Wuhan leaders became alarmed. The session was interrupted and those present immediately drew up a proclamation calling for moderation and caution. Hsü Ch'ien, Politburo member and minister of justice, was instructed to proceed at once to the scene of the commotion and read the proclamation to the demonstrators. The masses peacefully listened to Hsü Ch'ien and the crowds drifted away from the concession, but the agitation did not subside and meetings continued. Then for the first time the orators began to demand that the concession be reclaimed from the English.

Of all the governmental and public organizations in Wuhan only the Hupeh Trade Union Council demonstrated initiative and gave leadership to the movement. On the following day a special leaflet was printed by them formulating demands which they proposed to communicate to the English authorities. The unconditional return of the concession was not yet raised but the abolition of extraterritoriality was, along with demands that the English should no longer have troops in the concession, that the Chinese and not the English police should preserve order there, that the English volunteers should be disbanded, the barricades and barbed wire taken down, that Chinese could hold meetings and demonstrations within the concession and that English warships should leave Hankow, etc.

January 4 was not a holiday, yet even more people were on the streets. The minister of foreign affairs, Ch'en Yu-jen, began discussions with the English administration of the concession. On his demand, the English, in order to calm the masses, sent the marines back to their ships. But this did not help. In the evening the people destroyed the barricades and poured into the streets of the concession. Chinese troops stationed at the boundary did not offer any resistance.

The discipline with which the masses acted was astonishing. There was no pillaging, murder, or arson. The government's call to preserve the life and property of foreigners was at no time disregarded.

The seizure of the concession at first caused confusion in government circles. The leadership had not posed such a task. Foreign ships bristling with guns lay in the roadstead. The danger of intervention was quite real. However, it did not occur. It was the first time the British imperialists in China had made a concession of this order. They knew better than did the Wuhan leadership the strength of the forces which opposed them.

Several days later it was learned that the revolutionary masses of Kiukiang, a port on the Yangtse in Kiangsi province, had followed the example of Hankow and seized the local British concession. It was not until the morning of January 5 that my comrades and I succeeded in getting to the recovered territory. The British sentries had been removed and worker pickets stood at the crossroads. Smiling triumphantly at our appearance, they presented their sticks in imitation of a military salute. The imperialists did not dare to appear on the streets.

An impressively strong feeling of national unity arose in the masses of people in Wuhan. Formerly a foreigner could refuse to pay a Chinese, curse, and even strike him and the latter, knowing that it was best not to get involved with the foreigners, would not even protest. Now everything was changed. The Chinese demanded that the foreigners not forget who were the masters and who the guests in China.

At a much later date when passions had cooled and foreigners began to come out of their homes, I observed the following scene. A foreign car stopped in the middle of a street, its owner stood on the running board, his hands raised helplessly. In broken Chinese he was endlessly repeating "I won't go anywhere, I'm not planning on going away." Confusion and fear were written on his face. And not without reason. A furious, enraged crowd surrounded him; people shouted and clenched their fists. The car had knocked down a rickshaw puller and they were calling the owner to account. Would this have been possible in Hankow just a few months before, when foreign sailors amused themselves by purposely breaking or throwing rickshaws into the river and got away with it all?

The seizure of the concessions was evaluated as it deserved both within China and abroad. Really, what a triumphant beginning for the Kuomintang regime on the Yangtse! It seemed that the true desires of the Chinese people were beginning to be realized. Ch'en Yu-jen was holding discussions with the imperialists and hinting at the abolition of all the unequal treaties in general.

The people of Nanchang were growing excited. For the umpteenth time a decision was adopted to transfer the government to Wuhan. In the middle of September Chiang Kai-shek himself arrived in Hankow. Despite his disagreements with Wuhan a triumphal welcome was arranged for him. On its part the Wuhan bourgeoisie brought Chiang Kai-shek a million yuan as a gift. It became clear to everyone that this was an appeal over the head of the Wuhan group of the Kuomintang, a summons to establish "a firm authority" in Wuhan. There were many reasons for the dissatisfaction of the Wuhan bourgeoisie. After several days Chiang Kai-shek returned to Nanchang. His visit had not resolved the contradictions within the Kuomintang. On the contrary, they became even more exacerbated.

Blyukher arrived in Hankow together with Chiang Kai-shek, his patron from whom he soon parted.

On the first day of his visit Blyukher called on Borodin. Stern and smart-looking, in the ostentatious uniform of the National-Revolutionary Army, he walked into Borodin's office holding his proud, handsome head high as usual. He arrived in a car on the running-board of which as had been the case in Canton were Mauser-bearing troops, their fingers on the triggers. This was considered especially smart among the Chinese generals; such a guard was granted as a mark of honor by the National government. Later Blyukher recalled how when he told Chiang Kai-shek that he was leaving him, the latter came up to him and promising him whatever he wanted, implored him with tears in his eyes to stay. He understood how much Blyukher's military talent had contributed to the victories of the National-Revolutionary Army.

Soon the headquarters of the South China mission was established in Hankow. Of the China specialists E.M. Abramson, and M.I. Kazanin who had returned from assignment in England worked there. Subsequently, Kazanin — the author of many works on the Chinese economy — worked in the Scientific Research Institute on China and the Institute of World Politics and Economy. In 1937 he was arrested and returned to Moscow eighteen years later. In 1962 his book of reminiscences appeared: *Zapiski sekretaria missii* (Notes of a mission secretary) about the Far Eastern Republic's mission to China in 1920-1921.

In the middle of January Borodin's staff was assigned an imposing, grey building on Chinese territory behind the Japanese concession. The enormous rooms boasted forced air heating, were covered in damask wallpaper and furnished with rich, period furniture. The press bureau was to the right of the entrance. I was placed in the reception hall on which the doors of Borodin's office opened. I announced the arrival of visitors, translated Chinese manuscript materials, and sometimes acted as an oral interpreter. It happened on occasion that I was assigned to accompany Soviet delegations visiting Wuhan, and was sent as an interpreter to advisers working in various Kuomintang commissions.

The semi-official English organ of the Wuhan government was the *People's Tribune* which appeared in Peking until 1927 when Chang Tso-lin closed it down. The Chinese official organ of the Kuomintang CEC was the daily *Min kuo jih pao*. An English language weekly of the Kuomintang CEC, *Chinese Correspondence*, was also published but it was closed in the middle of May 1927 for its "overly red cover" as Ku Meng-yü, the head of the Agitprop Section expressed it. His concern of course was not its red cover but the revolutionary content which he could not tolerate.

The Soviet Colony in Hankow

In Hankow we had to settle in the territory of the former Russian and German concessions. Our closest neighbors turned out to be, on the one side, colonialists who seethed with indignation against the "Comintern agents" and on the other White emigrés headed by the former tsarist consul Belchenko. We had to put up with this. It would have been more difficult to guarantee our security in the Chinese part of town.

I made arrangements in Mrs. Rode's pension which was subsequently described by Tarkhanov in one of his talented Chinese novellas. There I encountered our entire finance commission headed by V.M. Shteyn[4], Ye. Yolk, O.S. Tarkhanov, and the typist of the Soviet consulate in Hankow, G.A. Kolchugina whom I had known in Peking and who was soon to become Blyukher's wife. The pension was overcrowded and I was given a tiny nook which was cold and uncomfortable.

Across from us was the so-called "First House of Soviets", peopled by the military advisers and their families. Both houses were very much alike and stretched the length of the block from corner to corner. The squat, two-storey brick buildings were constructed in the shape of detached houses merged together where every little porch led to a separate apartment. None of us, however, occupied an entire apartment.

Soon after when the relations between the Wuhan center and Chiang Kai-shek had become exacerbated to the point where almost all our advisers came to Wuhan a Second House of Soviets was opened on the next street. This was a four-storey Russian-style building with one three-room apartment on each floor. It was crowned with a real student garret with an arched ceiling and a view of the city. In this way a little Soviet town was created. We had no such club as there had been in Canton. Comrades met in each other's apartments. Meetings took place in the consular buildings. The consul was Pliche, the vice-consul was Bakulin, author of the diary *Zapiski ob Ukhan'skom periode Kitaiskoi revoliutsii* (Notes on the Wuhan period of the Chinese revolution; published in Moscow in 1930).

---

4. Victor Moritsovich Shteyn upon his return to the USSR wrote the book *Ocherki finansovogo krizisa v Kitae* (An outline of the financial crisis in China). He lived with his wife and young son in the pension.

The proprietor of the pension, Mrs. Rode, an elderly, resourceful German, had lived in Hankow for several decades. The pension was a profitable business. In April 1927 when the influx of Soviet workers increased, Mrs. Rode opened a branch of the establishment which housed the Comintern delegates to the Fifth Congress of the CCP, our trade union representatives, and the representatives of the Communist Youth International. There for the first time I met P. Mif, head of the Eastern Secretariat of the ECCI who up till then had been rector of Sun Yat-sen University in Moscow. Mrs. Rode soon became so rich that she sent her son Bubbi to study in Switzerland.

Mrs. Rode did not require any documents from her boarders. We were free if we desired to use any names at all. This is what most of the foreigners did. There was no registration for the boarders. The tenants of the house were answerable for everything. Mrs. Rode was terribly afraid that some time she might get in trouble for "having dealings with Bolsheviks." But what could she do? We paid her well.

Going downstairs for supper once, I encountered a distraught Mrs. Rode on the staircase. "Miss Vishnyakova," she whispered, taking me by the hand, "Look, what's going on in the lobby? What has happened? Two armed soldiers are standing in front of your friend Miss Kolchugina's room, and their faces are so cruel that, of course, they'll take her off to prison. Perhaps there has been a coup in the city and Soviet citizens are under arrest? Won't I have to answer for this?"

Glancing through the balustrade of the staircase I saw two Mauser-bearing soldiers standing immobile as carved figures in front of Kolchugina's door where Blyukher had gone for a visit. The enormous Mausers gleamed dully in their lowered hands. Evidently, Blyukher's personal bodyguard considered themselves bound to protect him under all conditions. When Blyukher heard of this he laughed and immediately sent his "bodyguards" to the car. Learning that the famous General Galen himself was beneath her roof, Mrs. Rode became radiant and her fears quieted down.

My former boss, the adviser Akimov, came to visit me one evening. He was now working as an instructor at the Central Military-Political Academy in Wuchang. It was cold in my cramped, uncomfortable little room with its lone window. The iron stove had long since lost its heat. We called and ordered another two yuan's worth of coal and supper for two. The evening passed in conversation. Akimov related the events which, as best I could, I have retold in the pages devoted to the Northern Expedition.

From that time on Akimov became a constant visitor and would leave at a late hour. Every time I worried thinking of the dangerous crossing of the Yangtse which awaited him. I would imagine the heavy, merciless waves and the frail little vessel crossing in the absolute darkness.

The Soviet colony in Hankow continued to increase. The comrades under Sinani arrived from Canton and found separate housing. Some of them even made arrangements with the Orthodox priests who lived nearby. They were known to us as the two priests—the red-haired one and the grey-haired one. At one time Hankow had been the center for the Russian tea trade. The Russian merchants Perlov, Botkin, and others had large real estate holdings here. They also built the Orthodox church in Hankow. Stalwart, bearded Cossacks in tsarist Cossack uniforms stood guard in the church vestibule.

Towards the end of January Soong Ching-ling paid a visit to the Borodins. I had not had occasion to meet her earlier. At that time she was living in Shanghai and paid flying visits to Canton. She had developed close, friendly relations with the Borodins. Together they had stood watch at the bedside of the dying Sun Yat-sen and recorded his last instructions, his testament and his letter to the government of the USSR.

Soong Ching-ling came to Hankow to support the demand of the left wing of the Kuomintang for the transfer of the government to Wuhan.

Entering the living room where the Borodins were entertaining Soong Ching-ling, I saw a woman of just above average height, very refined and slender. I knew that she was thirty-seven, but I could not believe this, it was impossible even to think of her as twenty-five. Her soft, restrained movements were full of dignity, her smile was charming but not gay. The shadow of sorrow lay upon her beautiful dark face. Soong Ching-ling wore a severe, high-collared black dress of traditional Chinese design which fastened on the right and had short sleeves and slits on the side. Her hair was brushed smoothly back and gathered into a tight knot on the top of her head. Soong Ching-ling spoke English freely and easily; she had been educated in America and often traveled abroad.

In the struggle which unfolded in Wuhan, Soong Ching-ling was always on the side of the leftists. In the middle of June the possibility of a rupture between the Kuomintang and the Communists became a real one, and it was probably at this time that Soong Ching-ling made the decision which she later acted upon to leave for the USSR if this came about. In any case it was then that Borodin suggested that I give Soong Ching-ling Russian lessons which she had suggested. I did not get to carry out this task. Events began to unfold so rapidly that at the end of June many of us, including myself, had to leave Hankow.

The last time I saw Soong Ching-ling was in Moscow in the Hotel Metropol where she lived in a room next to the Borodins. This was in early spring of 1928. Borodin requested that I show Soong Ching-ling around Moscow. I went to her at once but found her in tears. Soong Ching-ling thanked me and asked me to drop in another time. I left in utter confusion and only afterwards realized that I had gone to her on the anniversary of Sun Yat-sen's death—March 12.

New Successes and New Difficulties

The success of the Northern Expedition signified the colossal broadening of the base of the revolution and the appearance of the National Government within a broad political arena, but at the same time it brought new difficulties which had been unknown in Kwangtung.

The struggle within the Kuomintang which had subsided during the Northern Expedition now flared up again with new intensity. Increasingly, the Kuomintang split into a Wuhan group and those who remained in Nanchang under the leadership of Chiang Kai-shek. Relations with the imperialists also were exacerbated, and the economic situation deteriorated sharply.

The foreign policy of Wuhan, despite its brilliant beginning—the seizure of the British concessions in Hankow and Kiukiang—was very strained. All kinds of conflicts had to be dealt with constantly. True, England turned out to be isolated. Observing with malicious pleasure the position into which their rival had fallen, the other imperialist powers did not express a desire to manifest solidarity with England, especially since the seizure of the British concessions had been greeted all over China with such enthusiasm that even Marshal Chang Hsüeh-liang, the son of the old Japanese hireling Chang Tso-lin, declared publicly "If the British start a war against Wuhan, the North will fight alongside the South."

But the position of the imperialists was still harsher than that of armed neutrality. Wuhan was gripped by fear. Dozens of military vessels lay in the Hankow roadsteads and their numbers kept increasing. British, American, Japanese, and French flags fluttered over the gray silhouettes of the cruisers and gunboats.

When I read now of the outrages committed by American soldiers and sailors abroad, I remember Hankow in the spring of 1927 and the drunken hordes of foreign sailors on the streets. There wasn't any discipline to speak of. Once when an American cruiser sailed, a search of all the worst places in town was needed in order to locate the crew, and the sailing was delayed for days on end. A mood of racial intolerance, a contempt for people of a different skin color was always artificially cultivated among the sailors of the imperialist powers. It is not surprising that they did not view Chinese as human beings. Shoving a Chinese into the water or thrusting a knife into him were common occurrences.

During the negotiations which Ch'en Yu-jen was conducting with the English plenipotentiary, the embassy counselor O'Malley, concerning the administration in the British concessions, the imperialists continued to charge the atmosphere with tension. England sent twenty thousand soldiers to China. The families of British and American employees in the Yangtse basin were evacuated as a sign that the imperialists would not stop shy of beginning a war. American troops were landed in China and the Philippines. The USA recruited volunteers to send to China. In Shanghai the Shanghai English Defense Corps headed by General Duncan was established.

All over the world, especially in England, a workers' movement began against intervention in China. Everyone considered that the threat of intervention was quite real. But Ch'en Yu-jen did not submit to the pressure which the British imperialists tried to exert on him. He refused to sign the agreement which had already been drawn up and demanded that England first stop the dispatch of armed forces to China.

On January 20 a foreign policy declaration of the Wuhan government was published. It said that China had gotten stronger and become conscious of her strength and the question was no longer what the representatives of England and the other countries found agreeable, but rather what she herself found agreeable. Liberation from the foreign yoke did not necessarily entail armed conflict. Everything could be resolved through negotiations. The government was ready to hold these with any power on the basis of equality.

On February 19, however, Ch'en Yu-jen signed the agreement with O'Malley since England had promised not to send any more troops to China, but in fact the build-up in Shanghai continued. In response to this, mass protest demonstrations commenced and soon paralyzed the business life of Shanghai and other cities. In Hankow we witnessed a dramatization of the funeral of British imperialism. The coffin was festooned with wreaths from the inconsolable Chang Tso-lin, Wu P'ei-fu, Sun Ch'uan-fang, and Kuomintang rightists, while "they themselves" followed behind in paper coats and plumed hats, howling and "shedding tears."

The situation in Wuhan was complicated by serious economic difficulties. As early as November 1926 the Wuhan Chamber of Commerce adopted a resolution in which it protested against the "exorbitant workers' demands." But what the workers received was insufficient to sustain life. Moreover, the war along the Yangtse disrupted normal economic ties and caused inflation and unemployment. The National government was forced to raise taxes. Workers began to petition and go out on strike.

In a search for revenue the government ordered the confiscation of the homes and landed property of counter-revolutionaries who had fled. But it turned out to be impossible to implement the confiscation; no one would buy the land, they were afraid that the new government would prove of short duration. The economic blockade to which the foreign imperialists and the native bourgeoisie were subjecting Wuhan proved an especially difficult trial. In this respect Wuhan was very vulnerable. Its economic life was inseparably linked to that of Shanghai, the lower reaches of the Yangtse—the main commercial artery of the region. Without links to Shanghai Wuhan began to suffocate. Here is an example. More than ten thousand rickshaw men in Hankow were thrown out of work because of the absence of rubber tires on the market.

There began a colossal outflow of silver—the main currency of China at the time. The large bourgeoisie ran away and the petty bourgeoisie was ruined. There was a fall in the rate of exchange of the bank notes issued by the government's Central Bank. In Hankow's foreign stores the polished salesmen, dressed and combed like mannequins, calculated with haughty insolence the value of the Wuhan money according to the Shanghai rate of exchange and discounted it by ten per cent or even a higher percentage.

The soldiers of the National-Revolutionary Army were in a difficult situation. For a long time they received no salary and were not issued winter uniforms. The hospitals were overcrowded. It happened that sick soldiers would die right on the streets of Wuhan. I saw this with my own eyes.

It was the end of February. The sun was hot and buds swelled on the trees. The people walked the streets cheerful and happy. I also was in an excellent mood as I set off on some errand. It was far off and I had to take a rickshaw. Then as I rushed in a stream of rickshaws along Hsin Ma Lu, I suddenly saw a figure in a soldier's tunic stretched out on the sidewalk near a wall. The street was alive with its own activity. Rickshaws were rushing by, pedestrians were walking and no one was looking in that direction. I stopped my rickshaw and jumped down next to the prostrate man. He was a very young soldier, almost a boy—they took men scarcely older than children into the army then. He lay unconscious, his dull pupils stared out from under his half-open lids, his face twitched weakly. Next to him was a big pool of vomit.

Calling a policeman who was standing at his post right nearby, I asked him how he could allow a man to die on his beat without extending the slightest help. The policeman was surprised and said it was none of his business. When he had come on duty the soldier had already been lying there. Moreover, it was no longer cold.

Passers-by crowded around. Someone who had carefully looked at the soldier suddenly said *"ho luan"* (cholera). Suddenly the crowd shuddered and took to its heels. This word was a terrible one at the time. During the siege there had been a cholera epidemic in Wuhan which carried off thousands of victims. It stopped during the winter but it might flare up again in the spring.

Everyone looked at me inquisitively as if awaiting my decision. The main hospital of the Military Council of the National-Revolutionary Army was located in Wuchang. It was impossible to transport the sick man there in such a condition, moreover, as sometimes happened, they might not take him because of the shortage of space. I knew only one hospital in Hankow—the German missionary hospital where our comrades were sometimes treated. In the final analysis they admitted everyone there who paid. I went with the policeman to call them up to send over an ambulance. The policeman shouted *"wai, wai"* (which corresponds to our "hello") into the receiver for a long time, but he could not get through. The connection was very poor. Just then the rickshaw man ran up and said it was no longer necessary, the soldier had died.

Almost in tears I continued on my way.

Soong Ching-ling led the fight for the lives of the sick and the wounded soldiers. The Red Cross of the Northern Expedition which she created played an enormous role.

I attended one of the first charity benefits given by Soong Ching-ling. All of Wuhan's leading figures came as did our comrades including Blyukher. The gathering was held at a local theater on the territory of the former Russian concession. Family members of Wuhan's leading political figures took part in the first part of the presentation. I remember the performance of Sylvia and Iolanta Ch'en who sang some sort of English song and moved rhythmically in a simple dance. Professional artists performed during the second half.

The employees of the Red Cross of the Northern Expedition made a special contribution during the military activities in Honan. More than eight thousand wounded were gathered there in Wuhan in the middle of May and hospital trains kept bringing in new casualties. Soong Ching-ling worked indefatigably in those days. She succeeded in getting doctors from the missionary hospitals to take care of the wounded, and in organizing a campaign for contributions to a fund for helping wounded soldiers.

Guests from the Soviet Union

Meanwhile life in Wuhan took its normal course. Journalists, political figures, and international delegations arrived at the new revolutionary capital of China. At the end of February a representative of the Profintern, M. Kuznetsova (the wife of G. N. Voytinsky) arrived. I was assigned to her as an interpreter, and I accompanied her on tours of the textile factories in Hankow.

At that time Kuznetsova had already contracted the tuberculosis which carried her to the grave in the beginning of the thirties. It was not easy for her several times a day to enter the close, stuffy establishments where the cotton dust was never aired out. Yet she joyfully went to meet the Chinese textile workers. She was surrounded by women workers who had come straight from their machines without even having been able to shake off the cotton dust.

They stood in dusty jackets and trousers, many of them with nursing babies in their arms. The married women wore the small, black traditional hats with open crowns, the girls, all wearing long braids, had uncovered heads. Kuznetsova told them about the Soviet textile workers, the life of Soviet women, and much else. When she finished she said joyfully, "Well, I've said everything that I wanted to."

Some kind soul always tried to decorate in the Chinese fashion with paper flowers and lanterns the premises where she appeared. There were many people; the workers sacrificed their brief hours of rest to hear the woman from Moscow. They crowded about and stared at Kuznetsova. Everything about her interested them—her light-reddish hair, her high color, her manner of talking, her trusting, sweet smile. They all talked quietly about this among themselves, especially the young workers, the girls of seven or eight years old. When we were leaving the workers hurriedly hobbled after us, talking and talking . . .

In Chinese fashion Kuznetsova presented several banners and long silken cloths with revolutionary slogans to the workers. I went with her to order these gifts which were presented in the name of the Profintern.

Several days later I was assigned as an interpreter to a troop of barefooted dancers from the Isadora Duncan Studio who had come to Hankow. The famous dancer herself lived at that time outside of the USSR, but the school which her adopted daughter Irma directed was located in Moscow in one of the most beautiful houses on Kropotkin Street. By now the dances of the barefooted dancers are long forgotten in our country, but at one time they were very popular. In the circle dances which the girls conducted on the stage (barefoot and dressed in Grecian tunics), anyone who wanted to could participate. The directors of the studio did not concern themselves with preparing specialists. Isadora said that she wanted to teach people how to dance as they had in ancient Hellas, and to restore the native festivals in which the entire body of youth took part.

In Wuhan the performances of the barefooted dancers were received enthusiastically, although the moment of their arrival was not a fortunate one, as it seemed. In the middle of February when posters about the forthcoming tour appeared in the city, the troops of the Szechwanese General Yang Sen suddenly appeared in the western part of Hupeh. Yang Sen formally was an ally of Wuhan but, in fact, he was only waiting for a favorable moment to attack. This time, to be sure, the incident was liquidated at once. The troops of the National-Revolutionary Army blocked his path, and excusing himself for "the misunderstanding" he went back to Szechwan. Still the situation remained uneasy.

In Wuhan the studio gave not only paid but also several free performances for the poor. Undoubtedly, the interest shown in the barefoot dancers derived primarily from the fact that they were from the USSR. However, the performances themselves produced a strong effect on the Chinese viewers for various reasons. The dances performed by laughing young girls in bright, airy costumes expressed the joy of emancipated woman without any need for words. The Chinese saw in it a call to struggle against the barbaric habit of foot-binding.

This custom of old China was a horrible one, much worse than the purdah in the Middle East. No matter how terrible purdah is, shutting up a young being within a hairy, black prison, still one need merely throw it off and the woman is free. But bound feet remained crippled for all one's life.

"Golden lotus"—this was the poetic term for the woman's tiny feet in China. The object was to make them both in size and shape like the sharp-pointed bud of a lotus. From the age of five or six girls' feet were tightly bound with narrow, flat strips of cloth which bent the still unformed toes beneath the foot. Only the large toe remained above in order to form the sharp toe cap. It was necessary to rebind the foot two or three times daily otherwise the foot would lose the shape it was being given. The muscles atrophied, the ligaments between the toes and the foot formed a stinking crack, the calves began to dangle like an empty sack. The woman walked on her heels as if on stilts, and it was enough to give her a slight push and she would fall over. In the backward countries the burden of vestiges and superstitions weighs upon the oppressed classes the longest. So it was in China. The privileged and intellectual classes had long since abandoned this barbaric custom, but the workers and peasants, especially the women themselves, still clung to it. The mothers disfigured their daughters fearing that otherwise they would not be able to get married. Future mothers-in-law tried to find brides with bound feet since this was a faithful sign that she would live according to the old customs and would respect her elders. Marriageable girls spent many evenings preparing the tiny, colored satin slippers which they embroidered with many-colored silk.

Observing the street crowd in Hankow I was struck with how many women there were with bound feet. This cruel custom was especially wide-spread in the Yangtse Valley. I often had occasion to walk past a certain spinning mill where women and eight and nine-year-old girls worked. When a shift ended and the dense crowd of workers flocked out, every single one of them hobbled along on small, bent feet. It was especially painful to see the tiny girls who walked with an air of importance beside the adults, deprived as they were of the possibility of running and gamboling.

The women's organization in Wuhan developed a struggle under the slogan "Physical freedom must be guaranteed before anything else!" It was proposed that along with explanatory activity coercive measures be employed in the form of fines for women who did not unbind their feet by a certain date.

I especially remember one of the performances of the barefoot dancers in which Irma Duncan stood amid the dancing pupils with an enormous Kuomintang banner in her arms and tried through mime to underline the pathos of this scene. I remember her wide-open silently shouting mouth. The audience was beside itself with enthusiasm.

The Seizure of the Ship Pamyat Lenina

In the middle of February F. S. Borodina left for Shanghai. She took her youngest son who had to set out for the USSR. She spent about ten days in Shanghai and decided to return on the ship *Pamyat Lenina* which was sailing for Hankow with a cargo of tea.

Unexpectedly a completely improbable report was received in Hankow. On February 28 the *Pamyat Lenina* was detained in the vicinity of Pukow by White Guard detachments of the Shantung governor-general Chang Tsung-ch'ang (the lower reaches of the Yangtse were then still in the hands of the Northern militarists), the passengers and crew were under arrest and, with the exception of Borodina, had been placed in irons.[5]

There were three diplomatic couriers on board the ship who were carrying mail to the Soviet consulate in Hankow. In violation of the norms of international law the mails were opened and examined three times. Nothing of a

---

5. The ship was not returned to the Soviet Union. A month later when the Shantung forces were compelled to retreat from the north, the White Guardists sank it not far from Pukow.

criminal nature was uncovered. Later on the White Guardists invented some sort of falsehoods. When Borodina was arrested letters of Soviet representatives in China to Borodin and the consul were taken from her.

The arrested were removed to Tsinan, the main city of Shantung province. From there Borodina and the diplomatic couriers were sent to Peking to be judged, while the crew and the captain (forty-seven men in all) remained in the Tsinan prison where it was proposed to deal with them locally.

The situation was very serious for the arrested ones. The Chinese militarists paid little regard to the norms of justice and leveled the most fantastic accusations which were without any foundation at all. Borodina was charged under a statute which carried a death penalty or life imprisonment. It was intended to hand the sailors over to a military tribunal and two of them were also threatened with death.

Chang Tsung-ch'ang and Chang Tso-lin celebrated their victory in advance in the certain belief that they could now exert pressure on the Wuhan government since the wife of Borodin, to whose influence they ascribed the entire direction of Wuhan's policy, was in their hands. Borodin was sent an appropriate telegram although Fanya Semyonovna refused to intercede for herself before her husband.

Not knowing how the matter would turn out the militarists first threw her into prison and then arranged fancy banquets for her. The White Guardists disseminated the rumor that Chang Tso-lin had promised to display Borodina's head at the marketplace. In any case they strove mightily towards this end.

Borodina and the diplomatic couriers were freed by decision of the Peking court in the second half of July by the inspector Ho Ch'ung, but after several hours they had to go into hiding since Chang Tso-lin, learning of the decision, became enraged and ordered them to be judged anew. The chairman of the Supreme Judicial Chamber in Peking was removed from his post. Ho Ch'ung was threatened with death. Terrified, he fled to the foreign concession in Tientsin. His house was sealed up and his wife and two daughters and brother were sent to Tsinan to face Chang Tsung-ch'ang. After her return to the USSR Borodina described these events in detail in her pamphlet *V zastenkakh kitaiskikh satrapov* (In the torture chambers of the Chinese satraps).

The ship's crew was in a much worse position. For more than a year the sailors remained in the dirty, stinking prison without any charges or investigation. They slept on the bare brick floor and walked barefoot and half-naked. Some of them, including the captain, were kept in special isolators. Several times they declared hunger strikes.

Here is the content of one of the declarations which they addressed to the Tsinan judicial chamber in September 1927. "We are forty-seven sailors from the ship *Pamyat Lenina* arrested by the military authorities without any charges. We are being held under conditions such that many of us have fallen seriously ill. This place is not fit for living. Only after a five-day hunger strike were we even informed that our arrest was connected with the matter of Borodina. But according to press reports Borodina has long since been set free and we are still sitting here. Again we are declaring a hunger strike."

In the middle of December 1927 a shattering letter arrived at the offices of the Soviet commercial fleet in Vladivostok. In it the sailors wrote, "We are suffering from typhoid fever, malaria, and tuberculosis. We are exhausted and can endure no longer. Further tortures in this torture house shall prove fatal to us."

They were not freed until 1928.

The March Plenum of the Kuomintang

Let us return to the events in Wuhan. After a comparatively calm February the stormy March of 1927 arrived. On March 10 a group of cadets from the training regiment and the Central Military-Political Academy burst into the Wuhan headquarters of the Hupeh Trade Union Council whose leadership contained a great many Communists and dispersed a meeting of agitators with the cries "Down with all traitors who oppose the leader of the national revolution, Chiang Kai-shek!" Akimov and other advisers who worked in the academy said that there was even gunfire and casualties. The incident took place on the very day of the convening of the well-known March plenum of the Kuomintang CEC which was directed against Chiang Kai-shek's attempts to seize political power.

The academy which contained many Communists and Komsomols and where the influence of the Communist party was generally strong, had the reputation of being "Red," which gained it the hatred of the right wing of the Wuhan leadership. In April 1927 when the head of the Political Administration of the National-Revolutionary Army, General Teng Yen-ta, who was concurrently head of the academy, went with his troops to the Honan front, the members of the government who remained in Wuhan swiftly cut the academy's budget and even tried to break up the training regiment. But in May 1927 occurred the uprising of the reactionary general Hsia Tou-yin and the revolution was saved by the selfless fighting cadets headed by the well-known CCP activist Comrade Yün Tai-ying and the division of the Communist Yeh T'ing.

After the Nanchang Uprising of August 1, 1927, when an unrestrained White Terror commenced all over China the academy was disbanded and its training regiment shifted to Canton. But even there it did not give up the fight. During the Canton Commune in December 1927, it became the nucleus of the uprising and went down in history as the "Communist regiment."

Still, Chiang Kai-shek had his adherents in the academy who from time to time made themselves known by various provocative acts. Their activity was especially accelerated on the eve of the March plenum when the struggle of Wuhan against Chiang Kai-shek became exacerbated although it had not yet passed over into open conflict.

To be sure, in the beginning of February 1927 there were reports that Nanchang was amenable to the transfer of the government to Wuhan and, in fact, some of the leading Kuomintang figures began to gather there. However, the optimists' prognosis that "the conflict would end in a leftist victory" was not confirmed by events.

In the middle of February a campaign was already being waged in Wuhan, although not yet in the press, against Chiang Kai-shek's personal dictatorship. On Feburary 21, the Wuhanites whose patience had been exhausted by all the delays and excuses of the rightists, officially declared that the Kuomintang CEC and the National Government were beginning to function in Wuhan.

But meanwhile the chairman of the government, General T'an Yen-k'ai, had by no means resolved to break with Chiang Kai-shek and remained in Nanchang right up until the plenum.

The March plenum was one of the most important landmarks in the development of the inner-party struggle within the Kuomintang. The Kuomintang leftists prevailed at it. Chiang Kai-shek was demonstratively absent on the pretext of important affairs at the front. Subsequently the imperialist press criticized the rightists for boycotting the plenum and thereby allowing the leftists and Communists "to take over the Kuomintang apparatus on a Bolshevist footing." The decisions of the plenum were really very radical and aimed at preventing any sort of personal dictatorship. The principle of collective leadership in the work of the Kuomintang and the government prevailed; instead of chairmen everywhere there appeared presidia, councils, and committees.

The post of chairman of the CEC was liquidated and a nine-member presidium of the CEC was substituted for it. The list of members was headed by the name of Wang Ching-wei although he was still living abroad. Then came the names of T'an Yen-k'ai, Chiang Kai-shek, etc. In the same manner the post of chairman of the Military Council was liquidated and was also replaced by a presidium. Wang Ching-wei was assigned the first place there too.

A resolution was published affirming the stability of the alliance between the Communist party and the Kuomintang. For the first time the Communists entered the government. The plenum designated Su Chao-cheng as minister of labor and T'an P'ing-shan as minister of agriculture.

In the call for action which was adopted it was emphasized that the Kuomintang as before would support the revolutionary movement of the workers, peasants, and the democratic masses of the urban population in their struggle for the improvement of economic conditions, and would fight against those who sought to rein in the mass movement under the false pretext that it was supposedly interfering with the revolution.

On learning of the plenum's resolutions Chiang Kai-shek quickly resigned from all his posts although there was no longer any need for this. "I was on the front line all the time," he declared in his telegram, trying to ascribe nonexistent military virtues to himself "and did not have the opportunity to fulfill the duties of chairman of the Kuomintang CEC or of the Military Council. Now a reorganization is taking place and other people have come forward to do the work. I ask you to accept my resignation." In a series of declarations Chiang Kai-shek acknowledged the decisions of the plenum, but in reality he did not submit to them. Some of the political and military leaders in Wuhan began a flight to Nanchang.

Wang Ching-wei turned up in China in the beginning of April and declared that he approved of the decisions of the plenum. From Shanghai he sent a telegram to Wuhan in which, in the spirit of old Chinese etiquette, he said that obedient to orders he had returned and was respectfully awaiting further instructions. Almost simultaneously there arrived a circular telegram from Chiang Kai-shek saying, "Wang Ching-wei is my teacher and friend, his return is a piece of good fortune, he is the most faithful member of the Kuomintang. I have had a long and cordial conversation with him regarding the future direction of our policies. I will only lead the army. All political and economic questions should be decided by the Kuomintang CEC under the leadership of Wang Ching-wei." But Chiang was already getting ready for the seizure of power.

The imperialists conducted an extensive campaign against the decisions of the March plenum. Both of the foreign newspapers which appeared then in Hankow—*Hankow Herald* and the British *China Central Post*—called for "a return to Chiang Kai-shek" and indulged themselves in various attacks against the National Government. The imperialist press in China shamelessly interfered in its internal politics, but this time the provocateurs got what was coming to them. By decision of the pressmen's union the typesetters went out on strike and both newspapers did not appear for a long time. It is difficult to convey the fury of their publishers. On the way to work I had to pass by the editorial offices of the *Hankow Herald*. On the first day of the strike I saw a large sheet of white paper in its window on which it said in large letters, "Why isn't the paper coming out? Don't ask us, we don't know. Ask Borodin, he knows."

The *People's Tribune* administered a well-deserved rebuke to the presumptuous journalists from the *Hankow Herald* and the *Central China Post*. "In the course of many years these papers have attacked and defamed China, although they come out on Chinese soil. They know perfectly well that if they printed such attacks as foreigners in any of the western countries that they would be asked without any hesitation to remove themselves from the country which had mistakenly given them a friendly reception. Not for long will foreigners in China transgress propriety. The foreigners' rule in Hankow has ended. The same fate awaits them elsewhere in China."

The International Workers' Delegation

Revolutionary organizations abroad warmly supported the struggles of the Chinese people. On March 31, an International Workers' Delegation headed by Tom Mann, one of the most popular workers' leaders of the time, arrived in Wuhan. He was a handsome, sturdy old man, small in stature, with an amusing tuft of hair on his gray head, long mustaches, and an eagle eye. So straight and self-assured was his bearing, so enthusiastic and bold his speech, that no one would have guessed that he was already seventy-one. By trade a metallurgy worker, Tom Mann had entered upon the path of revolutionary struggle at an early age. He was a member of the Communist party of England from the moment of its founding. Engels called him one of the finest representatives of the English proletariat. Tom Mann came to China as a representative of the National Minorities Movement whose honorary chairman he was. This was an oppositionist movement of English workers directed against the traitorous policies of the trade-union leaders.

The purpose of the delegation was to establish a link with the Chinese revolutionaries and to hinder imperialist intervention. The delegation began its trip through China in Canton where it was met with great honors. It visited the Whampoa Academy and the strike committee, witnessed a parade of picketers, and was present at the training sessions of the city's Workers' Defense Corps and the Pioneers' military training. In honor of its arrival a meeting was held at which ten thousand persons took part.

Tom Mann, speaking at meetings in Canton, called for a struggle against British imperialism. The delegates laid wreaths on the grave of Liao Chung-k'ai and the main monument in the cemetery of the seventy-two heroes.

The delegation traveled to Hankow via Kiangsi. Chiang Kai-shek evidently did not want to meet with them so he wasn't there when they arrived in Nanchang. As the interpreter assigned to the delegation I was present at all the celebrations organized on the occasion of their stay in Wuhan. After a large meeting a banquet was arranged at which the delegates shared their travel impressions. They said that in Kiangsi, especially in the cities of Nanchang and Kiukiang, they had encountered open reaction. In Kanchow they came across memorial meetings of workers on the occasion of the murder of the chairman of the provincial trade union council, the Communist Ch'en Tsan-hsien, by Chiang Kai-shek's stooges. Tom Mann's speech was well-received. A stormy ovation burst forth when he said that he had already been struggling in the revolutionary cause for half a century.

In a report to the Executive Committee of the Profintern the delegation noted that the workers' movement in China had achieved many victories although the trade unions there were still very young. In Kwangtung they had existed for three or four years, while in the other provinces which the delegation visited—Kiangsi, Hupeh and Hunan—they were just six months old. Twenty per cent of their members were industrial workers, the remaining eighty per cent were handicraft workers and coolies. Since the development of the trade union movement the position of workers had significantly improved; the working day had been shortened, corporal punishment had been abolished, and for the first time in China a weekly day of rest had been instituted. Everywhere the leadership of the trade unions, as well as of the peasant unions, was in the hands of Communists.

An Incident in the Japanese Concession

April 1927 was a month of important political events in Wuhan. On April 3, while returning from work, my rickshaw man and I were stopped by a crowd which had gathered on the embankment. The exclamations of indignation and cursing resounded far off, clenched fists and enraged faces flashed by.

Suddenly the low, terrible whine of a siren pierced the air. It swelled up hoarse and threatening. I did not immediately understand what this meant but a terrible foreboding seized me.

Suddenly a Chinese voice shouted "Japanese soldiers!" In fact a landing had begun. In an instant the crowd began to run. The rickshaw man pulled me away at top speed.

Later I learned what had happened on the embankment. A drunken Japanese sailor, returning to his gunboat, refused to pay his rickshaw man the agreed upon fare. When the latter clutched at him, demanding payment, the Japanese drew his broadsword and in an instant ripped open his stomach. Passersby rushed the Japanese, but other sailors fought them off. The murderer and his confederates quickly jumped into a dinghy and made their getaway.

Everything seemed simple—the murderer should be tried. But the commander of the gunboat decided that the Japanese fleet had been insulted. Samurai honor propelled the gunboat captain to an act of aggression. The siren began to whine, a detachment of Japanese marines landed and began to build a barbed wire and sandbag barricade right on the spot. Several salvoes were fired at the crowd. Six persons were wounded and two killed.

The imperialists acted now with greater impudence. They knew about the difficulties of the Wuhan government and they understood that it was now disadvantageous for it to exacerbate its relations with the imperialists. Martial law was declared in all the concessions; marines and defensive works appeared at all the boundaries. In the foreign colony all the men were called up and with the comic importance of civilians incompetently performing military functions, they stood about leaning on their rifles, and demonstrating their martial intentions. The Russian White emigrés willingly participated in the provocation.

The Sixth of April

In the evening of April 6 the Soviet colony of Hankow was informed of preparations for a raid against it. An arrival from the headquarters of Akimov's group said that everything was in turmoil there, that they were moving further away from the Japanese concession where machine guns were being openly put into position around our quarters. There was confusion in the consulate as well. White Guards recruited as provocateurs came into the city to attack Soviet personnel. They were shown a map of Hankow in which all the places occupied by Soviets were marked with crosses. It was suggested to some of the advisers that they not spend the night at home; in the House of the Soviets an all-night watch was maintained. Several days passed like this, but the attack did not take place. Only on some of the streets of the former Russian concession groups of White Guards walked about at nightfall shouting threats at us.

This was a difficult time for Soviet citizens in China. On the imperialists' orders anti-Soviet provocations were organized in a number of Chinese cities. The raid conducted by Chang Tso-lin's troops on the Soviet Embassy in Peking had especially serious consequences. At 10:30 on the morning of April 6 five hundred soldiers, policemen, and detectives surrounded and occupied a section of the embassy grounds which was separated from the main grounds by an interior alley. All entrances and exits were closed off. The large court with its ten houses where the officials lived, the military compound, and the grounds of the CER administration where the buildings of the Far Eastern

Bank and the trade representative were also located were inundated with soldiers. Searches and pillaging which evolved into a real pogrom began. The bandits smashed the club, carried away the library, gathered up the bank's accounts, conducted a search on the premises of the commercial representative, and sacked the TASS office. The military attaché's office as well as various other private apartments were searched and sacked. A fire was set in one of the houses. Trucks carted away the furniture, rugs, and other valuable property. The police carried away enormous packages. All night one could hear the noise from the breaking of locks and the roar of trucks.

Most of the employees were at work in the main building, on the other side of the interior alley and therefore escaped the raid, but everyone who was in the occupied territory was arrested. The women and the children were freed about seven in the evening, the others were taken off to jail. The women had their money and valuables taken away, they were insulted and threatened with revolvers. Twenty of the sixty Chinese seized on the embassy grounds were Communists. Among them were Li Ta-chao and his two daughters. Alexandra Ilinichna Kantorovich, an eyewitness of the raid, saw Chang Tso-lin's troops leading away Li Ta-chao and the other Communists. Here is her story as I heard it in Moscow. "My husband had gone to work and I was at home with the child. Our Chinese servant ran in and shouted 'Missus, Chang Tso-lin is here!' I rushed outside. I saw them leading away Li Ta-chao and five other Chinese comrades. They had been bound and severely beaten, especially Li Ta-chao whom it was difficult to recognize. I knew him well, we used to meet in the embassy gardens where I would stroll with my infant son whom he always petted. Li Ta-chao loved children very much."

Along with the Chinese comrades fifteen Soviet citizens were arrested, among whom were the interpreter Gamberg (Maysky), Tonkikh and Ilyashenko, employees of the office of the military attaché, Skatkin, professor of Russian at Peking University, the watchman Grigorev, Vice-consul Morozov and others. All of the arrested, both Chinese and Russian, were beaten with rifle butts on the street in front of the foreign embassy employees who did not even think of interfering but who, on the contrary, expressed their satisfaction aloud. Morozov, who was ill with tuberculosis, was dragged by a rope along the ground to the police wagon. He was treated with particular cruelty simply because Li Ta-chao's daughters whom he had tried to conceal had been found in his room.

An exchange of diplomatic notes between the government of the USSR and the Peking government of Chang Tso-lin yielded no results and in Moscow the decision was taken to recall the entire embassy staff. Only the consulate and persons charged with protecting embassy property were left in Peking.

The most painful consequence of the raid was the death of twenty Chinese comrades headed by Li Ta-chao. Soon after the events of April 6, the Chinese wire service Kuowen reported, "The Head of the Justice Department declared that on interrogation Li Ta-chao manfully confessed that he is a Communist. His personality made a great impression even upon the Mukdenites. He is the greatest Chinese scholar."

Li Ta-chao, an exceptionally brilliant, talented man and a leading party organizer and political activist, was known widely all over China. He was called the first Communist in the Kuomintang where he had been accepted on the personal recommendation of Sun Yat-sen who had known him closely since 1919. He was chosen as a member of the CEC at the First Congress of the Kuomintang. Li Ta-chao participated in the 1911 Revolution and was one of the ideological leaders of the May 4, 1919 anti-imperialist movement. In 1920 in Peking he created a Marxist-Leninist circle, one of the first Communist groups in China. He attended the Fifth Congress of the Communist International.

Disregarding the fierce repression which threatened everyone who stood up for the Communists, the rectors of Peking and National Universities in Peking where Li Ta-chao worked appeared before Chang Tso-lin and requested that he free Li Ta-chao's two daughters and hand over his case to the civil courts, pleading that he was a leading scholar whom the Chinese people could be proud of. However, Chang Tso-lin did not take public opinion into consideration. Li Ta-chao and his nineteen comrades were handed over to a special military tribunal. At their trial they conducted themselves firmly and with dignity; they all admitted to being Communists. All of them were cruelly tortured.

On April 29, 1927, the terrible news spread around the world that Li Ta-chao and the Communists arrested with him had been slowly strangled. This agonizing, medieval punishment which had not been resorted to in China for a long time was chosen "in order to strike terror into the hearts of the Communists" as an English report phrased it. The trial lasted for two hours, and right after it before the eyes of the condemned preparations began for the execution. On May 1 police came to the embassy compound and confiscated the property of the executed men. In China and all over the world the May 1 celebrations were clouded by mourning for the heroes who had died in Peking.

On May 1, a three-hundred-thousand-man demonstration was held in Hankow. At the enormous hippodrome, Li Li-san (from the CCP) spoke, along with Teng Yen-ta, Borodin, Tom Mann, and representatives of the international trade union movement who had come to town for the Pacific Trade Union Conference. With anger and indignation they all spoke about the inhuman executions and summoned people to struggle for the cause for which Li Ta-chao and his comrades gave their precious lives.

On May 1, *Pravda* published an article entitled "Geroi kotorykh udavili" (The strangled heroes). It said "Today we celebrate May 1, but it is not only a day for the joyful enumeration of our victories but also a day for sorrow and for a summons to revenge. There stands before us today the shade of our friend and comrade Li Ta-chao, the scholar, fighter and Communist, as well as the shades of the nineteen other heroes who were strangled along with him. Not the Peking puppets but their masters—the imperialists—did this deed."

By this time it had been decisively established who the chief culprit was in the raid on our embassy and the death of the best sons of the Chinese people. James Fox, the editor of the *North China Star*, which was published in Tientsin, wrote in a special article for the American news service United Press, "I know that it was the American envoy MacMurray himself who played the most active part in instigating the raid on the Russian embassy. He acted together with the English envoy, the main instigator, who stayed calmly in the wings, and the Dutch envoy, the doyen of the diplomatic corps who gave Chang Tso-lin permission for the raid." According to the testimony of Chang Tso-lin's adviser, Lenox Simpson, the marshal complained that he had been deceived by the British diplomats. He was promised that if the raid on the Soviet embassy gave cause for active intervention that England would make use of it. However, this did not, in fact, occur.

This, it seems, is how matters stood. Not without reason, soon after the raid, the *London Daily Telegraph* wrote that the very existence of the Soviet embassy in the Legation Quarter of Peking was an anachronism, and that there was no place there for the hammer and the sickle. Li Ta-chao and his nineteen comrades who met their terrible death so manfully were murdered by foreign imperialists.

At the same time voices were heard among the colonialists condemning such a policy not from considerations of humanity, of course, but because the raid on the Soviet embassy might set an undesirable precedent dangerous to themselves.

The American-owned *China Weekly Review*, in discussing whether or not it was legal for Chinese Communists to be on the grounds of the Soviet embassy, wrote: "During the World War, the British and French embassies were centers for the dissemination of anti-German propaganda. The Americans were not innocent with respect to anti-Japanese propaganda. When the Anfu clique's Japanophile government fell in 1918 the entire cabinet fled to the Japanese embassy, and the ministers lived there for several months until they were secretly transferred to Tientsin. Now the Legation Quarter has dug its own grave. A different political faction may want to plunder the British, American, or any other embassy. A precedent has been created, the Boxer Protocol has been scattered to the winds."

One of the English papers in China, writing in the same vein, recalled that every ousted government in Peking always fled to the Legation Quarter. The remnants of the Manchu Dynasty in 1911, Chang Hsün in 1917, the Anfu clique in 1920, etc., all had taken refuge there. Now the administrators of the foreign concessions were destroying the former system. In November 1926, the authorities in Tientsin's foreign concession had handed over to Chang Tso-lin fourteen Kuomintang students who had been executed; now they had permitted the raid on the Soviet embassy. This was a dangerous policy.

After setting the Chang Tso-linites on the Soviet embassy, the British even took upon themselves the ignoble role of police detectives. During the raid the British soldiers stood alongside the wall of their embassy which adjoined the Soviet, so that the pursued Chinese Communists and Soviet embassy employees could not save themselves by crossing over.

The accusations leveled against the arrested Soviet citizens were ludicrous. Grigorev "undoubtedly aided the criminals, otherwise he would not have been designated as watchman," Skatkin "was a party to the crime since he was arrested in the barracks of the military compound," Tonkikh "was privy to secret documents and made summaries of newspaper reports of military affairs for the military attaché; in view of this he is accused of being a secret military agent of the Soviet government," etc., etc.

For a long time those arrested were not allowed to see anyone. On May 3 they declared a hunger strike and terminated it five days later only when they were told that their cases were being transferred to an ordinary public court with the right of defense. Many times the cases were set for a hearing and then postponed. It was not until the beginning of 1928 that the comrades were freed and left for home.

On the day of the raid on the Peking embassy, anti-Soviet provocations were also organized in other Chinese cities. Here, for example, is what happened in Shanghai. On April 6 the Soviet consulate was surrounded by armed White Guards and a detachment of British troops who tried to search everyone entering and leaving, even the Commissar for Foreign Affairs in the Chinese administration of Shanghai. Since he refused to submit to this degrading procedure, he was not allowed in to see the consul-general Linde.

In the following days despite Linde's protests, the police of the International Settlement, White Guards, and foreign volunteers continued to search the visitors. They examined footwear, hats, and underwear. Every scrap of paper was read attentively. The windows were smashed in one of the rooms on the ground floor. However, no one tried to break into the building. Evidently this had been forbidden. The doyen of the consular corps, the Norwegian Aal, responding to a phone call from Comrade Linde, said that he himself knew nothing, but that the chairman of the Municipal Council of the International Settlement, the American Fessenden, had declared that he took full responsibility.

The siege continued for two weeks. White Guards and helmeted troops of the imperialists in full battle dress—British, American, Filipinos, and Scots in colorful national costumes—relieved each other on the guard. All letters and telegrams were intercepted. Visitors were photographed and requested to give their address, the time of their arrival and departure was noted. Every means of humiliating and insulting them was employed. The White Guards were not shy about their language either. In the newspapers appeared photos of some of the comrades who had tried to get to the consulate. In one of these we saw the adviser Rogov surrounded by armed men. Evidently he had quarreled with his tormentors. His frightened wife had dragged him aside.

As in Peking, the provocations were caused by the imperialists. The imperialist press in Shanghai finally lost all sense of shame or reason. From their pages resounded calls for the arrest and expulsion of the consular employees. They published "letters" and declarations that in China only one man knew how to act properly—this was Marshal Chang Tso-lin. The White Guard newspaper *Rossia* expressed its gratitude towards him. Simultaneously with the anti-Soviet campaign the imperialists intensified their struggle against Wuhan. By the middle of April, more than forty warships were riding on the Hankow roadstead.

Koreyvo's Arrival from Feng Yü-hsiang's Headquarters

The links between the Wuhan government and the outside world were very tenuous. The telegraph lines were in British hands. On the ships anyone suspicious-looking was searched and documents were taken away. It was even impossible to send a package. One had to rely on oral contact and personal communications.

In the beginning of April, Feng Yü-hsiang's military adviser Koreyvo, "Grandfather Noga," arrived from the Kalgan mission. He was supposed to make a report to the national government and in general reach agreement on a series of important questions.[6]

Koreyvo had left Shensi at the end of January and gotten to Hankow only after two months. He had to travel through enemy territory. Moreover, he stayed in Shanghai after the seizure of the ship *Pamyat Lenina*. Grandfather Noga was happy to meet with his colleagues from Kalgan—Chernikov (Nikitin the second), Akimov, and me. At that time Akimov and I had just gotten married. Koreyvo, who had been friends with him from the USSR, clambered up to our fourth floor garret in the Second House of Soviets and warmly congratulated us. He had a collection of Chinese gods, and seeing a big pot-bellied ivory Buddha on my desk he began asking for it. I decided, though not without secret grief, to part with the idol since I did not want to grieve our general favorite Grandfather Noga for anything in the world.

On April 10 Koreyvo got ready for his trip back. Akimov and someone else were assigned to accompany him. Under conditions then prevailing the trip to Shanghai and Peking was a dangerous one. There remained the road

---

6. In June Feng Yü-hsiang's other advisers including Argentov and Lapin came to Hankow.

straight northward along the Han River through unfamiliar territory, where only unreliable troops of the "fellow-travelers" were stationed, and where one might encounter Wu P'ei-fu's troops. There was no other way. The party traveled with a small guard.

In order not to attract attention everyone wore civilian clothes. The new uniforms of the National-Revolutionary Army were packed away. Koreyvo even forbade people from seeing the party off. I said farewell to Akimov at home. However, he returned at night; it turned out that the departure of the boat had been delayed. We sat by the window of our garret until dawn. Akimov left when the uncertain features of the large, peacefully sleeping city began to appear in the first light of morning. Only later did I understand how dangerous was their assignment.

Several days passed. It had probably already become known at the headquarters that the situation in north Hupeh where Koreyvo's group was headed was unfavorable. On meeting me Blyukher looked away and my heart sank. Once during the lunch hour I hurried home. A fragrant Wuhan spring was in the air, the sunlight flooded the streets, gardeners stood on the sidewalks selling rosebushes in pretty pottery vases at incredibly cheap prices. On the way I ran into the wife of one of the advisers who lived in our house. "Where are you going?" she shouted at me. "Akimov has come and is looking all over the city for you." A rickshaw stood nearby. As if in a dream I called it, although I didn't really know where to look for my husband. Suddenly I saw Akimov. He was walking quickly towards me in a new spic and span uniform and a khaki-colored cork helmet. The rickshaw man looked at me expectantly. I felt that I was going to cry, I could not speak. Akimov was already next to me. Without saying a word I took some money from his pocket—I don't know how much—and gave it to the smiling rickshaw man. Then we went home.

It turned out that the Red Spears, indignant at the violence of the remaining militarist forces, had revolted in north Hupeh. Opposing "any alien troops" they spared no one who fell into their hands. Koreyvo's party succeeded in avoiding the danger since it had been forewarned by refugees from the region of the uprising. In two days the ship brought our comrades back to Hankow.[7]

---

7. Subsequently Koreyvo again left Hankow. I don't know how he managed to get to Feng Yü-hsiang. He did not succeed in returning to the homeland. He died of tuberculosis in Ulan Bator in 1927 on the way to the Soviet Union. Koreyvo had contracted consumption from the time of his tsarist days and evidently the condition became exacerbated under the difficult conditions of his service in Feng Yü-hsiang's army. He did not acquire literacy in Chinese, but he did give his last strength to the great cause of China's emancipation.

Chiang Kai-shek's Coup in Shanghai

Several days later Wuhan received the terrible news of the smashing of the revolutionary organizations in Shanghai—Chiang Kai-shek's famous coup of April 12, 1927. Thus Chiang Kai-shek repaid the Shanghai workers who three weeks before had opened the gates of the city to the National-Revolutionary Army at the cost of great sacrifices in battle against the northern militarists.

At that time there was reason for the imperialists to complain that Shanghai "had gone Red," that not only the workers but the students and even the petty bourgeoisie were following the Communists. Shanghai had not remained a passive observer of the Northern Expedition, it took an active part from the very beginning. Thrice the urban masses had risen up in the enemy's rear to support the revolutionary troops.

The first attempt was made in October 1926 during the fighting near Nanchang. It was not successful. The same fate awaited the second uprising begun on February 22, 1927, although its mass base was much broader. On the eve of the uprising the newspapers reported that two hundred thousand workers were on strike in Shanghai protesting against the imperialists' intention to block the city's liberation by the National-Revolutionary Army.

Sun Ch'uan-fang committed cruel outrages. The newspapers were filled with reports which made one's blood run cold. Eyewitnesses wrote that on all the main streets of Shanghai's Chinese section bamboo cages were hung with the heads of the executed. Relatives recognized their near ones, moaned and cried, women knocked their heads on the ground. In order to terrify people the executioners walked right through the dense crowds of pedestrians carrying several heads on sharp poles or on platters. Unclaimed, decapitated corpses lay in the squares. People inhaled the stench of corpses. Workers and students were executed right on the streets without any proof or evidence but merely on suspicion. It seemed that the worst period of China's medieval ages had returned.

Sun Ch'uan-fang's extraordinary measures did not shatter the Shanghai people's will to resist, on the contrary they evoked general rage and indignation and sharpened the desire to have done as quickly as possible with the hateful regime. On March 21-22, the third uprising took place in the city. This time it was successful. Shanghai was liberated by the workers' militia. It was not till thirty hours after power in the city passed into the hands of the revolutionary people that the advance units of the National-Revolutionary Army entered the city.

Chiang Kai-shek arrived in Shanghai on March 26. As the commander-in-chief of the Eastern Front a triumphal welcome was arranged for him. The worker-militiamen took part in the grandiose demonstration. Until this time they had dressed in civilian hats, jackets, and robes, and in short pants with puttees, but they appeared at the demonstration as if on parade in blue Kuomintang-type uniforms with a hammer and sickle on their caps. At that time the hammer and sickle were the emblem of the Shanghai trade unions.

But an ominous silence reigned in the territory of the International Settlement. Barricades of tangled barbed-wire were still standing there, patrols and tanks stood guard. The papers reported that "Shanghai's foreign population was in a panic." The imperialists threatened Chiang Kai-shek with armed intervention if he did not break with the Communists.

On the day of his arrival Chiang Kai-shek declared to correspondents that there was no schism in the Kuomintang and that he considered everyone who took part in the revolution to be members of one party. He wanted to conceal his true intentions. In fact as soon as he arrived in Shanghai, Chiang Kai-shek began to prepare reprisals against the Communists and the Red trade unions.

After the coup the foreigners in Shanghai openly declared that they had known of it in advance. Chiang Kai-shek also submitted plans for the approval of the Chinese big bourgeoisie of Shanghai with whom he had long had ties. Having carried out his criminal mission, he received his reward from them— a loan of fifteen million dollars. But Chiang Kai-shek had other allies as well. The imperialist press reported that on Chiang Kai-shek's side during the coup there were supposedly workers who had joined the troops in smashing the Red trade unions and shouting "Down with the Communists!" Even the appearance of these people was described—they wore civilian clothes with a black character *kung* (labor) on a white armband. But, in fact, the imperialists knew best of all what sort of people these were. In the struggle against the Communists Chiang Kai-shek made use of the Shanghai gangsters as well as the secret lumpen-proletarian organizations of the Greens and the Reds.

In those days Shanghai was considered to be the center of the Chinese criminal world, and its gangsters lived no worse than their brothers somewhere in Chicago. The names and addresses of the millionaires, the uncrowned kings of the Shanghai criminals, were well-known to the police and not to them alone. Many of them lived in their own houses in the International Settlement. They owned dives, opium dens, and gambling houses, traded in bodies, kidnapped for ransom, and engaged in the contraband and the illegal opium trade, but the police never disturbed them. The authorities and the police were in cahoots with them. There were hundreds of criminals at the beck and call of the big stockbrokers and financial bigwigs ready to respond to their first word. From his youthful years Chiang Kai-shek had ties with these circles.

In those years there were still very many "Reds" and "Greens", especially along the seacoast of central China and the banks of the Yangtse. They swarmed on every wharf. I was told that it was enough to affix the mark of the Reds or the Greens on one's things and one could leave them unattended. They would be closely guarded by the unknown "brethren" and he among them who transgressed the code or tried to take them would be swiftly disposed of.

The strongest organization of the Greens and the Reds (with many thousands of teamsters, rickshaw men, coolies, and lumpen-proletarian elements) was located in Shanghai. At the head of their hierarchy was a grand dragon, equivalent in the old Chinese system to the imperial title. Below him were little dragons, teachers, pupils, pupils-sons, pupils-grandsons, etc. Unconditional obedience was demanded of the members of the organization. Heavy penalties including death were prescribed for disobedience. A special jargon and secret signs were created. On entering the organization the novice had to pass through a series of secret procedures to which a magical power was ascribed. Originally the organization arose with the goal of self-defense. The defenseless, poverty-stricken coolie arrived in the city where he knew no one and where anyone might insult him. Unemployment, need and complete lack of justice, compelled him to band together with others like him to provide for mutual aid. Alas, the unions became the instruments of their leaders who were most often criminals. Anyone could purchase their aid for the most illegal activity. Fights, attacks, provocations, strike-breaking, and secret murders were among the activities of the Greens and the Reds. Their leaders were well-known to the police but the latter preferred not to have anything to do with them and were well paid for this. The dragons of the Greens and the Reds were men of wealth.[8]

---

8. I was told that the leaders of the Greens and the Reds in July-August 1927, having fallen out with Chiang Kai-shek, helped several leading CCP members to escape pursuit. They were driven about town in open cars next to the dragons. The police did not dare to interfere. In the Shanghai hurly-burly it was not easy to preserve your head if the grand dragon himself was angry at you.

Chiang Kai-shek's coup was prepared in the deepest silence. Even after his arrival the militia kept their arms. They were reorganized along military lines—regiment, company, platoon. In Chapei, the workers' section of Shanghai, military training and inspection proceeded. Fifteen hundred workers were under arms. Their headquarters were located in the club room of the Chinese publishing firm, the Commercial Press.

At the same time like crows the most dismal figures from the camp of reaction gathered in Shanghai—Ho Ying-ch'in, Hu Han-min, and others. The representatives from Chiang Kai-shek's clique began their meetings which resounded with anti-Communist slogans and the demand to get rid of Borodin. The relationship to the Soviet Union also changed. It is true that Chiang Kai-shek sent a sympathetic telegram to our chargé d'affaires in Peking, Chernykh, with expressions of protest against the raid on the Soviet embassy, but he himself did not lift a finger when the imperialists and White Guards besieged the Soviet consulate in Shanghai.

Unfortunately, Chiang Kai-shek's coup came as a surprise to the defenders of the revolution. They were taken unaware when before dawn on April 12 the troops of General Chou Feng-ch'i and Pai Ch'ung-hsi attacked the workers' militia in all the Chinese sections of Shanghai. Their headquarters was smashed, their commanders arrested, and union members including the chairman of the Shanghai Council of Trade Unions were thrown into prison. Armed skirmishes continued throughout the following day; the workers resisted desperately. Many were killed and wounded. Some vanished without trace.

A burst of indignation was the response to this base treachery. On April 13 a mass demonstration was held with the participation of women and children who marched in the front ranks. This did not stop the executioners. They fired upon the demonstration. The papers reported that more than a hundred were killed and about five hundred wounded. On April 15 *Pravda* appeared with the headline "Pravye gomin'danovtsy predali revoliutsiiu" (The Kuomintang rightists have betrayed the revolution). This was a heavy blow for the revolutionary movement in Shanghai and in China generally. A new period began in the history of the Chinese revolution. The Communist and trade union organizations in Shanghai went underground. Trade union headquarters were sealed up or occupied by troops. The building of the Shanghai Council of Trade Unions quartered the so-called Commission for Trade Union Unification organized by the political division of General Pai Ch'ung-hsi's staff which took up the job of exposing "dangerous elements" among the workers.

Two days later General Li Chi-shen carried out the same kind of counter-revolutionary coup in Canton. Purges began in Shanghai and Canton. The terror became especially severe on the eve of May 1. An underground printing shop printing leaflets for May 1 was uncovered in Shanghai during these days. The ferocious regime decreed that May 1 not be celebrated in Shanghai.

In the second week of May the curfew was already lifted in the foreign settlement although the barbed wire barricades still remained and tanks and foreign patrols were on the streets. The reactionary Shanghai press reported that "the crisis had passed" but, as it turned out, this was a premature judgment.

On May 30, the memorial day for the victims of the shootings by British police on Nanking Street, all Shanghai again took to the streets in response to the Communists' call. More than a hundred thousand demonstrators took part in a giant demonstration. They carried placards with anti-imperialist slogans. Among the foreign consulates only the Soviet lowered its flag as a sign of mourning. The culprits of the shooting, the British, with provocationist intent, illuminated their club supposedly in honor of the king's birthday, although this in fact fell on June 3. On June 3 they organized a parade and burned an effigy of the Kremlin. The Chiang Kai-shekists stooped so low that they sentenced two students to six weeks in jail for distributing proclamations on that day which they considered to be insulting to the British king.

The coup in Shanghai provoked confusion in Wuhan. Open betrayal had not been expected there. At this time the decision had already been taken to go north into Honan province against the Mukdenites. It was thought that Chiang Kai-shek at least for the immediate future would refrain from exacerbating relations with Wuhan and as the commander-in-chief of the forces of the Eastern Column (the western commander-in-chief at that time was Feng Yü-hsiang) would take part in the continuation of the Northern Expedition.

The Wuhan government published a resolution to the effect that Chiang Kai-shek had been removed from all his posts, expelled from the Kuomintang, and was subject to arrest.

In turn Chiang Kai-shek and the other rightists published a declaration about their final rupture with Wuhan.

The Nanking government began to function on April 18. Hu Han-min, the Kuomintang ultra-rightist, was appointed as chairman of the Chiang Kai-shek cabinet. Another extreme rightist, Wu Ch'ao-shu (S. S. Wu) became one of the ministers. About a month and a half later the Hsishan group entered the government. The former leader of the Kuomintang leftists Kan Nai-kuang and General Li Chi-shen were given cozy jobs in Nanking.

A comical incident took place during the formation of the government. Wu Ch'ao-shu demanded that Chiang Kai-shek renounce his former declaration that he, Wu, was a tool of the imperialists. He was referring to one of Chiang Kai-shek's speeches of May 1926 in which Chiang had declared that Wu Ch'ao-shu and Hu Han-min were carrying on secret negotiations with Hong Kong and in its name had offered him a bribe of fifteen million dollars to liquidate the anti-British boycott and bring about a general change in the policy of the Canton government.

The relations which developed between Wuhan and Nanking would in our time be called a "cold war." Troops faced each other ready to fire. Chiang Kai-shek declared an economic blockade of Wuhan. Trade there was sharply curtailed, shortages were felt in fuel and supplies, banking activity expired. The imperialist press called for military intervention against the Wuhan government.

In these circumstances discussion was resumed in Wuhan on the question of continuing the Northern Expedition.

The Second Phase of the Northern Expedition and the Wuhan Situation

At the morning Politburo session of the Kuomintang CEC on April 10 it was decided to move in an easterly direction which would have signified a campaign against Chiang Kai-shek. However, a special session was held in the evening at which the question was reexamined. As of April 9 the Twelfth Division had been stationed on board a ship which was supposed to transport it to the eastern front. On April 13 its officers were informed that the ship would not sail since a campaign in Honan was forthcoming.

In connection with the Shanghai events the dispatch of troops to the front was delayed once more and debates again flared up. Even among the leading cadres of the Chinese Communist party CC there was more than one opinion. There were even voices calling for a return to Kwangtung, the old revolutionary base, saying that everything should be begun anew. In the end it was decided to move on Honan. The proposal was to advance on Peking after linking up with Feng Yü-hsiang's troops. The liberation of the national capital would have made the National Government an all-Chinese regime after which, with Feng Yü-hsiang's help, they would finish off Chiang Kai-shek.

In the final analysis military activities in Honan were unavoidable. The Mukdenites, having defeated Wuhan's "fellow-travelers," in March conquered the center of the province—Kaifeng. After occupying Chengchow they began a movement along the Peking-Hankow Railroad towards Wuhan. The commander of the Thirteenth Army of the National-Revolutionary Army, Fang Shih-ming, who had remained in Honan after the defeat of the Second and Third Nationalist Armies there in the spring of 1926, was defeated by Wu P'ei-fu's troops. Feng Yü-hsiang's troops had just appeared in the west of the province. Wuhan had to secure itself against the north. The campaign in Honan began on April 19. The Fourth and Eleventh Armies from Chang Fa-k'uei's group, Ho Lung's Independent Fifteenth Division and later T'ang Sheng-chih's group, in all some seventy thousand men went to the front.

Almost all of our advisers showed up at the front. Ho Lung's adviser at the time was M. F. Kumanin. He had come to Canton in the autumn of 1926 and arrived in Wuhan together with the first contingent of the government members.[9] As before Gorev was Chang Fa-k'uei's chief adviser, while Faddey Ivanovich Olshevsky (Voynich) was T'ang Sheng-chih's adviser. Olshevsky was a hero of the civil war in Russia and commander of a Red Army division. Akimov was assigned as an adviser to T'ang Sheng-chih's troops.

As soon as military activities commenced the rightists began stirring in Nanking. In the beginning of May a conference was held there. A representative was sent to Feng Yü-hsiang and the Shansi *tupan* Yen Hsi-shan with a proposal for joint action against the Mukdenites. In Shanghai Pai Ch'ung-hsi declared, "Despite our political disagreements with Wuhan, we are maintaining contact with General T'ang Sheng-chih and will conduct joint operations against the northerners." In fact, on May 14, Ho Ying-ch'in's First Army forced the Yangtse and just managed to take Pukow. However, Chiang Kai-shek

---

9. M.F. Kumanin took part in the Nanchang Uprising of Ho Lung's and Yeh T'ing's troops on August 1, 1927. M.F. Kumanin's recollections of these events was published in the collection *Sovetskie dobrovol'tsy v Kitae* (Soviet volunteers in China). Moscow 1961.

set very limited tasks for himself; according to the operational plan he did not intend to go further than Pengpu in Anhui. Subsequently he conducted a series of operations in the northern section of Kiangsu but later he retreated from there.

Despite Chiang Kai-shek's betrayal and the economic difficulties the mood in Wuhan was optimistic. Victorious communiques came from the front and it seemed that the successes of the campaign might set everything straight. Wuhan remained the advance post of the anti-imperialist struggle, the center of the revolutionary movement.

Right up until April 1927 the CC of the Chinese Communist party remained in the French Concession of Shanghai. That city was the foremost industrial center of China and it was thought that the CC of the CCP should be located there. Not long before the Fifth Congress of the CCP the Central Committee transferred to Hankow. G. N. Voytinsky went there too.

I saw the general secretary of the CC of the CCP, Ch'en Tu-hsiu, only once, when soon after arrival he paid a visit to Borodin. Ch'en Tu-hsiu was recognized by everyone as the "patriarch" of the Communist party of China, as Borodin called him jokingly. For the rank and file Chinese Communist his authority and decisions were not open to dispute. I looked upon him with great interest and remember him well. He was dressed in a Western suit and was carefully groomed—a typical Chinese intellectual who had received his education abroad. A polite smile never left his lips; there was a certain ingratiating manner in his way of speaking. He was constantly agreeing with his interlocutor, evidently out of respect for the old Chinese etiquette.

By the first half of April all the members of the CC were already in Wuhan. Preparations for the Fifth Congress of the CCP were underway. The pre-Congress discussions which had begun about two months before continued on a whole range of basic questions about the Chinese Revolution, the agrarian question in the first place.

About three weeks before the CCP congress the well-known Kuomintang Agrarian Commission set to work in Hankow. It included Wang Ching-wei, Teng Yen-ta (chief of the Peasant Department of the Kuomintang CEC), T'an Yen-k'ai, the chairman of the Kuomintang National government, T'ang Sheng-chih, and many others. The CCP was represented by Mao Tse-tung (head of the Peasant Department of the CCP CC) and T'an P'ing-shan (minister of agriculture).[10] M. O. Razumov[11] and another person were advisers to the commission. Preliminary meetings took place before each session. I was present in my capacity as Razumov's interpreter. After innumerable sessions the committee closed up shop, having decided nothing concretely. But it was from this commission that there came the idea for the "political" confiscation only of the land of counter-revolutionaries.

One of Erdberg's most caustic novellas is dedicated precisely to this commission. Before the reader passes a line of Kuomintang politicians who desire to preserve the decorum of democratic institutions and at the same time do not want to move forward by a step the problem under discussion, landlords who shudder for their agrarian holdings, generals who are alarmed by the scope of the agrarian movement. These people, having put off decisions on the problem till the next time, with an obvious sense of relief sing in a discordant false chorus the Kuomintang hymn "Ta Tao Lieh Shen," the song which usually concluded all Kuomintang meetings at the time.

The Fifth Congress of the CCP opened on April 27, 1927, in Wuchang. Seventy delegates from every province were present along with twice that many guests—representatives from workers' and peasants' organizations, delegations from the Comintern, and from the Communist Youth International. The secretary of the Union of Railroad Workers of the USSR greeted the assembled in the name of the Soviet delegation which had arrived in Hankow for the Pacific Trade Union Conference.

The Fifth Congress was the first congress of Chinese Communists held under legal conditions, and a delegation from the Kuomintang attended for the first time. It included T'an Yen-k'ai, Hsü Ch'ien, and Sun Fo. Wang Ching-wei also spoke at the congress.

The workers' militia of Wuchang selected Ch'en Tu-hsiu and a representative of the Comintern as honorary militiamen and solemnly presented them with their uniform—dark-blue jackets and trousers and military caps.

The speeches of the Kuomintang representatives set the delegates on their guard. In his speech Hsü Ch'ien let it be understood that the Kuomintang was

---

10. The Communists who were a minority in the commission were unable to exert a decisive influence on its activity.
11. From the late twenties to middle thirties Razumov was secretary of the Tatar Oblast Committee and then of the East Siberian District Committee of the RCP(B). He was repressed in 1937.

opposed to the agrarian revolution. He declared that the CCP should be the party of the workers but that the peasants must be left to the Kuomintang. T'ang P'ing-shan, who as minister of agriculture considered himself a "specialist" on the agrarian question, at first did not want to reply to Hsü Ch'ien. Only after two days had passed, yielding to the delegates' demands, did he come out with an entirely inchoate declaration. He did not want to quarrel with the Kuomintang.

Ch'en Tu-hsiu's report lasted six hours; the discussion of it took four days. Resolutions were adopted on the agrarian question, the political situation, and the tasks of the CCP. A new Central Committee and Politburo were elected. The congress closed on May 10.

In the course of the congress we heard for the first time of the famous northwest theory which called for the transfer of the center of revolutionary activity to the northwest, Feng Yü-hsiang's area, the most backward region but the one furthest from the imperialist influence. This theory signified a flight from the resolution of the vital tasks of the revolutionary movement. It was correctly judged to be a retreat stemming from fear in the face of the forces of reaction and disbelief in the strength of the masses. The Fifth Congress of the Communist party of China has been sufficiently illuminated in our literature. For the first time an open criticism of Ch'en Tu-hsiu's line was heard, but no change in the party leadership occurred.

A week later the Pacific Conference of Trade Unions convened in Hankow. As early as 1922 at the Second Congress of the Profintern a proposal by the Australian delegation to convoke such a conference had been adopted. An armed conflict was expected then between Japan and the USSR. When the acute danger of conflict had passed the congress was postponed. Only in 1926 did it become an issue again. It was proposed that the following questions be placed on its agenda—support of the Chinese revolution, protest against intervention in China, struggle against the danger of war in the Pacific Basin, etc.

The delegation from the USSR suffered much unpleasantness on the way from Canton to Hankow. S. A. Lozovsky and several other delegates were detained in Hong Kong for two hours although they had transit visas. In Shanghai an English officer appeared on board the *Stravropol* which was taking two other members of the delegation—Korolev and Markov—from Canton, and forbade them to debark. While in port the *Stravropol* was kept under surveillance by a patrol cutter armed with machine guns. At night it was illuminated by scores of spotlights from military vessels. Korolev and Markov were unable to get to Hankow—they had to return to Vladivostok. The other delegates succeeded in getting through the enemy cordon.

Delegates from England, Australia, the USA, France, Indonesia, Korea, and Japan arrived for the Pacific Conference. Many of them could not get to Hankow. They were followed, refused visas, caught, and thrown into jail. Still fourteen and a half million organized workers were represented at the conference. The chairman of the Profintern Executive Committee, Lozovsky, gave the main report and the concluding speech.

At the final session a Pacific Trade Union Secretariat was formed and a decision was taken to publish a journal *Pacific Worker* in English.[12] The conference proclaimed the main tasks of the workers of the Pacific Basin to be the struggle against the threat of a new war and against racial prejudice as well as aid to the oppressed peoples struggling against imperialism. A special manifesto was dedicated to the tasks of the Chinese trade unions.

These and many other important events occurred in a city whose political life was tense. Conferences, meetings, and demonstrations followed one after the other. Even daily street life bore the mark of the masses' participation in the revolutionary changes. Every day we observed typical and quite curious scenes to this effect.

Here in the middle of the street is a band of Pioneers wearing red bands and white straw hats, armed with their traditional sticks, leading an entrepreneur who has violated the labor law. He is wearing a big dunce's cap on which his offense is written in large, black characters. He walks along with his head hanging low; it is evident that the punishment is very effective and that he would be happy to redeem himself in any way possible. The lads guffaw loudly. The majority of the Pioneers, especially the older ones, were self-supporting. They were young workers and with all the ardor of youth they were participating in the revolutionary movement, even speaking out at public meetings. Along with the workers' militia they were maintaining public order. They were also charged with the task of maintaining communications for the Wuhan trade unions. On March 8, International Women's Day,

---

12. The journal was published in Hankow until September and thereafter was based in Shanghai.

a Pioneers' parade was held in Hankow, in which more than twenty thousand young people, from six to sixteen, appeared.

Here, in plain view of everyone, police are leading two men and a woman. Their hands are tied behind their backs. In appearance they are average merchants. The policeman announces in a loud voice that they are guilty of spreading slanderous rumors to the effect that a parade of naked women has taken place in Wuchang and will soon be repeated. Passersby shout and laugh. This absurd canard was started abroad but almost all the reactionary papers in China gave it a place in their columns. The Hupeh Women's Union adopted a resolution that anyone who disseminated such rumors was a counter-revolutionary.

Here is a demonstration by the Sun Yat-sen Agitators' School. Girls are parading in white men's costumes with Kuomintang cockades on their caps. Among them, political workers of the National-Revolutionary Army—women carrying Mausers on straps—may be distinguished. The demonstrators are demanding a punitive expedition against Chiang Kai-shek.

Wuhan in the Critical Days

In Changsha in May events occurred which actually began the open crisis in the Wuhan camp which culminated in the final rupture of the Kuomintang and the Chinese Communist party and the liquidation of the Wuhan revolutionary center. I speak of the counter-revolutionary uprising in Hunan of General Hsü K'e-hsiang, one of the regimental commanders in T'ang Sheng-chih's army. The uprising occurred at a very difficult time. Still earlier, on May 16, General Hsia Tou-yin had betrayed the revolution. Yeh T'ing's division and the cadets of the Military-Political Academy succeeded in stopping his troops when they were already just forty kilometers from Wuhan. On May 19 Hsü K'e-hsiang rebelled.

Just at this time in Hankow at the headquarters of the Kuomintang CEC there took place a solemn ceremony establishing a Ministry of Agriculture headed by the Communist T'an P'ing-shan. This was done in accordance with the decision adopted already at the March plenum of the CEC, but whose implementation had been delayed. The Wuhan government, shaken by the new disaster, did not at once react to it and at first kept Hsü K'e-hsiang's action a secret. Armed guards were placed around the headquarters of the government and the Kuomintang CEC. Borodin's house was also guarded.

Soon it became known that worker-pickets had been disarmed in Changsha, a workers' demonstration shot into, the provincial government dispersed, and power passed into the hands of a committee of five officers. Hsü K'e-hsiang drove the Communists underground, and disbanded the trade unions and peasant leagues. Arrests and executions began.

In the next few days thousands of peasants under the leadership of local Communists advanced on Changsha intending to deal with the counter-revolutionaries. If not for Wuhan's prohibition the city would have been taken. The Kuomintang organization in Hunan was on the side of the masses, actively participating in their struggles.

The events in Changsha provoked disputes and disagreements among the members of the Central Committee of the CCP. Ch'en Tu-hsiu again took a position which one expected him to take. He censured the lack of discipline of Hunan's Communists, workers, and peasants.

When I arrived for work on May 26, emptiness and disorder greeted me in the reception room and Borodin's office. Obviously an extraordinary meeting had taken place during the night. It turned out that early in the morning Borodin and an official commission had left for Changsha. The commission included T'an P'ing-shan, Ch'en Kung-po (at that time chief of the Kuomintang CEC Merchants' Work Department), and two military men who were representatives of T'ang Sheng-chih. The commission was detained along the way, and only Ch'en Kung-po was allowed into Changsha. The others returned because Hsü K'e-hsiang threatened to have them executed.

With respect to the uprising Wuhan occupied a conciliatory position. A government decree was placed in the *People's Tribune* forbidding the Hunan organization of the Kuomintang from interfering in administrative matters. One day later a decree was published disbanding all the party and public organizations in Hunan including the women's league. T'ang Sheng-chih sent assurances from the front that he was opposed to the military mutiny and would punish the guilty severely. He was afraid that in his absence "the Communists would seize Hunan and Hupeh." Only one month later, after his return from the front, he declared that Hsü K'e-hsiang had acted properly in moving against "bandits and destroyers of order."

A delegation from the Hunan Provincial Committee of the Kuomintang arrived in Hankow in the beginning of June—more than a hundred persons, it seems. The leading Kuomintang members did not want to talk with them. One of the secretaries heard out their complaint that the White terror was continuing despite the presence of representatives of the Kuomintang CEC, that the revolutionary masses had gone underground, and that both leaders and rank and file revolutionaries were dying. The delegation accomplished nothing.

At the same time analogous events were occurring in Kiangsi, another province subordinate to Wuhan. On June 1 General Chu P'ei-te pulled off a coup. He expelled the Communists and political workers from his army and began to persecute the mass organizations. By now Wuhan was only an island in a raging sea. Kwangtung and Kwangsi were cut off, Chiang Kai-shek was threatening from the east, and a counter-revolutionary military clique had seized power in Hunan. In Wuhan itself after the events in Changsha the conflict between the Kuomintang and the CCP came to a head. And still the mood of the masses remained exalted, large hopes (alas, how vain they turned out to be) were inspired by the victories on the Honan front. On June 1 the troops of the National-Revolutionary Army took Chengchow, an important strategic point at the intersection of two railroads—the Lunghai and the Tientsin-Pukow. That same evening Feng Yü-hsiang's advance units entered the city. The following day there was a new victory—Chang Fa-k'uei had taken Kaifeng. Among the trophies were three tanks of Chang Tso-lin, whose very appearance previously had frightened the soldiers of the National-Revolutionary Army.

In the beginning of June the entire press in China noted the sharp change in the military situation in favor of the southerners. Panic set in in the imperialist camp. None of them had expected that the "Hunanese dwarfs" would smash what they had thought of as Chang Tso-lin's invincible army. But the alarm did not continue for long. Soon it became clear to everyone who was garnering the fruits of the victories.

On June 8 representatives of the government left Hankow for a conference of military leaders in Chengchow where Feng Yü-hsiang was also supposed to be present. The delegation included Wang Ching-wei, T'an Yen-k'ai, Sun Fo, Ku Meng-yü, and Hsü Ch'ien. The conference turned out to be a fatal dividing line—the Kuomintang members finally agreed to break with the CCP.

Chang Fa-k'uei's movement to the right commenced. He had been one of the most left of the generals in the National-Revolutionary Army. After the Chengchow conference he was already making all kinds of accusations against the peasant movements and the Communists.

For a long time in Wuhan great hopes were placed upon Feng Yü-hsiang. It was expected that sooner or later, gun in hand, Chiang Kai-shek would come out against the Wuhan army, and that such a strong ally as Feng Yü-hsiang might play a decisive role in the forthcoming engagement. As long as these hopes existed many wavering and discontented elements in Wuhan followed the Kuomintang leftists and the Communists. However, several Kuomintang leaders (Ku Meng-yü, Hsü Ch'ien, Wang Ching-wei) were working actively in a secret effort to line up Feng Yü-hsiang against the Communists. At the end of May Hsü Ch'ien and Wang Ching-wei sent him a telegram, in which they complained that the "hegemony in the revolutionary movement which should belong to the Kuomintang is passing into the hands of the CCP."

By that time Feng Yü-hsiang's decision to come out on the side of Chiang Kai-shek had already matured. As early as the night of May 10 all anti-Chiang posters in his troops' billets were torn down and several days later all agitation against Chiang was forbidden on the pretext that he was an ally in the struggle against Chang Tso-lin. On May 30, just prior to the union of his troops with those of Wuhan, Feng Yü-hsiang publicly declared that he could not consider the Nanking government to be counter-revolutionary.

But meanwhile no other campaign had cost the National-Revolutionary Army so many victims—it lost twenty per cent of its manpower. On the fields of Honan lay the bodies of thousands of Communists and Komsomols who had selflessly fought against the troops of Chang Tso-lin and Chang Tsung-ch'ang so that Feng Yü-hsiang might utter his weighty words in the cause of revolution.

I was in Hankow on June 16 when the return of the troops from the Honan front was being celebrated. The Hupeh Trade Union Council wanted to greet the generals with a general strike as a mark of protest against the unresolved conflicts with Changsha. But nothing came of this. The strike turned headlong into a welcoming demonstration. Still it proceeded under the slogan of struggle against the counter-revolutionaries in Hunan. This provoked the indignation of the leading members of the Kuomintang CEC who after the Chengchow conference had already come out openly against the CCP. They declared that the slogan was "put forth by the Communists, not by the masses." They were referring to the open letter of the CCP CC from June 15 concerning the events in Changsha. In it were advanced these demands: declare Hsü K'e-hsiang's mutinous committee to be counter-revolutionary, appoint a lawful government, swiftly dispatch a punitive expedition, arm the workers and peasants, and issue a decree concerning the free existence in Hunan of Communist and worker-peasant organizations. But these demands were too late. T'ang Sheng-chih's troops had already returned from the front and now he no longer feared anything.

The revolution in Wuhan declined sharply. During the third week of June in Hsüchou (on the north bank of the Yangtse) there took place a meeting between Feng Yü-hsiang and Chiang Kai-shek. Representatives from Wuhan, the Kuomintang leftists Hsü Ch'ien and Ku Meng-yü, were present at the meeting. The result of the meeting was a joint declaration and a letter from Feng Yü-hsiang to the Wuhan government. Referring to the events in Hunan, Feng Yü-hsiang declared that he had recently met with comrades from Nanking (he did not decide to say openly that it was with Chiang Kai-shek) and they had come to the following conclusions: 1) Borodin should quickly return to the USSR; 2) those members of the Kuomintang CEC who wanted to take a leave and travel abroad could do so, the others could adhere to Nanking, this was the only possible solution; 3) T'ang Sheng-chih, if he were a patriot, should send his forces to Chengchow to cooperate with the troops of the National Army.

On July 1 Feng Yü-hsiang returned to Chengchow. All the municipal and district committees of the Kuomintang in his territory were ordered to cease activity until new directions were forthcoming. Communists were expelled from the army.

It is impossible to say that Wuhan swiftly capitulated to the demands concerning the relief of Borodin, but in essence the objections were formalistic. They said that Borodin had been invited on the basis of a decision of the First Congress of the Kuomintang and that it was impossible to relieve him without a resolution of a new congress. Wuhan's resistance quickly grew enfeebled. In the first days of July T'ang Sheng-chih already asked as a favor that the Wuhan center not be liquidated entirely, but be reorganized in line with Nanking's principles. However, Feng Yü-hsiang objected saying that this was directly counter to the decisions of the Hsüchow meeting. He even sent an ultimatum to T'ang Sheng-chih demanding the dissolution of the Wuhan government and threatening a general offensive against the city. How quickly thereafter did Feng Yü-hsiang repent his mistaken line!

Meanwhile, as before Wuhan was the main attraction for revolutionary forces. At the national congresses and conferences held there representatives of the Kuomintang and the government appeared side by side with the Communists, but the process which was leading swiftly to the demise of the revolutionary center in Wuhan was inexorably continuing.

On June 20 the Fourth All-China Congress of Trade Unions, the last legal congress of Red trade unions in China during this period, began its work in Hankow. It was convened by Su Chao-cheng, a member of the CCP Central Committee and the minister of labor. Three hundred sixty delegates representing three million workers were in attendance. Representatives from the CCP, the Union of Chinese Pioneers, the Kuomintang, the political department of the National-Revolutionary Army as well as from the Profintern and the Pacific Conference, appeared with greetings. The representatives of the USSR delegation presented the assembled with a banner from the workers of the Soviet Union. On the following day the reports of the Kuomintang CEC and the government were heard.

The sessions continued for ten days. The delegates spoke of the fact that almost everywhere now the Chinese proletariat was living under conditions of terror, under the power of the counter-revolutionaries, and they called upon the proletariat to be prepared for struggle. The resolutions bore a militant, decisive character. The congress declared that the basic task of the Chinese working class at the present moment was the destruction of the counter-revolution headed by Chiang Kai-shek and the other traitors. In an appeal to the Kuomintang CEC the delegates demanded a punitive expedition against Chiang Kai-shek. The congress addressed an appeal to the workers of all countries to strengthen the united front against imperialism and a new war.

On June 23 the delegates took part in innumerable meetings on this, the second anniversary of the British imperialists' shooting of the demonstrators in Canton. In Shanghai flyers bearing the signature of one hundred three Shanghai trade unions in support of the congress were printed underground.

The Chiang Kai-shek sleuths ran their feet off searching for the responsible parties. A district committee of the Kuomintang was shut down for being pro-Communist. Three of its members were arrested, the rest fled.

And just then in plain view of the delegates who had come from every province of China the workers' militia in Hankow was disarmed. How did this happen? At that time the CC of the CCP adopted a resolution to create its own revolutionary army. It was proposed to bring worker and peasant detachments into Chang Fa-k'uei's troops among whom there were still many Communists in command positions, thereby creating a nucleus faithful to the revolution. It was in connection with this attempt which did not succeed that one of the most egregious errors of that period was committed—the worker pickets in Wuhan were disarmed "so that without arms it would be easier for them to enter Chang Fa-k'uei's army."[13] This took place on the day of the concluding session of the congress. On this occasion the *People's Tribune* came out with a laudatory article.

As soon as the workers' militia had been disarmed, soldiers occupied and partially pillaged the headquarters of the All-China Federation of Labor and the Hupeh Trade Union Council.

Emboldened, the entrepreneurs organized the destruction of several local trade unions. It is true that the commander of the Hankow garrison, General Li P'in-hsien, alleging a misunderstanding, excused himself, liberated the trade union quarters and returned the Mausers to the workers' guard, but this was simply a brief respite on the road to crushing the workers' movement. At a time when reaction was intensifying its attack the revolutionary leadership was persisting in a policy of concessions. In the beginning of July by decision of the Hupeh Trade Union Council even the Pioneer organizations were disbanded, their harmless sticks were taken away and handed over to the unions where they became the militiamen's only weapons. With the exception of special occasions, wearing the Pioneer uniform was prohibited.

I was no longer in Hankow when the Fourth All-China Congress of Trade Unions completed its work, but from the stories of comrades I know about the celebrations this occasioned. In the People's Palace on June 29, there took place a great meeting of workers and soldiers. Delegates and representatives of the military command spoke. Fraternization between the soldiers and

---

13. Simultaneously the cadets of the Military-Political Academy in Wuchang were also disarmed.

the workers took place after the speeches. The music resounded, the hall was brightly illumined, colorful flags were hung along with garlands of flowers. And only the unarmed worker pickets standing guard around the People's Palace served as a reminder that the workers' guard in Wuhan had ceased to exist.

The situation in Hankow was such that our advisers too had to fear for their lives. In the middle of June an attempt was made to poison Blyukher at one of the banquets given in honor of the victorious return of the troops of the National-Revolutionary Army from Honan. Blyukher took sick and recovered but one of the accompanying advisers—Zotov—was poisoned and died on the following day. The doctor from the German missionary hospital at first indignantly diagnosed poisoning. However, on the following day, when he was asked to confirm this officially, he declared with embarrassment that he had evidently made a mistake.

The Wuhan period is the most complex and contradictory in the history of the Chinese revolution of 1925-1927, a time of great victories and crushing defeats, heroic deeds and fatal errors. I remember how feverishly the pulse of Wuhan's political life beat. Opening the newspapers, each time we read about new events, each one of which at some other time might have become the subject of extended discussions, might have lent its color to the situation. But then they flashed by, one after the other, like woodchips in a whirlpool. Time was compressed to the limits. And unnoticed the moment crept up when I had to leave Wuhan.

Chapter VII

THE ROAD BACK

We Leave Hankow

About June 20 Borodin called me into his office and advised me to
return to the motherland. "I too will soon have to leave wearing blinders,"
he added. The word "blinders" was incomprehensible, but the general sense
of what he said needed no commentary. My heart began to thump. More
than once I had occasion to hear that the rupture of the Wuhan faction of
the Kuomintang with the Communist party was obviously an accomplished
matter. Wuhan inclined more and more to Nanking's position. The financial
situation was extremely difficult. The adviser V. M. Shteyn said, "We did
more than we could. It is amazing that we are still holding on." Everything
about the situation in Wuhan inclined one to sad thoughts. But still it was
bitter for me to hear Borodin's words.

And so I prepare for the road again, this time bound for home, and
I will soon see Moscow and the dear people whom I have missed. But how
heavy my soul! I departed together with my husband since the military
advisers too were leaving Wuhan one after another. Borodin left about a
month later and really was compelled, as he expressed it, "to leave wearing
blinders." He could not (as the others had) choose the shortest path via
Shanghai. His rabid enemy, Chiang Kai-shek, who threatened him with
violence, awaited him there. But the military advisers, even Blyukher, went
via Shanghai. In this period Chiang Kai-shek did not pursue them.

At that time navigation along the Yangtse was in essence monopolized
by the British commercial companies. We had to sail on one of the British
ships and sail at that time like prisoners. Fore and aft and at the captain's
bridge there jutted forth lanky figures in white naval uniforms with bayonets
at their waist and carbines slung from the shoulders. This absurd demonstration of the colonialists' military strength would have been comical had it
not been so insolent. After all nothing was threatening shipboard communications.

Following our comrades' advice, my husband and I took tickets in different cabins and arrived at the pier as if we were strangers. A dark blue

twilight cloaked the city. The large, pure white, very beautiful ship was brightly lighted; foreigners and wealthy Chinese milled about the gangplank hurrying to flee with their capital. Alongside in the roadstead, blinking their signal lights, stood the heavy hulks of the foreign warships. Their sinister appearance was wordless testimony to the dismal role played by the imperialists in what had occurred in Wuhan—the glorious city of two revolutions.

On that evening Hankow looked silent and sorrowful as if it were oppressed by the same foreboding of imminent disaster that we were. Tickets were checked at the gangplank, and at the same moment one of the navy men, without saying a word, took from me the small valise which I had wanted to keep in my cabin and carried if off before me. He did this without setting down his carbine. I do not know how to explain his kindness, perhaps he wanted a tip, but I didn't think of this then.

We walked along a corridor and around a corner suddenly bumped into persons among whom I recognized my husband. Two muscular sailors were interrogating him. Learning that he was a Russian they demanded clarification—was he White or Red? "I will not reply to such a question," declared Akimov, bursting with anger. The conflict was coming to a head and I decided to intervene. No one answered my anxious question "What's the matter?" but the atmosphere cooled off at once. Both fellows looked first at me, then indecisively at each other, and after hesitating for another moment they went away. I think that I owed my success to a large, stylish hat with sloping brims and an incredibly tall crown which I had specially purchased for the trip. Had I been wearing the student cap I had on two years before when I first landed on Chinese soil the result would have been different.

Soon after getting settled in my cabin I went out to the salon to see my husband and find out how things were going. The salon was jammed with passengers and people seeing them off. Seated at a small table in front of a large gilt-framed mirror with his back almost to the assembled people was a man in a light suit. My husband walked up to me. "We haven't done badly for ourselves," he said, nodding in this man's direction. "It's the English consul. And just whom is he seeing off? Look how he is following after us." I quickly glanced in that direction and met a cold, guarded look in the mirror.

Just then two more advisers entered the salon. Like us, they were returning home. In order to avoid any unpleasantness we pretended that we didn't know each other. We remembered well the provocative escapades of the British imperialists against Soviet officers and Soviet citizens in China, the more so since after the raid on Arcos in London in May 1927 diplomatic relations between the Soviet Union and England had been broken.

On British ships even the stand-offish first-class passengers often draw close to their fellow travelers and sometimes the relations take on a tone of familiarity but only for the duration of the voyage. I didn't know this yet and was very amazed when on the following day I was addressed from the table where the ship's officers dined. The captain's assistant, a young chap in short canvas trousers courteously inquired how I was. Later he spoke to me quite often until he noticed that I was conversing too often with the "Red" (this was my husband).

"Where are you coming from?" he asked once. "From Hankow? A terrible city, isn't it? It's become quite impossible to live there. You're quite right to give it up for Shanghai." Before Nanking we passed by the sunken ship *Pamyat Lenina*. The tops of its smokestacks and something that looked like its masts jutted out of the water. The passengers (British and American for the most part) crowded to the portside, and speaking animatedly among themselves, photographed its remains. It seemed that they hated it like a living thing. At that time Nanking was a sort of defensive point. There suspicious persons from Wuhan were taken off the boats and thrown into prison. That the boat was British was no defense. The local authorities had an agreement with the imperialists about this. We breathed more easily when the signal for departure was sounded.

In Shanghai, as before, we stayed in the furnished rooms let by Tarasov. Here too the change of circumstances was evident. We were shadowed regularly. A detective openly looked at his watch and recorded when we went out and when we returned. It was rather crowded in the pension. Many advisers and their families had already returned at this time. Chiang Kai-shek was informed, of course, of their presence in Shanghai, but for the time being he did not react to them. We ran across him in one of the central movie theaters of the International Settlement, a huge gilded hall with loges and a deep balcony, which held well over a thousand persons. Chiang Kai-shek was sitting in the

first row balcony while our party was some six rows behind. Turning about
he looked at us demonstratively, letting us know that he recognized us.
Perhaps he expected that we would go up to him to exchange greetings. He
was dressed not in uniform but in a simple Chinese gown and he seemed to
me not as frail and stooped as usual. Not knowing what he would do next
we hurried to leave the theater.

In Shanghai we had a meeting with yet another odious person—the
provocateur and White Guard Pick. In the spring of 1927 he insinuated himself into a position on Borodin's staff and the mission headquarters so that
later, after fleeing from Hankow, he could print all kinds of rubbish about
"the intrigues of the Bolshevists in China" in the imperialist press. His articles
which appeared daily in the so-called grand press of Shanghai were the greatest sensation among foreign residents at the time. He sprinkled these articles
with the names of Soviet workers in China, mercilessly confusing them[1]
and declaring interpreters to be agents of the OGPU. Pick recognized our
comrades on the street and turned on them with threats.

Before us once more were the noisy streets of Shanghai, the Settlement
with its arrogant masters, the haughty faces of people who lived and prospered
in China but who did not wish to recognize its laws. How embittered they
were now against the Chinese, how zealously they demanded "teach them
a lesson!" These were tragic times for Shanghai. Arrests and executions of
Communists took place almost daily. It was terrible to walk by the prisons
at night; terrible howling sounded forth from their gloomy walls. In Wuhan's
territory the authorities still refrained from such extreme measures, though
by no means everywhere even there. In Hunan Communists were being quietly
slaughtered by the hundreds. The effects of the terror and the sifting-out of
unstable petty-bourgeois elements was reflected in the numerical strength of
the Communist party—by the beginning of July only about three thousand
remained of the thirteen thousand Communists in Hunan. The Shanghai
organization also suffered great losses. It was not only the executioner's hand
which cut down the Communists. Many of them dropped from the ranks as
the result of unbelievably difficult living conditions. A representative from

---

1. For example Pick considered Victor Petrovich Rogachev, former adviser and subsequently military
attaché in Peking, and Alexey Petrovich Rogachev, China specialist who was working as a book-
keeper for Borodin, to be the same person.

the Soviet section of the MOPR[2] lived together with us in our furnished rooms. At that time this organization was very popular in China and in fact it succeeded in providing a lot of help to the victims of repression. In the course of this work a large amount of statistical information was collected. Our neighbor told us that seventy-five per cent of the leading personnel of the CCP suffered from tuberculosis. "Overwork, terrible living conditions, and poor food have a pernicious effect upon the leading Communist cadres," he said.

Wuhan after Our Departure

The contemporary situation in China was reflected in *Pravda*'s lead article of July 6, 1927.

Pravda wrote that reaction had struck the Chinese revolution in its most vulnerable place—its mercenary army. Following upon Chiang Kai-shek's betrayal came a whole series of betrayals by other generals. Feng Yü-hsiang turned traitor and then came the turn of T'ang Sheng-chih. In Wuhan itself the counter-revolutionary elements and groups came to life and Chiang Kai-shek's agents were active. They exerted pressure on the Kuomintang leadership, sowed panic, pushed people towards capitulation, and pressed for a bloc with Chiang Kai-shek. Today Wuhan was not blocking the militarists from disarming the workers, tomorrow it would be unable to prevent them from being shot. Wuhan followed a policy of self-liquidation as a revolutionary center. Wuhan didn't want to or could not go along the path which the Communists urged it to. It was going along the opposite path, coming out for the crushing of the agrarian revolution. But the possibility of revolution was still a serious one; there were no political calms. Despite the betrayals, the revolutionary struggle was seething and developing. The Wuhan upper leadership was trembling but the pressure of the masses was powerful.

An ideological preparation for a rupture with the Communists began in Wuhan at this time. Wang Ching-wei, Ku Meng-yü and Sun Fo published articles in which they polemicized against the CCP line. In an article "Sun Yat-senism against Nihilism" Ku Meng-yü declared communism to be nihilism. He wrote "Sun Yat-senism creates, nihilism only destroys." He accused the Communists of attempting to destroy the economy and basis of the revolutionary power in China.

---

2. International Aid to Revolutionaries. Translator.

In the beginning of July the Kuomintang CEC adopted a decision to propose the expulsion of Communists from the party at the upcoming plenum, which was scheduled for the middle of the month, and in the interim to entrust the presidium with taking decisive measures to crush the revolutionary movement. A harsh purge commenced in the army. Communist political workers were expelled from the Kuomintang. The reactionary militarists threw aside all restraints; Communists were arrested, workers and peasant unions liquidated.

Mid-July 1927 was the dividing line at which the decisive rupture between the Communist party of China and the Wuhan government occurred. The Central Committee of the CCP adopted a resolution to withdraw from the Wuhan government but not to withdraw from the Kuomintang. It was decided to build an illegal apparatus, to prepare the masses for decisive engagements, and to continue to develop the agrarian revolution.

Contrary to existing practice, Communists were not invited to the July plenum of the Kuomintang. On the same day (July 15), a declaration was adopted at a session of the Politburo of the CCP CC directed against the policy of the Kuomintang CEC. It did not appear in the Kuomintang press but on July 19 a communique of the Politburo of the Kuomintang CEC pronouncing the rupture with the CCP was published in response to it. This decision was taken despite the categorical protests of a number of leading Kuomintang leftists who understood its fatal significance. A crisis began in the leadership of the Wuhan group of the Kuomintang. The Kuomintang leftists began to abandon Wuhan.

General Teng Yen-ta declared that he was resigning from all of his positions because the Wuhan leadership was not observing Sun Yat-sen's three principles, and he could not follow the path which was being thrust upon Wuhan by the generals. "The situation is deteriorating," he wrote. "The principles of Sun Yat-sen are being distorted, many party members are openly abandoning them. If the Kuomintang does not take upon itself the defense of the interests of the workers and peasants, if it does not solve the agrarian question, the revolution will suffer defeat as it did in 1911." Soong Ching-ling left Hankow. The Kuomintang leftist Hsü Ch'ien went into retirement. A month later Ch'en Yu-jen went on leave and left for the USSR.

On the eve of her departure, Soong Ching-ling published a declaration dated July 14. The papers which printed it were closed or confiscated. Soldiers suddenly appeared at the offices of the *People's Tribune* and the issue of July 18 was burned on order of Ku Meng-yü, the director of the Bureau of Agitation and Propaganda of the Kuomintang CEC. The imperialist press in China printed Soong Ching-ling's declaration without commentary.

"The moment has come for precise formulations," wrote Soong Ching-ling. "Several members of the Kuomintang CEC are doing violence to the ideas of Sun Yat-sen, therefore I am removing myself from participation in the party's new policies. The third principle, the principle of People's Livelihood, has now been shelved, but Sun Yat-sen considered it basic for our revolution. The workers and peasants were the basis for the struggle against imperialism, and they are the foundation for the construction of a new, free China. A policy which weakens the support derived from them shakes the foundation of our party, deceives the masses, and destroys our loyalty to our leader. Such a policy is doomed to failure. We must not deceive people. We have aroused great hopes in them. They have greeted us with great faith and this faith binds us. We listen to the words of censure pronounced by the worker and peasant movement as if it were inopportune or alien. This is a lie. As long as twenty or thirty years ago Sun Yat-sen said that the revolution would change the condition of the peasants. As early as 1911 Sun Yat-sen wrote that agrarian reform must lie at the base of all the social and economic transformations in China. I am sure that all true members of the Kuomintang will choose the right path." Despite the terror, fifty thousand leaflets containing this declaration were distributed. The Wuchang municipal committee of the Kuomintang declared their solidarity with her.

On July 16-17 the counter-revolutionary generals in Wuhan pulled off a coup. Troops of the garrison commander of Wuhan, General Ho Chien (the commander of the Thirty-Fifth Army) occupied Hanyang and Hankow. They encountered no resistance. Obviously, everything had been arranged in advance, the Wuhan government did not object. Wuhan was placed under martial law. Posters opposing Borodin appeared.

The papers in Shanghai blossomed with headlines: "Panic in Wuhan," "Mass Arrests," "Raid on the CCP CC." But the raid was unsuccessful, the central party apparatus had already left Wuhan by that time. It paused in Kiukiang and then proceeded to Shanghai.

Anti-Soviet Provocations. Departure from Shanghai.

Simultaneously anti-Soviet provocations began. In Shanghai, on July 16, the municipal police of the Settlement and Russian White Guards carried out a raid on the Far Eastern Bank. A search continued from ten in the morning until four in the afternoon. Mobs of White Guards gathered in front of the building and noisily gave vent to their joy.

On the same day five Soviet establishments in the French concession in Tientsin were raided. Many papers were seized. The order for the search was approved by the French consul.

In the following days searches were carried out in the private apartments of Fromberg, the administrator of the Far Eastern Bank, Vaxman, an employee of the Central Union, Zefirov, administrator of the Shanghai branch of the CER, and Zaslavsky, special correspondent for *Izvestia*, who had just arrived from Hankow. Without any protocol or inventory being taken, documents, personal correspondence, books, and photographs were confiscated. The Shanghai police were actively looking for Borodin whom they knew to have left Hankow. Nanking was offering sixty thousand yuan for his head.

On July 18 a raid was carried out in the port of Shanghai on the ship *Genli* (chartered by the Soviet Commercial Fleet), on the eve of its sailing for Vladivostok. Chinese soldiers and White Guards of the municipal police, without producing their orders, began a check of the passengers. Several times they declared that they were looking for Borodin. They gathered the passengers on deck and threatened to shoot anyone who tried to get to the shore. Several Chinese including a woman were taken off the ship as were seven Soviet citizens including V. Sergeev, A. V. Blagodatov (Rollan) and others who had previously served as advisers in the National-Revolutionary Army. All of the arrested were put in chains.

The White Guard newspaper *Rossiia* reported triumphantly on the following day that "A court martial has already interrogated those arrested on the *Genli*. The Chinese have been decapitated, the others are wearing hand and leg irons. The Nanking authorities are not permitting them any visitors." All of this was true. The wives of the arrested advisers, who remained at liberty with their small children, were terribly worried.

The arrested persons were in terrible straits—filth and stench, heavy chains, which rubbed their skin till blood appeared, the mockery of their jailors. On the first day they declared a hunger strike and did not touch their food until they were freed through a personal telegram from Chiang Kai-shek, who hypocritically excused himself and assured them that everything had taken place without his knowledge.

Several of our comrades escaped arrest only by accident. They were already at the pier when the dock workers, complete strangers to them, warned them of the danger. My husband and I were saved thanks to our friend, the flyer Sergeev. Knowing that the Shanghai police were looking for Borodin and his co-workers, he gave us his own tickets for the boat which departed the evening before. He himself was imprisoned!

My husband and I boarded the ship safely. On this day, as before, White-Guard detectives kept watch at the doors of the pension and at the pier. Again we set off separately. Before the booth where tickets for the launch were sold, a White Guard came up to me and plied me with questions for a long time. In his presence I didn't want to name the quadrant where my ship was waiting. Time was passing, I might be late. Finally, having lost all patience and almost crying from rage, I really cursed him harshly. To my amazement he immediately quieted down and lost interest in me. Only later did I guess the truth. My insults had misled him, he took me for one of "his side," and decided that I was a "dancing girl."

So we were finally on a Soviet ship. We stepped onto the deck as if it were our native soil, and a marvelous feeling of peace and security came over us. The officers and crew treated us with exceptional cordiality. We could have been very happy if not for the oppressive thought of how difficult things would be for our Chinese comrades.

Borodin's Departure

Borodin left Hankow on July 14, on the eve of the plenum of the Kuomintang, declaring that he was taking a leave in Kuling and would soon return. He was not restrained since Borodin's presence at the plenum, which was to pass a decision about the rupture with the Communist party, was naturally not desired. Borodin was accompanied by two members of the CC of the CCP—Li Li-san and Ch'ü Ch'iu-pai. Two days later a raid was carried out on the house which had served as the headquarters of the chief adviser.

Borodin met in Kuling with the leading members of the CCP and Kuomintang leftists for several days. Sung Tzu-wen, still trying to pose as a "leftist," arrived from Shanghai. He tried to persuade Borodin to trust Chiang Kai-shek and return to the USSR via Shanghai, but Soong Ching-ling who was present decisively declared that this was a trap. In truth, it soon became known that the entire Shanghai police force, Chinese and foreign, was running its legs off looking for Borodin.

At the end of July Borodin returned to Hankow and on the morning of July 27 left for the Soviet Union. About thirty co-workers and journalists accompanied him. At first they went by railroad, then by car through Shensi and Kansu, through the shifting sands of the Gobi to Ulan Bator. The road was dangerous, scarcely used and little known, death from hunger and thirst was on the lookout for the travelers, but there was no other way. The usual road to Ulan Bator through Kalgan was closed. Chang Tso-lin's troops were stationed there. O. S. Tarkhanov who accompanied Borodin has left some interesting sketches of this journey.

The Wuhan government let Borodin go with great honors. He received a special train and a military guard. The most distinguished of Wuhan's leaders, including Wang Ching-wei and Sung Tzu-wen came to see him off. All the forms of Chinese etiquette were observed.

But several days later, after the Nanchang Uprising, which transported the Wuhan faction of the Kuomintang into a rage, when Borodin was Feng Yü-hsiang's guest in Chengchow, a telegram arrived with an order to arrest him. Feng Yü-hsiang, who had greeted Borodin with honors and conversed with him several times (although before this he had openly demanded his relief) hastened to usher Borodin out of his headquarters so that he might be able to reply "He has already left." The adviser Lapin (Seyfullin) joined Borodin in Chengchow since several of our advisers attached to Feng Yü-hsiang were also returning home.

Right up to the border of the Mongolian People's Republic Borodin was greeted as a high-placed official and provided with a convoy and the best quarters. Only in Sian, the center of Shensi province, did an article appear in the local newspaper calling Borodin an unwelcome guest and advising him to leave the city at once.

In Moscow Borodin more than once recalled the difficulties of the journey, especially the terrible loess roads of northwest China and the horrible sands of the desert where the cars floundered and not infrequently progressed only some ten to fifteen kilometers in the course of a whole day's tormenting efforts. Borodin was often sick along the way. Near Ulan Bator a French journalist died as the result of an accident, and several Chinese comrades in his car were seriously injured.

It was not until September 29 that Borodin flew into Verkhne-Udinsk.

Soon after my return to Moscow I paid a visit to Borodin in the Hotel Metropol where he was staying. He told me that he was preparing a book about China but he did not get to publish it. He was suspended from work having to do with China. For a time he worked for TASS, the Sovinformburo, and edited the English-language *Moscow News.* In the spring of 1949 he was arrested and died in prison.

The Struggle Continues

Let me say a few words about the political situation in China at the time the Russian advisers returned to the USSR.

On the way to Moscow we read in the papers about the Nanchang Uprising and the campaign of the rebellious troops in the South. It seemed that everything might still be redeemed, that the revolutionaries still had strength to establish themselves in their old revolutionary base—Kwangtung, and after consolidating themselves sufficiently, to begin a further offensive. Then, in October, came the news of their defeat.

The leaders of the Nanchang Uprising declared their solidarity with Soong Ching-ling's July 14 declaration. The Communist generals Ho Lung and Yeh T'ing informed Wuhan of this by telegram. Soong Ching-ling was chosen as chairman of a revolutionary committee. At this time she was in Shanghai where she publicly declared her solidarity with the participants in the uprising.

In the beginning of September Soong Ching-ling was triumphantly greeted in Moscow. In a speech at the station she said, "Before his death Sun Yat-sen asked me to spend some time in Moscow and I am happily fulfilling this behest. Greetings to you from revolutionary China which has nothing at all in common with the present feudal bureaucrats in Wuhan and Nanking.

The spirit of revolution in China is undaunted as before. The agrarian revolution will be completed."

M. F. Kumanin, who took part in the Nanchang Uprising as an adviser to General Ho Lung, was seized and thrown into prison after his defeat. He was not freed until eight months later.

The uprising called forth a new wave of repressions against the Communists, unprecedented in its cruelty. As always this was accompanied by anti-Soviet provocations. During the tenth anniversary of the October Revolution which was so triumphantly celebrated in Moscow, our colleagues in China were living through very hard times. Almost all of our consulates were attacked. In Shanghai the White emigrés smashed the front door and stormed into the lobby. The consular guard had to open fire. About ten of the Whites were wounded, several mortally. Demonstrators carrying tsarist flags and singing the tsarist anthem marched past the consulate. An attempt was made to seize our ship *Indigirka* which was in the port of Shanghai.

In those days the secretary of the Soviet consulate in Talien, Cherkasov, received twenty-two knife wounds. The fanatic who attacked him, the son of the dean of the local Orthodox church, when he was arrested expressed his regret that Cherkasov was still alive.

On December 11 in Canton the uprising which is famous as the Canton Commune began. It was suppressed with incredible cruelty. The insurrectionists who survived went off to join the guerillas. A carnival of White terror began in the city, mountains of corpses lay in the streets. Our consular employees and their wives and children were thrown into jail. Of the men only the consul Pokhvalinsky was spared, the other five employees were shot. They marched to the execution grounds singing the "Internationale."

A rupture of diplomatic relations followed, the staff of our consulates and other establishments left China. The employees of the consulate in Hankow were awakened at dawn and under convoy placed on a ship which was supposed to take them to Shanghai. Several of them hadn't even time to get dressed properly. Their property was pillaged. In Shantung the authorities seized two of our vessels—the *Simferopol* and the *Hsinp'inghai.*

On December 17 Soong Ching-ling sent a telegram to Chiang Kai-shek from Moscow in which she wrote, "The rupture with the USSR is a suicidal policy. Alliance with the USSR was the last desire of our leader."

Normal relations with the USSR were not restored until 1932 when the Japanese aggression began.

* * * * * * * * * * *

I have completed the final page of my memoirs. As an eyewitness of many important and gripping events in those years, I want to say in conclusion that the Soviet people, the Soviet government, and the Soviets then working in China always considered the cause of the Chinese revolution to be their very own and spared nothing on its behalf. We loved and now love the Chinese people and wish them happiness and prosperity. Years of persistent struggle unite us, the blood we jointly shed brings us together. Unity has always been the guarantee of our victories.

INDEX

HARVARD EAST ASIAN MONOGRAPHS

38.   Robert R. Campbell, *James Duncan Campbell: A Memoir by His Son*

39.   Jerome Alan Cohen, ed., *The Dynamics of China's Foreign Relations*

40.   Vishnyakova-Akimova, V.V. *Two Years in Revolutionary China, 1925-1927,* tr. Steven I. Levine